Fromm

D0825306

Vancouver Island, the Gulf Islands & the San Juan Islands

by Chris McBeath

Here's what the critics say about Frommer's:

"Amazingly easy to use. Very portable, very complete."

—*Booklist*

"Detailed, accurate, and easy-to-read information for all price ranges."
—*Glamour Magazine*

"Hotel information is close to encyclopedic."

—*Des Moines Sunday Register*

"Frommer's Guides have a way of giving you a real feel for a place."
—*Knight Ridder Newspapers*

BICENTENNIAL
1807
WILEY
2007
BICENTENNIAL

John Wiley & Sons Canada, Ltd.

John Wiley & Sons Canada, Ltd

6045 Freemont Blvd.
Mississauga, ON L5R 4J3

Library and Archives Canada Cataloguing in Publication Data

McBeath, Chris, 1953–
   Frommer's Vancouver Island, the Gulf islands & the San Juan Islands/by Christ McBeath
Includes index.
ISBN: 978-0-470-83978-2
   1. Vancouver Island (B.C.)—Guidebooks. 2. Gulf Islands (B.C.)—Guidebooks. 3. San Juan Islands (Wash.)—Guidebooks. I. Title. II. Title: Vancouver Island, the Gulf Islands & the San Juan Islands.

FC3844.2M32   2007   917.11'2045   C2007-900323-0

Editor: Robert Hickey
Project Manager: Elizabeth McCurdy
Project Coordinator: Pamela Vokey
Wiley Bicentennial Logo: Richard J. Pacifico
Cartographer: Mapping Specialists
Publishing Services Director: Karen Bryan
Publishing Services Manager: Ian Koo
Production by Wiley Indianapolis Composition Services

Front cover photo: Pacific Rim National Park, Schooner Cove, British Columbia
Back cover photo: Vegetation and tree limbs grow wildly in old growth forest, Vancouver Island

Special Sales

For reseller information, including discounts and premium sales, please call our sales department: Tel. 416-646-7992. For press review copies, author interviews, or other publicity information, please contact our marketing department: Tel. 416-646-4584; Fax: 416-236-4448.
Manufactured in Canada

1   2   3   4   5   TRI   11   10   09   08   07

Contents

List of Maps　　　　　　　　　　　　　　　　　　　　v

（1）The Best of Vancouver Island, the Gulf Islands
& the San Juan Islands　　　　　　　　　　　　　　1

1 The Best Family Experiences 2
2 The Best Adventure Activities 2
3 The Best Leisure Activities 3
4 The Best Hiking Trails 3
5 The Most Scenic Drives 4
6 The Best Wildlife Viewing 5
7 The Best Places to Experience First
　　Nations Culture & History 5

8 Best Spas 5
9 The Best Hotels & Resorts 6
10 The Best Bed-and-Breakfasts
　　 & Country Inns 7
11 The Best Culinary Inns 8
12 The Best Restaurants 8

（2）Planning Your Trip　　　　　　　　　　　　　　10

1 The Regions in Brief 10
2 Visitor Information 11
3 Entry Requirements & Customs 11
4 Money 14
5 When to Go 16
　　Vancouver Island, the Gulf Islands
　　& the San Juan Islands Calendar
　　of Events 18
6 Insurance 21
7 Health & Safety 22
8 Specialized Travel Resources 23

9 Planning Your Trip Online 25
　　Frommers.com: The Complete
　　Travel Resource 26
10 The 21st-Century Traveler 27
　　Online Traveler's Toolbox 28
11 Getting There 28
12 Tips on Accommodations 35
13 Getting Around 37
　　Fast Facts: Vancouver Island,
　　the Gulf Islands & the
　　San Juan Islands 38

（3）Suggested Itineraries　　　　　　　　　　　　41

1 The San Juan Shuffle 41
2 Gulf Islands Getaway in
　　One Week .42

3 The Wild West Coast in
　　One Week .44
4 An Adventure Travel Week 46

(4) Victoria   48

1 Essentials .48
   Victoria's Neighborhoods in Brief . . .50
2 Getting Around 51
   Fast Facts: Victoria 53
3 Where to Stay 54
4 Where to Dine 62
   Bargain Meals 66
   The Tea Experience 67

5 Exploring Victoria 68
   Eminent Victorian: Francis
   Mawson Rattenbury 69
6 Especially for Kids 76
7 Shopping .77
   Spas in Victoria 81
8 Victoria After Dark 82

(5) Southern Vancouver Island   87

1 The Saanich Peninsula 87
2 The Sooke Region 93
   Recipe for Gold Panning 97

3 En Route to Nanaimo:
   The Cowichan Valley 101
   Totem Poles 101

(6) Central Vancouver Island   109

1 Nanaimo 109
2 Gabriola Island 118
3 Parksville & Qualicum Beach 120
   Mark Your Calendar 121
   Teeing Up 124
4 Heading West: Port Alberni
   & Bamfield 128

   A Side Trip to Bamfield 132
5 Tofino, Ucluelet & Pacific Rim
   National Park 133
   About Clayoquot 135
   Camping in Tofino 142

(7) Northern Vancouver Island   147

1 Courtenay & the Comox Valley 147
2 Hornby & Denman Islands 156
3 Campbell River, Gold River & Tahsis,
   Nootka & Kyoquot Sounds 158
   Cruising the Queen Charlotte
   Strait 160
4 Quadra & Cortes Islands 167

   Tracking the Wild Side 169
5 En Route to Port Hardy 170
   Kayaking Adventures with
   a Twist .176
6 Port Hardy & Cape Scott
   Provincial Park 176

(8) The Gulf Islands   181

1 Essentials 182
2 Salt Spring Island 183
   Collect Island Dollars 183

   Palatable Diversions 188
3 The Pender Islands 193
   Nature Preserved 194

4 Galiano Island 198

5 Mayne Island 203

The Cob Wave 204

Respites from Bully Birds 205

6 Saturna Island 207

Island Legend: Warburton Pike 209

9 The San Juan Islands

211

1 Essentials .212

2 San Juan Island 215

3 Orcas Island 223

Get Potted 226

Shaw Island 229

4 Lopez Island 229

Index

234

General Index 234

Accommodations Index 244

Restaurant Index 245

List of Maps

Vancouver Island & the
North American Mainland   17

Vancouver Island   32

San Juan Island Itinerary   42

Gulf Island Itinerary   43

Vancouver Island Itinerary   45

Vancouver Island Adventure
Itinerary   47

Downtown Victoria   52

Southern Vancouver Island   92

Central Vancouver Island   112

Northern Vancouver Island   150

The Gulf Islands   184

San Juan Islands   213

Acknowledgments

Grateful thanks to Frommer's editor Robert Hickey, project co-ordinator Pam Vokey, and copy editor Allyson Latta, for their support and guidance in helping to make this book a reality.

An Invitation to the Reader

In researching this book, we discovered many wonderful places—hotels, restaurants, shops, and more. We're sure you'll find others. Please tell us about them, so we can share the information with your fellow travelers in upcoming editions. If you were disappointed with a recommendation, we'd love to know that, too. Please write to:

Frommer's Vancouver Island, the Gulf Islands & the San Juan Islands
John Wiley & Sons Canada, Ltd. • 6045 Freemont Blvd. • Mississauga, ON
L5R 4J3

An Additional Note

Please be advised that travel information is subject to change at any time—and this is especially true of prices. We therefore suggest that you write or call ahead for confirmation when making your travel plans. The authors, editors, and publisher cannot be held responsible for the experiences of readers while traveling. Your safety is important to us, however, so we encourage you to stay alert and be aware of your surroundings. Keep a close eye on cameras, purses, and wallets, all favorite targets of thieves and pickpockets.

About the Author

A full-time travel writer who globestrots and scribes to earn a living, author Chris McBeath makes her home in the islands of the Pacific Northwest. Although Chris maintains a travel website (www.greatestgetaways.com) and contributes to publications worldwide, this book represents an area close to her heart.

Frommer's Star Ratings, Icons & Abbreviations

Every hotel, restaurant, and attraction listing in this guide has been ranked for quality, value, service, amenities, and special features using a **star-rating system.** In country, state, and regional guides, we also rate towns and regions to help you narrow down your choices and budget your time accordingly. Hotels and restaurants are rated on a scale of zero (recommended) to three stars (exceptional). Attractions, shopping, nightlife, towns, and regions are rated according to the following scale: zero stars (recommended), one star (highly recommended), two stars (very highly recommended), and three stars (must-see).

In addition to the star-rating system, we also use **seven feature icons** that point you to the great deals, in-the-know advice, and unique experiences that separate travelers from tourists. Throughout the book, look for:

Finds	Special finds—those places only insiders know about
Fun Fact	Fun facts—details that make travelers more informed and their trips more fun
Kids	Best bets for kids and advice for the whole family
Moments	Special moments—those experiences that memories are made of
Overrated	Places or experiences not worth your time or money
Tips	Insider tips—great ways to save time and money
Value	Great values—where to get the best deals

The following **abbreviations** are used for credit cards:

AE	American Express	DISC	Discover	V	Visa
DC	Diners Club	MC	MasterCard		

Frommers.com

Now that you have the guidebook to a great trip, visit our website at **www.frommers.com** for travel information on more than 3,000 destinations. With features updated regularly, we give you instant access to the most current trip-planning information available. At Frommers.com, you'll also find the best prices on airfares, accommodations, and car rentals—and you can even book travel online through our travel booking partners. At Frommers.com, you'll also find the following:

- Online updates to our most popular guidebooks
- Vacation sweepstakes and contest giveaways
- Newsletter highlighting the hottest travel trends
- Online travel message boards with featured travel discussions

The Best of Vancouver Island, the Gulf Islands & the San Juan Islands

There's a geological reason, having to do with movement of the earth's various surfaces, that explains why these islands on the Northwest coast of the North American continent came into being. But to my mind, it is the words of one island resident that best describe this creation of nature: "When God made this continent, He finished up with Vancouver Island," he explains. "But there was a little material left, so God stood up, and brushed off His hands. The results are jewels in the water that we know today as the San Juans and the Gulf Islands."

However it happened, these islands in the Pacific Northwest are home to some of the most beautiful and pristine wilderness on earth today. An archipelago that stretches along the coastline of both sides of the 49th parallel, the islands number in the hundreds. Some are large enough to sustain small communities as diverse as the islands themselves, while others are no more than seagull perches that disappear at high tide.

Vancouver Island is the largest. Separated from the British Columbia mainland by the Georgia Strait, it offers the best of all worlds. In the south, the city of Victoria has the urban sophistication of a cosmopolitan center, and lies within easy reach of soft adventure activities such as hiking, whale-watching, and cycling. In the north, the countryside grows untamed, opening a door to exhilarating eco-adventures such as mountaineering, spelunking, surfing, and canoeing. This diversity consistently earns Vancouver Island high marks from leading travel publications.

The smaller Gulf Islands and San Juan Islands are equally appealing, and their communities reflect the isolation of their water-bound environments. Each has a different history and ambience, whether it is sleepy Lopez Island or eclectic Galiano Island. It's a sense of magic, though, that is their charm. Island residents prefer to live outside the mainstream: they are writers, artists, and craftspeople, city retirees looking for a sense of community, or specialty producers farming everything from llama and sheep to organic orchards and cottage dairies. They've chosen to live on "island time," an easygoing tempo that bewitches visitors the moment they set foot on the soil. Although visitors are certainly welcome (in summer they swell island populations tenfold), islanders like to keep outside influences at arm's-length, lest they change that special way of life too dramatically. Islanders are self-professed stewards of the land, and as such, keepers of the island faith. When writer James Michener wanted to describe his love of islands, he made up a word for it: *nesomania,* from the Greek *neso* (island) and *mania* (extreme enthusiasm). Explore these islands, and you'll discover that nesomaniacs abound—you might even become one yourself!

1 The Best Family Experiences

- **Visiting the Royal British Columbia Museum** (Victoria; ©888/447-7977 or 250/356-7226): This place is so diverse and inspiring that kids may want to stay all afternoon. How often can you say *that* about a museum? See p. 70.

- **Actually enjoying having stick insects navigate their way up your arm at the Victoria Bug Zoo** (Victoria; © 250/384-2847): The interaction with insects takes the creepy out of crawly. See p. 71.

- **Exploring at Horne Lake Caves Provincial Park,** (near Qualicum Beach): Armed with flashlights, helmets, and good shoes, you feel like intrepid adventurers, even though the darkened path has been well scouted. One of the most accessible networks of caverns on the island, the caves can also accommodate extreme spelunkers. See p. 124.

- **Wading through minnows and searching out sand dollars at Rathtrevor Beach Provincial Park** (Parksville): This is one of the most family friendly parks in British Columbia. The warm, ankle-deep waters seem to go on forever. So does the sand. See p. 122.

- **Exploring the sandstone-sculpted tide pools at Botanical Beach** (Port Renfrew): Discover hundreds of different species of intertidal life, including congregations of seastars, chitons, anemones, purple sea urchins, barnacles, snails, and mussels. Ridges of shale and quartz jut through the black basalt cliffs, creating some of the most photogenic landscapes on the island. See p. 98.

- **Harnessing up to zip along cables from one Douglas fir to another** at WildPlay at the Bungy Zone (Nanaimo; © 888/668-7874 or 250/714-7874): Zip trips can reach speeds of up to 100kmph (62 mph) and (unlike with bungee jumping) there's no age limit. See p 113.

- **Digging for fossils with the Courtenay & District Museum and Palaeontology Centre** (Courtenay; © 250/334-0686) along the Puntledge River: It's a dirty business (which kids love), and you get to keep any fossils you find. See p. 151.

2 The Best Adventure Activities

- **Kayaking through the Broken Group Islands** (Pacific Rim National Park): It's an oasis of calm waters, seal colonies, and other Pacific Ocean marine life. Better yet, travel there aboard the freighter MV *Lady Rose.* See p. 139.

- **Honing a new outdoor skill at Strathcona Park Lodge** (Strathcona Provincial Park; © 250/286-3122): Everything from hiking to rappeling is on offer here, for both the novice and extremist. See p. 154.

- **Learning to surf on Long Beach:** The waves just keep coming, and whether or not you manage to stand, it's a long and exhilarating ride to shore. See p 139.

- **Exploring Broughton Inlet's narrow fjordic waterways** aboard the heritage vessel *Columbia III* (Port McNeil; © 888/833-8887 or 250/202-3229): Paddle along two-kayak-wide channels and coves by day; enjoy ship comforts by night. Expect to see whales, eagles, and sea lions within feet of your paddle. See p. 176.

3 The Best Leisure Activities

- **Teeing off with kindred spirits at Crown Isle Resort** (Comox/Courtenay; ✆ **888/338-8439** or 250/703-5050): The entire resort is deliciously golf-nutty. See p. 153. (Crown Isle is one of more than 20 courses you'll find in the Central Island. See Chapter 7.)

- **Cruising on the *Aurora Explorer*** (Campbell River; ✆ **250/286-3347**): This 12-passenger packet freighter works her way up and down some of the most beautiful coastal inlets in British Columbia. Although cargo is priority, passengers are a lucrative sideline. A casual, offbeat way to travel. See p. 160.

- **Angling for a Tyee in Campbell River:** In fact, angling for anything in these waters is sport-fishing at its best. See p. 158.

- **Scooting around San Juan Island in a Scootcar from Susie's Mopeds** (Friday Harbor; ✆ **800/532-0087** or 360/378-5244): A Scootcar is a hybrid vehicle that shuttles along at a low speed giving you all the fun of a moped, and the cover of a car. See p. 215.

- **Whale-watching on the bluffs at Lime Kiln Point State Park** (San Juan Island; ✆ **360/378-2044**): This is the only park in the world dedicated to this purpose. Your chances of spotting orca, minke, or pilot whales are particularly good in late August and early September, during the salmon runs. See p. 219.

- **Storm Watching** (Tofino/Ucluelet): Pick a spot from anywhere along Vancouver Island's westernmost coast that's open to the fury of the Pacific Ocean and get set for an OMNI-MAX-style show. Suffice to say it puts the movie *The Perfect Storm* into perspective. See chapter 6.

- **Day sailing aboard MV *Uchuck III*** (Gold River; ✆ **250/283-2515**): A day trip with this converted minesweeper takes you to some of Vancouver Island's most isolated (and picturesque) communities from logging camps to water-bound hamlets. It's a great value cruise. Bring your binoculars. See p. 166.

4 The Best Hiking Trails

- **The boardwalks of the Wild Pacific Trail** (Ucluelet): You can make-believe you're in training for the West Coast Trail or a trek to Cape Scott. Great for 8- and 80-year-olds alike, it has all the dramatic views with absolutely none of the true-grit challenges. See p. 136.

- **The West Coast Trail** (Pacific Rim National Park): This trek is one of the world's best to test the mettle of the hardiest and most experienced hiker. Many don't make the grade. But if you do, you'll have bragging rights for years to come. Bring your camera and you'll also have some of the most spectacular coastal scenery shots to prove it! See p. 138.

- **The northernmost tip of Vancouver Island via the Cape Scott Trail:** A West Coast Trail alternative, this trail sees you through marshland, across beaches, and over suspension bridges with turn-back points to suit your stamina level. Choose the moderate 3-hour round trip to San Josef Bay or the full 8-hour trek to Cape Scott. The rain always turns this trail into a mucky quagmire. (Stay tuned for plans to construct a trail all the way from Cape Scott to Port Hardy, which, when complete, will be longer than the famous West Coast Trail.) See p. 178.

- **The Juan de Fuca Trail** (Sooke-Port Renfrew): Here's another West Coast Trail alternative with (almost) equally impressive scenic beauty, wildlife viewing, and roaring surf crashing against the coast. Moderate one-day hikes string together for a multi-day excursion that's a good rehearsal for more grueling expeditions. And all within an hour's drive of civilization.

- **Cathedral Grove** (Coombs-Port Alberni): This ancient stand of Douglas firs grow so close to the heavens, you feel you're in a medieval cathedral. The trails are easy—at the very least, pull into the parking lot to understand why tree-huggers fought so hard to save this area from logging. See p. 122.

- **Galloping Goose Trail** (Victoria–Sooke): A great trail for walking, and better still if you're on wheels—in-line skates or bicycle. The Goose is mostly graded, relatively level, and passes through some of Victoria's most picturesque neighborhoods and urban wilderness—all the way to Sooke. See p. 73.

- **East Sooke Coast Trail** (Sooke): It can be challenging in places (think raincoast forest to surf-beaten rocks), but this kind of wilderness hiking within a half-hour's drive of a major city is what makes Vancouver Island an eco-adventurer's dream destination. See p. 96.

- **The trail to Iceberg Point** (Lopez Island): Cutting through private property this trail delivers you to a windy walk along the cliff's edge. Good walking shoes—and perhaps a picnic, are all anyone needs to enjoy the bluffy landscape. See p. 232.

5 The Most Scenic Drives

- **Following the shoreline between Sooke and Port Renfrew:** The views are expansive, and the beaches along the way provide a delightful excuse to pull over and stretch your legs. If you can't make it all the way to Botanical Beach Provincial Park (well worth the effort), the restaurant at the **Point No Point Resort** (© 250/646-2020) is, well, a good point to regroup, refresh, and turn around. See chapter 5.

- **Taking Highway 4 across Vancouver Island from Parksville to Tofino:** Bisecting the island east to west is a topographical treasure. You'll pass through forests, rivers, and snow-capped mountains before hitting the windswept shores and beaches of the West Coast. See chapter 6.

- **Leaving the main highway (Hwy. 19) and following the starfish signs** along Highway 19A, the Oceanside Route: Take any exit near Parksville and meander up to Campbell River through seaside communities overlooking the Georgia Strait, past artisan studios, and across lush farmlands. A sage farmer once said that if the cows are lying down, inclement weather is brewing. Keep an eye open, and check the theory out. See chapter 7.

- **Cruising the Coastal Circle Route:** The drive from Victoria to Courtenay, over the Malahat, takes you from urban charm to mountain vistas and then down into a valley of wineries. From Courtenay, take the car ferry across to Powell River for a drive down along coastal rainforest to more ferry connections heading for Horseshoe Bay and Vancouver. See p. 147.

6 The Best Wildlife Viewing

• **Bald Eagles at Goldstream Provincial Park** (Victoria): When salmon run ends, thousands of eagles come to feast on their carcasses. From early December until late February, the park puts on many eagle-oriented programs, including a daily count that has reached as many as 276 sightings in one day. See p. 96.

• **Whale-watching at Robson Bight** (Port McNeill): There are many whale-watching opportunities throughout the islands, including a grey whale migration that passes by west coast. But nothing beats the orcas in Robson Bight, a one-of-a-kind ecological whale preserve. See p. 173.

• **Catching up with marmots** (Nanaimo): One of the most endangered species in the world, the marmot is found only on Vancouver Island. Take a hike into the wilds surrounding Nanaimo and you might get lucky and see these highly inquisitive creatures popping up from their underground burrows. See p. 114.

• **Hearing the breeding call of a bull Roosevelt elk** (San Juan River): It's a haunting refrain, heard every fall, as the bull searches out new females to add to his harem. Roosevelt elk are a formidable sight anytime of year and finding their shed antlers is high reward for a hike. This species of elk is found only on Vancouver Island and the Queen Charlotte Islands; herds hang out near Gold River, Jordan River Meadows, and in the Nanaimo Lake region. See p. 153.

7 The Best Places to Experience First Nations Culture & History

• **Quw'utsun' Cultural Centre** (Duncan; ✆ 877/746-8119): Owned and operated by the Cowichan Band, the center shares the band's cultural heritage through live demonstrations, dance, Native food, and the knitting of its famous Cowichan sweater. See chapter p. 103.

• **Eagle Aerie Gallery** (Tofino; ✆ 250/725-3235): Acclaimed artist Roy Vickers owns this stunningly moody and inspiring gallery, primarily a showcase for his own work, as well as a chosen few other artists. See p. 134.

• **U'Mista Cultural Centre** (Alert Bay; ✆ 250/974-5403): Even if you're not an aficionado of aboriginal art, a guided tour around the center's collection provides an invaluable perspective on First Nations culture. See p. 174.

• **Eagle Feather Gallery** (Victoria; ✆ 250/388-4330): Although you'll find many small studios scattered throughout Vancouver Island, if you're staying south and you've only time for one stop, this shop carries some of the best jewelry, arts, and crafts. See p. 79.

8 Best Spas

• **The Ancient Cedars Spa** (The Wickaninnish Inn; ✆ 250/725-3100): This spa offers hot stone massages in a little cedar hut perched on the rocks as the Pacific Ocean crashes below. Rock for rock, a very sensual experience. See p. 142.

• **Willow Stream Spa** (The Fairmont Empress; ✆ 250/384-8111): Regardless of what type of service you've booked, this spa throws in time in the steam room and in its mineral pool, so that you can turn a manicure into an afternoon event. See p. 81.

- **The Madrona del Mar Spa** (Galiano Inn; ✆ **250/539-3388**): This spa takes the concept of healing sanctuary to new levels with private glass and marble steam rooms, a sea-flotation bath and new guest rooms that even have a Murphy-bed-style massage table for fireside treatments. See p. 201.
- **The Spa at Ocean Pointe** (✆ **800/575-8882** or 250/360-5858): Prepare yourself for upscale pampering all the way, all the time, with a sauna, pool, and complete fitness facility thrown in for good measure. See p. 54.
- **The Grotto Spa** (Tigh-na-Mara Resort; ✆ **250/248-2072**): British Columbia's largest resort spa features a large cave-like mineral pool and two-story waterfall. See p. 126.
- **The Kingfisher Oceanside Spa** (Courtenay; ✆ **800/663-7929** or 250/338-1323): One of the first destination resort spas on the island, this is a great spot for group spa getaways. It offers the only Pacific Mist Hydropath in North America (a kind of "walking hydrotherapy") as well as tidal baths carved out of rock, mineral soaks, and a steam cave. See p. 150.
- **Essence of Life Spa** (Brentwood Bay Lodge; ✆ **888/544-2079** or 250/544-2079): The Couples Massage at this spa is just one more great reason why you won't want to leave this contemporary, and very romantic sanctuary. See p. 81.
- **Sante Spa** (Bear Mountain ✆ **888/533-2327** or 250/391-7160): One of the island's newest spa destinations, it's that rare breed of MediSpa where licensed services include medical esthetics. So why not add a little Botox to your facial? See p. 81.

9 The Best Hotels & Resorts

- **The Fairmont Empress** (Victoria; ✆ **800/441-1414** or 250/384-8111): Like a grand old dowager, this magnificent hotel commands the Victoria Inner Harbour as her fiefdom, and beckons her audience inside. If you're going for broke, stay here; the experience is what North Americans think England is all about. See p. 65.
- **Brentwood Bay Lodge & Spa** (Brentwood Bay; ✆ **888/544-2079**): As British Columbia's only Small Luxury Hotel, this contemporary lodge boasts an oceanfront location and a service ratio nearing three staff per one guest room. Expect all the amenities of a 5-star rated resort. See p. 90.
- **Clayoquot Wilderness Resort** (Clayoquot Sound; ✆ **888/333-5405** or 250/725-2688): Accessible only by water, the resort is quite isolated, so you feel as if you're completely one with the wilderness. But it's the luxurious safari-style campsites that steal the show. See p. 140.
- **Wickaninnish Inn** (Tofino; ✆ **800/333-4604** or 250/725-3100): With only floor-to-ceiling triple-glazed windows standing between you and the churning Pacific Ocean, this place elevates storm watching to an art. See p. 142.
- **Rosario Resort** (Orcas Island; ✆ **800/562-8820** or 360/376-2222): Situated on a peninsula, Rosario exudes an air of 1920s grace. Listed on the National Register of Historic Places, the beautifully refurbished resort has something for everyone: elegant dining, spa services, a children's program, and a see-it-to-believe-it 1,972-pipe Aeolian organ. Concerts nightly. See p. 226.
- **Sonora Resort** (Sonora Island; ✆ **888/576-6672** or 604/233-0460): Accessible only by air (the resort has its own state-of-the-art helicopter) or by

boat, this resort makes getting there half the fun. Fishing is the number-one activity, though spa-ing, hiking, and going on wildlife excursions are catching up quickly. The private lounge theater is like something made for reclusive movie moguls—and the popcorn's made to order. See p. 163

- **Poets Cove** (Pender Island; ☏ **888/ 512-POET** or 250/629-2100): This resort offers a wide variety of accommodations that beckon families (and boaters) in the summer and romantics at every other time of the year. It's so self-contained, you can eat, sleep, spa, and cocoon—all in one place. See p. 196.

- **Painter's Lodge Holiday & Fishing Resort** (Campbell River; ☏ **800/ 663-7090** or 250/286-1102): This is *the* place for fishing enthusiasts. These folks also own activity oriented April Point Lodge & Spa across the channel, and because guest privileges flow from one to the other, it's almost like staying in two resorts for the price of one. See p. 162.

10 The Best Bed-and-Breakfasts & Country Inns

- **Abigail's Hotel** (Victoria; ☏ **800/ 561-6565** or 250/388-5363): This inn is the essence of old-world charm and hospitality in a phenomenal downtown Victoria location. See p. 58.

- **Hastings House** (Ganges, Salt Spring Island; ☏ **800/661-9255** or 250/ 537-2362): Everything you would want in an English country inn is here, but so much better—Hastings House is a member of the exclusive Relais & Châteaux network. Expect wonderful gardens, inspired guest rooms, and world-renowned cuisine. See p. 190.

- **Sahhali Serenity Oceanfront B&B Inn** (North Pender Island; ☏ **877/ 625-2583** or 250/629-3664): This B&B packs so many pampering touches into its suites, there's no need to leave. Private panoramas of sunsets, storms, and eagles are yours. See p. 196.

- **Friday Harbor House** (Friday Harbor, San Juan Island; ☏ **360/378- 8455**): A modern, beautifully furnished inn sitting high above busy Friday Harbor. The views are outstanding. At night, the twinkling lights make the inn's restaurant a really romantic spot. See p. 220.

- **Inn at Swifts Bay** (Lopez Island; ☏ 800/375-5285 or 360/468-3636): Pull yourself away from the most sumptuously comfortable beds in the Northwest, and you'll find breakfasts that are more than an eye-opener. They're gastronomic adventures, island-renowned for being the best on the San Juans. See p. 231.

- **Oceanwood Country Inn** (Dinner Bay, Mayne Island; ☏ **250/539- 5074**): If you're lucky, from the dining room you'll see whales passing up Navy Channel. The inn offers a range of top-quality guest rooms (some more affordable than others), extravagant gardens, and lounges featuring heirloom furniture, antiques, and board games. See p. 206.

- **Woodstone Country Inn** (Galiano Island; ☏ **888/339-2022** or 250/ 539-2022): Tucked in between rain-forest and rambling meadows, this lovely inn epitomizes the country inn. The ambience is one of casual elegance, with fireplaces, fresh flowers, and excellent home-cooked food. See p. 202.

- **Wildwood Manor B&B** (San Juan Island; ☏ **877/298-1144** or 360/378- 3447): Staying here is like being an honored house guest. The proprietors' attention to detail is extraordinary, and hospitality is so genuine that you'll feel you've made lifetime friends. See p. 221.

- **Turtleback Farm Inn** (Orcas Island; ✆ **800/376-4914** or 360/376-4914): Set on a private 32 hectares (80 acres),

this working farm has been cited in *1000 Places to See Before You Die*, and I agree with that assessment. The 1800s green clapboard farmhouse has been lovingly restored. The pastoral views lull you into a relaxed state of Nirvana. See p. 228.

11 The Best Culinary Inns

- **Sooke Harbour House** (Vancouver Island; ✆ **800/889-9688** or 250/642-3421): Beyond its reputation as a hideaway for Hollywood's beautiful people, this place offers so much more. Many come for the Wine Spectator Grand Award winning wine cellar, and the food—an Epicurean feast of local and organic fare that seems to go on for as long as you can eat. Be prepared to make reservations at the restaurant sometimes weeks in advance. See p. 99.

- **The Aerie** (Malahat, nr. Victoria; ✆ **800/518-1933** or 250/743-7115): Located on the Malahat Mountain, this lavish Mediterranean-style mansion has ocean views—and food, that will take your breath away. Ingredients pay tribute to the region's diversity, from morels to asparagus to poultry and lamb, and change frequently as if

on an edible journey through the seasons. See p. 105.

- **Coopers Cove** (Sooke; ✆ **877/642-5727** or 250/642-5727): *Oprah* has featured the Cove's ex-Olympiad Chef Angelo Prosperi-Porta, who teams up with his guests to create mouth-watering interactive dinners. He claims you'll forge a "spiritual connection to the food you eat." However you interpret that, the results taste heaven-sent!

- **Fairburn Farm Culinary Retreat & Guesthouse** (Duncan; ✆ 250/746-4637): Part farm, part cooking school, and part country inn, Fairburn exemplifies what the Slow Food movement is all about. Chef Mara Jernigan creates a delicious experience that really raises your consciousness about foods of the land. See p. 105.

12 The Best Restaurants

- **Blue Crab Bar & Grill** (Victoria; ✆ **250/480-1999**): This restaurant serves the best seafood in Victoria, along with mouth-watering views of the harbor. See p. 62.

- **Pagliacci's** (Victoria; ✆ **250/386-1662**): Go for the late-night gossip, the showmanship of owner Howie Siegal, and a menu featuring items named after Hollywood royalty. See p. 67.

- **Deep Cove Chalet** (Saanich Inlet, nr. Victoria; ✆ **250/656-3541**): This place makes the list for its caviar:

Beluga, Ocietra, and Sevugra, from Russia, Iran, and China, which helps make the elegant French menu a standout. The wine reserve of 18,000 is remarkable too. See p. 91.

- **The Sushi Bar at the Inn at Tough City** (Tofino; ✆ **250/725-2021**): Surrounded by the bounty of the sea, you would think there would be a proliferation of sushi restaurants on the west coast of Vancouver Island. Not so, which is why this tiny cafe at the Inn at Tough City is such a treat. See p. 145.

- **House Piccolo** (Ganges; © 250/537-1844): The restaurant inside this tiny farmhouse is consistently recognized by the prestigious Chaine des Rôtisseurs, so you know the cuisine is top-notch. The ranking organization is an international gastronomic society devoted to finding and preserving the world's best fine dining restaurants. See p. 192.

- **Pointe Restaurant** (Tofino; © 250/725-3100): The eatery's food is as spectacular as its location, perched on a craggy bluff. This is where you come for an amazing multi-course, gourmet, culinary experience—albeit with gourmet prices to match. See p. 144.

- **Shelter Restaurant** (Tofino; © 250/725-3353): This upbeat restaurant gives the Pointe a run for its money, only here you'll save a few dollars. Perhaps that's because there's no view. But with such fresh and imaginatively blended flavors before you, you probably won't even notice. See p. 144.

- **Duck Soup Inn** (San Juan Island; © 360/378-4878): The eclectic atmosphere of artsy décor and offbeat paraphernalia is second only to the ever-changing menu, which is created on the fly depending on what the garden is producing at any given moment. The restaurant is rather hidden away among evergreens but that doesn't stop those-in-the-know from finding it. See p. 222.

2

Planning Your Trip

The islands of the Pacific Northwest are captivating, and their charm certainly invites impromptu getaway visits, but advance planning will save you time, money, and worry. This chapter covers the necessary nuts and bolts to help you plan a successful trip.

1 The Regions in Brief

As the largest of all the islands along the Pacific Northwest coast, **Vancouver Island** offers both urban sophistication and wilderness adventure; it can be as cosmopolitan or extreme as you want.

Victoria, the provincial capital of British Columbia, lies on the southern tip of Vancouver Island, not far from the international boundary. In fact, the U.S. border scoops below the 49th parallel, keeping the island—in its entirety—in Canada. With an ambience that's more English than England ever was, Victoria's beautifully preserved turn-of-the-century buildings dominate its harbor. The city's picturesque charm draws visitors in droves, especially in summer. Shopping, dining, and urban attractions, such as the **Royal BC Museum,** make the city a first-class family destination. From Victoria, there are a number of pleasant day and half-day trips around the southern part of Vancouver Island, including to the famed **Butchart Gardens.** It is also an ideal starting point for exploring farther afield.

As you travel north, the rest of Vancouver Island ranges from rural to wild, and nowhere is this better seen than in the central part of the island. Holiday resorts line the east coast overlooking the protected Georgia Strait, while the open Pacific Ocean pounds against Canada's wildest and most westerly coast. This is where to find the unpredictable **West Coast Trail,** the awe-inspiring **Pacific Rim National Park,** and some of the untouched wilderness areas of **Clayoquot Sound.** Much of the island is home to dozens of First Nations Canadian bands; throughout your travels there'll be opportunities to shop for Native arts and to experience the many different cultures.

At **Port Hardy,** Vancouver Island's most remote and northerly community, you can board a BC Ferries vessel and take a 15-hour trip through the famed **Inside Passage** to Prince Rupert, a port town on the mainland just shy of the Alaska Panhandle. A cruise aboard BC Ferries doesn't compare with the luxurious cruise ships that ply these waters, but you'll save yourself thousands of dollars and still travel through the same spectacular scenery.

The **Gulf Islands** and the **San Juan Islands** are actually a part of the same archipelago, yet, surprisingly, each group of islands has its individual appeal. While all are rural in character, each one offers a slightly different experience. For example, Galiano and Gabiola islands feel as if they're still hanging out in the sixties; Saturna Island is like a rainforest retreat; and in summer, Hornby and Denman islands are a bit like holiday camps, as holiday makers and day-trippers throng to these sun-drenched havens. The two most sophisticated islands are San Juan—it has a "real" town with a decent range of services save for big box stores—and Salt Spring Island, which is by far the most artsy of all the islands (although Orcas Island gives it a run for its money).

That said, all the islands are very rural. Many of the smaller ones are limited in the number of services they can provide (i.e., don't expect bank machines, let alone banks). The one thing they do share is a milder climate than the rest of B.C. or Washington State, in large part because they are protected by the coastal mountains, which means more sunshine and less rain than even on Vancouver Island.

2 Visitor Information

A great source for information on British Columbia is **Tourism British Columbia,** P.O. Box 9830, Parliament Building, Victoria, BC V8V 1X4, or P.O. Box 9830 Stn. Prov. Government, Victoria, BC V8W 9W5 (© **800/HELLOBC** [800/435-5622] or 604/HELLOBC [604/435-5622]; www.hellobc.com). Be prepared for lots of glossy magazines to whet your appetite.

For Vancouver Island specifics, contact the **Tourism Association of Vancouver Island,** 335 Wesley St., Suite 203, Nanaimo,

BC V9R 2T5 (© **250/754-3500;** www.islands.bc.ca). Another useful website is **www.vancouverisland.com.** There is a central reservations service for hotels and B&Bs in the Gulf Islands. Call © **866/539-3089.** You can also check out **www.gulfislandsguide.com** for general information. For the San Juan Islands, contact **San Juan Islands Visitor Information Services,** P.O. Box 1330, Friday Harbor, San Juan Island, WA 98250 (© **888/468-3701** or 360/378-9551; www.guidetosanjuans.com).

3 Entry Requirements & Customs

ENTRY REQUIREMENTS

ENTERING CANADA   All visitors to Canada must carry proof of citizenship and residence. United States citizens and permanent residents do not require visas; a passport, official birth certificate (photocopies may be refused), or certificate of naturalization is sufficient along with some form of photo ID with your home address. *Note:* As early as January 1, 2008, all travelers to and from Canada, including U.S. citizens, may be required to carry a passport or other documentation to enter or re-enter the country. U.S. residents should carry their passports and resident status cards or green cards, visitor or student visas, arrival–departure records, proof of sufficient funds for a temporary stay, and evidence of return transportation.

Citizens of most European countries, former British colonies, and certain other countries (Israel, Korea, and Japan, for example) do not need visas, but must carry passports. Entry visas for citizens of more than 130 countries must be applied for and received from the Canadian embassy in your home country. For further information, check with the **Canadian Consulate** in the city nearest you or contact the Canadian government's **800-Canada information line** (© **800/OCANADA,** 800/622-6232), which will link you to numerous government services and programs. Entry requirements to Canada are also on the Citizenship and Immigration website visitors' services page at www.cic.gc.ca/english/visit/index.html.

ENTERING THE UNITED STATES All visitors to the United States should carry passports along with arrival–departure information, proof of sufficient funds for a temporary stay, evidence of return transportation, and in many instances, student or visitor visas. Canadian citizens, too, now require a valid passport to enter or re-enter the United States. Since border security has become more stringent, a driver's license or other photo ID is no longer sufficient.

The U.S. State Department has a **Visa Waiver Program** allowing citizens of certain countries to enter the United States without a visa for stays of up to 90 days. At press time these included Andorra, Australia, Austria, Belgium, Brunei, Denmark, Finland, France, Germany, Iceland, Ireland, Italy, Japan, Liechtenstein, Luxembourg, Monaco, the Netherlands, New Zealand, Norway, Portugal, San Marino, Singapore, Slovenia, Spain, Sweden, Switzerland, and the United Kingdom. Citizens of these countries need only a valid passport and a round-trip air or cruise ticket in their possession upon arrival. If they first enter the United States, they may also visit Mexico, Canada, Bermuda, and/or the Caribbean islands and return to the United States without a visa. Further information is available from any U.S. embassy or consulate.

Citizens of all other countries must have (1) a valid passport that expires at least 6 months later than the scheduled end of their visit to the United States, and (2) a tourist visa, which may be obtained without charge from any U.S. consulate.

To obtain a visa, the traveler must submit a completed application form (either in person or by mail) with a 1½-inch-square photo, and must demonstrate binding ties to a residence abroad. Usually you can obtain a visa at once or within 24 hours, but it may take longer during the summer rush from June through August. If you cannot go in person, contact the nearest U.S. embassy or consulate for directions on applying by mail. Your travel agent or airline office may also be able to provide you with visa applications and instructions. The U.S. consulate or embassy that issues your visa will determine whether you will be issued a multiple- or single-entry visa and any restrictions regarding the length of your stay.

MEDICAL REQUIREMENTS   Unless you're arriving from an area known to be experiencing an epidemic (particularly cholera or yellow fever), inoculations or vaccinations are not required for entry into the United States or Canada. If you have a medical condition that requires **syringe-administered medications**, carry a valid signed prescription from your physician—the Federal Aviation Administration (FAA) no longer allows airline passengers to pack syringes in their carry-on baggage without documented proof of medical need. If you have a disease that requires treatment with **narcotics**, you should also carry documented proof with you—smuggling narcotics aboard a plane is a serious offense that carries severe penalties in both the U.S. and Canada. For **HIV-positive visitors,** requirements for entering either country are somewhat vague and change frequently. According to the latest publication of *HIV and Immigrants: A Manual for AIDS Service Providers*, the Immigration and Naturalization Service (INS) doesn't require a medical exam for entry into the United States, but INS officials may stop individuals if they look sick or if they are carrying AIDS/HIV medicine.

DRIVER'S LICENSES   Foreign driver's licenses are mostly recognized in the U.S. and Canada, although you may want to get an international driver's license if your home license is not written in English.

TRAVELING WITH CHILDREN
United States and Canada border officials pay particular attention to minors, especially if they are traveling solo or with a

single adult. Any person age 18 and under must carry a letter from a parent or guardian granting him or her permission to travel across the border, plus proof of identity. If parents are divorced, the non-traveling parent must write a similar letter granting permission for the child to accompany the ex-spouse.

TRAVELING WITH PETS Dogs, cats, and most other pets can travel with their owners between the United States and Canada provided you have proof of rabies vaccinations within the past 36 months. In Canada, contact the **Canadian Food Inspection Agency,** 59 Camelot Dr., Ottawa, ON K1A DY9 (✆ **800/ OCANADA,** 800/622-6232, or 613/225-2342; www.inspection.gc.ca). In the U.S., contact Centers for Disease Control & Prevention, Mail Stop C-14, 1600 Clifton Rd., Atlanta, GA 30333 (✆ **877/394-8747**; www.cdc.gov/ncidod/dg/animal/htm).

CUSTOMS
WHAT YOU CAN BRING INTO CANADA

Canadian Customs is fairly liberal except when it comes to firearms, plants, and meats. These are subject to rigorous inspection; without *precisely* the right paperwork, they won't make it across the border. Pepper sprays are also a big no. For a clear summary of Canadian rules, request the booklet "I Declare," issued by the Canada Border Services Agency ✆ **800/461-9999** in Canada, or 204/ 983-3500; www.ccra-adrc.gc.ca). Canada allows its citizens a C$750 (US$660) exemption, and you're allowed to bring back duty-free 1 carton of cigarettes, 1 can of tobacco, 1.5L (40 imperial oz.) of liquor, and 50 cigars. In addition, you're allowed to mail gifts to Canada valued at less than C$60 (US$53) a day, provided they're unsolicited and don't contain alcohol or tobacco (write on the package "Unsolicited gift, under C$60 value"). All

valuables should be declared on the Y-38 form before departure from Canada, including serial numbers of valuables you already own, such as expensive foreign cameras. *Note:* The C$750/US$660 exemption can only be used once a year and only after an absence of 7 days.

There is also a smaller 48-hour exemption (you can claim C$200/US$176 total) as well as a 24-hour exemption of C$50/ US$44. You must be over 19 to purchase tobacco products and alcoholic beverages, and purchases have to accompany you in your checked or hand luggage.

WHAT YOU CAN BRING INTO THE U.S.

Every visitor more than 21 years of age many bring in, free of duty, the following: (1) 1 liter (34 oz.) of wine or hard liquor, (2) 200 cigarettes, 100 cigars (but not from Cuba), or 3 pounds of smoking tobacco; and (3) C$100 (US$88) worth of gifts. These exemptions are offered to travelers who spend at least 72 hours in the United States and who have not claimed them within the preceding 6 months. It is altogether forbidden to bring into the country foodstuffs (particularly fruit, cooked meats, and canned goods) and plants (vegetables, seeds, tropical plants, and the like). Foreign tourists may bring in or take out up to $10,000 in U.S. or foreign currency with no formalities; larger sums must be declared to U.S. Customs on entering or leaving, which includes filing form CM 4790. For more specific information regarding U.S. Customs and Border Protection, contact your nearest U.S. embassy or consulate, or the U.S. Customs office (✆ **202/927-1770** or www.customs.ustreas.gov).

WHAT YOU CAN TAKE HOME
U.S. Citizens

For specifics on what you can bring back and the corresponding fees, download the invaluable free pamphlet "Know Before You Go" available online at **www.cbp.gov**.

(Click "Travel," and then click "Know Before You Go! Online Brochure") Or contact the **U.S. Customs & Border Protection (CBP),** 1300 Pennsylvania Ave., NW, Washington, DC 20229 (℃ 877/287-8667) and request the pamphlet.

Canadian Citizens

For a clear summary of Canadian rules, write for the booklet "I Declare," issued by the **Canada Border Services Agency** (℃ **800/461-9999** in Canada, or 204/983-3500; **www.cbsa-asfc.gc.ca**).

U.K. Citizens

For information, contact **HM Customs & Excise** at ℃ **0845/010-9000** (from outside the U.K., 020/8929-0152), or consult their website at **www.hmce.gov.uk**.

Australian Citizens

A helpful brochure available from Australian consulates or Customs offices is "Know Before You Go." For more information, call the **Australian Customs Service** at ℃ **1300/363-263,** or log on to **www.customs.gov.au**.

New Zealand Citizens

Most questions are answered in a free pamphlet available at New Zealand consulates and Customs offices: "New Zealand Customs Guide for Travellers, Notice no. 4." For more information, contact **New Zealand Customs,** The Customhouse, 17–21 Whitmore St., Box 2218, Wellington (℃ **04/473-6099** or 0800/428-786; **www.customs.govt.nz**).

4 Money

The Canadian dollar is stronger than it has been in many years, so you'll often find prices more or less at par between Canada and the United States.

CURRENCY

Canadian denominations are the same as in the United States: C$5, C$10, C$20, C$50, and C$100 (the last two are usually not welcome as payment for small purchases). Bills, however, come in different colors, which is why many Americans call them "Monopoly money"—rather a good-natured insult to Canadian ears. Although the U.S. still has the $1 bill, Canadians have long since replaced their paper dollar with a coin. It is nicknamed a "loonie" for the loon on one side, and the two-toned, two-dollar coin is commonly called a "toonie."

EXCHANGE RATES In Canada, United States currency is accepted at most shops and restaurants, but because exchange rates vary, you're better off changing your funds into Canadian currency.

Banks and other financial institutions offer a standard rate of exchange based on the daily world monetary rate. **Hotels** will gladly exchange your notes, but will usually give a slightly lower exchange rate. **Stores and restaurants** can set their own exchange percentages, so these are generally the lowest of all. Your best bet is to withdraw local funds from **bank ATMs**—they often provide the best rate of exchange. Your issuing company will automatically convert the transaction to your currency when you're billed.

In any transaction, always keep the rate of exchange in mind. The prices cited in this guide are given in Canadian dollars and U.S. dollars based on an exchange rate of US88¢ to C$1.

Note: The "foreign-exchange bureaus" so common in Europe are rare even at airports in the United States, and nonexistent outside major cities. It's best not to change foreign money (or traveler's checks denominated in a currency other than U.S. dollars) at a small-town bank, or even a branch in a big city; in fact, leave any currency other than U.S. dollars at home—it may prove a greater nuisance to you than it's worth.

ATMs

The easiest and best way to get cash away from home is from an ATM (automated teller machine), sometimes referred to as a "cash machine," or a "cashpoint." The **Cirrus** (© **800/424-7787;** www.mastercard. com) and **PLUS** (© **800/843-7587;** www. visa.com) networks span the globe; look at the back of your bank card to see which network you're on, then call or check online for ATM locations at your destination. Be sure you know your personal identification number (PIN) and daily withdrawal limit before you depart. *Note:* Remember that many banks impose a fee every time you use a card at another bank's ATM, and that fee can be higher for international transactions (up to $5 or more) than for domestic ones (where they're rarely more than $2). In addition, the bank from which you withdraw cash may charge its own fee. For international withdrawal fees, ask your bank.

Tip: Although ATMs are widespread on Vancouver Island, they are less prevalent on the Gulf and San Juan islands. Some of the Gulf Islands don't even have banks! If you plan to tour the Gulf and San Juan islands, be sure to travel with a **major credit card,** a **direct debit card,** or **traveler's checks,** and, of course, **cash.** Visa and MasterCard are accepted at most locations. Not as many businesses accept American Express.

TRAVELER'S CHECKS

Because most cities and towns have 24-hour ATMs, traveler's checks are not used as much as they once were. However, if you wish to carry larger denominations, banks, bigger stores, and hotels universally accept them. Cashing checks may sometimes incur a small fee, and you may be asked for photo ID to complete the transaction. Be sure checks are denominated in U.S. dollars, as foreign-currency checks are often difficult to exchange. The three traveler's checks that are most widely recognized—and least likely to be denied—are **Visa, American Express**, and **Thomas Cook.** Be sure to record the numbers of the checks, and keep that information in a separate place in case they get lost or stolen. Most businesses are pretty good about taking traveler's checks, but you're better off cashing them in at a bank (in small amounts, of course) and paying in cash. *Remember:* You'll need identification, such as a driver's license or passport, to change a traveler's check.

CREDIT CARDS

Credit cards are another safe way to carry money. They also provide a convenient record of all your expenses, and they generally offer relatively good exchange rates. You can withdraw cash advances from your credit cards at banks or ATMs, provided you know your PIN. Keep in mind that you'll pay interest from the moment of your withdrawal, even if you pay your monthly bills on time. Also, note that many banks now assess a 1% to 3% "transaction fee" on **all** charges you incur abroad (whether you're using the local currency or your native currency).

Canadian businesses honor the same credit cards as do those in the U.S. Visa and MasterCard are the most common, though American Express is also normally accepted in hotels and restaurants catering to tourists. Discover and Diner's Club cards are accepted less frequently.

5 When to Go

CLIMATE

There's a reason for the lush, green landscape, bountiful flowers, and rich agricultural fields in the Pacific Northwest. It's called rain. So, while you're enjoying the milder temperatures, always tote an umbrella.

In **March,** Victoria boasts the first spring blooms in Canada, parading its daffodils on television newscasts across a country still bound in much chillier climes. It's also a signal for travelers to hit the road. Although weather can still be a little unsettled, the deals in accommodation and uncrowded restaurants are worth the effort of carrying an umbrella. By **May,** cherry blossoms and tulips dot the islands, leading the way to a summer that enjoys at least 16 hours of daylight per day, temperatures that push the mercury to around 80°F/25°C, and a monthly rainfall that averages barely 2.5 centimeters (1 in.). This is **high season,** when the islands seem on perpetual parade. **September or October** is a golden time to visit. The days are still long, there's warmth in the air, and the leaves turn to hues of yellow, gold, and red. With the kids back in school, attractions aren't as jam-packed; getaway packages offer great savings. The winter season, from **November to February,** sees more rain than snow, which, if it falls at all, dissolves into the atmosphere within hours. But snow does settle in the mountains and on Vancouver Island's northernmost reaches, making skiing and snowboarding popular pastimes. Along the westernmost coast of Vancouver Island, **winter storms** from the open Pacific Ocean are so dramatic that savvy marketers have successfully created a new high season specifically geared to storm watchers. Yet, for all the rain, gray days are still outnumbered by beautiful, crisp weather, especially in the San Juans.

Vancouver Island's Average Temperature & Precipitation

	Jan	Feb	Mar	Apr	May	June	July	Aug	Sept	Oct	Nov	Dec
Temp. (°F)	39°	41°	45°	46°	52°	61°	66°	66°	63°	44°	44°	41°
Temp. (°C)	4°	5°	7°	8°	11°	16°	19°	19°	17°	7°	7°	5°
Precip. (inches/mm)	3.7/92	2.7/67	1.7/42	1.5/38	1/24	0.8/19	0.6/14	0.8/20	1.3/32	2.4/59	3.7/92	4/99

Note: Temperature and precipitation may vary among different parts of Vancouver Island by as much as 4 or 5 degrees. For example, you can expect the northern regions to be the coolest and the Cowichan Valley to be the warmest. Also, the west coast usually gets more precipitation than the east coast. The above chart can be used as a general gauge for conditions on the Gulf and San Juan islands, as well. For island-specific readings, contact the local chambers of commerce or visitor information centers.

HOLIDAYS

IN BRITISH COLUMBIA Although banks, offices, and government agencies close for holiday periods, tour operators and main shops remain open in the major cities, such as Victoria, to take advantage of holiday travelers. There are nine official public holidays: New Year's Day (January 1); Good Friday; Victoria Day (the Monday on or preceding May 24); Canada Day (July 1); B.C. Day (first Monday in August); Labor Day (first Monday in September); Thanksgiving (second Monday in October); Remembrance Day (November 11); Christmas Day (December 25).

IN WASHINGTON Banks, offices, and government agencies close for statutory holidays, as do most shops and

Vancouver Island & the North American Mainland

restaurants in outlying areas such as the San Juan Islands. In the United States, there are ten public holidays: New Year's Day (January 1); Martin Luther King Jr. Day (third Monday in January); President's Day/ Washington's Birthday (third Monday in February); Memorial Day (last Monday in May); Independence Day (July 4); Labor Day (first Monday in September); Columbus Day (second Monday in October); Veteran's Day (November 11); Thanksgiving (fourth Thursday in November); Christmas Day (December 25).

VANCOUVER ISLAND, THE GULF ISLANDS & THE SAN JUAN ISLANDS CALENDAR OF EVENTS

Island events tend to be community oriented and not as finessed as you would find in big city centers. Weather dictates that most activities take place in the summer months except for those celebrating wildlife migrations. Victoria and Nanaimo stage the most special events, though you're likely to find small festivities such as outdoor summer concerts and fall agricultural fairs on any one of the Gulf and San Juan islands as well as in Vancouver Island's rural communities. The San Juan Islands Visitors Information Centre (© 360/378-6822; www. visitsanjuans.com) or Vancouver Island Tourism (© 250/754-3500; www.vancouverisland. travel/art/events) can provide further details.

December/January

Annual Bald Eagle Count, Goldstream Provincial Park, Vancouver Island. When the salmon swim up Goldstream Provincial Park's spawning streams, more than 300 bald eagles take up residence with an eye to a month-long feast. Call © 250/478-9414 for exact dates and events.

February

Chinese New Year, Victoria, Vancouver Island. This is when the Chinese traditionally pay their debts and forgive old grievances to start the new lunar year with a clean slate. The Chinese community rings it in with firecrackers, dancing dragon parades, and other festivities. Late January or early February.

Trumpeter Swan Festival, Comox Valley, Vancouver Island. A week-long festival celebrating these magnificent white birds that gather in the Comox Valley. Call the **Tourism Association of Vancouver Island** (© 250/754-3500) for exact dates.

March

Pacific Rim Whale Festival, Pacific Rim National Park Region, Vancouver Island. Every spring, mid-March through early April, more than 20,000 grey whales migrate past Vancouver Island's west coast, attracting visitors from all over the world. A colorful celebration featuring live crab races, storytelling, parades, art shows, guided whale-spotting hikes, and whale-watching excursions in zippy Zodiacs. For information, call © 250/726-4641 or 250/725-3414.

April

Annual Brant Wildlife Festival, Parksville/Qualicum Beach, Vancouver Island. A birder's nirvana, this 3-day celebration focuses on the annual black brant migration through the area from Mexico to Alaska (20,000 birds). The event includes guided walks through old-growth forest and saltwater and freshwater marshes, goose-viewing stations, a birding competition, art, photography, and carving exhibitions, as well as numerous children's activities. For exact dates, call © 250/752-9171.

May

Swiftsure Weekend, Victoria and Vancouver Island. More than 200 vessels navigate the unpredictable coastal waters in this, the oldest and largest offshore overnight sailing race in the Pacific Northwest. In 2003, it celebrated its

60th anniversary. It is as exciting to watch as it is to participate. Call the **Royal Victoria Yacht Club** (© 250/ 592-2441) for information.

Harbour Festival, Victoria, Vancouver Island. This 10-day festival takes place in the downtown district and features heritage walks, entertainment, music, and more. Call Tourism Victoria for details (© 250/953-2033). Last week of May.

Artists' Studios Open House, San Juan Island. An island-wide open house featuring weavers, potters, and other craftspeople. Call © 360/378-5594 for information. Last weekend in May.

June

Jazz Fest International, Victoria, Vancouver Island. Jazz, swing, bebop, fusion, and improv artists from around the world perform at various venues in Victoria during this 10-day festival. Call © 250/388-4423 for dates and information.

Boat Festival, Cowichan Bay, Vancouver Island. Classic boats, a boat-building house for children, Dragon Boat races, folk singers, and dancing are some of the fun activities of this festival. The Fast-and-Furious Boat Building Contest is a highlight: entrants build a boat and race it within 4 hours! Call the Cowichan Bay Maritime Centre for exact dates (© 250/756-4955).

ICA Folkfest, Victoria, Vancouver Island. This free 8-day world-beat music festival takes place at the end of June or early July. Main venues are the Inner Harbour and Market Square in downtown Victoria. For dates and information, call © 250/388-4728.

July

Latin Caribbean Festival, Victoria, Vancouver Island. A nine-day celebration of music and food that draws folks from all over the Pacific Northwest. The Inner Harbour rocks with reggae, salsa, and funk. Call © 250/361-9433 for information.

Festival of the Arts, Salt Spring Island. Catch irreverent performances by the Hysterical Society. Call © 250/ 537-4167 for information. Begins first weekend in July and runs for entire month.

Nanaimo Marine Festival, Nanaimo, Vancouver Island. Lots of activities take place around the harbor, culminating in the famous Bathtub Race between the city of Nanaimo and Kitsilano Beach, in Vancouver. Yes, it's exactly what it sounds like—racers scrunched up in racer-designed bathtub look-alikes that may or may not make it across the chop. Contact the **Nanaimo Tourism Association** (© 800/663-7337) or the **Loyal Nanaimo Bathtub Society** (© 250/753-7223) for information.

Festival of Murals, Chemainus, Vancouver Island. Chemainus is known worldwide for its ever-changing murals. During the festival, visitors have the opportunity to see local and international artists "decorate" the sides of buildings, walls, and more with new murals. From mid-July to mid-August.

All Sooke Day and Annual Festival of History, Sooke, Vancouver Island. Loggers' sports fill All Sooke Day itself, while the festival continues to the following weekend. Activities include a fishing derby, heritage events, pioneer fashion shows, tea parties, and excursions. Call © 250/642-6351 for information. Third Saturday in July.

BC Open Sandcastle Competition, Parksville, Vancouver Island. Between mid- and late July, the wide sandy beaches are transformed with imagination and creativity. This event attracts more than 40,000 people.

Tips   Summer Markets

Over 10 community markets are held throughout Victoria, and area where local farmers sell their products and local artisans ply their wares. You can spend an entire weekend "market-hopping" from the peninsula located 20 minutes north of Victoria to the Cowichan Valley.

Call © 250/248-4819 for exact dates and information.

August

Victoria Dragon Boat Festival, Victoria, Vancouver Island. Traditional dragon boat races take place in the Inner Harbour, where 120 local and international teams compete. For details, call Tourism Victoria, at © 250/953-2033. Mid-August.

Symphony Splash, Victoria, Vancouver Island. It only lasts one day but this free event draws a crowd of 40,000 people to hear the Victoria Symphony play from a barge moored in the middle of Victoria's picturesque Inner Harbour. Traditionally, Tchaikovsky's 1812 Overture closes the concert, accompanied by fireworks. Call © 250/385-9771 for details. Early August.

Art in the Park, Orcas Island. Held at Moran Sate Park, this annual event brings together displays by local artists and traditional craftspeople that are normally scattered throughout the San Juan Islands. For information, call © 360/376-2273.

September

Saanich Fall Fair, Saanichton, Vancouver Island. The oldest agricultural fair in Western Canada showcases livestock, sheep shearing, show jumping, crafts, produce, home baking, and more. Lots of candy floss and old-style country fun, including a fiddle competition. Call © 250/652-2033 for information. Early September.

Cowichan Wine & Culinary Festival, Cowichan Valley, Vancouver Island. As the fastest growing wine region in Canada, the range of fruit-filled wines, cider, and mead you'll find in these islands are matched only by the variety of artisan cheeses, fresh produce, seafood, and herbs. This 3-day annual festival started in 2005 and is already among the top events for food and wine aficionados. Call Tourism Cowichan for details (© 250/746-1099). Last weekend in September.

October

Royal Victorian Marathon, Victoria, Vancouver Island. This annual race attracts runners from around the world. The air is fresh, and the temperature is usually just cool enough to keep the runners moving along a course that's not too strenuous. A good trainer for the Boston Marathon course. Call © 250/685-4520 for information. Canadian Thanksgiving weekend (second weekend in October).

November

The Great Canadian Beer Festival, Victoria, Vancouver Island. Held at the Victoria Conference Centre, this draws some of British Columbia's best microbreweries in a sampling extravaganza of beers from across Western Canada. Call Tourism Victoria for information (© 250/953-2033). Second week in November.

December

First Night, Victoria, Vancouver Island. The city's New Year's Eve performing-arts festival and alcohol-free party, specifically designed so the whole family can enjoy a safe and fun New Year's celebration. Victoria's Inner Harbour lights up with activity with streets reserved for pedestrian revelers only. Call ☏ **250/953-2033** for details. December 31.

6 Insurance

The cost of travel insurance varies widely, depending on the cost and length of your trip, your age and health, and the type of trip you're taking, but expect to pay between 5% and 8% of the vacation itself. You can get estimates from various providers through **InsureMyTrip.com**. Enter your trip cost and dates, your age, and other information, for prices from more than a dozen companies. Canada's national health insurance system will not cover non-Canadians; Canadian doctors and hospitals can bill U.S. health insurers or European health systems, so bring appropriate documentation or insurance cards.

TRIP-CANCELLATION INSURANCE

Trip-cancellation insurance will help retrieve your money if you have to back out of a trip or depart early, or if your travel supplier goes bankrupt. Permissible reasons for trip cancellation can range from sickness to natural disasters to the State Department declaring a destination unsafe for travel. Your credit card coverage may include coverage for lost luggage, canceled tickets, and medical expenses so review card policies before purchasing separate travel insurance.

For more information, contact one of the following recommended insurers: **Access America** (☏ **866/807-3982;** www. accessamerica.com); **Travel Guard International** (☏ **800/826-4919;** www.travelguard.com); **Travel Insured International** (☏ **800/243-3174;** www.travelinsured.com); and **Travelex Insurance Services** (☏ **888/457-4602;** www.travelex-insurance.com).

MEDICAL INSURANCE

Most health insurance policies cover you if you get sick away from home—but check, particularly if you're insured by an HMO. If you require additional medical insurance, try **MEDEX Assistance** (☏ **410/453-6300;** www.medexassist.com) or **Travel Assistance International** (☏ **800/821-2828;** www.travelassistance.com; for general information on services, call the company's Worldwide Assistance Services, Inc., at ☏ **800/777-8710**).

LOST-LUGGAGE INSURANCE

On international flights (including U.S. portions of international trips), baggage

---

Travel in the Age of Bankruptcy

Airlines go bankrupt, so protect yourself by **buying your tickets with a credit card**. The Fair Credit Billing Act guarantees that you can get your money back from the credit card company if a travel supplier goes under (and if you request the refund within 60 days of the bankruptcy). **Travel insurance** can also help, but make sure it covers against "carrier default" for your specific travel provider. And be aware that if a U.S. airline goes bust mid-trip, a 2001 federal law requires other carriers to take you to your destination (albeit on a space-available basis) for a fee of no more than $25, provided you rebook within 60 days of the cancellation.

coverage is limited to approximately C$9.07 (US$7.95) per .5kg (1 lb.), up to approximately C$635 (US$559) per checked bag. If you plan to check items more valuable than what's covered by the standard liability, see if your homeowner's policy covers your valuables, get baggage insurance as part of your comprehensive travel-insurance package, or buy Travel Guard's "BagTrak" product.

If your luggage is lost, immediately file a lost-luggage claim at the airport, detailing the luggage contents. Most airlines require that you report delayed, damaged, or lost baggage within 4 hours of arrival.

The airlines are required to deliver luggage, once found, directly to your house or destination free of charge.

CAR INSURANCE

Car insurance is compulsory in British Columbia. Basic coverage consists of "no-fault" accident and C$200,000 (US$176,000) worth of third-party legal liability coverage. If you're driving your own vehicle, check with your insurance agent to make sure your policy meets this requirement. If you are renting, your rental agreement will outline these insurance options.

7 Health & Safety

STAYING HEALTHY

Victoria and most of the major towns in the region have hospitals, but some of the Gulf and San Juan islands only operate clinics. These are well equipped for most medical needs but for life-threatening emergencies, airlift services are used.

WHAT TO DO IF YOU GET SICK AWAY FROM HOME

If you suffer from a chronic illness, consult your doctor before your departure. Pack **prescription medications** in your carry-on luggage, and carry them in their original containers, with pharmacy labels—

otherwise they won't make it through airport security. Carry the generic name of prescription medicines, in case a local pharmacist is unfamiliar with the brand name.

For travel abroad, you may have to pay all medical costs up front and be reimbursed later. See "Medical Insurance," under "Insurance," above.

STAYING SAFE

Because these islands are more laid-back than many other travel destinations, they have a stronger sense of community that is safe and genuinely friendly. This is

Avoiding "Economy Class Syndrome"

Deep vein thrombosis, or as it's know in the world of flying, "economy-class syndrome," is a blood clot that develops in a deep vein. It's a potentially deadly condition that can be caused by sitting in cramped conditions—such as an airplane cabin—for too long. During a flight (especially a long-haul flight), get up, walk around, and stretch your legs every 60 to 90 minutes to keep your blood flowing. Other preventive measures include frequent flexing of the legs while sitting, drinking lots of water, and avoiding alcohol and sleeping pills. If you have a history of deep vein thrombosis, heart disease, or another condition that puts you at high risk, some experts recommend wearing compression stockings or taking anticoagulants when you fly; always ask your physician about the best course for you. Symptoms of deep vein thrombosis include leg pain or swelling, or even shortness of breath.

Healthy Travels to You

The following government websites offer up-to-date health-related travel advice.

- Australia: www.dfat.gov.au/travel
- Canada: www.hc-sc.gc.ca/index_e.html
- U.K.: www.dh.gov.uk/PolicyAndGuidance/HealthAdviceForTravellers/fs/en
- U.S.: www.cdc.gov/travel/

especially true of the Gulf and San Juan Islands. That said, you should still use your common sense and discretion. Stow things in the trunk of your car, out of sight, hold on to your pocketbook when in a crowd, and keep expensive cameras or electronic equipment bagged up or covered when not in use. Vancouver Island, too, is regarded as pretty safe, though you might find Victoria busy enough to attract pickpockets and petty thieves. Further north, however, the population thins and some roads are fairly remote. Be sure that your gas tank is full and take along water and a snack, because if you get into trouble help may take a few hours to arrive.

8 Specialized Travel Resources

FOR TRAVELERS WITH DISABILITIES

The law requires that most hotels, restaurants, and other public places in British Columbia be **wheelchair accessible.** However, the nature of certain buildings and small-town layouts makes their compliance inconsistent, especially in the Gulf islands (and in the San Juans, for that matter). Except in towns like Ganges (on Salt Spring Island) and Friday Harbor (on San Juan Island), most streets are like country lanes. The charm or historical ambience of a building often means that access routes are difficult, which doesn't make for easy maneuverability. The **"British Columbia Accommodations Guide"** details accessibility options at lodgings throughout Western Canada. Contact **Tourism British Columbia,** P.O. Box 9820, Station Prov. Govt., 1803 Douglas St., Victoria BC VAW 9W5 (© **800/HELLOBC**, 800/435-5622; www.hellobc.com). For accessibility advice in the San Juans, contact the San Juan Islands Visitor Information Services, P.O. Box 1330, Friday Harbor, San Juan Island, WA 98250 (© **888/468-3701** or 360/378-9551).

Many travel agencies offer customized tours and itineraries for travelers with disabilities. Among them are **Flying Wheels Travel** (© **507/451-5005;** www.flyingwheelstravel.com); **Access-Able Travel Source** (© **303/232-2979;** www.accessable.com); and **Accessible Journeys** (© **800/846-4537** or 610/521-0339; www.disabilitytravel.com). **Avis Rent a Car** has an "Avis Access" program that offers such services as a dedicated 24-hour toll-free number (© **888/879-4273**) for customers with special travel needs; special car features such as swivel seats, spinner knobs, and hand controls; and accessible bus service.

Organizations that offer assistance to disabled travelers include **MossRehab** (www.mossresourcenet.org); the **American Foundation for the Blind (AFB)** (© **800/232-5463;** www.afb.org); and **SATH (Society for Accessible Travel & Hospitality)** (© **212/447-7284;** www.sath.org). **AirAmbulanceCard.com** is now partnered with SATH and allows you to preselect top-notch hospitals in case of an emergency.

The community website **iCan** (www.icanonline.net/channels/travel) has destination guides and several regular columns on accessible travel. Also check out the quarterly magazine *Emerging Horizons* (www.emerginghorizons.com), and *Open World* magazine, published by SATH.

FOR FAMILIES

Victoria is one of the most child-friendly, cosmopolitan cities on Vancouver Island, offering a great selection of family activities to enjoy. The **Victoria Bug Zoo** and **Miniature World** are wonderful diversions, rain or shine, and children of all ages will enjoy scooting around Victoria's Inner Harbour in the 12-passenger Harbour Ferries vessel, which looks like something out of Disneyland. (See chapter 4.) Tourism Victoria (812 Wharf St. (*©* 250/953-2033; www.tourismvictoria.com) publishes a good guide for parents, called "Things to Do with Kids." Check out www.kidfriendly.org, too. It's a great site for child-friendly things to do in British Columbia, places to stay, and other ideas.

FOR FEMALE TRAVELERS

British Columbia and the entire Pacific Northwest is safe, polite, and a great place for female travelers. As with any destination, common sense should dissuade you from hitchhiking, or walking alone late at night in a city. Otherwise, traveling should be a delight. If you're heading off the beaten track and into the wilds, hike or camp with a friend. A number of Canadian outfitters offer women-only adventure tours.

Check out the award-winning website **Journeywoman** (www.journeywoman.com), a "real life" women's travel-information network where you can sign up for a free e-mail newsletter and get advice on everything from etiquette and dress to safety; or the travel guide *Safety and Security for Women Who Travel* by

Sheila Swan and Peter Laufer (Travelers' Tales, Inc.), offering common-sense tips on safe travel.

FOR GAY & LESBIAN TRAVELERS

The larger cities in Western Canada are gay-tolerant, with a number of gay bars, gay-owned businesses, and after-hours clubs. In fact, same-sex union celebrations are one of Canada's hottest tourism products. In Victoria, Gay Pride stages an annual parade in early July, where transvestites and others really strut their stuff. The gay lifestyle is widely accepted throughout the islands, on either side of the border, although in some of the small, northernmost communities on Vancouver Island, discretion is advised. Public displays of affection will not be appreciated. Log into the chat channel at **www.gayvictoria.ca** for updates on events, and resources around the region.

The International Gay and Lesbian Travel Association (IGLTA) (*©* 800/448-8550 or 954/776-2626; www.iglta.org) is the trade association for the gay and lesbian travel industry, and offers an online directory of gay- and lesbian-friendly travel businesses; go to their website and click "Members."

Many agencies offer tours and travel itineraries specifically for gay and lesbian travelers. Among them are **Above and Beyond Tours** (*©* 800/397-2681; www.abovebeyondtours.com); **Now, Voyager** (*©* 800/255-6951; www.nowvoyager.com); and **Olivia Cruises & Resorts** (*©* 800/631-6277; www.olivia.com).

Gay.com Travel (*©* 800/929-2268 or 415/644-8044; www.gay.com/travel or www.outandabout.com), is an excellent online successor to the popular *Out & About* print magazine. It provides regularly updated information about gay-owned, gay-oriented, and gay-friendly lodging, dining, sightseeing, nightlife, and shopping establishments in every important destination worldwide.

FOR SENIORS

Travelers 65 years of age and over often qualify for discounts at hotels and attractions, so don't be shy about asking. Just be sure to always carry some kind of ID—such as a driver's license—that shows your date of birth. In Victoria and Nanaimo, seniors receive **discounts on public transit.** Passes for persons over 65 (with proof of age) may be purchased at shops in Victoria that display a Fare-Dealer sign (7-Eleven stores are a good bet, as are most newsstands). To locate a FareDealer vendor, contact **BC Transit,** 520 Gorge Rd., Victoria, BC V8W 2P3 (© 250/382-6161; www.bctransit.com).

Members of AARP (601 E. St. NW, Washington, DC 20049 (© **800/424-3410** or 202/434-2277; www.aarp.org), can get discounts on hotels, airfares and car rentals. Anyone over 50 can join; members receive a wide range of benefits including a monthly newsletter. The Canadian affiliate can be reached at www.aarpcanada.net.

Many reliable agencies and organizations target the 50-plus market. **Elderhostel** (© **877/426-8056;** www.elderhostel.org) arranges study programs for those aged 55 and over. **ElderTreks** (© **800/741-7956;** www.eldertreks.com) offers small-group tours to off-the-beaten-path or adventure-travel locations, restricted to travelers 50 and older. **INTRAV** (© **800/456-8100;** www.intrav.com) is a high-end tour operator that caters to the mature, discerning traveler (not specifically seniors), with trips around the world that include guided safaris, polar expeditions, private-jet adventures, and small-boat cruises down jungle rivers.

Recommended publications offering travel resources and discounts for seniors include: the quarterly magazine *Travel 50 & Beyond* (www.travel50andbeyond.com); *Travel Unlimited: Uncommon Adventures for the Mature Traveler* (Avalon); *101 Tips for Mature Travelers,* available from Grand Circle Travel (© **800/221-2610** or 617/350-7500; www.gct.com); and *Unbelievably Good Deals and Great Adventures That You Absolutely Can't Get Unless You're Over 50* (McGraw-Hill), by Joann Rattner Heilman.

FOR STUDENTS

Council Travel Service (© **800/226-8624;** www.counciltravel.com), which operates in Canada through **Travel Cuts,** is the biggest student travel agency operation in the world. It is a great resource for travel deals, as well as basic health and life insurance. It also has a **24-hour help line.** Here's where to obtain a **Student ID card** that will be your key to discounts on plane tickets, rail passes, and more. In Canada, you can find a Travel Cuts office at most university campuses across the country. They also have offices in Victoria, at 1312 Douglas St. (© **250/995-8556**) and Vancouver, at 567 Seymour St., Vancouver BC V6B 3H6 (© **604/659-2830**). You can call them toll-free, at © **800/667-2887,** or go online to **www.travelcuts.com.**

9 Planning Your Trip Online

SURFING FOR AIRFARE

The most popular online travel agencies are **Travelocity** (**www.travelocity.com,** or www.travelocity.co.uk); **Expedia** (**www.expedia.com,** www.expedia.co.uk, or www.expedia.ca); and **Orbitz** (**www.orbitz.com**).

In addition, most airlines now offer online-only fares that even their phone agents know nothing about. For the websites of airlines that fly to and from your destination, go to "Getting There," p. 28.

Frommers.com: The Complete Travel Resource

For an excellent travel-planning resource, we highly recommend **Frommers.com** (www.frommers.com), voted Best Travel Site by *PC Magazine*. We're a little biased, of course, but we guarantee that you'll find the travel tips, reviews, monthly vacation giveaways, bookstore, and online-booking capabilities thoroughly indispensable. Among the special features are our popular **Destinations** section, where you'll get expert travel tips, hotel and dining recommendations, and advice on the sights to see for more than 3,500 destinations around the globe; the **Frommers.com Newsletter**, with the latest deals, travel trends, and money-saving secrets; our **Community** area featuring **Message Boards**, where Frommer's readers post queries and share advice (sometimes even our authors show up to answer questions); and our **Photo Center**, where you can post and share vacation tips. When your research is finished, the **Online Reservations System** (www.frommers.com/book_a_trip) takes you to Frommer's preferred online partners for booking your vacation at affordable prices.

Other helpful websites for booking airline tickets online include:

- www.biddingfortravel.com
- www.cheapflights.com
- www.hotwire.com
- www.kayak.com
- www.lastminutetravel.com
- www.opodo.co.uk
- www.priceline.com
- www.sidestep.com
- www.site59.com
- www.smartertravel.com

SURFING FOR HOTELS

In addition to **Travelocity, Expedia, Orbitz, Priceline,** and **Hotwire** (see above), the following websites will help you with booking hotel rooms online:

- www.hotels.com
- www.quickbook.com
- www.travelaxe.net
- www.travelweb.com
- www.tripadvisor.com

Tip: It's a good idea to **get a confirmation number** and **make a printout** of any online booking transaction.

Canadian hotels are well represented on U.S.-based travel sites, especially Expedia.com (it has such a long list of deals) and Priceline. A particularly good site for B&Bs throughout Canada is www.bbcanada.com and for the west coast, www.bc-bed-and-breakfast.com. The Bed and Breakfast Association of San Juan Island also operates a good site: www.san-juan-island.net.

SURFING FOR RENTAL CARS

When booking rental cars online, the best deals are usually found at rental-car company websites, although all the major online travel agencies also offer rental-car reservations services. Priceline and Hotwire work well for rental cars, too; the only "mystery" is which major rental company you get, and for most travelers the difference between Hertz, Avis, and Budget is negligible.

10 The 21st-Century Traveler

INTERNET ACCESS AWAY FROM HOME
WITHOUT YOUR OWN COMPUTER

To find cybercafes in your destination check **www.cybercaptive.com, www.netcafeguide.com,** and **www.cybercafe.com**. In Victoria, most hotels have wireless access either in the lobby or lounge or as a guest room amenity. The larger ones are likely to have bedroom dataports as well. This cannot be said for inns on the San Juan or Gulf islands. Services are only just now reaching this part of the world, so if living "wired" is essential, call ahead to check. Don't expect to come across very many, if any, cybercafes.

Aside from formal cybercafes, most **youth hostels** and **public libraries** have Internet access. Avoid **hotel business centers** unless you're willing to pay exorbitant rates.

Most major airports now have **Internet kiosks** among their gates. These give you basic Web access for a per-minute fee that's usually higher than cybercafe prices.

WITH YOUR OWN COMPUTER

More and more hotels, cafes, and retailers are signing on as Wi-Fi (wireless fidelity) "hotspots." Mac owners have their own networking technology: Apple AirPort. **T-Mobile Hotspot** (www.t-mobile.com/hotspot) serves up wireless connections at more than 1,000 Starbucks coffee shops nationwide. **Boingo** (www.boingo.com) and **Wayport** (www.wayport.com) have set up networks in airports and high-class hotel lobbies. IPass providers (see below) also give you access to a few hundred wireless hotel lobby setups. To locate other hotspots that provide **free wireless networks** in cities around the world, go to **www.personaltelco.net/index.cgi/WirelessCommunities**.

For dial-up access, most business-class hotels throughout the world offer dataports for laptop modems, and a few thousand hotels in the U.S. and Europe now offer free high-speed Internet access. In addition, major Internet Service Providers (ISPs) have **local access numbers** around the world, allowing you to go online by placing a local call. The **iPass** network also has dial-up numbers around the world. You'll have to sign up with an iPass provider, who will then tell you how to set up your computer for your destination(s). For a list of iPass providers, go to www.ipass.com and click "Individuals Buy Now." One solid provider is **i2roam** (www.i2roam.com; **℃ 866/811-6209** or 920/235-0475).

Wherever you go, bring a **connection kit** of the right power and phone adapters, a spare phone cord, and a spare ethernet network cable—or find out whether your hotel supplies them to guests.

CELLPHONE USE

The three letters that define much of the world's wireless capabilities are GSM (Global System for Mobiles), a big, seamless network that makes for easy cross-border cellphone use throughout Europe and dozens of other countries worldwide. In the U.S., T-Mobile, AT&T Wireless, and Cingular use this quasi-universal system; in Canada, Microcell and some Rogers customers are GSM. If your cellphone is on a GSM system, and you have a world-capable multiband phone such as many Sony Ericsson, Motorola, or Samsung models, you can make and receive calls across civilized areas around much of the globe. Just call your wireless operator and ask for "international roaming" to be activated on your account. None of the islands mentioned in this book offer any cellphone rental services.

Online Traveler's Toolbox

Veteran travelers usually carry some essential items to make their trips easier. Following is a selection of handy online tools to bookmark and use.

- **Airplane Food** (www.airlinemeals.net)
- **Airplane Seating** (www.seatguru.com; and www.airlinequality.com)
- **Foreign Languages for Travelers** (www.travlang.com)
- **Maps** (www.mapquest.com)
- **Subway Navigator** (www.subwaynavigator.com)
- **Time and Date** (www.timeanddate.com)
- **Travel Warnings** (http://travel.state.gov, www.fco.gov.uk/travel, www.voyage.gc.ca, or www.dfat.gov.au/consular/advice)
- **Universal Currency Converter** (www.xe.com/ucc)
- **Visa ATM Locator** (www.visa.com), **MasterCard ATM Locator** (www.mastercard.com)
- **Weather** (www.intellicast.com; and www.weather.com)

Buying a phone can be economically attractive, as many nations have cheap prepaid phone systems. Once you arrive at your destination, stop by a local cellphone shop and get the cheapest package; you'll probably pay less than C$100 (US$88) for a phone and a starter calling card. Local calls may be as low as 10¢ per minute, and in many countries incoming calls are free.

Wilderness adventurers might consider renting a **satellite phone ("satphone").** It's different from a cellphone in that it connects to satellites and works where there's no cellular signal or ground-based tower. You can rent satellite phones from RoadPost (www.roadpost.com). InTouch USA offers a wider range of satphones but at higher rates. Per-minute call charges can be even cheaper than roaming charges with a regular cellphone, but the phone itself is more expensive. As of this writing, satphones were outrageously expensive to buy, so don't even think about it.

11 Getting There

AIRLINE DISCOUNTS   The smart traveler can find any number of ways to reduce the price of a plane ticket simply by taking time to shop around. For example, overseas visitors can take advantage of the APEX (Advance Purchase Excursion) reductions offered by all major U.S., Canadian, and European carriers. For the best rates, compare fares and be flexible with the dates and times of travel. Some large airlines (for example, Northwest and Delta) offer travelers on their transatlantic or transpacific flights special discount tickets under the name **Visit USA**, allowing mostly one-way travel from one U.S. destination to another at very low prices. These discount tickets are not on sale in the United States and must be purchased abroad in conjunction with your international ticket. If traveling to and around the San Juans is part of a larger itinerary to see the United States, this system is the best, easiest, and fastest way to see the U.S. at low cost. You should obtain information well in advance from your travel agent or the office of the airline concerned, since the conditions attached to these discount tickets can be changed without advance notice.

IMMIGRATION AND CUSTOMS CLEARANCE Visitors arriving by air, no matter what the port of entry, should cultivate patience and resignation before setting foot on U.S. soil. Getting through immigration control can take as long as 2 hours on some days, especially on summer weekends, so be sure to carry this guidebook or something else to read. This is especially true in the aftermath of the World Trade Center attacks in September 2001; since then, security clearances have been considerably beefed up at U.S. airports.

People traveling by air from Canada, Bermuda, and certain countries in the Caribbean can sometimes clear Customs and Immigration at the point of departure, which is much quicker.

BY PLANE

Western United States is linked with Canada, Europe, and Asia by frequent non-stop flights. Seattle's **Seatac International Airport** (② 206/433-5388; www.seatac.org) and **Vancouver International Airport** (② 604/207-7077; www.yvr.ca) are major hubs; regional airlines connect to Victoria, Bellingham, and smaller centers throughout the islands. Major carriers include: **Air Canada** (② 888/247-2262; www.aircanada.ca), **WestJet** (② 800/538-5696 or 888/937-8538; www.west

jet.com), **American Airlines** (② 800/443-7300; www.americanairlines.com), **Continental** (② 800/231-0856; www.continentalairlines.com), **Delta Airlines** (② 800/221-1212; www.delta.com), **Northwest Airlines** (② 800/447-4747; www.nwa.com), and **United Airlines** (② 800/241-6522; www.ual.com).

Air Canada and **Horizon Air** (② 800/547-9308; www.horizonair.com or www.alaskaair.com), Alaska Airlines' connector, offer direct connections from several U.S. and Canadian cities such as Washington, D.C., Anchorage, San Francisco, and Calgary, to Vancouver, Victoria, and Seattle. Provincial commuter airlines, including floatplanes and helicopters that fly between Vancouver Harbour on the mainland, and Victoria's Inner Harbour, also serve the Gulf Islands. They include: **Air Canada Jazz** (a subsidiary of Air Canada) (② 888/247-2262; www.flyjazz.ca), **Harbour Air Sea Planes** (② 800/665-0212 or 604/274-1277; www.harbour-air.com), **Helijet Airways** (② 800/665-4354 or 250/382-6222; www.helijet.com), **Kenmore Air** (② 800/543-9595; www.kenmoreair.com), **Pacific Coastal Airlines** (② 800/663-2872 outside Vancouver or 604/273-8666 in Vancouver; www.pacific-coastal.com), and **West Coast Air** (Floats) (② 800/347-2222; www.westcoastair.com). Commercial air service between the Seattle area and the San

---

ⓘ Tips Prepare to Be Fingerprinted

Starting in January 2004, many international visitors traveling on visas to the United States will be photographed and fingerprinted at Customs through a new program created by the Department of Homeland Security called **US-VISIT.** Non–U.S. citizens arriving at airports and on cruise ships must undergo an instant background check as part of the government's ongoing efforts to deter terrorism by verifying the identity of incoming and outgoing visitors. Exempt from the extra scrutiny are visitors entering by land or those from 28 countries (mostly in Europe) that don't require a visa for short-term visits. For more information, go to the Homeland Security website at **www.dhs.gov/dhspublic.**

Juan Islands includes: **Island Air** (charter only) (© **360/378-2376;** www.sanjuan islandair.com), **Kenmore Air** (seaplanes) (© **800/543-9595;** www.kenmoreair. com), **Northwest Seaplanes** (© **800/690-0086;** www.nwseaplanes.com), and **San Juan Airlines** (© **800/874-4434;** www. sanjuanairlines.com).

BY TRAIN

International visitors (excluding Canada) can buy a **USA Rail Pass**, good for 15 or 30 days of unlimited travel on Amtrak (© **800/USA-RAIL;** www.amtrak.com). The pass is available through many overseas travel agents. Current prices for a 15-day pass are US$305 off-peak, US$455 peak; a 30-day pass costs US$395 off-peak, US$565 peak. With a foreign passport, you can also buy passes at some Amtrak offices in the United States, including locations in San Francisco, Los Angeles, Chicago, New York, Miami, Boston, and Washington, D.C. Reservations are generally required and should be made for each part of your trip as early as possible. If a stopover to the islands is in your overall touring plans, such a pass is a good option. Because **Amtrak** services, and Canada's VIA Rail services across Canada, end in Vancouver, travel to Victoria and Vancouver Island requires connecting to either ferry or plane transportation. **VIA Rail** (© **800/561-8630;** www.viarail.com) connects Vancouver to the rest of Canada. **Amtrak** (© **800/872-7245;** www.amtrak.com) offers a daily service (a combination of train and coach) between Seattle and Vancouver. Schedules for both VIA Rail and Amtrak are posted at **Pacific Central Station,** 1150 Station St. (at the corner of Main St. and Terminal Ave.), Vancouver, and at King Street Station, 303 South Jackson St., Seattle.

BY BUS & FERRY

Although bus travel is often the most economical form of public transit for short hops between U.S. cities, it can also be slow and uncomfortable—certainly not an option for everyone (particularly when Amtrak, which is far more luxurious, offers similar rates). **Greyhound/Trailways** (© **800/231-2222;** www.greyhound. com), the sole nationwide bus line, offers an **International Discovery Ameripass** that must be purchased before coming to the United States, or by phone through the Greyhound International Office (© **888/454-7277**). The pass can be obtained from foreign travel agents or through Greyhound's website (order at least 21 days before your departure to the U.S.) and costs less than the domestic version. The passes cost as follows: 7 days for US$283, 15 days for US$415, 30 days for US$522, or 60 days for US$645. You can get more info on the pass at the website, or by calling © **402/330-8552.** In addition, special rates are available for seniors and students.

TO VICTORIA Pacific Coach Lines (© **800/661-1725** or 604/ 662-7575; www.pacificcoach.com) operates bus service between Vancouver and Victoria. The 4-hour trip from the **Vancouver bus terminal** (Pacific Central Station, 1150 Station St.) to the **Victoria Depot** (700 Douglas St.) includes passage on the **Tsawwassen–Swartz Bay ferry.** One-way fares are C$37 (US$32) for adults, C$25 (US$22) for B.C. seniors; return fares are C$71 (US$62) for adults, C$47 (US$41) for B.C. seniors. Discounts are not offered to out-of-province seniors. Fares for children 5 to 11 are half the adult fare. Departures are daily, every 2 hours, between 5:45am and 7:45pm.

The Victoria Express (© **800/633-1589** in season, or year round © 360/ 452-8088 from the U.S. and 250/361-9144 from Canada; www.victoriaexpress. com) operates a seasonal passenger-only ferry service, June through September, between Port Angeles and Victoria. Crossing time is 1 hour. There are two crossings per day. Reservations are available. Fares are US$13 per passenger; children 1 year and under travel for free.

Clipper Navigation (✆ **800/888-2535** or 250/383-8100; www.victoria clipper.com) runs a year-round passenger-only service between Seattle and Victoria aboard a high-speed catamaran called the **Victoria Clipper.** From mid-May to mid-September, there are up to three crossings per day. The rest of the year this is reduced to one crossing per day. The trips are approximately 3 hours. One-way fares mid-May through mid-September are US$84, return fares are US$139. From mid-September to mid-May, in the off-season, one-way fares are US$66–$77; return fares are US$110–$129. From mid-May to mid-September, there is one daily crossing aboard the Victoria Clipper from Seattle to Friday Harbor, on San Juan Island. One-way fares for all passengers are US$65; return fares are US$80. Reservations are not accepted.

TO THE GULF ISLANDS Travelers should take the **Pacific Coach Lines coach** from Vancouver to Victoria, as mentioned above, but disembark in **Tsawwassen,** where **BC Ferries** (✆ **888/ BCFERRY [888/223-3779])** or 250/386-3431; www.bcferries.com) sails year-round to the island of your choice. On Vancouver Island, BC Ferries departs from **Swartz Bay,** north of Victoria. Fares and sailing times range from 1 to 3 hours depending on your final island destination. See "Getting There," in chapter 8 for information about schedules and fares to specific islands.

TO THE SAN JUAN ISLANDS From Seattle's **Seatac International Airport** (✆ **206/433-5388;** www.seatac.org) and from the **Bellingham Airport** (✆ **360/ 671-5674), Airporter Shuttle** (✆ **800/ 235-5247;** www.airporter.com) and **Skagit County Bus** (✆ **360/757-4433;** www. skat.org) transport passengers to Anacortes, north of Seattle on the Olympic Peninsula, just east of the San Juans. Connections can be made between Bellingham Airport and Vancouver on **Quick Shuttle** (✆ **800/665-2122;** www. quick coach.com). There is no bus transportation for travelers from Anacortes to the San Juans; you travel either on foot or in your own vehicle. Once there, visitors traveling on foot have a choice of taxis, car rentals, moped rentals, or bicycle rentals. See chapter 9.

BY CAR & FERRY

Car travel is the most cost-effective, convenient, and comfortable way to travel around this westernmost part of North America. The interprovincial highway system connects cities and towns all over the country; in addition to these high-speed, limited-access roadways, there's an extensive network of federal, provincial, and local highways and roads. Some of the national car-rental companies include **Alamo** (✆ **800/462-5266;** www.alamo. com), **Avis** (✆ **800/230-4898;** www. avis.com), **Budget** (✆ **800/527-0700;** www.budget.com), **Dollar** (✆ **800/800-3665;** www.dollar.com), **Hertz** (✆ **800/ 654-3131;** www.hertz.com), **National** (✆ **800/227-7368;** www.nationalcar. com), and **Thrifty** (✆ **800/847-4389;** www.thrifty.com).

If you plan to rent a car in either the United States or Canada, you probably won't need the services of an additional automobile organization. If you're planning to buy or borrow a car, automobile-association membership is recommended. **AAA, the American Automobile Association** (✆ **800/222-4357**), is the country's largest auto club and supplies its members with maps, insurance, and, most important, emergency road service. The cost of joining runs from US$63 for singles to US$87 for two members, but if you're a member of a foreign auto club with reciprocal arrangements, you can enjoy free AAA service.

Vancouver Island

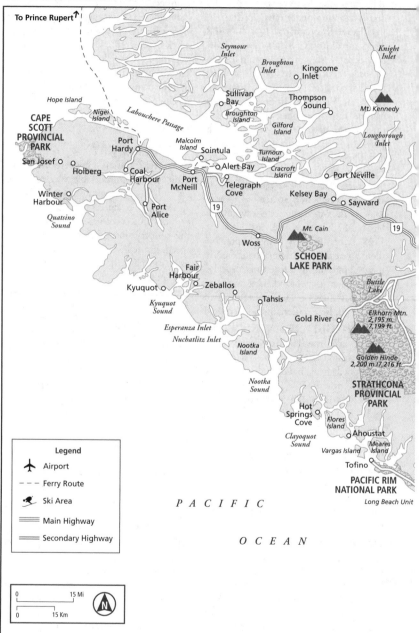

To Prince Rupert↑

Seymour
Inlet

Broughton
Inlet

Kingcome
Inlet

Knight
Inlet

Sullivan
Bay

Thompson
Sound

Mt. Kennedy

Hope Island

Nigei
Island

Labouchere Passage

Broughton
Island

Gilford
Island

Loughborough
Inlet

**CAPE
SCOTT
PROVINCIAL
PARK**

Port
Hardy

Malcolm
Island

Sointula

Turnour
Island

San Josef

Holberg

Coal
Harbour

Port
McNeill

Alert Bay

Cracroft
Island

Port Neville

Winter
Harbour

Port
Alice

Telegraph
Cove

Kelsey Bay

Sayward

Quatsino
Sound

19

Woss

Mt. Cain

**SCHOEN
LAKE PARK**

19

Buttle
Lake

Fair
Harbour

Kyuquot

Zeballos

Tahsis

Gold River

Elkhorn Mtn.
2,195 m.
7,199 ft.

Kyuquot
Sound

Esperanza Inlet

Nuchatlitz Inlet

Nootka
Island

Golden Hinde
2,200 m./7,216 ft.

Nootka
Sound

**STRATHCONA
PROVINCIAL
PARK**

Hot
Springs
Cove

Flores
Island

Ahoustat

Clayoquot
Sound

Vargas Island

Meares
Island

Tofino

**PACIFIC RIM
NATIONAL PARK**

Long Beach Unit

Legend

✈ Airport

- - - Ferry Route

🎿 Ski Area

═══ Main Highway

══ Secondary Highway

P A C I F I C

O C E A N

0   15 Mi
0   15 Km

N

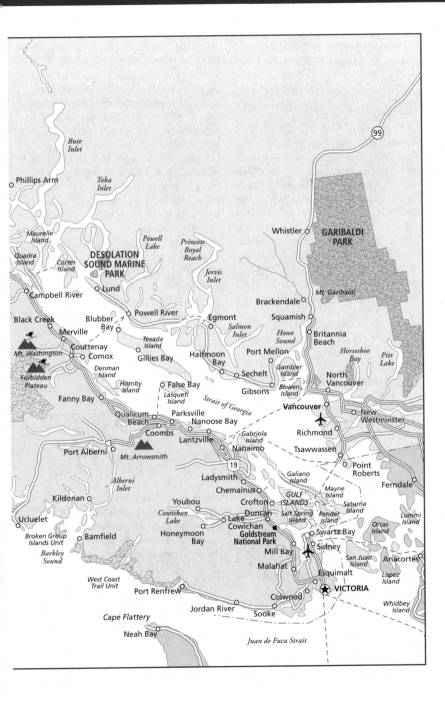

TO VANCOUVER ISLAND Hopping across the United States/Canadian border by car is easy, with the main crossing located right on the **I-5 at Peace Arch Park,** just north of **Blaine.** Once in Canada, drive to **Tsawwassen** to catch any number of ferries leaving for Vancouver, Nanaimo, and the Gulf Islands.

From the United States, daily ferry services link Port Angeles, Seattle, and Anacortes, Washington, with port facilities near Victoria. These include **Blackball Transport** (© **360/457-4491** in Washington, © **250/386-2202** on Vancouver Island; www.cohoferry.com), which runs a year-round, first-come first-served car and passenger service aboard the MV *Coho* between Port Angeles and Victoria. One-way fares are US$43 for a standard-size vehicle and driver, US$11 for adult passengers, US$5.50 for children. There are four 1½-hour daily crossings, from June to mid-September. There is one crossing daily from October to January, and two crossings daily from February to May.

Washington State Ferries (© **800/843-3779** in Washington, or 888/808-7977 in Canada, or 206/464-6400; www.wsdot.wa.gov/ferries) runs a passenger and car ferry service from Anacortes, through the San Juan Islands, to Sidney, 26km (16 miles) north of Victoria, and returns. There are two crossings daily, and vehicle reservations are strongly recommended in summer. Reservations must be made by 5:30pm the day prior to travel. From May to early October, one-way fares are US$16 for adults, US$7.80 for seniors, US$13 for children 6 to 18, and US$53 for a standard-size vehicle and driver. From mid-October to April, one-way fares remain the same for adults, seniors, and children; the fare for a standard-size vehicle and driver is reduced to US$42. Crossing time is 3 hours.

Alternatively, you can choose to cross the border just north of Blaine, and catch a **BC Ferries** vessel from Tsawwassen on the mainland to Swartz Bay, a 32-km (20-mile) drive from Victoria's city center, or to Duke Point Terminal, near Nanaimo. Ferries leave every hour on the hour during the summer season, June through Labor Day, and on the odd hour for the rest of the year. Extra sailings are often added for holiday periods. Reservations are available, but not always necessary. One-way fares average C$12 (US$11) for adults, C$5.50 (US$5) for B.C. students, and all children 4 to 11; C$48 (US$42) for a standard-size vehicle and driver. B.C. seniors travel free Monday through Thursday, except on holidays. All BC Ferries have a restaurant and/or coffee bar on board, serving a wide range of soups, sandwiches, burger platters, salads, and snack food.

TO THE GULF ISLANDS BC Ferries (© **888/BCFERRY** (888/223-3779 or 250/386-3431; www.bcferries.bc.ca) operates an extensive network of ferries to the Gulf Islands, linking the islands to one another, to the B.C. mainland, and to Vancouver Island. There are at least two crossings daily, year round, to each of the Gulf Islands, but departure times vary according to your destination. Ferry travel can be expensive if you're taking a vehicle, and long boarding waits are not uncommon. Ticket prices vary seasonally; midweek travel is slightly less than on weekends and holidays. During these peak periods, book at least 3 weeks in advance to avoid disappointment. Reservations can be made by phone or online. One-way fares from Tsawwassen average C$12 (US$11) per passenger; C$52 (US$46) for a standard-size vehicle and driver. One-way fares from Swartz Bay average C$7 (US$6) per passenger; C$32 (US$27) for a standard-size regular vehicle and driver. Return fares are less, and vary according to which island you are returning from. Return fares from the islands to Swartz Bay are free. Inter-island trips average C$4 (US$3.50) per passenger; C$9 (US$8) for a standard-size vehicle.

TO THE SAN JUAN ISLANDS From mid-May to September, **Clipper Navigation** (✆ **800/888-2535** or 250/383-8100; www. victoriaclipper.com) runs one crossing daily from Seattle to Friday Harbor, on San Juan Island, aboard the **Victoria Clipper** passenger-only ferry. One-way fares are US$84 per adult; US$78 senior; return fares are US$139 per adult; US$129 senior. Children 1 to 11 years are US$42 one way; US$70 return. Crossing time is 2½ hours. Reservations are not accepted. **Washington State Ferries** (✆ **888/808-7977** or 206/464-6400; www.wsdot.wa.gov/ferries) provide multiple crossings daily between Anacortes and each of the larger San Juan Islands. No reservations are available. If you're taking a vehicle, you should arrive at least an hour before scheduled sailings; up to 3 hours at peak travel times on summer and holiday weekends. Some food service and a picnic area are available near the terminal. Check out **www.ferry cam.net** to see live images of the ferry lanes. From May 3 to October 1, one-way fares are US$13 for adults, US$6.40 for seniors, US$10 for children 6 to 18, and US$50 for a standard-size vehicle and driver; seniors taking a vehicle travel at half the adult fare (a discount of US$6.40). Fares are lower in the off season, October 2 through May 2. Inter-island travel is US$9.35 for a standard-size vehicle and driver; passengers are free.

12 Tips on Accommodations

Between the large hotels in Victoria, and the picturesque B&Bs and inns in the rest of the region, there really is something for everyone in terms of charm, character and comfort. Other than in Victoria, you won't come across major chains. The inns and B&Bs on the islands have a special appeal because they're far from cookie-cutter guest houses. Be aware, however, that accommodation tends to get a little more basic the farther north you travel. In Canada, a big deal is made about the term "Canada Select," which refers to a provincial rating program. If a place is part of the program, then you know to expect a level of cleanliness and service that won't disappoint. Hence, most don't advertise their rating until it reaches in excess of 2—the top being "we've got absolutely everything" 5 stars. That includes having a paved driveway, which some rural destinations have forgone for the sake of ambience, costing themselves half a star in the process.

SAVING ON YOUR HOTEL ROOM

The **rack rate** is the maximum rate that a hotel charges for a room. Hardly anybody pays this price, however, except in high season or on holidays. To lower the cost of your room:

- **Ask about special rates or other discounts.** You may qualify for corporate, student, military, senior, frequent flyer, trade union, or other discounts.
- **Dial direct.** When booking a room in a chain hotel, you'll often get a better deal by calling the individual hotel's reservation desk rather than the chain's main number.
- **Book online.** Many hotels offer Internet-only discounts, or supply rooms to Priceline, Hotwire, or Expedia at rates much lower than the ones you can get through the hotel itself.
- **Remember the law of supply and demand.** Resort hotels are most

House-Swapping

House-swapping is becoming a more popular and viable means of travel; you stay in their place, they stay in yours, and you both get an authentic and personal view of the area, the opposite of the escapist retreat that many hotels offer. Try **HomeLink International** (homelink.org), the largest and oldest home-swapping organization, founded in 1952, with over 11,000 listings worldwide (US$75 for a yearly membership). **HomeExchange.org** (US$50 for 6,000 listings) and **InterVac.com** (US$69 for over 10,000 listings) are also reliable.

crowded and therefore most expensive on weekends, so discounts are usually available for midweek stays. Business hotels in downtown locations are busiest during the week, so you can expect big discounts over the weekend. Many hotels have high-season and low-season prices, and booking even one day after high season ends can mean big discounts.

- **Look into group or long-stay discounts.** If you come as part of a large group, you should be able to negotiate a bargain rate. Likewise, if you're planning a long stay (at least 5 days), you might qualify for a discount. As a general rule, expect 1 night free after a 7-night stay.

- **Avoid excess charges and hidden costs.** When you book a room, ask whether the hotel charges for parking. Use your own cellphone, pay phones, or prepaid phone cards instead of dialing direct from hotel phones, which usually have exorbitant rates. And don't be tempted by the room's minibar offerings. Finally, ask about local taxes and service charges, which can increase the cost of a room by 15% or more.

- **Book an efficiency.** A room with a kitchenette allows you to shop for groceries and cook your own meals. This is a big money saver, especially for families on long stays.

- **Consider enrolling in hotel "frequent-stay" programs**, which are upping the ante lately to win the loyalty of repeat customers. Frequent guests can now accumulate points or credits to earn free hotel nights, airline miles, in-room amenities, merchandise, tickets to concerts and events, discounts on sporting facilities—and even credit toward stock in the participating hotel, in the case of the Jameson Inn hotel group. Perks are awarded not only by many chain hotels and motels (Hilton HHonors, Marriott Rewards, Wyndham ByRequest, to name a few), but individual inns and B&Bs. Many chain hotels partner with other hotel chains, car-rental firms, airlines, and credit-card companies to give consumers additional incentive to do repeat business.

- **Check with the local island tourism offices for lead**s: some island homes, usually the more modest ones, aren't advertised too far off-island. Once you're on one of the smaller islands, you're likely to come across cards posted on the bulletin board at the local hardware store advertising short-term and long-term lets.

LANDING THE BEST ROOM

Somebody has to get the best room in the house. It might as well be you. You can start by joining the hotel's frequent-guest program, which may make you eligible for upgrades. A hotel-branded credit card usually gives its owner "silver" or "gold" status in frequent-guest programs for free. Always ask about a corner room. They're often larger and quieter, with more windows and light, and they often cost the same as standard rooms. When you make your reservation, ask if the hotel is renovating; if it is, request a room away from the construction. Ask about nonsmoking rooms, rooms with views, rooms with twin, queen- or king-size beds. If you're a light sleeper, request a quiet room away from vending machines, elevators, restaurants, bars, and discos. Ask for a room that has been most recently renovated or redecorated.

If you aren't happy with your room when you arrive, ask for another one. Most lodgings will be willing to accommodate you.

13 Getting Around

BY CAR

All the islands are a pleasure to explore and best done by car. In Victoria and Nanaimo, you'll find a number of rental car companies, including **Avis** (© **800/879-2847;** www.avis.com), **Budget** (© **800/268-8900;** www.budget.com) and **Hertz** (© **800/263-0600;** www.hertz.com).

ON VANCOUVER ISLAND   Although highways are well maintained on Vancouver Island, getting from point A to point B can take longer than anticipated. Traffic in and around Victoria tends to be heavy and frustratingly slow—perhaps because so many drivers appear to be cautious retirees. Also, many of the region's more interesting attractions are off the highway on roads that twist and turn through picturesque communities. If you have the time, this beats highway asphalt. Gas is sold by the liter, averaging around C97¢ a liter (US85¢ a liter). Speeds and distances are posted in kilometers (1 kilometer = 0.6 miles). Logging roads lead to some of the best places on the island, but if you drive on one, remember that logging trucks have absolute right-of-way.

Members of the **American Automobile Association (AAA)** can get emergency assistance from the **British Columbia Automobile Association (BCAA)** (© **800/ 222-4357;** www.bcaa.com).

IN VICTORIA   This is a walking city, so don a good pair of shoes and park your car. Those few attractions that are not close to the city core are only a short taxi ride away. Victoria also has a comprehensive public transit system (see "Essentials" in chapter 4).

ON THE GULF & SAN JUAN ISLANDS   The easiest way to tour these islands is by car, although some communities have rental scooters, mopeds, and bicycles. (For details, see "Essentials" in chapter 8 or 9 for the specific island.)

BY TRAIN

VIA Rail's Malahat (© **800/561-8630;** www.viarail.ca) travels between Victoria and Courtenay, winding through the Cowichan River Valley and Goldstream Provincial Park. Travelers on the Horseshoe Bay–Nanaimo ferry board the train in Nanaimo. It departs from Victoria's

---

Tips **Distances and Driving Times from Victoria**

Victoria to Sidney: 26km (16 miles), approximately ½ hour
Victoria to Nanaimo: 111km (67 miles), approximately 1¾ hours
Victoria to Port Alberni: 195km (117 miles), approximately 3 hours
Victoria to Campbell River: 264km (158 miles), approximately 4 hours
Victoria to Tofino: 316km (190 miles), approximately 4¾ hours
Victoria to Port Hardy: 502km (312 miles), approximately 7 hours

VIA Rail Station (450 Pandora Ave.). The service runs Monday through Saturday, and the trip takes about 4½ hours. One-way fares from Victoria to Courtenay are C$48 (US$42) for adults, C$43 (US$38) for seniors, C$31 (US$27) for students, C$24 (US$21) for children 2 to 11. There are 7-day advance-purchase discounts and other specials available.

FAST FACTS: Vancouver Island, the Gulf Islands & the San Juan Islands

American Express To report lost or stolen traveler's checks, call ② **800/ 221-7282.**

Automobile Organizations Auto clubs will supply maps, suggested routes, guidebooks, accident and bail-bond insurance, and emergency road service. The **American Automobile Association (AAA)** is the major auto club in the United States. If you belong to an auto club in your home country, inquire about AAA reciprocity before you leave. You may be able to join AAA even if you're not a member of a reciprocal club; to inquire, call AAA (② **800/222- 4357**). AAA is actually an organization of regional auto clubs, so look under "AAA Automobile Club" in the White Pages of the telephone directory. AAA has a nationwide emergency road service telephone number (② **800/AAA- HELP**). In British Columbia, the reciprocal organization is the BCAA (② **604- 293-2222**).

Business Hours In Victoria and other major urban centers, banks are open Monday through Thursday from 10am to 3pm, Friday from 10am to 6pm, and sometimes on Saturday mornings. Stores typically open Monday through Saturday from 10am to 6pm. Stores in Victoria are also open Sunday in summers. Although business hours on the San Juan Islands and Gulf Islands tend to follow this pattern, you may come across unexpected closures of individual stores, especially early in the week when tourist traffic is slower.

Car Rentals See "Getting There" and "Getting Around," earlier in this chapter.

Currency Exchange See "Money," earlier in this chapter.

Dentists Most Gulf Islanders commute to Victoria for dental services. However, **Pender Island Dental Clinic** (5715 Canal Rd. ② **250/629-6815**) offers family and emergency dental care. San Juan islanders find major services in Anacortes and Seattle. **Tooth Ferry Dental Office** is located in Friday Harbor (385 Court St. ② **360/378-5319**).

Doctors On most of the islands, doctors operate out of medical clinics (see also "Hospitals" below). These include **Galiano Island Health Centre**, 908 Burrill Rd. (② **250/539-3230**); **Pender Island Health Care**, 5715 Canal Rd. (② **250/629- 3326**); **Mayne Island Health Centre**, 526 Felix Jack Rd. (② **250/539-2312**); **Orcas Island Family Health Center**, 1286 Mt. Baker Rd. (② **360/376-7778**), and **Inter- Island Medical Center**, 550 Spring St., Friday Harbor (② **360/378-3655**).

Drinking Laws In British Columbia, the minimum drinking age is 19. Liquor is sold only in government-run liquor stores, although in the larger communities such as Victoria and Nanaimo, you may find beer and wine sold from independent, government-licensed specialty shops. In the Gulf Islands, liquor is sold over a specific counter in one of the local stores. In Washington State, the minimum drinking age is 21. Spirits, wine, and beer are available for purchase in most grocery stores.

Drugstores You'll find outlets throughout the Islands. In Canada, pharmacists are extremely helpful for casual medical advice and are a good preliminary stop for minor ailments.

Electricity Like Canada, the United States uses 110 to 120 volts AC (60 cycles), compared to 220 to 240 volts AC (50 cycles) in most of Europe, Australia, and New Zealand. If your small appliances use 220 to 240 volts, you'll need a 110-volt transformer and a plug adapter with two flat parallel pins to operate them here. Downward converters that change 220–240 volts to 110–120 volts are difficult to find in the United States, so bring one with you.

Emergencies Dial 911 for fire, police, or ambulance, in either the US or Canada. This is a toll-free call. (No coins are required at public telephones). In British Columbia, the Royal Canadian Mounted Police (RCMP) administer a **Tourist Alert** program, by posting emergency notices at visitor information centers, at provincial park sites, and on B.C. ferries.

If you encounter serious problems, contact Traveler's Aid International (🕐 202/546-1127; www.travelersaid.org) to help direct you to a local branch. This nationwide, nonprofit, social-service organization geared to helping travelers in difficult straits offers services that might include reuniting families separated while traveling, providing food and/or shelter to people stranded without cash, or even giving emotional counseling. If you're in trouble, seek them out.

Gasoline (Petrol) Petrol is known as gasoline (or simply "gas") in Canada and the United States, and petrol stations are known as both gas stations and service stations. Gasoline costs about half as much here as it does in Europe (about C97¢ per liter at press time), and taxes are already included in the printed price. One U.S. gallon equals 3.8 liters or .85 Imperial gallons. Canadian gas is sold by the liter.

Hospitals Most major cities and towns, such as **Victoria, Nanaimo,** and **Campbell River,** have hospitals. These include Royal Jubilee Hospital, 1900 Fort St., Victoria (🕐 250/370-8000) and Lady Minto Hospital, 135 Crofton Rd., Salt Spring Island (🕐 250/ 538-4800). On the Gulf and San Juan islands, however, there are only medical clinics; for life-threatening situations, airlift services are used. (See "Doctors" and "Dentists" above.)

Internet Access Although you will find wireless access and Internet cafes in Victoria, public Internet access becomes increasingly scarce away from the city center, particularly on the Gulf Islands and San Juan Islands.

Newspapers & Magazines For regional and world news, Gulf Islanders have access to Victoria's major newspaper, *The Victoria Times-Colonist* and the *Vancouver Sun*. **The Gulf Islands Driftwood** is a small community newspaper published every Wednesday. Local papers on the San Juans include *The Journal* (San Juan Island), *The Sounder* (Orcas Island) and on Lopez, the *Islands Weekly*, all owned by the same publisher but each reporting on their specific island news.

Measurements See the chart on the inside front cover of this book for details on converting metric measurements to U.S. equivalents.

Post Office At press time postal rates within Canada are C51¢ for standard letters and postcards, C89¢ to the U.S., and C$1.49 overseas. For more information, log on to **www.canadapost.ca**. Postal rates within the U.S. are US39¢, US63¢ to Canada and US84¢ overseas. For more information, go to **http://pe.usps.gov**.

Radio There are no local radio stations on the islands (other than in Victoria—see "Victoria Fast Facts"). Islanders pick up signals from Victoria and Bellingham. CBC Radio One is Canada's equivalent to the BBC and can be heard on 90.5 FM in Victoria, and 91.5 FM in Tofino.

Smoking British Columbia by-laws prohibit smoking in a public place, including restaurants, offices, and shopping malls. Although this is adhered to in the larger cities, individual pubs and bars in the island communities try to turn a blind eye to the legislation. Ask before you light up publicly anywhere in the province. No smoking is also the "norm" in most public places in Washington State.

Taxes See "Entry Requirements & Customs," earlier in this chapter.

Telephone Although the Canadian and U.S. phone systems are the same, the systems are run by private companies, so rates, especially for long-distance service and operator-assisted calls, can vary widely. Generally, hotel surcharges on long-distance and local calls are astronomical, so you're usually better off using a public pay telephone which you'll find clearly marked in most public buildings and private establishments as well as on the street. Most public phones accept prepaid phone cards, sold at drugstores and convenience stores. Many public phones also accept American Express, MasterCard, and Visa credit cards. Numbers are made up of the 3-digit area code and the 7-digit local number. On Vancouver Island and the Gulf Islands, this prefix is 250. For the San Juan Islands, the area code is 360. "1" is the long-distance prefix. For directory assistance within Canada, dial **411**; in the U.S., dial **1 + area code + 555-1212**.

Note: Other than in the major centers, cellphone signals may vary in strength in different areas of all these islands, ranging from nonexistent to mediocre.

Time Zone British Columbia and Washington State are in the Pacific Time Zone, 3 hours behind Eastern Standard Time. As of 2007, daylight saving time applies from the second Sunday in March through the first Sunday in November.

Tipping Tipping etiquette is the same in Canada and the United States. In restaurants, tip 15% to 20% for good service. Tip 10% to hairdressers and taxi drivers. Tip on par, U.S. or Canadian funds, for baggage handling at $1 a bag, and tip chamber staff $1 to $2 per day.

Toilets You won't find public toilets or "restrooms" on the streets, but they can be found in hotel lobbies, bars, restaurants, museums, department stores, railway and bus stations, and service stations. Not all the islands have all these facilities; on the San Juans, for example, you're more likely to find an outhouse or two, strategically placed at a trailhead or public beach.

Weather Call ⓒ **604/664-9010** for weather updates; ⓒ **604/666-3655** for marine forecasts.

3

Suggested Itineraries

The coastal islands of the Pacific Northwest are almost as diverse as they are numerous, so explorations can be virtually custom-created according to mood and preference. City lovers can hover around Victoria; urban escapees will likely enjoy touring the San Juan and Gulf Islands; while outdoor devotees should head for Vancouver's Islands westernmost coast or to its most northern regions. The best thing about this part of the world, though, is that you can even mix and match activities to get a little of everything.

1 The San Juan Shuffle

Whether you arrive by ferry from Sidney or Anacortes, this short getaway feels like a world away. Traveling from Sidney means you can spend extra days in and around Victoria. If you head for San Juan Island from Anacortes, you can work your way back through the other islands with free inter-island ferry trips.

Day ❶: San Juan Island

After stopping off at **Friday Harbor** (p. 216) to see the sights and shops, take the perimeter road south to **American Camp** (p. 217). It's a long stretch of road (watch out for cyclists) with expansive views. On your return, take a slight detour to the **Pelindaba Lavender Farm** (p. 220) before heading along the westerly coast road to **English Camp** (p. 218). Farther along the road, you'll come to the new **Westcott Bay Sculpture Park** (p. 219). From there you can either walk or drive down to **Roche Harbor** (p. 218)—a good stop for the evening.

Day ❷: Orcas Island

Hop onto an early morning inter-island ferry and 35 minutes later you'll arrive at Orcas Island. Local traffic tends to head straight up the main road to Eastsound, but as visitors, choose to make the picturesque, winding drive west to **Deer Harbor** (p. 225) to get a sense of how pretty parts of this island can be. Then head north to **Eastsound** (p. 224), where you can browse specialty shops and enjoy lunch. Exploring the eastern arm of Orcas Island, including **Moran State Park** and **Olga** (p. 225), will take the better part of your afternoon.

Day ❸: Shaw Island/Lopez Island

Shaw Island (p. 229) is a pleasant morning detour en route to Lopez Island, although you'll need to coordinate your day carefully around sailing times. Once on Lopez, there's little left to do but kick back and relax. Enjoy the bucolic atmosphere and go on rambles along the bluff at **Iceberg Point** (p. 232) and around **Spencer Spit State Park** (p 229).

Day ❹: Return options

Take the return ferry to Anacortes, or plan to sail to Sidney to continue your adventure on Vancouver Island.

San Juan Island Itinerary

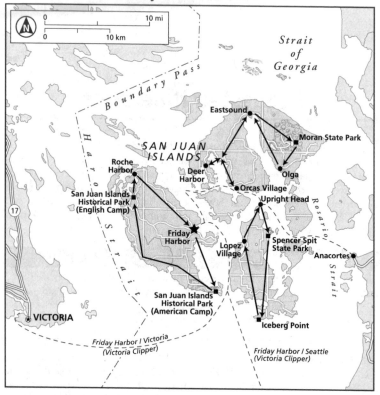

0   10 mi
0   10 km

Strait of Georgia

Boundary Pass

Eastsound

Moran State Park

SAN JUAN ISLANDS

Roche Harbor

Deer Harbor

Olga

Orcas Village

Upright Head

San Juan Islands Historical Park (English Camp)

17

Friday Harbor

Lopez Village

Spencer Spit State Park

Anacortes

San Juan Islands Historical Park (American Camp)

Iceberg Point

VICTORIA

Haro Strait

Rosario Strait

Friday Harbor / Victoria (Victoria Clipper)

Friday Harbor / Seattle (Victoria Clipper)

2 Gulf Islands Getaway in One Week

Island hopping around the Southern Gulf Islands will treat you to scenery that's breathtakingly beautiful: dense rainforest, wild shorelines, pretty coves, and pastoral landscapes. Every island has a distinct charm. Just be sure to bring along a book or crossword puzzle to help while away the inevitable hours you may have to linger a little longer than anticipated on an island as you wait for your ferry to come in! Ferry connections aren't always back to back and ferries can run later than scheduled. This itinerary assumes you're starting from Vancouver. Reverse it for Victoria departures.

Day ❶: Galiano

Galiano is the closest island from Van-couver, but it's a laid-back community that's worked hard to maintain its rural roots. The road that runs the length of the island's long, skinny shape takes you from a cluster of buildings near the ferry terminal, past pretty coves and marinas, and up to densely packed forests. There are wonderful walks in and around **Galiano Bluffs Park** and **Montague Provincial Park** (p. 199). Head north to experience the island's 'wild' side in and around **Dionisio Point Provincial Park.** Kayaking out of **Montague Harbour**

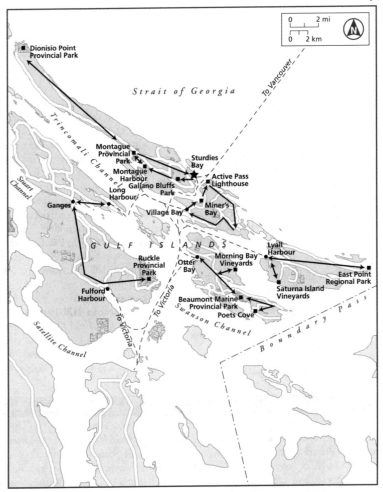

(p. 199) is another great way to fully appreciate the gentleness of this island.

Day ❷: Mayne Island

The small village area around **Miners Bay** (p. 204) boasts a bakery, a few worthwhile eateries and country inns, and sandy beaches. Of all the islands, this one is where you'll find the most accessible history: visit the tiny church, **St. Mary Magdalene** (p. 204); **Active Pass Lighthouse** (p. 204); **Mayne Island Museum**, which is housed in a historic

jail; and the **Agricultural Hall** (p. 204), which often hosts Saturday night bingo and second-run movies, for those seeking true local flavor.

Day ❸: The Penders

The marinas and coves here make the Penders a favorite destination for sailors, and with a permanent population base of approximately 2,000, these hilly islands have lots for you to see and do. **Beaumont Marine Provincial Park** (p. 195) is one of the prettiest destinations for hiking. It's also ideal for a picnic—be sure to pick up a bottle of wine from **Morning Bay Vineyards** (p. 194). If you're interested in **kayaking** (p. 194), it's especially easy to reach neighboring Saturna and Mayne islands from here. **Poets Cove** (see p. 196) is one of the best destination resorts in the Gulf Islands archipelago.

Day ❹: Saturna

You can tour around Saturna in less than a day; but staying longer means you have time to really appreciate the remote tranquility of this rainforested island. **East Point Regional Park** (p. 208) is a beautiful spot to picnic; en route, be sure to pick up some wine at the **Saturna Island Vineyards** (p. 208).

Days ❺ & ❻: Salt Spring

As the largest and most commercial of all the Southern Gulf Islands, Salt Spring's proximity to Victoria makes it a popular weekend escape. Although developers are catching the wave of recreational property seekers, they haven't yet affected the pastoral and artsy charm of Salt Spring. The **shops, galleries** and **pubs** in Ganges (p. 186) alone will take at least a half-day to explore (longer if it's **market day** (p. 186). Take the second day to tour the island's art studios, galleries, farms, and parks (**Ruckle Provincial Park** being the prettiest).

Day ❼: Victoria/The Inner Harbour

Park the car and enjoy the more refined atmosphere of Victoria's Inner Harbour. Here's where you'll find the **Provincial Legislature** (p. 70) and the ivy-clad **Fairmont Empress** (p. 55), both landmark buildings that, not surprisingly, conjure up the era of the city's Victorian namesake. Fun attractions, particularly if you're traveling with children, include **Miniature World** (p. 70), **Pacific Undersea Gardens** (p. 70), and the terrific-at-any-age **Royal BC Museum** (p. 70). When your feet have had enough, hop into a **horse-drawn carriage** (p. 75) for a trip through **Beacon Hill Park** (p. 72), or simply take a **Kabuki Cab** to **Fisherman's Wharf** (p. 72) for a meal of chips and just-caught fish, served in newspaper with salt and traditional malt vinegar.

3 The Wild West Coast in One Week

To follow this itinerary, you'll need a car; it's the only way to experience the full diversity of what Vancouver Island has to offer. Your trip starts in Victoria with the option to stay in the urban center, or venture into the surrounding countryside. Think of it as a teaser of what's to come on the wild west coast, where nature still has the upper hand. The changes in countryside during the drive from Victoria to Tofino, over mountains, through orchards, by seashores, and past fast-moving rivers, are mesmerizing.

Day ❶: Victoria

If you've already enjoyed Victoria's main attractions (described in day 7 of the previous itinerary), explore some of those attractions outside of the Inner Harbour, such as **Craigdarroch Castle** (p. 68), and **Butchart Gardens** (p. 75). If you've been to Victoria before, try going farther afield: count eagles at **Goldstream Provincial Park** (p. 96), cycle the **Galloping Goose Trail** (p. 95), or make a day trip of hiking and tide-pool exploring along the **Juan de Fuca Trail** (p. 95) to **Botanical Beach** (p. 98). The latter two suggestions are great family excursions.

Day ❷: Cowichan Valley/Duncan

The drive north from Victoria takes you over the vista-filled Malahat before descending into the Cowichan Valley, one

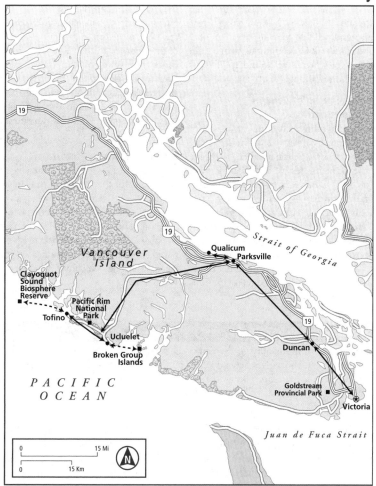

of Canada's fastest growing agri-tourism regions. Take your time exploring the backroads and you'll be rewarded with a range of small, quality **wineries** (p. 103), orchards, specialty farms, and dairies. You get a good impression of the island's Native culture in Duncan with its host of totem poles. Nearby Cowichan is home of the must-see **Quw'utsun Cultural Centre** (p. 103), which illustrates the story of the Cowichan people, the original inhabitants of the valley.

Days ❸ & ❹: Tofino/Long Beach

From Duncan, continue north to Parksville and the junction with Highway 4, the start of the beautiful, windy, and mountainous drive west. Allow 3 hours to cross the island—longer if you stretch your legs in **Cathedral Grove** (p. 129), through which you'll pass. Rain or shine, Tofino and the Long Beach section of the **Pacific Rim National Park** (p. 133) make the journey worthwhile. Hiking through these rainforests is stunning.

Many trails are easy walks; some are strenuous hikes. Whale-watching, surfing, and wildlife viewing are first rate; and sea-kayaking around the usually calm waters of **Clayoquot Sound** (p. 137) is easy and rewarding.

Day ❺: Ucluelet/Broken Group Island

Located within a 20-minute drive south of Tofino, Ucluelet is less touristy; some might even say a little rougher. It is home base to the impressive **Wild Pacific Trail** (p. 136) with easy-to-navigate **boardwalks** through forested terrain and solidly packed pathways that follow the coast. Ucluelet is nearest to the **Broken Group Islands** (p. 139) and you'll find several boat charters and kayaking outfitters in the marina that run tours across the Pacific Ocean swells directly into this oasis of exceptionally calm waters.

Day ❻: Qualicum/Parksville

Surrounded by six major **golf courses** (p. 124), all within a few minutes' drive of one another, this is tee-off central. For those not fond of the links, there's **Rathtrevor Beach** (see p. 122), where you can beachcomb for sand dollars, or take time out to relax in British Columbia's largest spa at **Tigh-Na-Mara Resort** (p. 126).

Day ❼: Return to Victoria

The drive back to Victoria is a chance to catch some of the attractions you missed on the way up. And if the week's adventuring has worked up an appetite, book a table at **The Aerie** (p. 105) atop the Malahat. Savor the immaculately prepared food and your memories of your week exploring Vancouver Island's wild west coast.

4 An Adventure Travel Week

If you start your itinerary in Nanaimo, all sorts of extreme (and soft) adventure options present themselves beyond what you find in Victoria's environs. This adventure itinerary is geared to take in the best eco-activity in the different regions while showcasing the wild side of Vancouver Island.

Day ❶: Spelunking and Rappeling

From Nanaimo, take Hwy 19 north to Parksville and Qualicum Beach, keeping your eyes open for the turnoff to **Horne Lakes Provincial Park** (p. 124). Pitch your tent here or in nearby Englishman's River and take the afternoon to explore the fossil-filled caverns at **Horne Lake Caves** (p. 124). Tours range from family excursions to extreme adventures.

Day ❷: Hiking and Mountaineering

Continue north and just before Campbell River, take the turnoff to **Strathcona Provincial Park.** Strathcona was British Columbia's first provincial park and it includes Elkhorn Mountain, Golden Hinde, and trail access to Mount Washington (p. 152). Whether you're a neophyte or an experienced adventurer, you'll find plenty of challenges, from rock climbing to wilderness hikes through meadow-filled mountain back-country.

Day ❸: Fishing

Campbell River is nicknamed the Salmon Capital of the World and is where eco-activist and fishing expert Roderick Haig-Brown cast his rod. Fishing diehards may want to go for the great Tyee—a Chinook salmon in excess of 14 kilograms (30 lb.) (p. 158) or follow in Haig Brown's footsteps to fly-fish the fast-moving waters of Campbell River.

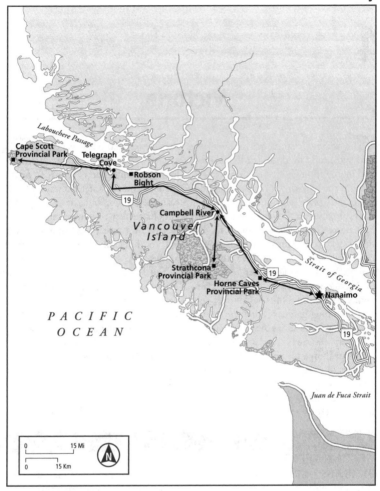

Day ❹: Sea-kayaking in Whale Waters

The road north leads up **Telegraph Cove** (p. 172), one of the remaining communities built on stilts over the water. Spend the afternoon sea-kayaking near **Robson Bight** (p. 172), a unique ecological reserve for whales; sightings are almost guaranteed.

Days ❺ & ❻: Extreme Hiking

Cape Scott Provincial Park (p. 178) lies at the end of the road, literally. Its extreme wilderness takes you from relatively easy trails through always damp rainforest to much harder muddy bogs, craggy shorelines, and naturally wild beaches. You need to be self-sufficient to make it through to the very tip of Vancouver Island, and have a plan to keep at least one pair of socks dry.

Day ❼: Return to Nanaimo

Allow 6 hours for the drive back from Cape Scott to Nanaimo; the distance is approximately 450km (280 miles).

4

Victoria

Whoever said Victoria was for the newly wed and nearly dead needs to take a second look. Although it certainly has its fair share of the blue-rinse brigade, Victoria is a romantic place, and in the past decade has evolved into a thriving city. Described by painter Emily Carr as "more English than England," Victoria's charm is moving beyond its quaint facade. Sure, there are still plenty of double-decker buses, heritage brick buildings covered with clambering vines, English-style taverns, and ever-blooming gardens, but there's also a definite zip in the air as the city's staid and sedentary pleasures give way to hipper places to shop and dine, and more active pursuits to enjoy. In fact, Victoria is now nicknamed the "recreational capital" of British Columbia, and its range of activities reads like an exhaustive shopping list:

year-round golf, whale-watching, fishing, cycling, and much more. Victoria is located around one of Canada's prettiest harbors, and the water is always busy with seaplanes, ships, and kayaks. Accommodations are first-class, many attractions are worthy of a repeat visit, shopping is varied, and restaurants are cosmopolitan and always busy.

You'll want to spend at least two days here, just to get a taste of what Victoria is becoming. It's also the ideal base from which to explore the rest of Vancouver Island. Extending more than 450km (280 miles) from Victoria to the northwest tip of Cape Scott, the island offers some of the most dramatic stretches of coastal wilderness you'll find in the Pacific Northwest. (See chapters 5, 6, and 7 for coverage of the rest of Vancouver Island.)

1 Essentials

GETTING THERE

BY PLANE   Most visitors arrive via a connecting flight from either **Vancouver International Airport** (© 604/207-7077; www.yvr.ca), or **Seatac International Airport** in Seattle (© 206/433-5388; www.seatac.org). Airlines flying into the rapidly expanding **Victoria International Airport** (© 250/953-7500; www.victoriaairport. com) include **Air Canada** (© 888/247-2262; www.aircanada.ca), Horizon Air (© 800/547-9308; www.alaskaair.com), and WestJet (© 888/937-8538; www.west jet.com). The Victoria International Airport is near the BC Ferries terminal in Sidney, 26km (16 miles) north of Victoria off Highway 17. Highway 17 heads south to Victoria, becoming Douglas Street as you enter downtown.

Airport bus service, operated by **AKAL Airport** (© 877/386-2525 or 250/386-2526; www.victoriaairporter.com), takes about 45 minutes to get into town. Buses leave from the airport daily, every 30 minutes from 4:30am to midnight. The adult fare is C$15 (US$13) one-way. Dropoffs and pickups are made at most Victoria area hotels. **Empress Cabs** (© 250/381-2222), and **Blue Bird Cabs** (© 250/382-4235) make airport runs. It costs about C$45 (US$40) one way, plus tip.

Several car-rental firms have desks at the Victoria International Airport, including: **Avis** (© **800/879-2847** or 250/656-6033; www.avis.com), **Budget** (© **800/668-9833** or 250/953-5300; www.budgetvictoria.com), **Hertz** (© **800/654-3131** or 250/656-2312; www.hertz.com), and **National (Tilden)** (© **800/227-7368** or 250/656-2541; www.nationalcar.com). Car reservations are recommended from June to September and during peak travel times on holiday weekends.

BY TRAIN **VIA Rail** trains arrive at Victoria's **VIA Rail Station,** 450 Pandora Ave., near the Johnson Street Bridge (© **800/561-8630** in Canada or 800/561-3941 in the U.S., or 250/383-4324; www.viarail.com).

BY BUS The **Victoria Bus Depot** is at 700 Douglas St. (behind the Fairmont Empress Hotel). **Pacific Coach Lines** (© **800/661-1725** within North America or 250/385-4411 in Victoria; www.pacificcoach.com), offers daily service to and from Vancouver, and includes the ferry trip across the Georgia Strait between Tsawwassen and Sidney. **Laidlaw Coach Lines/Island Coach Lines** (© **800/663-8390** or 250/385-4411; www.victoriatours.com) provides daily service up island to Nanaimo, Port Alberni, Campbell River, and Port Hardy.

BY FERRY BC Ferries offers crossings from the mainland to various points on Vancouver Island (© **888/BCFERRY** [888/223-3779] in B.C. outside the Victoria dialing area, or 250/386-3431; www.bcferries.com). For more information, see "Getting There" in chapter 2.

VISITOR INFORMATION

The **Tourism Victoria Visitor Information Centre,** 812 Wharf St., Victoria, BC V8W 1T3 (© **250/953-2033;** www.tourismvictoria. com) is an excellent resource for brochures, ideas for itineraries, and maps. Tourism Victoria also operates a **reservations hotline** (© **800/663-3883** or 250/953-2022) for last-minute bookings at hotels, inns, and B&Bs. The center is open September through April daily from 9am to 5pm, May and June daily from 8:30am to 6:30pm, and July and August daily from 9am to 9pm. Bus nos. 1, 27, or 28 to Douglas and Courtney streets.

CITY LAYOUT

Victoria was settled around the Inner Harbour in the mid 1800s and grew out from there. Because of the *curvy* shoreline, the grid system of streets doesn't kick-in immediately, but there are three main **north-south arteries** that will get you almost anywhere you may want to reach in Victoria.

Government Street leads from the Inner Harbour to downtown (Wharf Street merges with Government Street in front of the hotel); **Douglas Street** runs behind the Fairmont Empress, parallel to Government Street. It is the city's main business thoroughfare as well as the highway north to Nanaimo and beyond. It's also the Trans-Canada Highway 1—Mile Zero is at the corner of Douglas Street and Dallas Road. **Blanshard Street,** which runs parallel to Government and Douglas streets, becomes

---

Give Your Umbrella a Break

Greater Victoria is one of Canada's driest areas, with an average snowfall of only 25 centimeters (9¾ in.) and an average rainfall of 592 millimeters (23 in.), less than recorded precipitation in Vancouver, B.C. or Seattle, Washington.

Hwy 17, the route to the Saanich Peninsula including the Butchart Gardens and the ferry terminals to Vancouver and the San Juan Islands.

Three major east–west streets of note are **Johnson Street**, in Old Town/Downtown—the Johnson Street Bridge divides the Upper Harbour and the Inner Harbour. **Belleville Street** runs in front of the Parliament Buildings, along the Inner Harbour's southern edge up to Fisherman's Wharf. It then loops around to become **Dallas Road,** which follows the water's edge towards Oak Bay.

When you're looking for an address, be aware that the suite number precedes the building number, and generally speaking, these go up in increments of 100 per block as you travel north and east. Addresses for all east–west downtown streets (Fort, Yates, Johnson, and so on) start at 500 at Wharf Street. This means all buildings between Wharf and Government streets fall between 500 and 599 with the next block, between Government and Douglas streets are numbers 600 through 699, and so on. Detailed maps of downtown and farther afield are available for free at the Tourism Victoria Visitor Info Centre. Invariably, hotels have maps they will mark up with a highlighter pen, showing you the quickest, easiest, and most interesting routes.

VICTORIA'S NEIGHBORHOODS IN BRIEF

Victoria central is so compact that it's hard to draw definitive lines dividing the three major neighborhoods. Suffice to say that the nearer you are to the water, the more expensive the hotel room, so unless you're absolutely hooked on having a view, save yourself a few dollars by heading a block or two inland.

Inner Harbor

For most visitors, this is where it's at, and it's what those glossy tourism brochures depict in their Victoria sell. Framed by the Parliament Buildings on one side, and the Fairmont Empress on another, the Inner Harbour is where to find cabs, horse-drawn carriage rides, double-decker tour buses, ferries, floatplanes, whale-watching outfitters, and a host of other tourist services. Attractions such as the **BC Royal Museum** and **Undersea Gardens** are here, alongside some of the city's most expensive hotels. There's an easy waterside stroll that takes you around the harbor perimeter; in summer it fills up with artist-vendors selling photographs, Native carvings, and inexpensive jewelry. It's touristy and expensive, but also picturesque.

Downtown & Old Town

Head away from the water, and within two to three blocks you're in Victoria's social and commercial centers. Because the two neighborhoods blend together, Victorians usually refer to them together. **Old Town** tends to include Bastion and Market Squares—the areas that grew up around the original Fort Victoria at View and Government streets. **Downtown** tends to include everything east of Wharf Street, and is where you'll find the bulk of the city's shopping, banking, restaurants, bars and hotels. Staying here may save you a few dollars but it can be noisy, especially when the pubs and nightclubs let out.

Chinatown

The size of this area belies its history. Although only two square blocks, Victoria's Chinatown is the oldest in North America. The historic alleyways and buildings make for an intriguing visit, especially **Fan Tan Alley,** Canada's narrowest commercial street. Just over a meter (4 ft.) wide, this narrow alleyway cuts a divide between brick buildings that once housed gambling joints and opium dens, but has given way to curiosity and souvenir shops.

James Bay, Oak Bay, & Ross Bay

Largely residential, these peaceful and postcard-pretty neighborhoods boast some large turn-of-the-century manor homes and gardens—some are distinctive B&Bs—as well as newer homes. Oak Bay in particular has retained a quieter English ambience and offers excellent beaches, golf courses, and tea houses. Although away from Victoria central, the property taxes are hefty enough here to warrant higher-than-expected room rates. These areas are easiest to reach by car.

2 Getting Around

BY PUBLIC TRANSPORTATION

The **Victoria Regional Transit System** (BC Transit) (✆ **250/382-6161;** www.bc transit.com) operates approximately 40 bus routes throughout **Greater Victoria** and the outer suburbs of **Sooke** and **Sidney.** Regular service on the main routes runs Monday to Friday from 6am to midnight. Call for schedules on the weekends. Consult the **"Victoria Rider's Guide"** for schedules and routes, available at the **Tourism Victoria Visitor Information Centre** (see "Visitor Information," above). The guide outlines transit routes for many of the city's neighborhoods, landmarks, and attractions. Popular routes include no. 2 (Oak Bay), no. 11 (Downtown, James Bay, Beacon Hill Park), no. 14 (Craigflower, University of Victoria), no. 23 (Art Gallery of Victoria), no. 61 (Sooke), no. 70 (Sidney, Swartz Bay), and no. 75 (Butchart Gardens). This route includes a pickup at the Sidney ferry terminal and is handy for those arriving from the mainland without a vehicle.

Fares are based on the number of geographic zones a passenger crosses and are defined by boundaries. For example, downtown Victoria is one zone, traveling to Sooke crosses two zones, as does traveling from Sidney to Victoria. One-way, single-zone **fares** are C$2 (US$1.75) for adults, C$1.25 (US$1.10) for seniors and children to grade 7, but children 5 and under are free. Two-zone fares are C$2.75 (US$2.40) for adults, C$2 (US$1.75) for seniors and children. Transfers are good for travel in one direction with no stopovers. A **DayPass,** which costs C$6 (US$5.30) for adults, C$4 (US$3.50) for seniors and children, is available at the Tourism Victoria Visitor Information Centre, at convenience stores, and at outlets displaying the FareDealer symbol. See chapter 2, "Specialized Travel Resources."

BY CAR

If you must bring your car (exploring downtown is really best done on foot), make sure your hotel has parking. Parking spaces around the city-center are at a premium. (Hotels that have parking are included in "Where to Stay.") For out-of-town activities, car-rental agencies include **Avis,** at 1001 Douglas St. (✆ **800/879-2847** or 250/386-8468; www.avis.com), **Budget,** at 757 Douglas St. (✆ **800/268-8900** or 250/953-5300; www.budget.com), **Hertz Canada,** at 2634 Douglas St. (✆ **800/263-0600** or 250/385-4440; www.hertz.com), and **National (Tilden),** at 767 Douglas St. (✆ **800/387-4747** or 250/386-1213; www.nationalcar.com). Renting a car costs approximately C$50 (US$44) per day but may be less with various discounts.

BY TAXI

Empress Cabs (✆ **800/808-6881** or 250/381-2222) and **Blue Bird Cabs** (✆ **800/655-7055** or 250/382-4235) are good bets. But do call ahead—very few stop for flagdowns, especially when it's raining. Rides around the downtown area average C$6 to C$8 (US$5.30–US$7), plus 15% tip.

Downtown Victoria

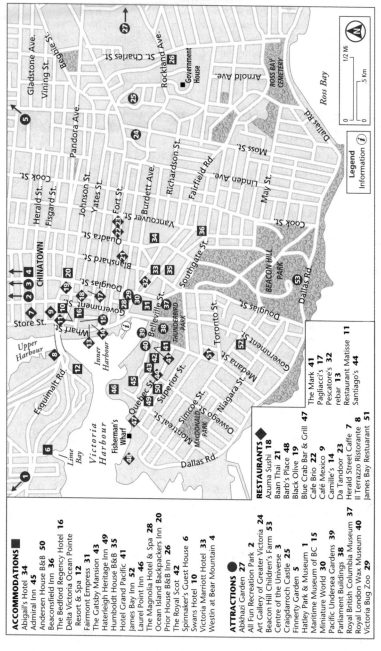

ACCOMMODATIONS
Abigail's Hotel **34**
Admiral Inn **45**
Andersen House B&B **50**
Beaconsfield Inn **36**
The Bedford Regency Hotel **16**
Delta Victoria Ocean Pointe Resort & Spa **12**
Fairmont Empress **31**
The Gatsby Mansion **43**
Haterleigh Heritage Inn **49**
Humboldt House B&B **35**
Hotel Grand Pacific **41**
James Bay Inn **52**
Laurel Point Inn **46**
The Magnolia Hotel & Spa **28**
Ocean Island Backpackers Inn **20**
Prior House B&B Inn **26**
The Royal Scot **42**
Spinnaker's Guest House **6**
Swans Hotel **10**
Victoria Marriott Hotel **33**
Westin at Bear Mountain **4**

ATTRACTIONS
Abkhazi Garden **27**
All Fun Recreation Park **2**
Art Gallery of Greater Victoria **24**
Beacon Hill Children's Farm **53**
Centre of the Universe **3**
Craigdarroch Castle **25**
Finnerty Garden **5**
Hatley Park & Museum **1**
Maritime Museum of BC **15**
Miniature World **30**
Pacific Undersea Gardens **39**
Parliament Buildings **38**
Royal British Columbia Museum **37**
Royal London Wax Museum **40**
Victoria Bug Zoo **29**

RESTAURANTS
Azuma Sushi **18**
Baan Thai **21**
Barb's Place **48**
Black Olive **19**
Blue Crab Bar & Grill **47**
Cafe Brio **22**
Café Mexico **9**
Camille's **14**
Da Tandoor **23**
Herald Street Caffe **7**
Il Terrazzo Ristorante **8**
James Bay Restuarant **51**
The Mark **41**
Pagliacci's **17**
Pescatore's **32**
rebar **13**
Restaurant Matisse **11**
Santiago's **44**

Legend
Information *i*

1/2 Mi
.5 Km

BY FERRY

Once you're downtown, scooting across the harbor in one of the tiny, 12-passenger ferries operated by **Victoria Harbour Ferry** (✆ **250/708-0201;** www.victoria harbourferry.com) is great fun—and expedient—in getting from one part of the city to another. The squat, cartoon-style boats have big wraparound windows that allow everyone a terrific view. Ferry connections to the Fairmont Empress, the Coast Harbourside Hotel, and the Delta Victoria Ocean Pointe Resort run May through October daily every 15 minutes from 9am to 9pm. From November to April, the ferries run only on sunny weekends from 11am to 5pm. When the weather is "iffy," call the ferry office to check whether the ferries are running that day. The cost per hop is C$4 (US$3.50) for adults, C$2 (US$1.75) for children. See "Organized Tours" for other ways to enjoy a ferry ride.

FAST FACTS: Victoria

American Express There is no Victoria office. To report lost or stolen traveler's checks, call ✆ **800/221-7282.**

Business Hours **Banks** in Victoria are open Monday to Thursday from 10am to 3pm, Friday from 10am to 6pm. **Stores** are open Monday to Saturday from 10am to 6pm. Many stores are also open on Sunday in summers. Last call at the city's bars and cocktail lounges is 2am.

Currency Exchange The best rates of exchange are at bank ATMs. Try the **Royal Bank,** 1079 Douglas St. (✆ **250/356-4500**), in the heart of downtown. **Calforex Foreign Currency Services** is open 7 days a week, 724 Douglas St., and 606 Humboldt St. ✆ **250/384-6631. Custom House Currency Exchange** (✆ **250/389-6007**), is also open daily, and has locations at 815 Wharf St., Bastion Square, Bay Centre, and the airport, among others.

Dentists Most major hotels have a dentist on call. You can also visit the **Cresta Dental Centre,** #28–3170 Tillicum Rd., at Burnside Street, in Tillicum Mall. Open Monday to Friday from 8am to 9pm, Saturday from 9am to 5pm, and Sunday from 11am to 5pm. Call ahead for appointment: ✆ **250/384-7711.**

Doctors Hotels usually have a doctor on call or are able to refer you to one. Clinics include the Downtown Medical Clinic, 622 Courtney St. ✆ **259/380-2210,** open Monday to Friday 8:30am to 5:30pm; and the **James Bay Treatment Centre,** 100–230 Menzies St., open Monday to Friday from 9am to 6pm, Saturday 10am to 4pm. Call for appointment: ✆ **250/388-9934.**

Drugstores Pick up your allergy medication or refill your prescription at **Shoppers Drug Mart,** 1222 Douglas St. ✆ **250/381-4321.** Open Monday to Friday from 7am to 8pm, Saturday from 9am to 7pm, and Sunday from 9am to 6pm. **McGill and Orme,** 649 Fort St. ✆ **250/384-1195,** is open Monday to Saturday from 9am to 6pm, and Sunday and holidays from noon to 4pm.

Emergencies Dial 911 for police, fire, ambulance, and poison control.

Hospitals Local hospitals include the **Royal Jubilee Hospital,** 1900 Fort St. ✆ **250/370-8000** or 250/370-8212 for emergencies; and **Victoria General Hospital,** 1 Hospital Way ✆ **250/727-4212** or 250/727-4181 for emergencies.

Hotlines Emergency numbers include: **Royal Canadian Mounted Police** (*C* 250/ 380-6261); **Crime Stoppers** *C* 250/386-8477); **Emotional Crisis Centre** (*C* 250/386- 6323); **Sexual Assault Centre** (*C* 250/383-3232); and **Poison Control Centre** (*C* 800/567-8911).

Internet Access Nearly all hotels have either high-speed access in a public lounge or in guest bedrooms; Wi-Fi is increasingly common. The greater Victoria Public Library, 735 Broughton St. (*C* 250/382-7241) has a dozen terminals and is open Monday, Wednesday, Friday, and Saturday 9am to 6pm, Tuesday and Thursday to 9pm. Or try The James Bay Coffee & Books, 143 Menzies St. *C* 250/386-4700; it's just around the corner from the Parliament Buildings.

Newspapers The **Victoria Times-Colonist** comes out daily. The weekly entertainment paper, **Monday** magazine, comes out, curiously, on Thursday, and is widely distributed in grocery stores, information centers, and elsewhere.

Police Dial 911 for emergencies. For non-emergencies, the **Victoria City Police** can be reached at *C* **250/995-7654**.

Post Office The main **Canada Post office** is at 714 Yates St. (*C* 250/953-1352). The **Oak Bay post office** is at 1625 Fort St. (*C* 250/595-2552). There are also postal outlets in **Shoppers Drug Mart** (see "Drugstores," above).

Safety Crime rates are quite low in Victoria, but transients panhandle throughout the downtown and Old Town areas. Lock items in the glove compartment or trunk when you park your car, and avoid dark alleys and uninhabited areas.

Weather For local weather updates, call *C* **250/363-6717**; Victoria is extension #3502.

3 Where to Stay

Victoria has a wide choice of fine accommodations, and all are in, or within walking distance of, the **Inner Harbour** and **downtown core.** In Sooke, Brentwood Bay, and on the Malahat, there are some spectacular options. See chapter 5 for places to stay on the South Island.) If you're looking for a bed-and-breakfast, get in touch with **Born Free Bed & Breakfast of BC** (4390 Frances St., Burnaby, BC V5C 2R3; *C* **800/ 488-1941** (U.S. only) or 604/298-8815; www.vancouverbandb.bc.ca), which seems to have the inside scoop on availability. **Tourism Victoria** (*C* **800/663-3883** or 250/ 953-2022; www.tourismvictoria.com) can book rooms at hotels, inns, and B&Bs. Another great source is **www.hellobc.com**, Tourism British Columbia's official site for researching and booking accommodation.

INNER HARBOUR & NEARBY
VERY EXPENSIVE

Delta Victoria Ocean Pointe Resort and Spa 𝒜𝒜   Huge rooms, spacious bathrooms, and great bedding are all part of the relatively clutter-free decor, which highlights the gleaming woods and the soft, natural colors throughout. Located on the north side of the Inner Harbour, many of the guest rooms have floor-to-ceiling windows that view the Parliament Buildings and the Fairmont Empress; they're worth the extra dollars since back-of-house rooms look out onto an industrial landscape. And for still a few dollars more, you get Signature perks of breakfast, evening hors d'oeuvres, and turndown service. All rooms come with the usual toiletries, down duvets, and cuddly robes. The European-style spa rivals the Fairmont's Willow Stream for top spa billing, and is a destination in itself. Though the hotel's fitness facilities will satiate the needs of most obsessives; the large indoor pool is worth a visit; it's surrounded by glass and makes you feel as if you're swimming outdoors. **Lure Seafood Restaurant and Bar** boasts the best dining-room views in the city and offers a great weekday, prix fixe dinner from 5 to 6:30pm, before the crowds roll in to savor the very pretty night lights of the city's harborfront.

45 Songhees Rd., Victoria, BC V9A 6T3. ⓒ **800/667-4677** or 250/360-2999. Fax 250/360-1041. www.deltahotels. com or www.oprhotel.com. 250 units. Apr to mid-Oct C$169–C$419 (US$149–US$369) standard; C$439–C$799 (US$386–US$703) suite. Mid-Oct to Mar C$119–C$$319 (US$105–US$281) standard; C$329–C$$629 (US$289–US$554) suites. Extra person C$30 (US$26). Children 11 and under stay free in parent's room. AE, DC, DISC, MC, V. Valet parking C$14 (US$12). Bus: 6, or 24 to Colville. Pets accepted (C$35/US$31). **Amenities:** 2 restaurants (both Pacific Northwest); ozonated indoor swimming pool; 2 night-lit outdoor tennis courts; 1 indoor racquetball and squash court; extensive health club & spa; children's programs; car-rental desk; free shuttle to/from downtown; secretarial services; 24-hour room service; in-room massage; babysitting; laundry service; dry cleaning. In room: A/C, TV, dataport, minibar, coffeemaker, hair dryer, iron.

Fairmont Empress ⓐⓐ   It's an ivy-adorned iconic harborside landmark and staying here is the quintessential Victoria experience. Although ongoing renovations maintain the old girl's elegance, the Fairmont folks couldn't make many of the 1908 rooms any larger, so this still means small rooms (billed as "cozy"), narrow corridors, and a disparity of views that might just as easily include the unsightly working rooftops of the hotel's working areas as they might the harbour. If you're slightly claustrophobic, don't even think about these. They're a lot of money for what you get, too. That said, the deluxe guest rooms, studio-, one- and two-bedroom suites, and all of the Fairmont Gold guest rooms are superb: all have extra-large beds and windows that let the light pour in. Fairmont Gold rooms also have extras such as TVs in the bathrooms and CD players, and guests have private check-in, their own concierge, and a private lounge that has an honor bar, complimentary hors d'oeuvres (sometimes enough for a light supper), and breakfast. The **Willow Stream Spa** is one of the, if not the, city's finest spa retreats and some of the services are priced accordingly. Dining choices include the Bengal Lounge—its ceiling fans and tall palms are very colonial India; the Empress Dining Room, and Kipling's. The famous afternoon tea is served year round in the Main Tea Lobby, spilling into surrounding areas as the number of tea drinkers dictates.

721 Government St., Victoria, BC V8W 1W5. ⓒ **800/441-1414** or 250/384-8111. Fax 250/381-4334. www.fairmont. com/empress. 477 units. Jul–Sept C$299–C$809 (US$263–US$712) double; C$429–C$1,509 (US$378–US$1,328) suites; C$399–C$1,509 (US$351–US$1,328) Fairmont Gold. Oct–Jun C$179–C$$479 (US$158–US$422) double; C$219–C$1,269 (US$193–US$1,117) suites, C$219–C$1,269 (US$193–US$1,117) Fairmont Gold. Packages available. Children 11 and under stay free in parent's room. AE, DC, DISC, MC, V. Underground valet parking C$25 (US$22). Bus 5. Small pets accepted C$25 (US$22). **Amenities:** 2 restaurants (East Indian, Pacific Northwest); bar/lounge; tearoom; large heated indoor pool; health club & spa; concierge; tour desk; car-rental desk; business center; 24-hour room service; in-room massage; babysitting; laundry service; dry cleaning. In room: A/C, TV w/pay movies, Internet, minibar, coffeemaker, hair dryer, safe.

Hotel Grand Pacific ⓐⓐ   The "grandness" begins as you approach the hotel beneath a canopy of trees—beside ducks paddling in waterfall-fed pools. Located next to the Parliament Buildings, the Grand Pacific sits right on the waterfront. Guest rooms are more spacious and elegantly contemporary than those in the other waterfront hotels, and because of the wide range of accommodation, from standard rooms facing the Olympic Mountains and smallish bathrooms, to multi-room harborview suites with fireplaces and lavishly large bathrooms, you might be able to afford top-notch luxury here for less than what's offered elsewhere. Executive suites feature double Jacuzzis, fireplaces, multiple balconies, and wet bars. The hotel has a quality spa; fitness facilities (with a huge ozonated indoor pool) that are the most extensive in the city, and dining options that include The Mark, geared to high-end, romantic encounters (see "Where to Dine").

450 Quebec St., Victoria, BC V8V 1W5. ℰ 800/663-7550 or 250/386-0450. Fax 250/380-4473. www.hotelgrand pacific.com. 304 units. Mid-May to Sept C$219–C$$389 (US$193–US$342). Oct–mid-May C$159–C$$269 (US$140–US$237) double. 1-bedroom suites from C$389 (US$342). Children 17 and under stay free in parent's room. AE, DC, DISC, MC, V. Parking C$10 (US$9). Bus 30 to Superior and Oswego sts., 27, or 28. **Amenities:** 2 restaurants (all Pacific Northwest); lounge; indoor zone-filtered lap pool; 2 squash and racquetball courts; health club & spa; concierge; secretarial services; 24-hour room service; babysitting; laundry service; dry cleaning. In room: A/C, TV w/pay movies, high-speed Internet, minibar, coffeemaker, hair dryer, iron, safe.

EXPENSIVE

Andersen House B&B ☆ This small 1891 house, with its high ceilings, stained-glass windows, and ornate Queen Anne–style fireplaces, is filled with furnishings and art that echo the old British Empire. Every room has a private entrance and is unique. The sun-drenched Casablanca Room has French doors and a window seat overlooking the Parliament Buildings; the Captain's Apartment comes with a clawfoot tub and an extra bedroom; the Southside Room enjoys a private, garden entrance; and the Garden Studio has the hot tub. Rates include a sumptuous breakfast. The Andersens also operate Baybreeze Manor (3930 Telegraph Bay Rd.; ℰ **250/721-3930;** www.baybreeze manor.com) a restored 1885 farmhouse with two rooms, 15 minutes from downtown.

301 Kingston St., Victoria, BC V8V 1V5. ℰ **250/388-4565.** Fax 250/721-3938. www.andersenhouse.com. 4 units. C$95–C$275 (US$84–US$242) Rates include full breakfast. MC, V. Free off-street parking. Bus 30 to Superior and Oswego sts. Children under 12 not accepted. **Amenities:** Jacuzzi, nonsmoking rooms. In room: TV/VCR, Wi-Fi, coffeemaker, hair dryer, iron, CD player.

The Gatsby Mansion Overlooking the Inner Harbour, just across from where the Seattle–Port Angeles ferry docks, this hundred-year-old heritage mansion is trapped in a time warp, with its antique furniture, Italian stained glass, velvet tapestries, frescoed ceilings, and meandering hallways. Staying here is like staying in a museum; if you're drawn to the eccentric, this place will appeal. Each guest room has a different configuration, so you might get a square room or one that has a few corner nooks, or even a 1.5-m (5-ft.) corridor into a sitting area. Bathrooms are on the small side and functional rather than spa-like. All beds feature the comforts of down duvets and fine linens. A gracious high tea is served every afternoon beneath twinkling chandeliers in what was once the front parlor, drawing room, and dining rooms. Breakfast and dinner are served in the same space. *Tip:* If you want space, forgo the harbor view and opt for a room at the back. These folks also own the **Ramada Huntingdon Hotel & Suites** (ℰ **800/663-7557** or 250/381-3456) next door, which, thankfully, has been refurbished so that the large rooms, pullout beds, and in-room fridges make it a value option for families and folks on a budget.

309 Belleville St., Victoria, BC V8V 1X2. ℰ **800/563-9656** or 250/388-9191. Fax 250/920-5651. www.bellevillepark. com. 20 units. Mid-May to Sept C$169–C$309 (US$149–US$272) double. Oct to mid-May C$129–C$199 (US$113–US$175) double. Rates include full breakfast. Packages available. AE, MC, V. Free parking. Bus 5 to Belleville and Government sts., 27, 28, or 30. **Amenities:** Restaurant (Pacific Northwest); lounge; Wi-Fi. In room: TV w/pay movies, coffeemaker, iron.

Haterleigh Heritage Inn 🌟 Located only two blocks from the harbor, this turn-of-the-century inn exudes the essence of old world Victoria with antique furnishings, European wall coverings, original stained-glass windows, and attentive touches such as sherry and chocolates at night, and gourmet breakfasts in the morning. Rooms are large, with sitting areas, large windows, and good-sized bathrooms, all of which have soaker tubs. The inn scores high on the romance quotient, especially with the Day Dreams suite on the main floor, dedicated to honeymooners. The Angels Suite on the third floor has two bedrooms; the Victoriana Suite has an original clawfoot soaker tub.

243 Kingston St., Victoria BC V8V 1V5 ⓒ **866/234-2244** or 250/384-9995. Fax 250/384-1935. www.haterleigh.com. 7 units. Mid-Mar to mid-Oct C$225–C$340 (US$198–US$299) double. Mid-Oct to mid-Mar C$135–C$225 (US$119–US$198) double. Rates include full breakfast. Off-season discounts available. MC, V. Free parking. Pets not accepted. Children under 12 not accepted. Bus: 30 to Superior and Montreal sts. **Amenities:** Jacuzzi; Internet. *In room:* Hair dryer, no phone.

Laurel Point Inn 🌟 One of the first modern hotels built on the Inner Harbour, the Laurel Point Inn's simple Japanese-style design still retains a certain grace with its newer earth-toned West Coast style furnishings. Japanese visitors love the place. There are two wings and all guest rooms have balconies with views; the scene, harbor or inland, helps determine the price you'll pay. Try for a room in the newer south wing. Rooms here are more spacious and have an Asian theme, including shoji-style sliding doors, down duvets, and plenty of Asian art. The Japanese Garden features a large reflecting pond and a waterfall that cascades over a whopping 21,300 kilograms (47,000 lb.) of rock. The two restaurants are fine (one is seasonal), but nothing to write home about. The inn is within easy walking distance of Fisherman's Wharf, the Parliament Buildings, and the Royal BC Museum.

680 Montreal St., Victoria, BC V8V 1Z8. ⓒ **800/663-7667** or 250/386-8721. Fax 250/386-9547. www.laurelpoint. com. 200 units: 135 harbor view, 65 suites. Jun 1–Oct 15 C$254 (US$224) double; C$394 (US$347) studio suite. Oct 16–May 31 C$144 (US$127) double; C$239 (US$210) suite. Packages available. Extra person C$15 (US$13). Children 11 and under stay free in parent's room. AE, DC, MC, V. Parking C$7. Small pets C$50 (US$44). **Amenities:** 2 restaurants (Pacific Northwest); lounge bar; small heated pool; access to nearby health club; Jacuzzi; sauna; concierge; activities desk; business center; 24-hour room service; in-room massage; babysitting; laundry service; dry cleaning; Internet. *In room:* A/C, TV w/pay movies, Internet, coffeemaker, hair dryer, iron, safe.

MODERATE

James Bay Inn (Value) There aren't many budget rooms around the Inner Harbour but this is one of them. Granted, the 1907 manor has a faded quality about it and rooms are on the small side and very simply furnished, but at least you can say you slept in the same house where Emily Carr, one of Canada's most beloved painters, once lived. Guests get a discount at the on-premises restaurant and pub. The real bargain is the renovated heritage cottage next door. The four suites may be small, but they come with full-size kitchens and somewhat better furnishings. High-season rates here start at C$197 (US$173). A third building sleeps eight and runs at C$240 (US$211) per night, making it the best deal in town.

270 Government St., Victoria, BC V8V 2L2 ⓒ **800/836-2649** or 250/384-7151. Fax 250/385-2311. www.jamesbay inn.bc.ca. 45 units. Jul–Oct C$130–C$240 (US$114–US$211). Nov–Jun C$75–C$145 (US$66–US$128). AE, MC, V. Free limited parking. Bus: 5 or 30 to Niagara St. **Amenities:** Restaurant; bar; tour desk; nonsmoking rooms; Wi-Fi. *In room:* TV, dataport, hair dryer, iron.

The Royal Scot 🌟 (Value) (Kids) Situated a block from the Inner Harbour, this suite hotel provides excellent value, particularly if you're not hooked on a waterfront view. Converted from an apartment building, the hotel has large guest rooms with lots of cupboard space. Studio suites include a living/dining area and kitchen; one-bedroom suites have separate bedrooms with king-size, queen-size, or twin beds. Kitchens are fully equipped (including microwaves) and living areas come with sofabeds. This is an ideal home base for families; weary parents in need of a few zzz's will love scooting their off-spring to the children's games room. The indoor pool gets heavy use, as does the video arcade room. Jonathan's restaurant is fully licensed and has a summer patio. There are nine room types ranging from guest rooms to two-bedroom corner suites, so you're bound to find a good fit. Parking is free (a bonus anywhere in Victoria central) and if you didn't bring your car, the Royal Scot operates a complimentary guest shuttle to downtown. Off season, this becomes the hot location for bargain-conscious retirees.

425 Quebec St., Victoria, BC V8V 1W7. © 800/663-7515 or 250/388-5463. Fax 250/388-5452. www.royalscot.com. 176 units. C$155–C$185 (US$136–US$163) double; C$185–C$415 (US$163–US$365) suite. Weekly, monthly, and off-season rates available. Children 11 and under stay free in parent's room. AE, DC, MC, V. Free parking. Bus 30. **Amenities:** Restaurant (Pacific Northwest); small heated indoor pool; hydrotherapy pool; access to nearby health club; sauna; games room; concierge; business center; 24-hour room service; babysitting; laundry service; dry cleaning; Internet. *In room:* TV, coffeemaker, hair dryer, iron.

DOWNTOWN & OLD TOWN
EXPENSIVE
Abigail's Hotel 🎇🎇 Tucked into a quiet residential cul-de-sac, only three blocks from downtown Victoria and the Inner Harbour, this European-style Tudor inn is just about as romantic as it can get. Guest rooms are superbly decorated with antiques, wood-burning fireplaces, two-person Jacuzzis, fresh-cut flowers, and welcoming treats such as truffles and fruit. The six "Celebration" suites in the Coach House addition have extravagant touches such as four-poster beds, Jacuzzi tubs and leather loveseats. Breakfast is fit for royalty—literally—since the chef has cooked for the Queen, and will be brought to your bedside if that's your preference. The small Pearl Spa offers a full range of quality spa services. Abigail's is geared to adults; children are discouraged.

906 McClure St., Victoria, BC V8V 3E7. © 800/561-6565 or 250/388-5363. Fax 250/388-7787. www.abigailshotel.com. 23 units. Mid-May to mid-Oct C$289–C$450 (US$254–US$396) double. Mid-Oct to mid-May C$199–C$339 (US$175–US$298) double. Rates include full breakfast and evening hors d'oeuvres. Spa, Honeymoon, and Wine Tour packages available. AE, MC, V. Free parking. Bus 1. **Amenities:** Spa; concierge; business center; laundry service; dry cleaning. *In room:* Some with TV/VCR, dataport, hair dryer, iron, some with Jacuzzi.

Beaconsfield Inn Designed by famed local architect Samuel Maclure in 1905 (he was also responsible for Maclure House), there's a pleasant English feel to this person-able B&B. Touches include fir paneling, mahogany floors, antique furnishings, and stained-glass windows. Guest rooms are sumptuously decorated, and very romantic. Some have fireplaces. The Gatekeeper Suite has French windows leading onto a flow-ery patio and the Garden Suite has a double hot tub. The Emily Carr Suite remains one of the showpiece rooms, with its romantic double hot tub in front of a fireplace, queen-size bed, and separate sitting area. Another suite features a flowery patio and similar double hot tub. As a bonus, the full breakfast served in the sunroom, afternoon tea, and evening sherry in the library are all included in the rate.

998 Humboldt St., Victoria, BC V8V 1Z8 © 888/884-4044 or 250/384-4044. Fax 250/384-4052. www.beaconsfield inn.com. 9 units. Jun–Sept C$169–C$299 (US$149–C$263). Oct–May C$109–C$199 (US$96–US$175). Full breakfast, afternoon tea, and sherry hour included. AE, MC, V. Free parking. Bus: 1 or 2 to Humboldt and Quadra sts. Pets not accepted. Children 12 and over accepted. Nonsmoking. **Amenities:** Jacuzzi; access to nearby health club. *In room:* Hair dryer, no phone.

Humboldt House B&B ❀ (Finds)   Located on a quiet tree-lined street, this beautifully renovated, turn-of-the-century home overlooks the orchards of St. Ann's Academy, a heritage convent and chapel, and is only minutes away from the Inner Harbour. Each guest room has a different theme, such as the Japanese Mikado Suite; the Edwardian, and the Celebration Room with its Victorian-lace-canopied bed. In-room touches include large Jacuzzis, wood-burning fireplaces, goose-down comforters, fresh flowers, and homemade chocolate truffles, and as an ultimate touch of pampered privacy, a romantic champagne breakfast in bed is passed to you through a two-way pantry—you don't even have to open the door. Although older children are accepted, the B&B's style is among the best for romantic trysts. This B&B also operates a self-contained renovated 1925 English cottage nearby with two rooms—ideal for couples traveling together.

867 Humboldt St., Victoria, BC V8V 2Z6. ⓒ 888/383-0327 or 250/383-0152. Fax 250/383-6402. www.humboldt house.com. 6 units. May–Sept C$245–C$315 (US$216–US$277); Oct-Apr C$147–C$189 (US$129–US$166). Extra person C$40 (US$35). Rates include full breakfast. Packages available. Children 11 and under stay free in parent's room. MC, V. Free parking. Bus: 1 or 71. **Amenities:** Concierge; in-room massage; babysitting; laundry service; dry cleaning. *In room:* TV/ VCR/DVD, high-speed Internet, fridge, hair dryer, iron, no phone.

The Magnolia Hotel & Spa ❀❀   This sophisticated boutique hotel appeals to business travelers and international visitors alike. It has a terrific downtown location and lots of finishing touches to make you feel immediately welcome: a huge bowl of apples, a larger arrangement of fresh flowers, crisp daily newspapers. Guest rooms are bright, with floor-to-ceiling windows, custom-designed furniture, two-poster beds, and oversize desks. Executive Diamond suites have gas fireplaces. There's also an umbrella on hand—Victoria does get its fair share of rain, after all. Of special note is the **Aveda Lifestyle spa** (www.spamagnolia.com), which is professional, if small, with special services for men as well as women. The hotel houses the new **Sanuk Restaurant** (ⓒ **250/920-4844;** www.sanukrestaurant.com). This is an innovative Asian styled restaurant in food and décor.

623 Courtney St., Victoria, BC V8W 1B8. ⓒ 877/624-6654 or 250/381-0999. Fax 250/381-0988. www.magnolia hotel.com. 64 units. Jun to mid-Oct C$229–C$$349 (US$202–US$350). Mid-Oct to May C$159–C$229 (US$140– US$202). Rates include continental breakfast. Children 11 and under stay free in parent's room. AE, DC, DISC, MC, V. Valet parking C$15 (US$13). Bus: 5. Small pets accepted C$60 (US$53). **Amenities:** Restaurant (Pacific Northwest); pub; access to nearby health club; spa; concierge; limited secretarial services; limited room service; laundry service; dry cleaning. *In room:* A/C, TV w/pay movies, dataport, minibar, coffeemaker, hair dryer, iron.

Prior House B&B Inn   Out in the quiet and pretty Rockland neighborhood, this luxurious B&B was formerly an English governor's manor. Consequently, both the house and gardens are among the most picturesque in Victoria. Everything here takes you back to an earlier time: oak-paneled rooms with wood-burning fireplaces, stained-glass windows, hardwood floors, and a blend of antique and replica Edwardian furnishings. Every guest room is sumptuously comfortable with custom-made goose-down duvets and bathrooms fashioned in marble and sporting air-jetted tubs for two. Although the Lieutenant Governor's Royal Suite is the inn's pièce de résistance with its 1880 king-size canopied bed, crystal chandeliers, and spa-style bathroom with gilded walls, the less-ostentatious Windsor Penthouse Suite is just as much of a private sanctuary. The Hobbit Garden Studios are more simply decorated, but no less appealing, with private patios into the well-tended garden. Attention to detail is what this inn is all about; you can even choose to have breakfast served to you in bed.

620 St. Charles St., Victoria BC V8S 3N7. ⓒ 877/924-3300 or 250/592-8847. Fax: 250-592-8223. www.priorhouse.com. 6 units. Mid-Jun to Labor Day C$179–C$299 (US$158–US$263) double. After Labor Day to mid-Oct & Apr to mid-Jun

C$149–C$269 (US$131–US$237). Mid-Oct to mid-Mar C$119–C$199 (US$105–US$175) double. Rates include gourmet breakfast and afternoon tea. MC, V. Free parking. **Amenities:** Lounge; in-room massage; library. *In room:* TV/VCR/ CD player, hair dryer, fireplace.

Victoria Marriott Inner Harbour
Although its modern and urban ambience makes it seemed geared more to the business executive than a casual visitor, the young and enthusiastic staff will give you a warm welcome. In fact, their service has earned this high-rise hotel both the 2006 Outstanding Customer Service Award from Victoria's Chamber of Commerce and international recognition from its parent company. Rooms have all the usual Marriott amenities, including a concierge level that offers a pleasant lounge where you can enjoy complementary hors d'oeuvres in the evening and a continental breakfast. The hotel's location is central, and although set behind the Empress, from the upper-floor guest rooms the views stretch to the Olympic Mountain Range in Washington State. Hotel amenities include a cozy bar, full-size indoor pool, a health club, and the **Fire & Water Fish and Chop House**, a fine-dining restaurant featuring high-quality steaks and seafood.

728 Humboldt St., Victoria BC V8W 3Z5 ✆ **877/333-8338** or 250/480-3800. Fax: 250/480-3838. www.victoria marriott.com. 236 units. C$139–C$229 (US$122–US$202) standard double. AE, DC, MC, V. Valet or self-parking C$12 (US$11). Bus: 2 to Convention Centre. **Amenities:** Restaurant; lounge; indoor pool; health club; Jacuzzi; 24-hr room service; babysitting; laundry service; same-day dry cleaning; nonsmoking rooms. *In room:* A/C, TV, Internet, minibar, fridge, coffeemaker, hair dryer, iron, safe.

Westin at Bear Mountain
Canada's first (and to date only) 36-hole Nicklaus-designed golf course (18 holes are open; the second 18holes open in 2008) is the focal point of this new master-planned resort and residential community. They are situated on what includes a mountain-lodge style resort, five restaurants that range from fine dining to a sushi bar, a MediSpa and state-of-the-art health club. Guest rooms have an earth-tone, natural decor with spacious sitting areas, a fireplace, bathrooms with slate tile floors, well-stocked kitchenettes, and either a balcony or terrace overlooking the fairways and Mount Finlayson.

1999 Country Club Way, Victoria BC V9B 6R9. ✆ **888/533-BEAR** or 250/391-7160. Fax 250/391-3792. www.bear mountain.ca. 156 units, nonsmoking. Jun–Sept C$229–C$459 (US$202–US$404). Oct–May C$159–C$389 (US$140–US$342). AE, MC, V. Free parking. **Amenities:** 3 restaurants; lounge; pub; golf course; health club; spa. *In room:* TV w/movies; DVD (in suites), high-speed Internet, fridge, coffeemaker, hair dryer.

MODERATE

Admiral Inn *Value Kids* The harbor views here will more than make up for the small, motel-like rooms and bathrooms. Besides, they are comfortable and immaculately clean and available at rates that attract couples, families, seniors, and others in search of a multimillion-dollar vista without the expense. Larger rooms have fridges, microwaves, pullout sofabeds and balconies; the suites have full kitchens. The inn is a family run operation, so service is empathetic and includes extras like free bicycles, free local calls, free Internet access in the lobby, and lots of friendly advice on what to see and do.

257 Belleville St., Victoria BC V8V 1X1. ✆ **888/823-6472** or ✆/fax 250/388-6267. www.admiral.bc.ca 32 units. Mid-Jul to Sept C$219 (US$193). Oct to mid-Jul C$99–C$219 (US$87–US$193). Extra person C$10 (US$8.80). Children under 12 stay free in parent's room. Rates include continental breakfast. AE, DC, MC, V. Free parking. Bus: 5 to Belleville and Government sts. **Amenities:** Complimentary bikes; coin laundry; dry cleaning; nonsmoking rooms; complimentary Internet access. *In room:* A/C, TV, kitchen/kitchenette (in some units), fridge, coffeemaker, hair dryer, iron.

The Bedford Regency Hotel ✿
Located on the main commercial drag (the entrance gives the impression that you're entering a shopping mall), the Bedford is one

of Victoria's oldest hotels. Although tasteful renovations have brought it up to modern standards, the quirky layout of guest rooms reflects its heritage. All are elegantly comfortable with down duvets and quality toiletries. Some are so tiny, however, that the foot of the bed is just inches from the pedestal sink. Some have a fireplace "around the corner" beside a reading chair, while others are quite spacious, with two queen-size beds facing each other because the room is long and narrow. Bathrooms are small and very Art Deco. The 12 Superior rooms have Jacuzzis and fireplaces. Window boxes mask the busy street scene below, which in summer can be a bit noisy, at least until midnight. Belingo 1140 is an Art Deco-styled jazz/martini lounge located on the mezzanine. If you're looking for something more casual, head for the Garrick's Head Pub.

1140 Government St., Victoria, BC V8W 1Y2. ✆ 800/665-6500 or 250/384-6835. Fax 250/386-8930. www.bedford regency.com. 40 units. Mid-May to mid-Oct C$140–C$200 (US$123–US$176). Mid-Oct to mid-May C$89–C$159 (US$78–US$140). AE, MC, V. Parking C$10 (US$8.80). Bus: 5 to Douglas and Johnson sts. **Amenities:** Restaurant (Pacific Northwest); pub; martini lounge; dry cleaning; laundry; Internet; Wi-Fi. *In room:* TV, coffeemaker.

Ocean Island Backpackers Inn *(Finds)*

This quirky, historic, four-level youth hostel cum apartment building attracts all age groups and families. Dorm accommodations sleep four to six people, and are co-ed as well as women-only. If you're a twosome, the rates are reasonable enough that it's worth booking a whole dorm to yourself. Special family rooms are more hotel-like, and have a private bathroom, multiple beds, and a fridge. This is not a place for shrinking violets. The lounges, bar, and dining room are magnets for lively and multilingual conversations with fellow travelers. In addition, Ocean Island operates a 1907 character house in the James Bay area that contains three self-contained, self-catering suites.

791 Pandora Ave., Victoria BC V8W 1N9 ✆ 888/888-4180 or 866/888-4180 or 250/385-1788. Fax: 250/385-1780. www.oceanisland.com. 74 units C$19–C$24 (US$17–US$21) dorm, C$25–C$68 (US$22–US$60) private room, C$80–C$110 (US$70–US$97) family room. AE, MC, V. **Amenities:** Lounge; communal kitchen; laundry; Wi-Fi; bike lockup. *In room:* No phone.

Spinnaker's Guest House

Located right on the waterfront at the entrance to Victoria Harbour, Spinnakers is best known by locals for its brewpub (see "Where to Dine") and although it can get a bit noisy around closing, the guesthouse operation is a terrific alternative to central lodgings, provided you don't mind a 15-minute walk to downtown or a 5-minute ferry ride. The complex includes two superbly renovated circa-1880 buildings, the Heritage House, and the Garden Suites, which are more like self-contained studio apartments. All rooms feature queen-size beds, soft earth-toned Westcoast style furnishings, in-room Jacuzzis (except for shower-only room 4), and some have wood-burning fireplaces. Room 9 is one of the nicest and most spacious. It has a vaulted ceiling close to 14 ft. high, a fireplace, sitting room, full kitchen, and south-facing private sun deck.

308 Catherine St. Victoria BC V9A 3S3 ✆ 877/838-2739 or 250/384-2739. Fax: 250/384-3246. www.spinnakers.com. 10 units. Jun–Oct C$159–C$249 (US$140–US$219). Nov–May C$129–C$209 (US$114–US$184). Rates include continental breakfast. AE, DC, MC, V. Free parking. Bus: 24 to Catherine St. **Amenities:** Nonsmoking rooms. *In room:* TV (some rooms), kitchen (some units), coffeemaker, hair dryer, iron, fireplace (some units), Jacuzzi.

Swans Hotel *(★★)*

The charming Swans offers a warm welcome in an intimately comfortable modern-day tavern. But it's more than a bed-and-beer experience. One of Victoria's best-loved heritage restorations, this 1913 warehouse now provides guests with 30 distinctive—and really spacious—suites. Most of the one- and two-bedroom suites are in fact two-story lofts with 11-foot, exposed-beam ceilings and nifty layouts that have many, if not most, of the comforts of home. Accommodating up to six adults, they feature fully equipped kitchens, separate living and dining areas, and private patios. Here you'll also find one of Canada's largest private art collections, which sounds more impressive than it really is because you only get to see what's in the lobby: many pieces are in guest rooms. They add to the atmosphere nonetheless. Check out the stylized totem pole in the restaurant lobby. The **Wild Saffron Bistro & Wine Bar** is open daily. Other facilities include **Swans Pub** and **Buckerfields' Brewery**.

506 Pandora Ave., Victoria, BC V8W 1N6. (© **800/668-7926** or 250/361-3310. Fax 250/361-3491. www.swanshotel.com. 30 suites. Mid-Apr to Sept C$189–C$199 (US$166–US$175) studio, C$259–C$359 (US$228–US$316) suite. Oct to mid-Apr C$179 (US$158) studio, C$259 (US$228) suite. Weekly and monthly rates available. Extra person C$30 (US$26). Up to 2 children 11 and under stay free in parent's room. Rates include continental breakfast. AE, DC, MC, V. Parking C$9 (US$7.95). Bus: 23 or 24 to Pandora Ave. **Amenities:** Restaurant (Pacific Northwest); wine bar; brewpub; brewery; nightclub; access to nearby health club; secretarial services; limited room service; babysitting; laundry service; dry cleaning. *In room:* TV, Internet, kitchen, fridge, coffeemaker, hair dryer, iron.

4 Where to Dine

With more than 700 restaurants in Victoria, there's something for every taste and budget, and refreshingly, you don't always have to pay through the nose to get good quality. In fact, one or two holes-in-the-wall have excellent food. What you will pay for is the restaurant's proximity to a waterfront view. The best restaurants are all within walking distance of downtown hotels, so you don't have to worry about who'll be the designated driver. Although there's still a tendency for Victorians to eat early (restaurants are packed between 7 and 9pm), many trendier restaurants accept late-night reservations.

For a taste of Britain in the heart of Victoria, brewpubs are great gathering-places for a before- or after-dinner pint, or an anytime pint, for that matter. Favorites include the **Swans Brewpub** (506 Pandora Ave. (© **250/361-3310**) in the Swans Hotel (see "Where to Stay," earlier), **Spinnakers** (308 Catherine St. (© **250/386-2739**), and the **Sticky Wicket Pub** (919 Douglas St. (© **250/383-7137**).

And remember, no one does tea better than the Victorians. Sure, it's a bit touristy, but this isn't just dunking a tea bag in warm water. Tea in Victoria is an Epicurean affair offering a host of caloric delicacies. If you're a visitor, you must experience it at least once. In addition to the famed tea at the **Fairmont Empress** (721 Government St. (© **250/384-8111**) (see "Where to Stay," earlier) are summer teas served on the lawns at **Point Ellice House** (2616 Pleasant St. (© **250/380-6506**).

INNER HARBOUR & NEARBY
EXPENSIVE

Blue Crab Bar & Grill 🦀🦀 SEAFOOD   This is the best seafood spot in the city, with killer views of the harbor to boot, so naturally, it's always busy and has a tendency to get noisy. Blue Crab's seafood specials, featured on their signature blackboards, are what keep this restaurant at the top. Dishes are extraordinary inventions, such as blue crab fish pot, grilled salmon with crispy yucca-root spaetzles, or smoked Alaskan black cod poached in coconut milk with a hint of red curry. For a real treat, the platters for two include sampler morsels from several menu items. There's also a good selection of landlubber dishes for those whose tastes run away from the sea. The wine list is excellent, particularly when it comes to acclaimed B.C. and other West Coast wines.

In the Coast Hotel, 146 Kingston St. (© **250/480-1999**. Reservations required. Main courses C$24–C$35 (US$21–US$31). AE, DC, MC, V. Daily 6:30am–10pm. Nibbles available until 1am.

The Mark ★★ CONTINENTAL WEST COAST   The Mark has no view, preferring to create an intimate dining experience within the confines of a discreet, wood-paneled room, but it's perfect for memorable and romantic encounters—it seats only 26 diners. The upscale menu matches the high-end wine list with dishes such as Moroccan roasted venison striploin with a king-oyster-mushroom strudel and marsala demi-glace, and a scorched sashimi albacore tuna, with sun-dried golden-tomato tabbouleh and fennel cream, as well as a mouth-watering frangipane Gala apple pie, with Tugwell honey cream, almond brittle and hand-made Kashmiri chai gelato. Waiters are well informed on dishes, and the service has gracious finesse (extra butter arrives quietly almost before you realize it's running out), without staff hovering.

In the Clarion Hotel Grand Pacific, 450 Quebec St. ✆ 250/380-4487. Reservations recommended. Entrees C$29–C$48 (US$26–US$42); 6-course tasting menu C$70 (US$62). AE, DC, DISC, MC, V. Daily 5–9:30pm.

Pescatore's Fish House ★★ SEAFOOD   Consistently ranked among Victoria's best seafood restaurants, this spot's artsy decor, good service, and extensive, seasonal menu create a great dining alternative to the Blue Crab, even though it hasn't got the view. The daily fresh sheet usually features at least ten items, and whether you go for oysters at the raw bar, crab, clams, salmon, or halibut, you won't be disappointed. Non-fish entrees—pastas, steak, and lamb—are said to be good, though why you would order these at such a great fish place? There's a late-night tapas-style menu offered after 10pm, and weekend live-jazz brunches.

614 Humboldt St. ✆ 250/385-4512. www.pescatores.com. Reservations recommended. Main courses C$17–C$35 (US$15–US$31). AE, DC, MC, V. Mon–Fri 11:30am–midnight; Sat & Sun 11am–midnight.

MODERATE & INEXPENSIVE

Barb's Place FISH & CHIPS   Absolutely no frills here; this floating restaurant at Fisherman's Wharf serves fish and chips at their very tastiest, although it's received such rave reviews that the eatery is on the verge of being overrated. After all, this is only fish and chips, and it's served in newspaper pouches, not on bone china. Get your cod, oysters, or halibut grilled, steamed, or deep-fried any way you like it. Barb serves it all up with hand-hewn chips. Douse your chippies in salt and vinegar, the way they do in England, and enjoy the feast at picnic tables while watching the boats, seagulls, and other harborside activities. A safe bet for hungry appetites.

Erie Street, Fisherman's Wharf (at the entrance to the Inner Harbour). ✆ 250/384-6515. Reservations not accepted. Main courses C$5.50–C$17 (US$4.85–US$15). MC, V. Mar–Oct daily 10am–sunset. Closed Nov–Feb.

The James Bay Tea Room & Restaurant *Finds* BRITISH   British cooking doesn't deserve a bad rap—at least not here. Home-style bangers and mash, Welsh rarebit, liver and bacon, and roast beef and Yorkshire pudding are hearty and great-tasting This is one of the few places that actually serves kippers for breakfast. The decor includes Tiffany lampshades, brass knickknacks, and sepia-tinted family portraits. Tables are crowded with locals and the atmosphere is lively with English-accented chatter. Tarot card readings are offered on the weekend.

332 Menzies St. (behind the Parliament Buildings). ✆ 250/382-8282. Reservations recommended. Breakfast and lunch C$5.50–C$10 (US$4.85–US$8.80); dinner C$11–C$17 (US$9.70–US$15). AE, MC, V. Mon–Sat 7am–7pm; Sun 8am–7pm. Winter to 5pm.

Santiago's *Finds* LATIN AMERICAN   Although the colorful ornamental lights make the place look like a Mexican fiesta, they also indicate the upbeat personality of this cheery cafe. The menu is a creative mix of tasty dishes from Malaysia, Spain, and

South America, so you get tapas dishes alongside items like Pollo Naraja (chicken with oranges) and a mouth-watering spicy paella that brims with mussels, shrimp, sausage, chicken, and artichoke hearts. Meals come with tortilla chips and salsa, sour cream, and quacamole, and the service is friendly and fast.

660 Oswego St. ✆ 250/388-7376. Reservations not accepted. Main courses C$8–C$14 (US$7.05–US$12). MC, V. Daily 8am–9pm.

DOWNTOWN & OLD TOWN
EXPENSIVE

Cafe Brio 🍴🍴 WEST COAST   This award-winning, bistro-style restaurant serves delicious Tuscan-inspired, West Coast fare, likely because its two chefs, one Canadian and one Italian, blend their styles into the ever-changing menu that's based on whatever fresh organic produce they purchased that day. The result is a creative mix of natural flavors zinging with just the right amount of added spices. In winter, expect substantial items such as venison shank, free-range chicken, and confit of duck. In summer, items are lighter: beef tartar complemented by curly-leafed frisee lettuce, goat cheese, and olive oil; Salt Spring Island mussels; and seared scallops topped with crisp potato rösti. Service is top-notch and the wine list is exceptional, with more than 200 wines by the bottle and 30 by the glass or half liter. Local artwork decorates the walls, and wide-planked wooden floors add warmth to the decor.

944 Fort St. ✆ 250/383-0009. www.cafe-brio.com. Reservations recommended Main courses C$14–C$32 (US$12–US$28). AE, MC, V. Daily 5:30–10:30pm.

Il Terrazzo Ristorante 🍴 ITALIAN   Locals have voted this Victoria's best Italian restaurant year in, year out, so if you find your way to its location in an alley between Yates and Johnson streets, it will be worth the effort. The restaurant's three talented chefs create specialties of their homeland that include wood-oven-roasted pizzas, fresh grilled seafood, and a wide variety of homemade pastas, as well as steaks, osso bucco, and other mostly northern Italian specialties. Set in a converted heritage building, its atmosphere is warmly romantic and features a flower-filled heated courtyard, surrounded by brick fireplaces and lit by wrought-iron candelabras. Inside, exposed brick walls, wooden beams, and intimate nooks and crannies are a delight.

555 Johnson St., Waddington Alley (off Johnson St. at Wharf St.). ✆ 250/361-0028. www.ilterrazzo.com. Reservations recommended. Lunch C$9–C$19 (US$7.90–US$17); dinner C$16–C$38 (US$14–US$33). AE, MC, V. Mon–Sat 11:30am–3pm (Oct–Apr no lunch Saturday); dinner nightly 5–10pm.

Restaurant Matisse 🍴🍴 CLASSIC FRENCH   Wrought-iron gates give way to an alluring Parisian ambience. Filled with soft lights and a profusion of fresh flowers, this award-winning 40-seat restaurant has been noted for its service, elegance, and quality, and justifiably so. Savor fresh bread, rack of lamb, filet bordelaise, duck, rabbit, bouillabaisse, and a feathery-light crème brûlée. Menus items are always fresh and innovative, presenting new recipes and ideas garnered during annual pilgrimages to France. The 7-course chef's sampler prix-fixe dinners are C$85 (US$75); add C$40 (US$35) for wine pairings.

512 Yates St. (at Wharf St.). ✆ 250/480-0883. www.restaurantmatisse.com. Reservations recommended. Main courses C$19–C$32 (US$17–US$28); 4-course prix-fixe dinner C$49 (US$43). AE, MC, V. Wed–Sun 5:30–10pm.

MODERATE & INEXPENSIVE

Azuma Sushi 🍴*Value* JAPANESE SUSHI   A relative newcomer to the Victoria sushi scene, this modern, busy, and bright restaurant has the best-value sushi in town.

Best Breakfast

One of the best breakfasts in town is at the **Blue Fox Café** (919 Fort St. ℂ **250/ 380-1683**), a small, always jammed-packed cafe that oozes with mouth-watering smells of down-to-earth but mountain-high pancake stacks, eight varieties of eggs Benny, and homemade granola. Get there early to avoid long lineups.

Rumor has it that at his previous restaurant Azuma's chef developed quite the following for his special rice sauce, the secret of which he has brought with him. The seafood is top quality (not an imitation crab in sight), and the unagi nigiri and spicy tuna sashimi are especially good. The daily two-for-one bento boxes are a real bargain for hungry appetites.

615 Yates St. (between Broad and Government).ℂ **250/382-8768.** Reservations recommended. Main courses C$10–C$20 (US$8.80–US$18). Daily 11am–10pm

Baan Thai THAI   Original art from Thailand creates an elegant restaurant where food and spices are taken seriously. The Singha beer and many ingredients are imported directly from Thailand. The menu has a good variety of classic dishes, pad Thais, stir-fries, and burning hot (count the peppers) garlic prawns. The green curry with eggplants, bamboo shoots, and sweet basil leaves in coconut milk is especially good. Most items can be adapted to accommodate vegetarians, and dishes can be made as hot or as mild as you prefer. Portions are on the small side, however, so if you're sharing, order an extra item.

1117 Blanshard St. ℂ **250/383-0050.** Main course C$10–C$18 (US$8.80–US$16). Mon–Sat 11:30am–10pm; Sun 5–10pm.

Black Olive CONTINENTAL   With over 25 years in the restaurant biz, owner Paul Psyllakis has created an elegant dining room that exudes a Mediterranean warmth. The menu has a West Coast, and overly olive-oriented flare, as in the salmon with artichokes and black olive pesto. Thankfully, a handful of non-olive dishes give the menu broader appeal: an excellent roasted vegetable dish in phylo pastry as well as Greek-style beef tenderloin medallions, pan seared with a mushroom and red wine sauce. Paul's extra virgin olive oil is made from his own olives in Crete, Greece.

739 Pandora St. ℂ **250/384-6060.** www.theblackolive.com) Reservations recommended. Main courses: C$18–C$34 (US$16–US$30). AE, DC, MC, V. Mon–Fri 11:30am–2:30pm; Mon–Sat 5:30–10pm; Sunday 10:30am–2pm.

Café Mexico *Kids* MEXICAN   If you've a sophisticated palate you'll probably find the food too generic, but when hungry children are in tow, you won't go wrong here. The menu has all the standards: sizzling fajitas, burritos, nachos, and tacos, served with the usual order of refried beans, as well as daily specials based around seafood, beef, and chicken. Vegetarian versions are available on many items and the delicious deep-fried ice cream makes up for the limited dessert menu. Besides, part of the reason you go is for the atmosphere—the decor is chock full of color and fun, with Mexican piñatas hanging from the ceiling.

1425 Store St. ℂ **250/386-1425** or 250-386-5454. Reservations not accepted. Main courses: C$10–C$15 (US$8.80– US$13). AE, DC, MC, V. Daily 11am–9:30pm.

Camille's *&* PACIFIC NORTHWEST   The restaurant's owner was one of the founders of the Vancouver Island Farm Co-operative, so, true to form, the ever-changing menu is seasonal and packed with locally sourced ingredients. This might mean tender fiddleheads in spring, and wild salmon and blackberry desserts in the fall. Canadian bison, wild boar, and caribou might also be on the menu—wild game is a specialty, alongside pheasant, quail, and partridge. Everything has an unexpected touch, such as prawn bisque with ginger and lemon, or fennel cakes in a champagne sauce. Camille's is a very romantic spot with cliché, crisp white linens, exposed brick walls, stained glass lamps, soft jazz, and candlelight. Wine tastings are held on Sunday evenings.

45 Bastion Sq. ⓒ 250/381-3433. www.camillesrestaurant.com. Reservations recommended. Main courses: C$22–C$34 (US$19–US$30). AE, MC, V. Daily 5:30–10pm.

Da Tandoor INDIAN Tandoori chicken, seafood, and lamb are the house specialties, though the menu is so extensive you may want to go for the tantalizing sampler plates that have a little of everything—masalas, vindaloos, and vegetarian dishes. Every item is prepared differently, some using ancient moghul techniques that add to the dishes' authenticity. Even if you ask that the spice (heat) ratio be reined in for blander preferences, dishes are all very flavorful, so choose another restaurant if you're looking for milder tastes. The desserts, such as fried cheese dunked in sugared rosewater, are overly sweet for the Western palate (typical of Indian food). If you like what you've eaten here, the restaurant sells its own line of spices and chutneys.

1010 Fort St. ⓒ 250/384-6333. Reservations recommended. Main courses C$11–C$23 (US$9.70–US$20). MC, V. Sun–Thurs 5–9pm; Fri–Sat 5–10pm.

Herald Street Caffe ⓚ PACIFIC NORTHWEST Consistently great, and sometimes inspired, the food here is combined with an imaginative martini menu, and a wine list offering French and Canadian labels, along with a selection of local reds and whites. Located in a renovated 19th-century warehouse on the far side of Chinatown, it has a casual, lively atmosphere that's geared to the younger crowd. All desserts, breads, pastas, soups—even the jam—are made in-house. Main dishes focus on fresh, local seafood and organic produce. The clams are superb, and the crab cakes have been written up by *Bon Appétit* and *Gourmet* magazines. Portions are large enough that small eaters might want to share. In topping off your meal with exceptionally good service, this restaurant earns its reputation as one of the city's best.

⟨*Value* **Bargain Meals**

These tiny and inexpensive Asian eateries aren't much on decor (wear your jeans) but they're big on flavor and small in price. **My Thai Café** (1020 Cook St. ⓒ 250/472-774) doesn't offer a huge variety on the menu but what there is, is excellent home-cooked Thai food. The beef salad is tasty. **Wah Lai Yuen** (560 Fisgard St. (in Chinatown) ⓒ 250/381-5355) offers an authentic Chinese dining experience. If you can put up with the sometimes offhand service, the humongous servings make this a real deal.

And for gamblers? Order the C$10 (US$8.80) Mahoney at **Floyd's Diner** (866 Yates St. ⓒ 250/382-5114) and let the kitchen cook up whatever it wants. After eating, flip a coin, and if you win, the meal is free. If you lose, you pay double.

The Tea Experience

When the Duchess of Bedford (1788–1861) complained about a "sinking feeling" in the late afternoon, she invented afternoon tea to keep her going until dinner. Today, however, tea has come to mean everything from a genteel cuppa of Earl Grey to a full-blown meal in itself with scones with whipped cream, savory crustless sandwiches, sweet tartlets, and home-baked biscuits. Among the top choices are:

- **The Fairmont Empress** (721 Government St. ✆ **250/384-8111)** serves its famed epicurean feast in the Tea Lobby and elsewhere as the throngs of tea-takers dictate. It's expensive (C$54/US$48 in high season) and, quite frankly, overrated, although the inflated price does include a keepsake of nicely packaged Empress tea.

- **The Blethering Place Tearoom** (2250 Oak Bay Ave., Oak Bay ✆ **250/598-1413)** is slightly less pretentious and has the art of tea down pat. Tea menus start at C$17 (US$15) and are what a quintessential Victorian tea house is all about.

- **White Heather Tea Room** (1885 Oak Bay Ave. ✆ **250/595-8020)**, is a local favorite just down the road. Small, bright, and exceptionally friendly, the Big Muckle Giant Tea for Two (C$37/US$33) is the grand slam of all teas. Smaller options are available.

- **Point Ellice House** (2616 Pleasant St. ✆ **250/380-6506)** was where Victoria's social elite gathered in early 1900s. Located only a 5-minute ferry ride from the Inner Harbour, it's a place where today you can enjoy tea (summer only) near the water on beautiful lawns. The cost of C$18 (US$16) includes a half-hour tour of the mansion and gardens.

- Further afield, taking tea in the elegant **Butchart Gardens Dining Room** (800 Benvenuto Ave. ✆ **250/652-4422)** is worth the drive, although you can only enjoy the experience if you've also paid for admission to the gardens. A full tea is C$25 (US$22).

- **Murchie's Tea and Coffee**, 1110 Government St. (✆ **250-383-3112)**, offers the best selection of teas in the city, plus good coffee and everything from snacks to full-blown sandwiches and salads (C$5–C$12/US$4.40–US$11).

546 Herald St. (in Chinatown). ✆ 250/381-1441. Reservations required. Main courses C$16–C$39 (US$14–US$34). AE, DC, MC, V. Daily 5–10pm; Sat–Sun brunch 11am–3pm.

Pagliacci's ⟨R⟩ ITALIAN   Opened in 1979 by expatriate New Yorker Howie Siegal, Pagliacci's is not your ordinary Italian restaurant. Named after the Ital0ian word for *clown*, it's elbow-to-elbow most nights, and tables are quite close together. This is the place neither for those wanting a private tête-à-tête nor for connoisseurs in search of exquisite Italian cuisine (those folks need to go to Il Tarrazzo, see above). Pagliacci's is just fun. You can mix and match selections from the menu in true *Harry Meets Sally* style, especially when items have such a quirky Hollywood take that you'll want to experiment: take the Veronica Lake Salad or the Mae West Veal Medallions as examples. You'll also find more traditional menu items such as veal parmigiana and almost two dozen a la carte freshly made pastas. And if all this isn't entertainment enough, there's live jazz Sunday through Wednesday. The likes of Diana Krall and Etta James have played Pagliacci's.

1011 Broad St. ℂ **250/386-1662.** Reservations not accepted. Lunch C$7–C$12 (US$6.15–US$11); dinner C$12–C$25 (US$11–US$22). AE, MC, V. Mon–Thurs 11:30am–11pm; Fri–Sat 11:30am–midnight; Sun 11am–11pm.

rebar Modern Food *(Kids)* VEGETARIAN   This bright and funkily decorated basement restaurant is likely the best vegetarian cafe on the West Coast. The juice bar alone boasts more than 80 varieties of deliciously healthful smoothies, shakes, wheatgrass drinks, and power tonics. The stress-busting Soul Change—a blend of carrot, apple, celery, ginger, and Siberian ginseng—is a winner. The menu is geared (though not exclusively) to vegetarian and vegan diners, featuring international cuisine from Thai curries and pastas to hummus and fresh shrimp quesadillas. The homemade muesli is dynamite and the Cascadia Bakery produces everything from decadent vegan Belgian chocolate fudge cake to hand-shaped whole-grain specialty breads. The small wine list offers predominately B.C. wines, and even when it's really busy (which is most of the time), the service remains fast and friendly. rebar is a number one choice for juices; a top spot for lunch, and good for dinner only if you're still in your jeans and needing something fast and nutritious.

50 Bastion Sq. (downstairs). ℂ **250/361-9223.** www.rebarmodernfood.com. Reservations not accepted. Main courses C$8–C$16 (US$7–US$14). AE, MC, V. Mon–Thurs 8:30am–9pm; Fri–Sat 8:30am–10pm; Sun 8:30am–3:30pm. Reduced hours in winter.

5 Exploring Victoria

If you're staying anywhere near the downtown core, trade the car for a good pair of walking shoes because virtually everything in this chapter is doable on foot. Besides, walking is by far the best way to appreciate some of Victoria's diverse architecture: heritage residences, refurbished turn-of-the-century warehouses, and ornamental showpieces. Start with the attractions around the Inner Harbour and fan out from there for a refreshing walk through Beacon Hill Park, or head in the opposite direction for great shopping. The waterfront is also the departing point for most of the city's tours, whether you're off to Butchart Gardens (see chapter 5), or up for whale-watching or a kayaking excursion. Attractions that are out of the Victoria Central, such as Craigdarroch Castle, Abkazi Garden, and Hatley Park, are only a 10-minute cab ride away.

THE TOP ATTRACTIONS

Art Gallery of Greater Victoria   Located near Craigdarroch Castle, the AGGV, as it's often called, exhibits more than 15,000 pieces of art, drawn mainly from Asia, Europe, and North America. Permanent collections include a life-size dollhouse and an authentic Shinto shrine that is part of Canada's most extensive Japanese art collection. Most compelling is the Emily Carr exhibit, which integrates her visual and written work alongside images from the B.C. provincial archives, together creating an in-depth portrait of this pre-eminent Victoria artist.

1040 Moss St. ℂ **250/384-4101.** www.aggv.bc.ca. Admission C$8 (US$7.05) adults, C$6 (US$5.30) students and seniors. Daily 10am–5pm (Thurs to 9pm). Bus: 11, 14, or 22.

Craigdarroch Castle *★★*   If you've got it, flaunt it. That's what coal baron Robert Dunsmuir (the wealthiest and most influential man in British Columbia back in the 1880s) decided to do. More than a home, this Highland-style castle rises 87 stairs through five floors of Victorian opulence—and there's not an elevator to be had! Children might think it's like something out of Disneyland. The nonprofit society that runs Craigdarroch does so with impressive care; the stained glass, Persian carpets, and intricate woodwork are treasures to behold. Visitors receive a self-guided tour booklet and volunteers delight in sharing sidebars of Dunsmuir's family history. Head to the top for a fabulous view of Victoria, the Strait of Juan de Fuca, and the Olympic Mountains. Allow about an hour to tour the castle.

1050 Joan Cres. (off Fort St.). ℰ 250/592-5323. www.craigdarrochcastle.com. Admission C$12 (US$10) adults, C$11 (US$9.50) seniors, C$7.50 (US$6.60) students, C$3.50 (US$3.10) children 6–18, free for children 5 and under. Jun 15–Aug 31 9am–7pm; Sept 1–Jun 14 10am–4:30pm. Take Fort St. out of downtown, just past Pandora Ave., and turn right on Joan Cres. Bus: 11 or 14.

Maritime Museum of British Columbia   Located in a former Victoria courthouse, this museum celebrates British Columbia's seafaring history in film and exhibits, from whalers and grand ocean liners, to military conflict and 20th-century explorers. Highlights include a replica of the HMS Temeraire, constructed entirely of beef and chicken bones by French naval prisoners captured during the Napoleonic Wars. Check out the heritage courtroom renovated by Francis Rattenbury, as well as one of Victoria's most ornate elevators. Plan to stay 1½ hours, longer if you have salt

Eminent Victorian: Francis Mawson Rattenbury

As one of Victoria's most famous people, **Francis Mawson Rattenbury** ("Ratz," as he was known) not only left his architectural mark on the city (including the Parliament Buildings and the Empress Hotel), but also was among Victoria's most controversial residents. In 1892, at 25 years of age, he arrived here from England, having won a competition to design the Parliament Buildings. It was an impressive start to an illustrious career, during which he only ever sought the largest commissions and boldest opportunities. These included branches for the Bank of Montreal, The Vancouver Hotel, and provincial courthouses in Nanaimo, Nelson, and Vancouver.

Rattenbury's reputation, however, suffered when, in his mid-50s, he left his wife Florrie and appeared publicly with his mistress, Alma Packenham—a beautiful woman 30 years his junior and already twice married. After divorcing Florrie, Rattenbury married Alma and in 1930, when they realized they had become social pariahs, they left for England. But the age differences began to tell, and increasingly, Rattenbury took solace in the whiskey bottle.

In 1934, when 17-year-old George Stoner was hired as their chauffeur, Alma quickly seduced the young man and installed him in the spare bedroom as her lover-in-residence. But, driven wild at the prospect of being discovered, Stoner came upon a dozing Rattenbury in the living room, and clubbed him to death. Both Alma and Stoner were charged with murder, and after a sensational trial, Alma was acquitted and Stoner sentenced to hang. Alma, however, was unable to face Stoner's execution, and within four days she committed suicide by stabbing herself through the heart. Stoner was later released from prison.

in your veins; the museum maintains a registry of heritage vessels, and a wealth of resource information for maritime buffs. The gift shop has an excellent selection of nautical paraphernalia. Kids programs include a sleepover in this purportedly haunted place!

28 Bastion Sq. ⓒ 250/385-4222. www.mmbc.bc.ca. Admission C$8 (US$7.05) adults, C$5 (US$4.40) seniors & students, C$3 (US$2.65) children 6–11, free for children 5 and under, C$20 (US$18) family pass. Daily 9:30am–4:30pm. Bus: 5 to View St.

Miniature World *Kids*   If you ever wondered what Gulliver felt like in the land of the Lilliputians, this little world reveals all. Children and the young at heart will love the more than 80 miniature displays (many of them moving) of solar systems, battle scenes, fancy 18th-century dress balls, a three-ring circus, and dozens of scenes from beloved fairy tales. A big favorite is the Great Canadian Railway, one of the world's largest model railways, although close contenders are the world's smallest operational sawmill, 11 years in the making, and two of the world's largest doll houses. Allow an hour.

649 Humboldt St., ⓒ 250/385-9731. www.miniatureworld.com. Admission C$9 (US$7.90) adults, C$8 (US$7.05) children 12–17, C$7(US$6.15) children 3–11, free for children 2 and under. Jun14–Labor Day daily 9am–9pm; after Labor Day–Jun 13 9am–5pm. Bus: 5, 27, 28, 30, or 31.

Pacific Undersea Gardens *Kids*   The stark exterior looks out of place in Victoria's Inner Harbour, but descend the sloping stairway and you're in another world—below the waterline. From a glass-enclosed sunken vessel, you get to experience the harbor's marine life, which swims all around you in natural aquariums. All manner of fish—from brilliant red snapper to stonefish and octopi—swim through the kelp forest. Divers descend every hour to show the audience some of the harder-to-see creatures, like starfish tucked in rocks, wolf eels, and sharks. The observatory also cares for injured and orphaned seals, many of which prefer to stay in the area after their release. Buy a bag of herring in the gift shop and feed them a feast. Plan to stay about an hour, although feeding the seals is so captivating, you may want to hang around longer.

490 Belleville St. ⓒ 250/382-5717. www.pacificunderseagardens.com. Admission C$8.95 (US$7.90) adults, C$7.95 (US$7) seniors, C$6.95 (US$6.10) children 12–17, C$4.95 (US$4.35) children 5–11, free for children 4 and under. Jun–Sept daily 10am–7pm; Oct–May daily 10am–5pm. Closed Jan–Feb Tue–Wed. Bus: 5, 27, 28, or 30.

Parliament Buildings   By night, this architectural gem is lit by thousands of lights so that it looks more like the Hogwarts School for Wizards than the provincial Parliament Buildings. Designed by then 25-year-old Francis Rattenbury, one of the most sought-after architects of the day, the buildings were constructed between 1893 and 1898 at a cost of nearly C$1 million (US$880,000). The interior is equally mystical, filled with mosaics, marble, woodwork, and stained glass. If the Legislature is sitting, head up to the visitor's gallery. There's not a lot of room there, but it's fun to watch politicians in action. British Columbia is known for its eccentric politics, and Question Period, in the early afternoon, can be particularly entertaining. The "been there, done it" crowd could do this in 20 minutes; guided tours (summer only) last about 40 minutes and leave every half hour from the central lobby.

501 Belleville St. ⓒ 250/387-3046. www.victoriabc.ca/victoira/parliamentbuildings. Free admission. Daily 9am–5pm. Bus: 5, 27, 28, or 30.

Royal British Columbia Museum *Kids*   This museum is one of the best regional museums in the world and is worthy of at least a half day. The dioramas are so lifelike, you'll feel as if you're stepping back in time—whether it's coming face to

Symphony Splash

The highlight of the long weekend in early August is the free on-the-water per-formance of the Victoria Symphony Orchestra. As it plays atop a floating barge, the entire Inner Harbour becomes a concert venue with orchestral renderings carried across the water via loudspeakers. Traditionally, the concert closes with *The 1812 Overture*, complete with guns and the carillon.

tusk with a wooly mammoth, tracking through a B.C. forest or to the edge of a glacier, or meandering down the cobblestone streets of a pioneer town. Feel the train rattle the timbers of the old train station each time it passes, or enjoy old Charlie Chaplin movies in the movie theater. Just like an IKEA store, the museum has a route that doesn't bypass a thing, so start at the top in the Modern History Gallery (the showcases have items from the early 1900s through to the power eighties that highlight the lifestyles of each decade), and work your way down through the second-floor Natural History Gallery and the First Peoples Gallery with its totems, Native longhouses, and artifacts. The museum also has an IMAX theater, showing an ever-changing variety of large-screen movies (© **250/953-IMAX** or 250/953-4629; www.imaxvictoria.com). Thunderbird Park, beside the museum, houses a cedar longhouse, where Native carvers work on new totem poles. *Note:* Admission rates are sometimes higher during special exhibitions.

675 Belleville St. © **250/356-7226**. www.royalbcmuseum.bc.ca. Admission C$14 (US$12) adults, C$9.50 (US$8.35) seniors, students, children 6–18, free for children 5 and under, C$38 (US$33) family pass. Daily 9am–5pm. Bus: 5, 28, or 30.

Royal London Wax Museum *(Kids)*   If you've been to Madame Tussaud's in London, then you'll be disappointed, but for those who have never seen a wax-works exhibi-tion, it can be quite fun. You'll find celebrities, world leaders, and historical figures mixing and mingling in groupings never dreamed of. There's a gaggle of waxy royal figures (Camilla included) along Royalty Row, an Einstein-esque Wizard of Oz in Sto-rybook Land, and a host of significant others past and present. The Chamber of Hor-rors doesn't exactly scare up a flutter, even in the faint of heart. The average price tag for each figure is C$10,000 (US$8,800), depending on how popular it is. U.S. presi-dents go cheap; Canadian prime ministers are pricey. Plan to spend 1½ hours if you're with kids—they love the place; half that time if you've done wax museums elsewhere in the world and are just trying to get in out of the rain.

470 Belleville St. © **250/388-4461**. www.waxmuseum.bc.ca. Admission C$10 (US$8.80) adults, C$9.50 (US$8.35) seniors, C$7 (US$6.15) students, C$5 (US$4.40) children 6–12, free for children 5 and under. May–Sept daily 9:30am–8:30pm; Oct–Apr daily 9:30am–5pm. Bus: 5, 27, 28, or 30.

Victoria Bug Zoo *(Kids)*   In the heart of downtown Victoria, enter an amazing world of international insects: walking sticks, praying manti, tarantulas, and scorpi-ons, to name a few. Although all the creepy-crawlies are behind glass, an entomologist (bug scientist) is on hand to answer questions and show you how to handle some of the multilegged creatures, which include a 400-leg millipede that stretches the length of your forearm. Even if you're spider-wary, this is a fascinating place. Kids will want to spend a couple of hours here.

631 Courtney St. © **250/384-2847**. www.bugzoo.bc.ca. Admission C$7 (US$6.15) adults, C$5 (US$4.40) seniors, C$6.50 (US$5.70) students, C$4.50 (US$3.95) children 3–16, free for children 2 and under. Daily Mon–Sat 10am–5pm and Sun 11am–5pm. Any downtown bus.

PARKS & GARDENS

Victoria is famed for its garden landscapes and for its abundance of flowers. Even if there's not a horticultural bone in your body, you really can't help but appreciate the efforts that have earned the city such acclaim. Look overhead and chances are that there'll be an overstuffed hanging basket trailing with colorful blooms. And in most of the residential neighborhoods, private home owners take special pride in their gardens.

Among the most spectacular examples are **The Gardens at Government House** (1401 Rockland Ave. ℭ **250/356-5139**), the official (and private) residence of British Columbia's Lieutenant Governor. The formal gardens are free to wander from dawn to dusk, and for rose lovers in particular, they're well worth the visit. Guided tours are C$10 (US$8.80) and include areas not normally open to the public.

Nearby **Abkahzi Garden** (1964 Fairfield Rd. ℭ **250/598-8096;** www.conservancy. bc.ca) is a dramatic, half-hectare (1-acre) jewel of a garden created by Prince and Princess Nicholas Abkhazi in the 1940s. Amid the woodland, rocky slopes, and rhododendrons is a quaint tearoom and gift shop. The gardens are open April to September, Wednesday through Sunday, 1 to 5pm. Another once-private-residence is **Hatley Park & Museum** (2005 Sooke Rd. ℭ **250/391-2666;** www.hatleygardens.com). This is actually a National Historic Site, and boasts one of the few Edwardian estates in Canada, complete with Italian, Rose, and Japanese gardens. There are hundreds of heritage trees, including 250-year-old Douglas firs, an ecologically important salt marsh estuary, and a series of natural springs. Garden and castle tours are offered weekdays, 1 to 4pm. Admission is by donation. Next door, **Royal Roads University** (ℭ **250/391-2511**) also features extensive floral gardens, which are open to the public, free of charge. The University of Victoria, too, has gardens that are free to wander: **Finnerty Gardens** (3800 Finnerty Rd.,ℭ **250/721-7606**) contain one of Canada's best collections of rhododendrons, many of which were started from seed from famous plant explorers. There are over 500 different varieties as well as 1,600 trees, shrubs, companion plants, and ornamentals. The gardens cover 2.6 hectares (6½-acres) and are open daily from dawn to dusk. The entrance to the gardens is near the University Chapel, on the southwest edge of the campus. Proceed around the Ring Road to parking lot 6.

If you're staying put around the downtown core, a walk through **Beacon Hill Park** is a must. Originally gifted to the city by the Hudson Bay Company in 1882, today it stretches from just behind the Royal BC Museum to Dallas Road. Without doubt, it's the top park in Victoria—an oasis of indigenous Garry oaks, floral gardens, windswept heath, ponds, and totem poles. There's also a children's farm (see "Especially for Kids"), aviary, tennis courts, lawn-bowling green, putting green, playgrounds, and picnic areas. En route, be sure to drop by tiny **Thunderbird Park** (at the corner of Bellevue and Douglas streets, beside the Royal BC Museum). It has several totem poles, and in summer, there's an outdoor studio for experienced carvers to

---

On the Waterfront

Be sure to visit **Fisherman's Wharf** near the Laurel Point Hotel. It's a delightful 15-minute walk along the waterfront from the Inner Harbour, at the end of which you'll find a picturesque flotilla of working fishing boats, houseboats, yachts, and other sailing vessels. Reward yourself with fish and chips at wharfside.

---

create new poles. Adjacent to the park lies **Helmcken House**, the oldest house still on its original site in British Columbia.

OUTDOOR ACTIVITIES

Vancouver Island, and even urban Victoria, is garnering quite a reputation for its range of outdoor activities. Hiking and biking are big pastimes for both residents and visitors, and there is an abundance of whale-watching companies. Victoria is also a good resource for activities farther afield such as scuba diving (Ogden Point Dive Centre, 199 Dallas Rd.; ✆ **250/380-9119;** www.divevictoria.com) and birding (Victoria Natural History Society; www.nicnhs.bc.ca).

BIKING   Cycling is a popular mode of transportation, and bike paths abound here. There's a scenic **Marine Drive bike path** that takes you around the peninsula and over to Oak Bay. The Inner Harbour also has a bike lane alongside the pedestrian pathway. The city's jewel, however, is the 60-km (about 37-mile) **Galloping Goose Trail** (✆ **250/478-3344** for maps and information). This terrific rails-to-trails conversion starts in Victoria at the south end of the Selkirk Trestle, at the foot of Alston Street in Victoria West, and travels the back roads through urban, rural, and semi-wilderness landscapes. There are access points along the entire trail route with many parking areas. It is named after a gawky and noisy 1920s gasoline-powered passenger car that operated on the abandoned CNR line between Victoria and Sooke.

   Great Pacific Adventures, 811 Wharf St. (✆ **877/733-6722** or 250/386-2277; www. greatpacificadventures.com) rents bikes from C$8/US$7.05 per hour or C$35/US$31 per day (call ahead in winter), as does **Cycle BC**, with two locations at 747 Douglas St. (year round) or 950 Wharf St. (May–Oct) (✆ **250/885-2453;** www.cyclebc.ca).

CANOEING & KAYAKING   **Ocean River Sports,** 1824 Store St. (✆ **800/909-4233** or 250/381-4233), on the waterfront, caters to novice and experienced paddler alike, with rentals, equipment, dry storage camping gear, and a number of guided tours. Beginners should opt for the 2½-hour "Explorer" around Victoria Harbour (C$59/US$52). More adventuresome kayakers can go for the multi-day adventure to explore the Gulf Islands (C$595/US$524) inclusive of tent accommodation on secluded beaches, and meals. Rentals are C$25 (US$22) for 2 hours; C$40 (US$35) for an 8-hour day. *Tip:* Because of Ocean River's waterfront location, absolute beginners can rent a kayak for a try-out paddle in the harbor's protected waters.

   Sea Wharf Kayaks (950 Wharf St. ✆ **250/216-5646;** www.victoriakayak.com) does 2½-hour naturalist tours to Seal Island (C$59/US$52) and a 6-hour excursion to the Strait of Juan de Fuca (C$125/US$110).

FISHING   Saltwater fishing is very popular in this part of the world, and guides will show you the current hot spots. **Adam's Fishing Charters** (✆ **250/370-2326,** www. adamsfishingcharters.com) and **Beasley Fishing Charters** (✆ **866/259-1111** or 250/ 381-8000; www.beasleyfishingcharters.com) are good starting points. Fishing charters run around C$95 (US$84) an hour, for a minimum 4 hours.

   To fish, you need a **saltwater fishing license,** available at Adam's and the Marine Adventure Centre. For nonresidents, a 1-day license costs C$7.40 (US$6.55), a 3-day license C$20 (US$18), and a 5-day license C$33 (US$29). For B.C. residents a 1-day license is C$5.75 (US$5.05), a 3-day C$12 (US$10) and a 5-day C$17 (US$15). There is a salmon surcharge of C$6.35 (US$5.60).

If you're interested in taking the wheel yourself, Great Pacific Adventures, 811 Wharf St. (© **877/733-6722** or 250/386-2277; www.greatpacificadventures.com) rents watercraft, including 16-foot powerboats at C$49 (US$43) an hour.

For fly-fishing, **Robinson's Outdoor Store,** 1307 Broad St. (© **250/385-3429;** www.robinsonsoutdoors.com), is an excellent resource for information and gear from specialty flies for area waters, to rods, reels, and a number of resource books. They also sell freshwater fishing licenses. For nonresidents, a one-day license is C$21 (US$19) and an eight-day is C$38 (US$43). For B.C. residents, a one-day license is C$11 (US$9.35) and an eight-day is C$21 (US$19).

GOLF Victoria has an enviable number of good courses. The fees are reasonable, the scenery is spectacular, and most courses are open year round. The **Olympic View Golf Club,** 643 Latoria Rd. (© **800/I-GOLFBC [800/445-5322]** or 250/474-3671; www.golfbc.com), is one of the top 35 golf courses in Canada, with 2 waterfalls and 12 lakes sharing space with the greens. The 6,414-yard course is par 72, and green fees range from C$35 (US$31) winter season to C$75 (US$66) on a summer weekend. There's a VIP package, for C$90 to C$130 (US$79–US$114) per person, which includes a cart and a warm-up bucket of range balls. The **Cedar Hill Municipal Golf Course** at 1400 Derby Rd. (© **250/475-7151**) is a more modest 18-hole public course located only 3.5km (2 miles) from downtown Victoria. Daytime fees are C$38 (US$33), twilight, junior and winter fees are C$23 (US$20). Tee-off times are first come, first served. The **Cordova Bay Golf Course** at 5333 Cordova Bay Rd. (© **250/ 658-4444;** www.cordovabaygolf.com) is midway between the Victoria International Airport and downtown Victoria—about a 20-minute drive from either location. It's par 72; expect some tight fairways and 66 sand traps. May to September, daytime green fees Friday to Sunday are C$65 (US$57), and Monday to Thursday are C$60 (US$53), when booked 7 days in advance. Tee times within 7 days are reserved for members. From October to April, green fees range from C$45 (US$40) weekdays to C$55 (US$48) weekends (including Friday).

If you're tight for time, call the **Last Minute Golf Hotline** at © **800/684-6344** for substantial discounts and short-notice tee times at courses in and around Victoria. Book on line at www.lastminutegolfbc.com.

SAILING Sailors have often remarked that the Juan de Fuca Strait is some of the best and prettiest sailing in the world. **Sail Piraeus Adventures** (© **250/360-6184;** www.sailpiraeus.com) leaves right from the Inner Harbour for 3-hour excursions aboard a restored 54-foot ketch. There are three sailings daily (C$60/US$53 per person), including a sunset cruise. You can participate or just relax. Binoculars are provided. For an even more romantic option, with **Tall Ship Adventures** (© **877/788-4263** or 250/885-2311) you can hop aboard the 55-foot tall ship *Thane.* It's a 1978 vessel modeled after Joshua Slocum's *Spray,* the first vessel to circumnavigate single-handed in 1895. Departures are also from the Inner Harbour; 3-hour trips are C$60 (US$53) per person.

⌒Moments Dance of the Sugar Plum Ferries

Every Sunday at 10:45am, June through Labor Day, Victoria Harbour is the stage for an extraordinary dance: a "water ballet" of ferries waltzing through the waves to *The Blue Danube.*

⌒Moments An Overview of the Islands

If time doesn't let you see everything this book has to offer, take a shortcut with a Harbour Seaplane Islands Extravaganza tour—a C$269 (US$237), 75-minute flight through the Gulf and San Juan islands, and perhaps even a fly over Vancouver Island's wild, most westerly coast (see chapter 5).

WHALE-WATCHING Orcas (killer whales), harbor seals, sea lions, porpoises, and gray whales ply these waters year-round, so whale-watching outfitters abound. Competition keeps prices in line—expect to pay about C$95 (US$84) for a 2- to 3-hour excursion—so the real choice is between riding the waves in a zippy 12-person Zodiac or in a larger, more leisurely craft. Some reputable outfits include **Orca Spirit Adventures** (© **250/383-8411;** www.orcaspirit.com), which departs from the Coast Harbourside Hotel dock; **Prince of Whales,** 812 Wharf St. (© **888/383-4884** or 250/383-4884; www.princeofwhales.com); and **Seafun Safaris Whale Watching**, 950 Wharf St. (© **877/ 360-1233** or 250/360-1200; www.seafun.com).

ORGANIZED TOURS

BUS TOURS Gray Line of Victoria (© **800/663-8390** or 250/388-5248; www. grayline.ca) conducts tours of the city and, notably, of **Butchart Gardens.** The 1½-hour **"Grand City tour"** costs C$21 (US$18) for adults, C$10 (US$9) for children 5 to 11, and is free for children 4 and under (one child per adult). In July and August, daily tours depart every 30 minutes from 9:30am to 4:30pm. In spring and fall, tours depart hourly, and in winter there are only three departures a day. Call ahead for exact times. Gray Line also offers seasonal tours such as Ghost Tours and Murder Mysteries. Check the website for details.

FERRY TOURS Departing from various stops around the Inner Harbour, **Victoria Harbour Ferries** (© **250/708-0201;** www.victoriaharbourferry.com) offers terrific 45- and 55-minute tours of the harbor. See shipyards, wildlife, marinas, fishing boats, and floating homes from the water. Tours cost C$17 (US$15) for adults, C$15 (US$13) seniors, and C$9 (US$7.90) for children 12 and under. From March 1 to April 30 and for the month of October they operate daily, every 15 minutes from 10am to 5pm. From May 1 to September 30 they run daily from 9am to 9pm. If you want to stop for food or a stroll, you can get a token that's good for reboarding at any time during the same day.

SPECIALTY TOURS In the mood for something a little different? Climb into one of the bicycle-rickshaws operated by **Kabuki Cabs** (613 Herald St. © **250/385-4243;** www.kabukikabs.com). They hold up to four people, operate seasonally, and run just like regular taxis; you can flag one down or (usually) find them parked in front of the Fairmont Empress. Rates run about C$1 (US88¢) per minute for a two-person cab, and C$1.50 (US$1.30) per minute for a four-person cab. A typical 30-minute tour (you can set your own itinerary) runs about C$30 to C$45 (US$26–US$40).

Tallyho Horse Drawn Tours (© **866/383-5067** or 250/383-5067; www.tallyho tours.com) has conducted horse-drawn carriage tours and trolleys in Victoria since 1903. Trolleys hold up to 20 strangers and are by far the most affordable at C$15 (US$13) adult, C$12 (US$11) senior, and C$7 (US$6.15) children for a 45-minute roll around the city. In summer, tours depart daily, every half hour from 9 am to dusk.

Sunday's Best

The **Old Cemetery Society of Victoria's** (© 250/598-8870; www.oldcem.bc.ca) Sunday-only cemetery tours have become so popular that the group now has a full summer program. Guides take you through Ross Bay Cemetery as well as the Old Burying Ground of Pioneer Square Cemetery (the evening Lantern Tour is quite eerie). Visit the graves and hear Victoria's history through the lives of Emily Carr, Gold Rush prospectors, and others. Meet at 2pm in front of Starbucks, Fairfield Plaza, 1516 Fairfield Rd. Tours are C$5 (US$4.40). No reservations needed.

By far the most romantic are the turn-of-the-century two-person carriage tours—from a short and sweet 15-minute harbor tour for C$40 (US$35) to a ride through Beacon Hill Park at C$80 (US$70) or a 100-minute Romance tour for C$240 (US$211). All Tallyho rides start at the corner of Belleville and Menzies streets (across from the Royal London Wax Museum). To get a bird's-eye view of Victoria, **Harbour Air Seaplanes** (950 Wharf St. © **800/665-0212** or 250/384-2215; www.harbour-air.com) provides 30-minute sky-tours of Victoria's panorama for C$99 (US$87) as well as a romantic Fly 'n' Dine tour that combines a flight to Butchart Gardens, garden admission, and dinner, and a Daimler limo ride back into town. The cost is C$209 (US$184) per person.

You can also take a limousine-only tour with **Heritage Tours and Daimler Limousine Service** (713 Bexhill Rd. © **250/474-4332**) around Victoria; rates start at C$75 (US$66) per hour. Stretch limos for 8 to 10 people are also available; hourly rates are C$75 to C$85 (US$66–US$75).

WALKING TOURS Victoria is such a great walking city that guided walks proliferate. Sure, there are self-guided walks (maps are available at the Visitor Information Centre), but to get the most out of what you're seeing, nothing beats hearing the history, gossip, and anecdotes that tour guides can offer. **Discover the Past** (© 250/384-6698; discover thepast.com) is the leader of the pack, offering walks conducted by historian and entertaining storyteller John Adams. Tours run year round (by appointment) and cover eight themes or areas, from ghostly walks in Old Town to historical walks around Chinatown; starting points may vary. Tours run June through September and cost C$15 (US$13).

Walkabout Historical Tours (© 250/592-9255) is the only company that tours the Fairmont Empress. Dressed in turn-of-the-century clothes, guides are exceptionally well informed about this historical hotel (which is said to be haunted). Their knowledge adds a whole new dimension to enjoying high tea there later. The 70-minute, C$10 (US$8.80) tour departs daily at 10am sharp; meet at the Fairmont Empress store located next to the Tea Lobby (on the Belleville Street end of the hotel).

Victoria Bobby Walking Tours (© 250/995-0233; www.walkvictoria.com) offers a variety of walks around the city neighborhoods; they depart from the Visitor Information Centre May through mid-September daily at 11am. Your guide is an English ex-bobby—just look for that distinguishing helmet.

6 Especially for Kids

There's no doubt that Victoria caters well to getaway travelers, whether looking for romance, or simply a quality urban destination. But families with children of all ages also find much to enjoy here. There are the obvious city attractions such as the touchy-feely, creepy-crawly **Victoria Bug Zoo** (p. 71) that's bound to be a sure-fire hit; the watery kingdom of **Pacific Undersea Gardens** (page 70); the diminutive displays at **Miniature World** (p. 70); and the **Royal London Wax Museum** (p. 71)—although jaded teenagers may not think the House of Horrors is macabre enough. Then there's the very unstuffy **Royal BC Museum** (p. 70), which really does have something for all ages, especially when combined with a visit to the **IMAX** theater.

For youngsters, the **Beacon Hill Children's Farm** (Circle Drive, Beacon Hill Park Ⓒ **250/381-2532**) is a well-established petting zoo with rabbits, goats, and other barn-yard animals, which makes for a great outing, especially when coupled with some kite flying on Beacon Hill or picnicking at the wading pool and playground area nearby.

Outside of the downtown core, remember to check out the **Butterfly Gardens** (p. 89), **Fort Rodd Hill & Fisgard Lighthouse** (p. 94), and **Mineral World & Scratch Patch** (9891 Seaport Place, Sidney; Ⓒ **250/655-4367**; www.scratchpatch. com), an outdoor garden containing two gold-panning pools, a pond filled with trop-ical shells, and mounds of semi-precious gemstones. Admission is free, though if you're stone-digging, you must buy a collector's bag for C$6 to C$10 (US$5.30–US$8.80); anything you find, you can keep. The Patch is open Monday to Saturday 9:30am to 6pm, Sunday 11am to 5pm.

For more kid-friendly suggestions, take a look at *The Kids' Guide to Victoria*, which details more than 50 places to go and things to do around Vancouver Island. You can get this guide by contacting Tourism Victoria (Ⓒ **250/953-2033**; www.tourism victoria.com).

All Fun Recreation Park   If the weather is really hot, the waterslides will be a life-saver for heat-weary kids. The park also has two go-kart tracks, mini golf, and batting cages, all priced separately, so it can get expensive. For example, the cost of go-karting ranges from C$6 to C$12 (US$5.30–US$11) per session; golf is C$5.50 (US$4.85) per adult, C$4 (US$3.52) per child, and swinging at 25 balls will set you back C$3 (US$2.65).

2207 Millstream Rd. Ⓒ **250/474-3184**. www.allfun.bc.ca. Mid-Jun–Labor Day, daily 11am–7pm. Admission C$15–C$20 (US$13–US$18) depending on the age and height of the slider. Observers are C$6 (US$5.30), which includes access to an 80-person hot tub and beach volleyball courts.

Centre of the Universe   The larger of the two telescopes trained to the heavens was once the largest in the world, so you know that the stargazing is good—depend-ing on the cloud cover. Nighttime vigils for the public are offered somewhat sporadi-cally (especially in winter) as they're scheduled between bookings by professional astronomers. The daytime 75-minute tour of the aging observatory is still a fun excur-sion from the downtown core.

5071 West Saanich Rd. Ⓒ **250/363-8262**. www.cu.hia.nrc.gc.ca. Admission C$9 (US$7.90) adults, C$8 (US$7.05) senior and students, C$5 (US$4.40) children. Apr–Oct daily 10am–6pm; Nov–Mar Tues–Sun 10am–4:30pm.

7 Shopping

GREAT SHOPPING AREAS

Victoria has dozens of specialty shops that make browsing a real delight. Nearly all are within walking distance of one another. Stores are generally open Monday through Saturday from 10am to 6pm; some are open on Sundays from noon to 5pm.

The first shopping foray for most visitors is to head up the brick-paved **Government Street promenade,** about five blocks north from the Inner Harbour. Many of the stores are housed in beautiful heritage buildings and stepping inside is like stepping back a century. You'll find various specialty shops here, including ones featuring First Nations art. But be warned: Amid the jewels is an excess of souvenir shops, each hip-deep in bottles of maple syrup and Taiwanese knickknacks.

The largest shopping area runs north–south along Douglas Street and east–west along several cross streets, in particular Yates—the focal point of many restaurants and bars, too. It's where to find banks, camera suppliers, music stores, and other outlets. The multi-level **Bay Centre** (© 250/952-5690; www.thebaycentre.ca) anchors this city core and is where to shop for top-name fashions and mainstream goods. **The Bay** itself is also a popular department store; it got its start over 330 years ago as a series of trading posts across the country and is the oldest corporation in North America. Aside from designer labels and general housewares, you can still buy their famous red-green-and-yellow-striped point blanket, an item that was originally traded for beaver pelts.

Just off Government Street, adjacent to The Bay Centre, are intriguing shopping streets: **Trounce Alley,** Victoria's former red-light district now transformed into chic and hip, and nearby **Broad Street,** a small and bustling strip packed with gift shops, galleries, and specialty stores. Farther north, **Old Town/Market Square** features a fascinating blend of turn-of-the-century buildings housing funky, up-to-date shops. The area is reminiscent of San Francisco's Garibaldi Square, but quainter, with live performances in summer. Nearby, Victoria's **Chinatown** is so tiny you might miss it. Search out **Fan Tan Alley.** It's Canada's thinnest commercial street, just over a meter (4 ft.) wide at either end, yet crammed with oddball paraphernalia and a maze of doors leading to small courtyards—and even more doors leading to more back alleys, stairs, and living quarters. When the police used to raid gambling clubs, participants could easily escape through the myriad passageways. If antiquing is your thing, make your way to **Fort Street,** fondly known as Antique Row, on the eastern edge of the downtown core.

THE GOODS A TO Z
Antiques & Collectibles

Renowned for its high-quality British collectibles, Antique Row is a three-block stretch along Fort Street between Blanshard and Cook streets. Here's where to find some of the finest in estate jewelry, silverware, heritage china, and furniture. In addition to those listed below, check out **Charles Baird,** 1044A Fort St. (© **250/384-8809**), for antique furniture; **The Glass Menagerie,** 1036 Fort St. (© **250/475-2228**), for its collectible plates, china, and pottery; and **Romanoff & Co.,** 837–839 Fort St. (© **250/480-1543**), for its impressive collection of coins and silverware. For the recreational antiquer looking for a bargain, the **Old Vogue Shop,** 1034 Fort St. (© **250/380-7751**), and **Recollections,** 817A Fort St. (© **250/385-1902**), are both generalist shops with a hodgepodge of items and styles.

Classic Silverware   A gorgeous shop that specializes in discontinued sterling silver and silver-plated flatware and tea service sets, it also maintains a registry for missing and discontinued china. 826 Fort St. © 250/ 383-6860.

David Robinson Antiques   Come here for high-quality period furniture, silver, oriental rugs, paintings, and other fine antiques. 1023 Fort St. © 250/384-6425.

Faith Grant's Connoisseur Shop   Housed in an 1862 heritage building, this store has a myriad of rooms filled with high-end household furnishings. 1156 Fort St. © 250/383-0121.

Vanity Fair Antique Mall   With more than 40 dealers of crystal, glassware, furniture, and jewelry all under one roof, this mall offers a range of items ranging from those requiring a mortgage to purchase to others more affordable that might even leave change in your pocket. 1044 Fort St. ℭ 250/380-7274.

Art/Contemporary

Fran Willis Gallery   With its spacious 5-m (17-ft.) high ceilings and high arched windows, Victoria's oldest and largest contemporary gallery is certainly one of the nicest display spaces in the city. Look for established and emerging Western Canadian artists. 1619 Store St. ℭ 250/381-3422. www.franwillis.com.

The West End Gallery   This open, airy gallery features works by over 100 Canadian artists. Its specialty is original paintings, sculpture, and art glass. 1203 Broad St. ℭ 250/388-0009. www.westendgalleryltd.com.

Winchester Galleries   Offering a diversity of original Canadian art, both historical and contemporary, Winchester Galleries features names that include the Group of Seven, Jack Shadbolt, Mary Pratt, and Toni Onley. The main gallery is in Oak Bay at 2260 Oak Bay Ave. 1010 Broad St. ℭ 250/386-2773. www.winchestergalleriesltd.com.

Art/Native

Alcheringa Gallery   Recognized for its museum quality (and expensive) aboriginal work from all over the world, this gallery offers many pieces that have a West Coast and Australasia influence. 665 Fort St. ℭ 250/383-8224. www.alcheringa-gallery.com.

Eagle Feather Gallery   This gallery carries one of the finest First Nations' collections of authentic jewelry, arts, and crafts, all exclusively created by First Nations artists. A percentage of all profits are donated to First Nations' Youth programs. 904 Gordon St. ℭ 250/388-4330. www.eaglefeathergallery.com.

Hills Native Art   One of the most respected stores for established B.C. First Nations artists, this is the place to find exquisite traditional pieces, such as wooden masks, drums, and talking sticks alongside items for the less serious collector, such as dream catchers and souvenir totem poles. 1008 Government St. ℭ 250/385-3911.

Books

Chapters Downtown   The mothership of all Chapters bookstores, this location has three floors of book titles, DVDs, and stationery. In addition to the usual bargain tables on the main floor, there are some great deals on kids' books in the basement. 1212 Douglas St., ℭ 250/ 380-9009.

Chronicles of Crime   Every one of the more than 15,000 new and used book titles is spy-related, criminal, and mysterious. 1067 Fort St. ℭ 250/721-2665.

Munro's   The range of titles within the 1909 former bank building, described as Canada's most magnificent (architecturally speaking) bookstores, is impressive, and the remainder tables are filled with good discounts. 1108 Government St. ℭ 250/382-2464.

Crafts

Cowichan Trading Company   Best known for its authentic Cowichan sweaters and hand-made moccasins, this store also sells a slew of junky T-shirts, giftware, and souvenirs. 1328 Government St. ℭ 250/383-0321. www.cowichantrading.com.

Starfish Glass Works   A former bank building now serves as a gallery-cum-workshop. Watch from the mezzanine level as award-winning artists transform molten glass into imaginative works of art. **Note:** Glass is blown during afternoons only, and not at all on Mondays or Tuesdays. 630 Yates St. ℂ **250/388-7827.**

Fashion/Women

Although The Bay Centre holds court for many mainstream retailers such as La Senza, Guess?, and Jacob, specialty stores are your better bet for that more memorable purchase.

Edinburgh Tartan Shop   Looking for the *right* custom-fitted kilt in the *right* family plaid? Tartans can also be purchased by the yard and come with a huge collection of kilt pins as well as Highland scarves, brooches, sweaters, and blankets. 909 Government St. ℂ **250/953-7788.**

Hughes Clothing   Look for names such as Eileen Fisher (USA), Nougat (London), Xandres (Belgium), and J. Lindeberg (Sweden). 564 Yates St. ℂ **250/381-4405.** www.hughes closthing.com.

Not Just Pretty   Shop with a conscience. This sweatshop-free store carries organic, natural-fiber fashions (cotton, wool, and silk) where the production emphasis is on sustaining communities. Items range from T-shirts and skirts to dresses, jackets, cashmere sweaters, scarves, and hats. 1036 Fort St. ℂ **250/414-0414.**

She She Bags   The most discriminating of bag fetishists will be satiated here, with all manner of offbeat and jewel-studded bags. Most of the whimsical designs are for the bold at heart, with the occasional classic design thrown in for good measure. 616 View St. ℂ **250/388-0613.** www.she-shebags.com.

Smoking Lily   This tiny, home-bases 4-sq.-m (44-sq.-ft.) store—one of the smallest in the world—is like a test-run showcase for new ideas in women's clothing and accessories. Consequently, there's always something new and innovative on hand. 569A Johnson St. ℂ **250/382-5459.** www.smokinglily.com.

Fashion/Men

British Importers Men's Wear   This exceptionally stylish showroom features high-end continental imports from Arnold Brant, Canali, Hugo Boss, and others. 1125 Government St. ℂ **250/386-1496.** www.britishimporters.com.

Outlooks for Men   Victoria's most fashion-forward menswear store will appeal to the younger demographic. Cutting-edge designer labels include Hugo Boss, Orange Label, Z Zegna, Melting Pot, and Horst. 554 Yates St. ℂ **250/384-2848.** www.outlooksfor men.ca.

W&J Wilson   The Wilson family has operated this clothing store since 1862. Although the store certainly doesn't carry fashions from that era, they do lean toward sensible casuals for men, largely from England, Scotland, and Ireland. 1221 Government St. ℂ **250/383-7177.**

Jewelry

Jade Tree   Here's where to find jewelry made from British Columbia jade. Mined in northern Vancouver Island, the jade is crafted and polished for a variety of items including necklaces, bracelets, pendants, and small ornaments. 606 Humboldt St. ℂ **250/388-4326.**

The Patch   This is the island's largest purveyor of body jewelry—for your nose, navel, nipple, and ears. Many of the studs, baubles, and rings are quite funky and colorful. 719 Yates St. ℂ **250/384-7070.**

Spas in Victoria

Whether nestled in the rainforest, perched on craggy shores, or presented as urban getaways of serenity, spas are plentiful on Vancouver Island. Some of the best ones are in and around Victoria.

Sapphire Day Spa   Although located in a small space, this spa feels fresh and spacious with its clean and contemporary look. It is the only spa in Victoria offering Ayurvedic treatments (alongside European services). It even has a Swedana herbal cedar steam chest, one of the hallmarks of quality Ayurveda services. 714 View St. ✆ **250/385-6676**. www.sapphiredayspa.com.

The Spa at Delta Victoria   A luxurious, European-style sanctuary, this spa includes a complete fitness facility, pool, and sauna. It's consistently rated one of the city's best spas. Ocean Pointe Resort, 45 Songhees Rd. ✆ **800/575-8882** or 250-360-5858. www.thespaatdeltavictoria.com.

Willow Stream Spa   Chic, expensive, and a true spa oasis, Willow Stream Spa's treatments include time in the sauna, steam room, and Hungarian mineral pool, so you can turn a pedicure into a spa getaway. The Fairmont Empress, 721 Government St. ✆ **866/854-7444** or 250-995-4650. www.willowstream.com.

Essence of Life Spa   A 30-minute drive from Victoria, this oceanfront spa and aroma garden pulls out the stops on a wide range of European services, especially the Signature Couples Massage. Brentwood Bay Lodge, 849 Verdier Ave. ✆ **888/544-2079** or 250/544-2079.

Spa Magnolia   Veteran spa-goers know the name Aveda, and this spa does the name proud. It's small, cozy, and tucked away on the second floor of the hotel, almost as if it's trying to keep itself a secret. Magnolia Hotel, 623 Courtney St. ✆ **877/624-6654** or 250/381-0999. www.spamagnolia.com.

Sante Spa   Run by Institue de Sante, the premier MediSpa folks in Canada, this is one of the few places where traditional spa treatments are offered alongside medical esthetics such as Botox, Laser hair removal, and microdermabrasion. The location atop a mountain is pretty spectacular too. Bear Mountain, 1999 Country Club Way, ✆ **888/533-2327** or 250/391-7160. www.bearmountain.ca.

Shi Studio   Chinese silk brocades, often using traditional dynastic patterns, is fused into pendants, belt buckles, brooches, cuffs, and ear rings. This is a working studio, so it's best to call ahead. 420-620 View St. ✆ **250/995-2714**. www.shistudio.com.

Violette Veldor   If you love accessories, check out this store's eclectic mélange of jewelry. Look for terrific designs from local talent and international names such as Alex & Chloe and Sugar Lime. 1223 Government St. ✆ **250/388-7752**.

Markets
Market Square   This eclectic little shopping and restaurant complex is made up of former warehouse and shipping offices from the 1800s. Shops here sell everything from used cameras, second-hand books, and a gourmet dog-biscuit deli to teddy bears and condoms. The central courtyard comes into its own in the summer with live performances, and casual patio dining. 560 Johnson St. ✆ **250/386-2441**.

Specialty Gifts/Souvenirs

As in all touristy destinations, souvenir stores that sell T-shirts and tacky memorabilia are a dime a dozen in Victoria. For ideas that say "Victoria" in a different way, try these suggestions.

Irish Linen Stores   A fixture in this 1884 Victoria Italianate heritage building since 1917, this store sells fine Irish damask towels, linens, laces, and sweaters. 1019 Government St. (℃ 250/383-6812. www.irishlinenvictoria.com.

Rogers' Chocolates   A Victoria institution for more than a hundred years, Rogers' offers exquisite cream-filled specialty chocolates that have been enjoyed by royalty and others. The store is equally delightful, filled with original Tiffany glass, ornamental tile-work, and old-fashioned, highly polished wooden counters. 913 Government St. (℃ 250/384-7021. www.rogerschocolates.com.

Silk Road Aromatherapy & Tea Company   This small but impressive tea emporium in the heart of Chinatown features loose-leaf teas, equipage, and even tea-based aromatherapy products. A basement spa offers green-tea facials and the like. 1624 Government St. (℃ 250/704-2688. www.silkroadtea.com.

Simply the Best   Small in size it may be, but the price tags and range of goods are quite the opposite. Simply the Best boasts more than 10,000 items, many of which sport the world's most exclusive brand names in clothing, housewares, and office and dining accessories. 1008 Broad St. (℃ 250/386-6661.

Sydney Reynolds China   Located in an old bank building, Victoria's oldest china shop was established in 1929 and now offers fine porcelains, hand-painted tea sets and Victorian dolls. 801 Government St. (℃ 250/383-3931. www.sydneyreynolds.com.

The Wine Barrel   You'll find the largest selection of B.C. VQA (Vintner Quality Alliance) wines in the province here. Walls are stacked with more than 300 varieties, including ice wines and limited editions, as well as an enormous selection of wine accessories. 644 Broughton St. (℃ 250/388-0606. www.thewinebarrel.com.

8 Victoria After Dark

As vibrant as Victoria is by day, once the hour hand passes 10pm, city activity just seems to fade into the darkness. Granted, the pubs and the Yates Street area remain pretty busy, especially at weekends, but all in all, when the theatres, concert venues, and movie houses close up shop, so does downtown.

Monday magazine (www.monday.com) covers everything going on in town, from nightclubs and the performing arts, to films and poetry readings. You name it, *Monday's* got it. You can also call the **Community Arts Council of Greater Victoria's** events hotline, at (℃ **250/381-ARTS** (250/381-2787). Tickets and schedules are also available at the **Tourism Victoria Travel Visitor Information Centre,** 812 Wharf St. (℃ **250/953-2033.**

THE PERFORMING ARTS

Although Victoria is a primary tourist destination, visitors aren't the mainstay of the city's performing arts. Consequently, there's still a community feel to the audiences and venues, many of which are shared among the professional groups.

VENUES   The **Royal Theatre,** 805 Broughton St. ((℃ **250/361-0800**), dates from the early 1900s. Renovated in the 1970s, it hosts concerts (including the Victoria

Symphony), dance recitals, and touring plays, as well as performances by Pacific Opera Victoria. The **McPherson Playhouse,** 3 Centennial Sq. (✆ **250/361-0800**), was built in 1914 as the first Pantages Vaudeville Theatre. It hosts smaller stage plays and performances by the Victoria Operatic Society. The Royal and the McPherson share a box office at the **McPherson Playhouse** (✆ **888/717-6121** or 250/386-6121; www.rmts.bc.ca). Box office hours are Monday to Saturday from 9:30am to 5:30pm, and on performance days for the 2 hours prior to showtime. Take bus no. 6 to Pandora and Government streets.

CLASSICAL MUSIC   The **Victoria Symphony Orchestra,** 846 Broughton St. (✆ **250/385-9771;** www.victoriasymphony.bc.ca), kicks off its season in August with **Symphony Splash,** a free concert performed on a barge in the Inner Harbour. The regular season begins in September and runs through May at the Royal Theatre or the University Farquhar Auditorium. Tickets average C$60 (US$53) for adults depending on the series, with discounts for seniors and students.

DANCE   Dance recitals and full-scale performances by local and international dance troupes such as **Danceworks** and the **Scottish Dance Society** are scheduled throughout the year. To find out who's performing while you're in town, call **Tourism Victoria** (✆ **250/953-2033**) or the **Community Arts Council of Greater Victoria** (✆ **250/381-ARTS,** or 250/381-2787, 1001 Douglas St.).

OPERA   The **Pacific Opera Victoria,** 1316B Government St. (✆ **250/385-0222;** box office ✆ **250/386-6121;** www.pov.bc.ca), presents productions during the months of October, February, and April. Tickets are available at the McPherson Playhouse and Pacific Opera box offices. The **Victoria Operatic Society,** 798 Fairview Rd. (✆ **250/381-1021;** www.vos.bc.ca), stages old-time musicals and other popular fare year round at the McPherson Playhouse. They may not be to the standard of Carnegie Hall, but they make for a good evening out.

THEATER   The nationally acclaimed **Belfry Theatre Society,** 1291 Gladstone St. (✆ **250/385-6815;** www.belfry.bc.ca; bus no. 22 to Fernwood St.), stages contemporary productions in an intimate church-turned-playhouse space. Works are generally of Canadian origin and are often interspersed with visiting productions, such as *The Syringa Tree.* The **Intrepid Theatre Company,** 301-1205 Broad St. (✆ **250/383-2663;** www.intrepidtheatre.com), runs two theater festivals annually. In late April and early May it's the **Uno Festival of Solo Performance,** a unique event of strictly one-person performances with tickets at C$18 (US$16) adult, C$15 (US$13) senior and student. Multi-show passes are also offered. From late August to early September, Intrepid stages the **Victoria Fringe Festival** (✆ **250/383-2691 box office,** or 250/383-2662), an amazingly eclectic selection of alternative theatre. More than 50 performances from all over the world are staged in six venues around the city, including the Victoria Conservatory of Music, St. Andrew's School, and the Downtown Community Activities Centre. Compared to mainstream theater, festival tickets are cheap (the artists set their own prices to a maximum of C$9/US$7.90); performances are about an hour, and content is unpredictable. **Theatre Inconnu** (✆ **250/360-0234;** www.islandnet.com/~tinconnu) produces Victoria's annual **Shakespearean Festival,** which takes place in the historic St. Ann's Academy, 835 Humboldt St., in July and August. Ticket prices (C$12/US$11) reflect the groups' semi-professional status, but don't be deterred: plays are of an exceptionally high caliber. Every year, Theatre Inconnu also stages a two-man adaptation of Charles Dickens's *A Christmas*

Carol. The **Langham Court Theatre,** 805 Langham Ct. (© **250/384-2142;** www. langhamcourttheatre.bc.ca), performs works produced by the **Victoria Theatre Guild,** a local amateur society dedicated to presenting a wide range of dramatic and comedic works that are surprisingly good for average theatre-goers. New York critics, however, may disagree. Tickets are a bargain at C$15 to C$17 (US$13–US$15) Take bus no. 14 or 11 from downtown to Fort and Moss streets.

THE BAR SCENE

There are few places outside of England that do pubs as well as Victoria does, even though some of them lean toward lounge status. Here are the best drinking places; pick according to your mood. Some, like The Bengal Lounge, are classy and elegant; others like the Sticky Wicket are as you would find in the old country. Most are hybrids.

The Bengal Lounge ✪   This lounge salutes Queen Victoria's role as the Empress of India with a colonial elegance that includes huge leather coaches, oversize palms, ceiling fans, and a lengthy cocktail list. It's the chic place to go, especially for the live jazz on Friday and Saturday nights. Fairmont Empress Hotel, 721 Government St. © 250/384-8111.

Big Bad Johns   Without doubt, this is the rowdiest spot in town. Despite a decor that includes an ever-increasing collection of bras hanging from the ceiling, and a floor inches deep in discarded peanut shells, it's a clean-cut place where half the fun is letting it all hang out. Strathcona Hotel, 919 Douglas St. © 250/383-7137.

Darcy's Wharf Street Pub   This large, bright, waterfront watering hole is where you'll find the lively younger crowd enjoying fine brews and pool tables. Live bands play occasionally on the weekends. 1127 Wharf St. © 250/380-1322.

Harbour Canoe Club   Be prepared for a crowd here; it's always busy, especially with the after-work crowd, many of whom will stay on for dinner. The atmospheric heritage brick-and-beam building has an on-site micro-brewery that produces some excellent brews; the six-small-glass taster option is the best deal in town. 450 Swift St. © 250/361-1940.

Hugo's Brewhouse   Another in-house micro-brewery and hot spot for whiling away an evening, it's a popular choice for ladies wanting to have some fun together, without feeling they're in a meat market. 625 Courtney St. © 250/920-4844.

The Reef   Strictly speaking, The Reef is a restaurant, though as the evening progresses its upbeat Caribbean tone gives it the feel of a reggae hangout with a mix of martinis, rum punches, and DJ and live music. 533 Yates St. © 250/388-5375.

Spinnakers Brewpub ✪   It all started here. The original brewpub in town remains one of the best. Though the view across Victoria Harbour almost makes it reason enough to come here, its brewed-on-premises ales, lagers, and stouts are the big draw. There's even an on-site bakery selling beer breads. The pub fare is good too. 308 Catherine St. © 250/386-2739.

A Quiet Pint

Away from the downtown in quieter Oak Bay Village, the **Penny Farthing Pub** (2280 Oak Bay Ave. © 250/370-9008) is a charming, quintessential English country pub complete with cozy fireplace, great brews and pub fare.

Feeling Lucky?

The Great Canadian Casino (1708 Old Island Hwy. Ⓒ **250/391-0311**; www.gc gaming.com) can't compete with the high-stake tables in Las Vegas; it's the sort of outing you could take your grandmother to. Games include blackjack, roulette, sic bo, red dog, and Caribbean stud poker. The casino operates a complimentary shuttle service from downtown Victoria.

The Sticky Wicket Reminiscent of a turn-of-the-century Irish pub, this is as close as you'll get to a traditional pub (including its pub grub), as you can get. Most of its stained glass windows, dark wood interior furnishings, and long teak bar were shipped over from Ireland. Thankfully, it feels like another world to Big Bad John's in the basement and the volleyball sands of the rooftop patio. Strathcona Hotel, 919 Douglas St. Ⓒ **250/383-7137**.

Suze Lounge & Restaurant One of *the* places for martinis and Sinatra-flavored schmoozing. Aim for a seat at the 7.6-m (25-ft.) mahogany bar. 515 Yates St. Ⓒ **250/383-2829**.

Swans Brewpub Swans is a local favorite, and if there's a live band scheduled for the weekend, the place gets very busy and noisy. It occupies the ground floor of a heritage warehouse, above which is one of Victoria's most unique inns (see "Where to Stay"). The decor features the original brickwork and beams, and it's a showcase for an ever-changing display of First Nations art. The signature British-style ales and German and Canadian beers are brewed on site. 506 Pandora Ave. Ⓒ **250/361-3310**.

THE CLUB SCENE
DANCE CLUBS & LIVE MUSIC

New venues come and go with regularity so what's listed below are the tried-and-trues—those clubs that have found a winning formula. Most places are open Monday through Saturday until 2am and Sunday until midnight. Drinks are from C$4 to C$9 (US$3.50–US$7.90); some clubs have covers (usually weekends only) ranging from C$3 to C$7 (US$2.65–US$6.15).

Hermann's Jazz Club Although not chic, for 25 years Hermann's has consistently delivered Victoria's best live jazz and Dixieland. Martinis are named after famous musicians such as Duke Ellington and Ella Fitzgerald. The club's usually open Wednesday through Sunday (call ahead to check) and if you play jazz and bring your instrument, there'll likely be an opportunity to jam. 753 View St. Ⓒ **250/388-9166**.

Legends The nightclub at "The Strath" is, well, legendary. Quality live music makes this a pop-music palace, running the gamut from afro-pop to blues, to R&B and zydeco. Strathcona Hotel, 919 Douglas St. Ⓒ **250/383-7137**. www.legendsnightclub.com.

The Lucky Bar This is probably one of Victoria's hottest nightspots. Drinks in the long, darkly lit lounge are a natural follow-through to an earlier meal at Suze, or you can go just for the martinis and music, which is a mix of DJ-spun and live bands. 517 Yates St. Ⓒ **250/382-5825**.

The Red Jacket There are two rooms, one for boozing and schmoozing, the other for dancing. Either way, you'll want to dress to impress and express. The DJs spin mainly Top 40, retro, hip-hop, funk, and R&B. Friday is ladies night, and Saturday fills up quickly so get there early. 751 View St. Ⓒ **250/384-2582**.

Steamers ⟨*⟩ Although it claims to be "blues central," you can expect some of the nightly acts to play Celtic, world beat, or even zydeco. If you don't like the music, there are pool tables and darts. More important, this is a pub with cheap beer. 570 Yates St. ⟨*⟩ 250/381-4340.

GAY & LESBIAN BARS

The gay scene is so small in Victoria that most gay-friendly bars have relaxed any gays-only policies in order to keep their doors open. Indeed, out of the five clubs that existed last year, only two remain. One resource that might put you in contact with some of the private parties held in peoples' homes is www.gayvictoria.ca.

Hush (1325 Government St. ⟨*⟩ **250/385-0566;** www.hushnightclub.ca) is one of the few clubs that has stayed the course, although the crowd is becoming increasingly straight. Loud music (often live) and electronics pack the place at weekends. With techno, progressive, drum-'n'-bass, and trance, the experience is more like a rave. Hush is open Wednesday to Sunday. **Prism Lounge** (642 Johnson St.; ⟨*⟩ **250/388-0505;** www.prismlounge.com) is Victoria's only true gay and lesbian nightclub. It has a full menu and a lounge that's spacious enough to host drag shows. Enjoy a fairly off-beat selection of techno, disco, and hip-hop music, pick up a mic and sing a little karaoke—there are thick binders full of song titles. Prism is open daily, Monday to Friday 3pm to 2am; and from 1pm on the weekend. There's no cover charge.

5

Southern Vancouver Island

Exploring the South Island is a relaxing change of pace from visiting downtown Victoria. The entire area can be reached within a day, so itineraries are easy to plan. Or, you can stay in the city and simply make an afternoon of touring the countryside. Places like East Sooke Regional Park, with one of the most accessible and prettiest trails in Canada, Fort Rodd Hill & Fisgard Lighthouse National Historic Site, the picturesque seaside community of Sidney, and the world famous Butchart Gardens are about 21km (13 miles) from Victoria. All are worthwhile destinations where you can spend a few hours, with or without the kids.

If you're an outdoor enthusiast who really wants to taste the island's wild west coast without traveling too far, the Juan de Fuca Trail delivers raincoast forest, wilderness beaches, and spectacular landscapes. It has earned the reputation of being the easier-to-hike cousin of the famed West Coast Trail. Unlike its arduous relative, the Juan de Fuca can be enjoyed in an afternoon (or multi-day) outing. Botanical Beach lies farther up the coast and is a beachcomber's paradise, with tidal pools and sandstone rock formations to explore.

Goldstream Provincial Park is another terrific outing, offering hikes for all abilities through well-maintained forested trails. One of the more challenging hikes is a direct ascent of Mount Finlayson, while an easier walk leads to an abandoned mine—Goldstream got its name during the 1860s gold rush, and if you arm yourself with a gold pan, the river still yields flecks of gold.

Agri-tourism is one of Vancouver Island's fastest growing movements, and nowhere is this better seen than in the Cowichan Valley, Canada's hottest new food and wine destination. Here's where driving through the back country really pays dividends with farms, orchards, artisan cheese factories and quality cottage wineries to visit. Little wonder that slow-food fans have even dubbed the area The New Provence. The valley deserves a day to do it justice.

If you're staying in Victoria but want to sample its urban wilderness or pastoral beauty, taking in the southern part of Vancouver Island is a great way to do so. When heading north toward Nanaimo, you'll discover some attractions worth building into your itinerary (see "En Route to Nanaimo: The Cowichan Valley," later in the chapter).

1 The Saanich Peninsula

A bustling seaside village, Sidney is filled with scenic parks and gardens, waterfront restaurants, galleries, and more bookstores than any other community on Vancouver Island. It is small-town Canada gift-wrapped in beautiful scenery. Sidney is located 26km (16 miles) north of Victoria, and approximately 6km (4 miles) south of the BC Ferries terminal in Swartz Bay. Washington State ferries, arriving from Anacortes, dock at Sidney.

ESSENTIALS
GETTING THERE
BY CAR AND FERRY   If you're driving out of Victoria, head north on **Blanshard Street,** which becomes **Highway 17,** or take BC Transit bus nos. 70, 72, or 75, from downtown Victoria. If you're driving from Swartz Bay (BC Ferries terminal), Sidney is a 6-km (4-mile) drive south on **Highway 17. BC Ferries** (© **888/223-3779** or 250/386-3431; www.bcferries.com) runs a passenger- and car-ferry service between Swartz Bay and **Tsawwassen,** on the mainland.

June through August, crossings are every hour on the hour, from 7am to 11pm. September through May crossings are every other hour. Additional ferries are often scheduled during holiday periods. One-way fare is C$11(US$9.50) for adults, C$5.40 (US$4.75) for children 5 to 11, C$38 (US$33) for a standard-size vehicle. B.C. seniors travel free Monday through Thursday, except on holidays.

BY FERRY   The Washington State Ferry terminal is located in Sidney, at 2499 Ocean Ave., (© **888-808/7977** or 206/464-7977; www.wsdot.wa.gov/ferries). Ferries sail once a day, midmorning, between Sidney and Anacortes. Crossing time is 3 hours. Summer vehicle reservations are highly recommended, and must be made by 5:30pm the day prior to travel. One-way passenger fares during the high season (May to early October) are C$18 (US$16) for adults, C$14 (US$13) for students 6 to 18 years, C$9 (US$7.90) for seniors, and C$60 (US$52) for a standard-size vehicle. Fares are lower in the off season (October 2 to May 2).

VISITOR INFORMATION
The Sidney Chamber of Commerce operates two visitor information centers on the Saanich Peninsula. One is located at 10382 Pat Bay Hwy., Sidney BC V8L 3S3 (© **250/656-0525;** www.spcoc.org). It is open year-round, Monday through Friday, from 8:30am to 5:30pm. The other information center is located in Sidney, opposite the Washington State Ferry terminal, at A-2295 Ocean Ave. (© **250/656-3260;** mailing address is 10382 Pat Bay Hwy., Sidney BC V8L 3S3). The center is open April through October 15, Monday through Saturday, from 10:30am to 12:30pm, to coincide with ferry arrivals, and closed October 16 through March.

THE TOP ATTRACTIONS
British Columbia Aviation Museum   You'll want to dig out your bomber jacket for a visit to this hangar on the edge of the Victoria International Airport. It's a working museum that illustrates the province's aviation history. Volunteers restore vintage aircraft to add to the collection, which already has several reconditioned vintage airplanes, helicopters, and kit planes. Most are in working order. Look for a 1930s Bush Plane, an A26 World War II Bomber, a Gibson Twin (built in Victoria in 1911), a replica of the Chanute Glider, built in 1897, a Bell 47 Helicopter (best known as the busy MedEvac-type chopper in *M.A.S.H.*), and more. This may not stack up to the great aviation museums in Europe, but for aviation nuts or for a family looking to while away an hour or two, it's an enjoyable attraction.

1910 Norseman Rd. © **250/655-3300.** www.bcam.net. Admission C$7 (US$6.15) adults, C$5 (US$4.40) seniors, C$3 (US$2.65) students. Children 11 and under free, but must be accompanied by an adult. Summer daily 10am–4pm; winter daily 11am–3pm. Closed Dec 25. Take the airport turnoff from Hwy. 17. The museum is on your right, as you approach the airport. Bus: 70 (Airport Bus).

Butchart Gardens ✿✿✿   Converted from an exhausted limestone quarry back in 1904, Butchart Gardens is an impressive place: 20 hectares (50 acres) of gardens and not a blade of grass out of place! Every flower blooms so as to be a perfect match to the other in height, color, and tone, including the 300,000 bulbs that bloom in spring. On summer evenings, the gardens are illuminated with soft colored lights. Musical entertainment is provided June through September, Monday through Saturday evenings. In July and August, watch for fireworks every Saturday night, and in December, enjoy lavish displays of Christmas lights. An excellent lunch, dinner, and afternoon tea are offered in the **Dining Room Restaurant;** more casual fare is served in the **Blue Poppy Restaurant.** The gift shop sells seeds for some of the plants on display. If you're not traveling by car, your best bet is to take a Grayline Tour (see "Organized Tours" in chapter 4) that includes admission (C$35/US$31) and an optional stopover at the Victoria Butterfly Gardens (C$44/US$39). In the summer, Grayline also offers an hourly shuttle (C$6/US$5.30 each way) between the gardens and downtown Victoria.

800 Benvenuto Ave., Brentwood Bay. ✆ **866/652-4422** or 250/652-4422. Dining reservations. ✆ 250/652-8222. www.butchartgardens.com. Admission C$23 (US$20) adults, C$12 (US$10) children 13–17, C$2.50 (US$2.20) children 5–12, free for children 4 and under. Daily 9am–sundown (call for seasonal closing time). Take Blanshard St. (Hwy. 17) north toward the ferry terminal in Saanich, then turn left on Keating Crossroads, which leads directly to the gardens. Bus: 75. Grayline shuttle leaves from Victoria Bus Station, hourly. Call for exact times ✆ 250/388-6539.

Sidney Historical Museum   If you're an ambler who loves funky detours, this attraction is bound to delight. Tucked away in the basement of the 1939 post office building, the tiny museum is lovingly tended by volunteers and includes a surprisingly varied range of monthly exhibits from toys and quilts, to model railways and radio-controlled boats. It also has a number of historical photographs and artifacts portraying the early lives of Coast Salish, European, and Asian local peoples. A half-hour visit will probably suffice unless you hit upon an exhibit of personal interest and get talking to one of the knowledgeable, and enthusiastic, curators.

2423 Beacon Ave., Sidney. ✆ **250/655-6355.** www.sidneybc.com/museum. Admission by donation. Suggested: C$2 (US$1.75) adults, C$5 (US$4.40) groups. Daily 10am–4pm. Closed Dec 25. Take Hwy. 17 to Sidney, turning right down Beacon Ave., to 4th St. Bus: 70 from downtown or Swartz Bay.

Victoria Butterfly Gardens ✿✿ *Kids*   Hundreds of exotic species of butterflies flutter through this lush tropical greenhouse, from the tiny Central American Julia to the Southeast Asian Giant Atlas Moth (its wingspan is nearly a foot). Pick up an identification chart before you enter so you can put names to the various flying wonders around you. Then wander freely through the gardens. Along the way, you'll encounter naturalists happy to explain butterfly biology, who pepper their speech with slightly bizarre factoids, such as "Butterflies taste with their feet," and "If a human baby grew at the same rate as some caterpillars, it would weigh 8 tons in only two weeks." Hmm. Food for thought. If you're visiting between November and February, you need to make a reservation to see the gardens. A good way to see the gardens is in combination with the Butchart Gardens (see listing above). Together, they make a full day's excursion.

1461 Benvenuto Ave., Brentwood Bay. ✆ **877/722-0272** or 250/652-3822. www.butterflygardens. com. Admission C$10 (US$8.80) adults, C$9 (US$7.90) seniors and students, C$5.50 (US$4.85) children 5–12, free for children 4 and under. 10% discount for families. Mar–May and Oct daily 9:30am–4:30pm; June–Sept daily 9am–5:30pm. Closed Nov–Feb. Bus 75.

Got Extra Time?

If the ferry schedules don't co-operate, Island Camping (© **250/656-4826;** www.islandcamping.ca) operates an 11-passenger water taxi service out of Sidney to your gulf island of choice. The service is great for day visits, touring, or for transport to a "base-camp" beach for kayaking. Trips costs C$125 (US$110) per hour, generally split among the number of passengers. For a point of reference, Pender Island is a half-hour boat ride from Sidney.

PARKS & BEACHES

Located off Highway 17 in Saanich, **Elk Lake/Beaver Lake Park** is a lovely place to spend an afternoon. The park's big draw is a 240-hectare (593-acre) freshwater lake rimmed by four beaches, with plenty of play areas and picnic tables. The lake provides for all sorts of aquatic recreation, and is a particularly good place for beginner windsurfers. It is also home to the University of Victoria Rowing Club, and the site of the annual International Boat races, one of the five top rowing events in the world. Nearer to Victoria, off Cordova Bay Road, is **Mount Douglas Park,** a 10-hectare (25-acre) park in its natural state. The park is located 8km (5 miles) northeast of Victoria at the north end of Shelbourne Street. Another 1.5km (1 mile) up Churchill Drive brings you to the summit parking lot, and to several great viewpoints of the surrounding area. There are several **easy hiking trails** to the mountaintop. These include the **Irvine Trail** off Cordova Bay Road, and the **Merriman Trail** (it has an easy start but takes a little scrambling near the top). Both trails are well signposted from the road.

The lower park can be accessed near the intersection of Ash and Cordova Bay roads. A trail to the beach leads down from a large parking lot. There's also a playground and picnic area. For a fairly level, easy walk, look for the **Norn Trail,** which roughly parallels Cordova Bay Road, and takes you through some very tall Douglas firs.

WHERE TO STAY

Brentwood Bay Lodge & Spa 𝕲𝕲   Nestled among arbutus trees at the water's edge, this sophisticated boutique resort is a showcase for West Coast style with picture windows, rust-colored cedar and steel-framed terraces, and interior spaces that combine subtle browns, greens and stone-floor finishes, along with handmade light wood furniture, fir wood beams, and high-gabled ceilings. Each of the 33 suites has a balcony or patio view of the inlet, forested peaks and marina, gas fireplaces, hand-crafted furnishings, and local art. The rooms' spa-like bathrooms feature hard-to-resist double jetted baths, and shuttered windows let you sit in the tub and bask in the views. This is only outdone by the spa itself—a lavish affair. There's a fine-dining restaurant that offers an ever-changing gourmet menu of primarily local seafood and regional game, as well as a marine pub serving distinctive craft beers and upscale comfort foods. The chunky roast chicken brick-oven pizza with wild mushrooms is a favorite. The hotel is a licensed PADI dive center and has an eco-marine center with kayak rentals and charters.

849 Verdier Ave. (on Brentwood Bay), Victoria, BC V8M 1C5 © **888/544-2079** or 250/544-2079. Fax 250/544-2069. www.brentwoodbaylodge.com. 30 units, 3 suites (some with fireplaces and hot tubs). C$299–$C409 (US$263–US$360) double, C$599–C$659 (US$580) suite. Rates include breakfast. AE, DC, MC, V. Free parking. Take Pat Bay Hwy. north to Keating Crossroads, turn left (west) to Saanich Rd., turn right (south) to Verdier Ave. **Amenities:** Restaurant; pub; cafe; heated outdoor pool; full service spa; steam room; Jacuzzi; concierge; 24-hr. room service; laundry; dry cleaning; nonsmoking facilities. *In room:* A/C, TV/DVD, dataport w/high-speed Internet, minibar, coffeemaker, hair dryer, iron.

Miraloma on the Cove 𝄞𝄞   With stunning West Coast scenery and the sophistication of a European boutique hotel, this inn features warm, honey-toned woodwork and atrium-style architecture for glimpses of sky, and many of the studio, one- and two-room suites have views. All rooms feature locally made furniture and custom-made linens, gas fireplaces, impressive ensuite bathrooms (complete with heated towel racks and floors), flatscreen TVs, gleaming, fully appointed kitchens, and decks. The superior suites also have washer–dryer facilities. **The Latch**, one of the region's destination restaurants (see "Where to Dine," below), is right next door and serves as the hotel's dining room.

2326 Harbour Rd., Sidney, BC V8L 2P8. ℂ 877/956-6622 or 250/656-6622. Fax 250/656-6212. www.miraloma.ca. 20 units. July to mid-Sept C$169–C$325 (US$149–US$286) studio, C$249–C$425 (US$219–US$374) 1-bedroom, C$450–C$475 (US$196–US$418) 2-bedroom; mid-Sept to June C$135–C$175 (US$120–US$154) studio, C$195–C$299 (US$172–US$163) 1-bedroom, C$299 (US$263) 2-bedroom. Rates include continental breakfast. Extra person C$25 (US$22). AE, DC, MC, V. Free parking. **Amenities:** Restaurant; lounge; mountain bikes; concierge; business center; massage. *In room:* A/C, TV w/pay movies, DVD, dataport, high-speed Internet, minibar, fridge, coffeemaker, hair dryer, iron.

WHERE TO DINE

Deep Cove Chalet FRENCH   A local favorite for special occasions, this charming 1914 chalet was originally the terminus building of the British Columbia Electric Railway. Perched on a grassy bank overlooking a beautiful inlet, the restaurant offers top-notch service, a superb menu that emphasizes local seafood, lamb, and game, and a cellar that boasts some 18,000 bottles in its reserve, some dating from 1902. If you're looking for a classic fine-dining experience, the chalet makes the drive worthwhile, especially on a sunny day. The a la carte menu selection can be pricey (La Soupe aux Truffles is C$45/US$40); prix fixe dinners won't break the bank and feature items such as roast caribou, Dungeness crab, and sometimes even a terrific selection of caviars from Russia, China, and France.

11190 Chalet Drive Rd. ℂ 250/656-3541. Reservations recommended for Sunday brunch and dinner. Lunch C$25 (US$22), dinner C$55 (US$48), brunch C$35 (US$31). Prix fixe dinner C$55–C$80 (US$48–US$70). AE, MC. Wed–Sun noon–2:30pm; daily 5:30–9:30pm. Closed Mon–Tues lunch.

Side Grill - loved it!

DOCK ~~503 Waterfront~~ Café PACIFIC NORTHWEST   You can't dine nearer to the water than this—perched on the pier, virtually on top of Van Isle Marina. View windows give the room a contemporary ambience, although in summer the heated and covered patio is the favored spot. The menu focuses on local and seasonal items: regional seafood—the Thai-influenced Pacific seafood hot pot is a must for zest-loving palettes, Cowichan Valley chicken cooked with minted quinoa and lemon yogurt, artisan cheeses and homemade breads, desserts, and ice cream. If you're not up to a full meal, at least treat yourself to the latter.

2320 Harbour Rd. Sidney, BC ℂ 250/656-0828. Lunch C$12 (US$11), dinner C$28 (US$25). AE, MC, V. Mon–Sun 11:30am–2:30pm and 5–11pm; Sunday 10:30am–2:30pm.

The Latch WEST COAST   Built in the 1920s for then Lieutenant-Governor Walter C. Nichol, The Latch was once a summer retreat for dignitaries and debutantes. The restaurant's small dining rooms still retain an intimate heritage feel, and although the antiques hark back to that era, the food certainly does not. New West Coast flavors are prepared in a classic Tuscan style with an emphasis on local produce. House specialties include veal scallopini served in white-wine lemon sauce, and the Seafood Platter featuring halibut, king crab, salmon, and prawns. The Latch creates its own

Southern Vancouver Island

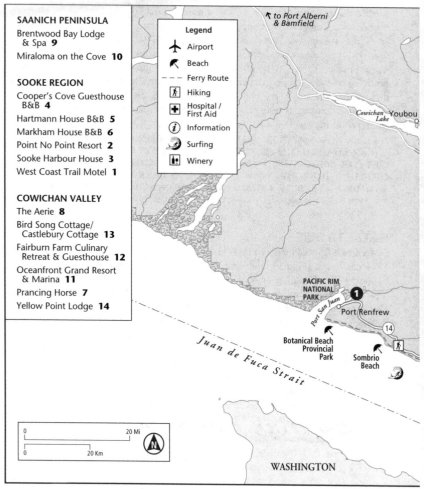

SAANICH PENINSULA
Brentwood Bay Lodge
  & Spa **9**
Miraloma on the Cove **10**

SOOKE REGION
Cooper's Cove Guesthouse
  B&B **4**
Hartmann House B&B **5**
Markham House B&B **6**
Point No Point Resort **2**
Sooke Harbour House **3**
West Coast Trail Motel **1**

COWICHAN VALLEY
The Aerie **8**
Bird Song Cottage/
  Castlebury Cottage **13**
Fairburn Farm Culinary
  Retreat & Guesthouse **12**
Oceanfront Grand Resort
  & Marina **11**
Prancing Horse **7**
Yellow Point Lodge **14**

Legend
✈ Airport
↖ Beach
– – – Ferry Route
🚶 Hiking
✚ Hospital /
  First Aid
ⓘ Information
🏄 Surfing
Winery

↖ to Port Alberni
& Bamfield

Cowichan Youbou
Lake

PACIFIC RIM
NATIONAL
PARK
Port Renfrew
14

Botanical Beach
Provincial
Park
Sombrio
Beach

Juan de Fuca Strait

0 ————————— 20 Mi
0 ————————— 20 Km

N

WASHINGTON

artisan breads and is known for its homemade Italian ice cream. This restaurant is an excellent choice for romantic, candlelight dining. The Latch also has six sumptuously decorated guest rooms upstairs; they're popular, however, so if you're thinking of staying overnight, advance reservations are recommended.

2328 Harbour Rd., Sidney. 📞 **250/656-6622**. www.latchinn.ca. Reservations recommended on weekends. Main courses C$17–C$32 (US$15–US$28). AE, DC, MC, V. Daily 5–10pm.

Stonehouse Pub *(Finds* PUB FARE   For many regulars using the ferry system, this little eatery provides more than simple sustenance. If there's a long wait in store before sailing, locals know to leave their car in the ferry lineup and take the 15-minute walk through the woods to this 80-year-old English-style pub. Set amid a garden filled with perennials, you can enjoy soups, salads and appetizers like chicken wings and nachos

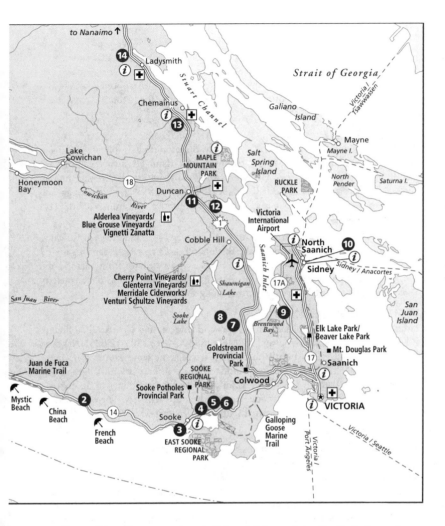

as well as traditional bangers and mash, fish and chips, and shepherd's pie. It sure beats what you'll find at the ferry terminal, especially when you can wash it down with a pint of local ale. In summer, the stone patio is sun-drenched. In winter, the wood-paneled, slightly tired decor—appropriately so for a pub—is nevertheless warm and inviting.

2215 Canoe Cove Rd., Sidney BC V8L 5V5. © **250/656-3498.** www.stonehousepub. C$10–C$16 (US$8.80–US$14). MC, V. Daily 11am–11pm.

2 The Sooke Region

To the west of Victoria lies Southern Vancouver Island's wild side. Within a couple hours' drive of the city, you are met with windswept beaches and trails through old-growth forest. Whether you're an urbanite looking for a spectacular afternoon side trip, a soft adventurer, or a hardy hiker, this drive along **Highway 14,** toward Port Renfrew, delivers. Set aside a day, or make the tranquility of Sooke your home base. Just 32km (20 miles) out of Victoria, you're on the edge of outdoor adventure country. Sooke is one of those wish-you-were-here coastal towns. Its name is derived from the first inhabitants of the region, the T'sou-ke band. The "e" in both T'sou-ke and Sooke is silent, just like the morning mist that lingers over the harbor.

ESSENTIALS
GETTING THERE
BY CAR   Driving from Victoria, take **Douglas Street** north and follow the signs to **Highway 1,** toward Sooke. Take the **Highway 14 (Island Highway) exit** at **Colwood,** and you're on your way. Highway 14 follows the coast all the way through Sooke, and along to Port Renfrew. Remember to get gas in Sooke; it's the last gas station before Port Renfrew. Sooke is a 32-km (20-mile) drive west from Victoria; Port Renfrew is 74km (46 miles) west from Sooke.

BY BUS   Board at the Western Exchange on Highway 14 (Island Hwy.) at Colwood (about 20 minutes out of Victoria). Take **Bus no. 50** (get a transfer), then **Bus no. 61** to Sooke. Depending on traffic, the trip can take up to an hour from Victoria and because of the transfers, might be a frustrating journey, especially as once you're in Sooke, you'll be tempted to explore farther along the coast.

VISITOR INFORMATION
Head to the **Sooke Region Museum Visitors and Information Centre,** 2070 Phillips Rd. (right off Sooke Road/Highway 14) (Ⓒ **866/888-4748** or 250/642-6351). It's open July through August daily from 9am to 5pm. It keeps the same 9am to 5pm hours from October to May, but it's closed Mondays. The staff here is knowledgeable and very enthusiastic, with all kinds of ideas for places to stay and things to do, particularly when it comes to both soft- and rugged-adventure activities. There are options for self-guided explorations or escorted tours. The center is wheelchair accessible.

THE TOP ATTRACTIONS
Fort Rodd Hill & Fisgard Lighthouse National Historic Site *Kids*   The Fisgard lighthouse is the oldest lighthouse on Canada's west coast. From its vantage point atop a volcanic outcrop, it has guided ships toward Victoria's sheltered harbor since 1873. Although the beacon has long been automated, the site has been restored to its original appearance and the lighthouse, which you can climb, houses some displays that show how keepers lived some 100 years ago. The surrounding park is filled with old military installations: camouflaged searchlights, underground armories, and guns dating from the 1890s, which, in more than half a century, have never fired a shot in anger. Canada has designated it a National Historic Site. This is a great attraction for individuals and families alike to pass an hour or so; longer if you're tossing a Frisbee, picnicking, or beachcombing.

603 Fort Rodd Hill Rd. Ⓒ **250/478-5849.** www.parkscanada.pch.gc.ca. Admission C$4 (US$3.50) adults, C$3.50 (US$3.10) seniors, C$2 (US$1.75) children 6–16, C$10 (US$8.80) family pass, free for children under 6. Mar–Oct daily 10am–5:30pm, Nov–Feb daily 9am–4:30pm. Follow Hwy. 1 out of Victoria, taking the Colwood exit (#10) onto Hwy. 1A. Continue for 2km (1 mile), turn left at the third traffic light onto Ocean Blvd. Follow the signs to the sites.

Sooke Region Museum   Fittingly, the museum is housed in Moss Cottage (built in 1870), Sooke's oldest building and somewhat of a museum piece itself. Sharing space with the Visitor Information Centre (see "Essentials," earlier in the chapter), the

museum houses a charming, compact collection of diorama exhibits and pioneer memorabilia. On summer weekends, an interpretive guide in the character of "Aunt Tilly," the original owner of Moss Cottage, will chat with visitors while bustling about doing her household chores. A 30-minute stop here is well worth the extra time while you're picking up information on the area.

2070 Phillips Rd. (right off Sooke Road/Hwy. 14). © 250/642-6351. Admission by donation. Suggested: C$2 (US$1.75). July–Aug daily 9am–5pm; Sept–June Tues–Sun 9am–5pm.

HIKING TRAILS

Whether you like to cycle, hike, horseback ride, or just stroll, the **Galloping Goose Trail** and **Peninsula Trail** are the place to be. Laid out like a green ribbon from Sidney to Sooke, their 100km (60 miles) of pathways link the region's parks to form a continuous chain of greenspaces. Named for the gawky and noisy gas rail car that carried passengers between Victoria and Sooke in the 1920s, the popular **Galloping Goose Trail** follows the abandoned rail beds and trestles of that railway legacy. **Leechtown,** once the site of a gold mining community, marks the westernmost reach, and terminus, of "The Goose," as it's affectionately called. For more information on the Galloping Goose and Peninsula trails, many of which make for easy half-day outings, contact the **Capital Region District Parks,** at © 250/478-3344.

Stretching 47km (29 miles) along the near-wilderness coastline from **China Beach** to **Botanical Beach,** is the 47-km (29-mile) **Juan de Fuca Marine Trail** ✮✮✮. A neighbor to the famed (and very strenuous) West Coast Trail (see below), the less demanding Juan de Fuca Marine Trail offers similar scenic beauty, yet can be completed as a comfortable, albeit strenuous, 4- or 5-day trek or as several 1-day hikes from different trailheads. It isn't easy going, though—you'll be hiking through muddy trails, over fallen trees, across suspension bridges and along wilderness beaches. If you're not up to the full distance, each of the four main trailheads at China Beach, Sombrio Beach, Parkinson Creek, and Botanical Beach offer parking lots that allow day hikes and smaller family hikes down to the beach. If you're more interested in the 4- or 5-day trek, you can start at either **Botanical Beach** or **China Beach.** Because this is a wilderness trail, conditions are always changing, so check the trailhead information centers for updates. Be sure to wear proper footwear and appropriate clothing. Campsites are regularly spaced along the trail. A great online resource is www.vancouver islandoutdoors.com. The site has maps, photos, safety pointers, and camping information for the Juan de Fuca Marine Trail.

Note: As you hike, watch for orange balls that mark exits from the beach to the trail. Be aware, however, that beaches may be cut off from the trail during high tides and storms. Of all the trails on Vancouver Island, the **West Coast Trail** ✮✮✮ is the most famous. It is known as one of the most extreme, rigorous, and beautiful trails in the world. With its easternmost trailhead just outside of Port Renfrew, the West Coast Trail is virtually the town's only raison d'être. Now a part of **Pacific Rim National Park,** the trail originally was constructed for the rescue of mariners shipwrecked along the rugged west coast, appropriately referred to as the "graveyard of the Pacific." Running approximately 75km (46 miles) north between Port Renfrew and Bamfield, it takes an average of 5 to 7 days to complete, and is a challenge for even the most experienced hikers. For more information about the West Coast Trail, check out www.westcoasttrailbc.com. See chapter 6 for more on the West Coast Trail and Pacific Rim National Park.

PARKS & BEACHES

Goldstream Provincial Park is a favorite escape for Victoria residents and visitors alike. Picnic beneath 600-year-old red cedars (the best spot is near the parking lot), or hike through beautiful rain forest. Watch out for old mine shafts where, in the late 1800s, prospectors mined for gold (hence, the park's name); or try panning for gold yourself in the river. All you need is a 30.5- or 38-centimeter (12- or 15-in.) steel pan, and a whole lot of patience. You can take several easy loop hikes that explore a range of ecosystems: deep forests of Douglas fir, dry upland ridges with arbutus and Garry oak, and a salt marsh estuary at the head of Saanich Inlet. Favorite hikes include the 419-m (1,375-ft.) climb up the Mount Finlayson Trail. Although only a 1-km (.5-mile) ascent, the hike is very steep and rigorous enough that you should allow 3 hours for the round trip. The Upper Goldstream Trail is much easier and although approximately the same distance, most hikers complete the return in half the time. This trail takes you through some of the oldest and biggest Douglas firs in the park, and at the end, you're rewarded with waterfalls. It's a good choice for kids, but not those in strollers. From mid-October through November, thousands come to Goldstream Provincial Park to watch salmon spawn, while in December and January, they come for the Bald Eagle Count (see the "Calendar of Events," in chapter 2). Many areas of the park are wheelchair accessible. For information on Goldstream Provincial Park and all other provincial parks on the South Island, contact BC Parks (© 250/391-2300; www.env.gov. bc.ca/bcparks). The park's Freeman King Visitor Centre (© 250/478-9414; www. goldstreamnaturehouse.com) is open daily from 9am to 4:30pm, and offers a nature house and year-round guided walks, as well as programs geared to children. Interested in camping in the park? Choose from among 173 sites. Reserve through Discover Camping (© 800-689-9025 or 604-689-9025; www.discover camping.ca).

In Sooke, you'll find **Sooke Potholes Provincial Park,** featuring an unusual rock formation, over which the Sooke River flows onto a series of ledges and waist-deep swimming holes, and from there into rock pools below. In summer, the chilly waters are just warm enough to attract a swarm of swimmers. The park has picnic facilities, while easy hiking trails are firm under foot. A network of over 50km (31 miles) of trails can be found in **East Sooke Regional Park** ⚓, lacing through the park's 1,421 hectares (3,512 acres) to beaches, secluded coves, forested areas, petroglyphs, and an abandoned copper mine. In the heart of the park, stumps of Douglas fir and red cedar—some measuring 2 to 3m (7–10 ft.) in diameter, hold clues to the era when loggers felled their riches with the springboard, axe, and crosscut saw. One of these trails, the **East Sooke Coast Trail,** is considered a premier day hike. Though it covers only 10km (6 miles), the trail is rough, winding, and a challenging 6- to 8-hour trip. You can access East Sooke Regional Park at **Aylard Farm,** off Becher Bay Road (popular with picnickers and those looking for easy excursions); at **Anderson Cove** (for hikers heading to Babbington Hill and Mount Maguire); or at **Pike Road,** off East Sooke Road, an old logging road that winds through forest to meadow and beach. Information posted at these trailheads will help you choose a trail suitable to your hiking ability. Many trails are wheelchair accessible. As you wind your way west along Highway 14 (also known as the West Coast Road) toward Port Renfrew, you'll pass a series of beaches—many of which are worth pulling over to explore. Some are more accessible than others, and trails often link one stretch of sand to another, but sometimes, only at low tide. *Note:* If you park your car, remove all valuables. Thefts are common; rental cars are favored targets.

(Moments Recipe for Gold Panning

Goldstream Park got its name during the 1860s gold rush for the gold the river contained. There is still gold in them thar waters, and panning for gold flecks can be a fun family activity if you've youngsters in tow. With patience, you'll probably produce some tiny flecks – enough to cover your pinky fingernail.

Ingredients
- One darkened gold pan, preferably 12–15 inches in order to see the gold flecks more clearly, (most hardware stores have suitable pans which you can darken by placing it over a burner or in a campfire)
- Oodles of patience

Location
- Rivers or streams with gravel bars
- Downstream of large boulders
- On the inside of a river bend
- In the middle of heavy water run-off
- On and around tree roots

Method
- Using the pan, scoop up a thin layer of silt from under water.
- Pick out large stones and break up lumps of mud.
- Hold pan level with both hands; rotate it with a swirling motion.
- Tilt the pan slightly downward to carefully discard the dirty water, sand, and gravel (heavier gold will settle to the bottom of the pan).
- Rotate the pan with increasingly lighter material by raising and lowering the pan's lip so water will flow over it.
- Continue this process until nothing but heavier minerals—and possibly gold—are left.

The first beach you'll come to, ironically, is called **Second Beach,** a small sand and cobblestone beach, subject to strong storm and tidal action. At low tide, it's possible to walk along the beach to **Jordan River,** a popular wintertime surfing and windsurfing area, or to **China Beach,** where fine sand makes it an ideal spot for picnicking, building sandcastles, wading, and relaxing. There's a hidden waterfall at the west end of the beach. From the parking lot, follow the wide gravel trail through lush forest, to the beach itself. The trail is easy to navigate, and therefore suitable for children as well as older travelers. It takes about 20 minutes, one-way; watch for some steep sections. China Beach is the southern terminus of the Juan de Fuca Marine Trail. Camp overnight in your vehicle (it's allowed), or at one of the beach campsites.

Getting to **Mystic Beach** involves a fairly strenuous, 2-km (1-mile) hike along a steep rain-forest trail, which can take up to 45 minutes to complete. But you'll be rewarded by a sandy beach surrounded by sandstone cliffs, shallow waves, and a waterfall. If you can manage it, the trip is worth making. Beachfront campsites are available, but pit toilets are the only amenity. Bring your own water, or if you take water from the streams, remember to purify it. Farther along is **French Beach,** a sand and gravel beach that's a hot spot from which to watch for passing grey whales. Picnic tables and an adventure playground are located on an open, grassy area between the parking lot and beach, making this a good family destination. Sixty-nine campsites are right on the beach. The winds, breakers, and rollers of the Pacific Ocean make **Sombrio Beach** a favorite spot for surfers. An old logging road winds down from Highway 14 to a large parking lot. From there, it's an easy 10-minute walk to the beach. Sombrio Beach is another entry route to the Juan de Fuca Marine Trail. Overnight camping in your vehicle is allowed, and there are a number of beach sites. But the real treasure is **Botanical Beach Provincial Park** 𝒜𝒜, about 4km (2.5 miles) south of Port Renfrew. A terrific place for kids, it's one of the richest intertidal zones on North America's west coast, and a magnet for avid poolies, who gather to enjoy the ocean's bounty. Over the millennia, tidal action has carved out spectacular pits and pools that have filled with purple sea urchins, gooseneck barnacles, fiery red blood stars, and other marine flora and fauna. Check local tide tables: a low tide of 1 meter (4 ft.) or less is best for viewing. In spring and fall, watch for passing grey whales. Camping is prohibited at this park.

For information about camping at any of these beaches, and to reserve campsites, contact **Discover Camping** (© **800/689-9025** or 604/689-9025; www.discover camping.ca).

PORT RENFREW

Port Renfrew is a sleepy fishing village quite literally at the end of the road (Hwy. 14), and unless you're heading to the West Coast Trail (see "Hiking Trails," above, and chapter 6), there aren't a whole lot of reasons to stay. Most accommodations are geared to hikers, and include a complete range of camping facilities for both tents and RVs. You might want to try the **Port Renfrew Recreational Retreat** (© **250/647-0058**). Thirty-three full RV hookups are C$29 (US$26) per night; tents are C$5 (US$4.40) per night. There's a 6-person self-contained cabin at C$150 (US$132) per night. **The West Coast Trail Motel,** on Parkinson Road (© **877/299-2288** or 250/647-5565; www.westcoasttrailmotel.com), is your best bet for anything resembling a decent hotel room. Rates range from C$83 to C$89 (US$73–US$78) per room. It's located next to the **Lighthouse Pub & Restaurant** (© **250/647-5505**), the main gathering place in town, and a good pit stop before turning the car around for the drive back to Sooke.

WHERE TO STAY

Cooper's Cove Guesthouse B&B *(Finds)*　This guest house is a real find for foodies. The owner is an ex Olympiad chef and his culinary school and interactive dinners are legendary. Few places let you muse over dinner preparations—with an option to participate as an elaborate, multi-course, dinner is created before your very eyes. Guest rooms are tasteful also, with downy soft duvets on comfortable king- and queen-size beds, warm pine furniture and touches like homemade truffles on your pillow to sweeten the night. All rooms have water views and a fireplace. Although you don't have to love food to enjoy your stay, the culinary packages are where this inn excels.

5301 Sooke Rd., Sooke BC V0S 1N0 © **877/642-5727** or 250/642-5727. Fax 250/642-5749. www.cooperscove.com. 4 units. C$165–C$215 (US$145–US$189). Culinary packages available. AE, MC, V. **Amenities:** Golf nearby; hot tub; Internet. *In room:* Fridge, hair dryer, massage.

Hartmann House B&B 𝒜𝒜　Hartmann House is at its best in spring: shrouded by wisteria and surrounded by hydrangeas, peonies, rhododendrons, azaleas, and other flowering plants. It has an English country-garden style setting (that's very private), with distant views of the water. Inside is just as welcoming. The cedar finish throughout

the home adds warmth and character, and is accented by a roaring fire and overstuffed rattan couches. These touches extend into each of the two private, self-contained and spacious suites, each with its own entrance, private veranda, and oversize whirlpool tub. You can expect complimentary chilled wine waiting for you upon arrival alongside Belgian chocolates, and a fruit and cheese plate. Breakfast is delivered to your door through a butler's pantry. A truly one-of-a-kind romantic retreat.

5262 Sooke Rd., Sooke, BC V0S 1N0. ✆ **250/642-3761**. Fax 250/642-7361. www.hartmannhouse.bc.ca. 2 units. May–Oct C$195–C$225 (US$172–US$198); Nov–Apr C$175–C$195 (US$154–US$172). Rates include full breakfast. V. No pets. Nonsmoking. **Amenities:** Golf nearby, dataport. *In room:* TV/DVD, fridge, hair dryer, microwave, Jacuzzi, fireplace.

Markham House B&B and Honeysuckle Cottage ☆☆

Nestled into a 4-hectare (10-acre) hillside, this Tudor-style home is bordered by towering firs and flowering perennials. A golf tee and bocce ball court are set up on the lawns and intriguing pathways lead to mossy bluff lookouts. Guests enjoy afternoon tea on the veranda or in the old English-style living room filled with antiques. Each guest room has all the trimmings necessary for cocooning: featherbeds, duvets and comfortable sofas, as well as luxurious bathrobes and double Jacuzzis. There's a separate cottage tucked away in the woods that has its own private deck, outdoor Jacuzzi, plus woodstove, full kitchen and barbecue.

1853 Connie Rd., Victoria BC V9C 4C2. ✆ **888/256-6888** or 250-642-7542. Fax 250-642-7538. www.markhamhouse. com. 3 units, cottage. C$105–C$195 (US$92–US$172) guest room, C$225 (US$198) cottage. Extra person C$25 (US$22). Special packages and off-season discounts available. AE, DC, MC, V. **Amenities:** Lounge; golf nearby; hot tub; wireless Internet. *In room:* TV/DVD/VCR, hair dryer.

Point No Point Resort ☆

It's the ultimate getaway—a private cabin, the ocean as your front yard, and 16 hectares (40 acres) or so of wilderness "out the back." Since this waterfront resort has been in business more than 50 years, the size and relative quality of the cabins varies depending on when they were built. Some are large enough for families; others are romantic retreats that are as private as they are cozy. All have wood-burning fireplaces, full kitchens, private bathrooms, stunning oceanviews, and a strip of private beach, which includes a beach house and fire pit. Lunch and traditional tea are served daily in a central teahouse overlooking the Juan de Fuca Strait. Dinner is served Wednesday through Sunday.

1505 West Coast Hwy. (Hwy. 14), Sooke, BC V0S 1N0. ✆ **250/646-2020**. Fax 250/646-2294. www.pointnopointresort. com. 25 cabins, 10 w/Jacuzzi and private deck. C$180–C$260 (US$158–US$229). 2-night minimum stay on weekends; 3-night minimum stay July–Aug, holiday weekends, Christmas. AE, MC, V. Free parking. Small pets accepted C$10 (US$8.80). **Amenities:** Restaurant. *In room:* Kitchen, fireplace.

Sooke Harbour House ☆☆☆

Poised on the end of a sand spit, this little inn is a celebrity hideaway for Hollywood types such as Gillian Anderson, Robert DeNiro, and Richard Gere. The ambience is understated elegance with a friendly, yet completely unobtrusive staff. An eclectic blend of antiques, original art, and whimsical crafts is showcased throughout the inn. In fact, the collection is one of the largest public art displays on Vancouver Island. Each of the 28 guest rooms is decorated in a unique way, though they all express a Northwest theme. All have wood-burning fireplaces, exquisite views, and all but one have sundecks. Many have Jacuzzis and showers with beautiful stained-glass doors. Speaking of showers, guests will find rooms well equipped if the day is rainy; umbrellas, rubber boots, and rain jackets are provided for all. The experience wouldn't be complete without enjoying a meal at the **Sooke Harbour House** restaurant, which is the best in the region (see "Where to Dine," below). If you're not a guest at the hotel, dining here often means making a reservation weeks in advance, especially in summer. Be sure also to try the **Sea-renity Spa;** it offers an excellent range of massage and esthetic services. Among the spa's specialties are seaweed treatments, many of which have been created for Sea-renity. In fact, seaweed is so abundant in Sooke that seaweed byproducts have quickly become much more than a cottage industry.

1528 Whiffen Spit Rd., Sooke, BC V0S 1N0. ⓒ 800/889-9688 or 250/642-3421. Fax 250/628-6988. www.sooke harbourhouse.com. 28 units, 23 w/Jacuzzi. May–Sept C$335–C$495 (US$195–US$436); Oct–Apr C$250–C$355 (US$220–US$312). Rates include breakfast and picnic lunch. Off-season discounts available. Children 12 and under stay free in parent's room. DC, MC, V. Free parking. Take Island Hwy. to the Sooke–Colwood turnoff (junction Hwy. 24); continue on Hwy. 14 to Sooke; turn left onto Whiffen Spit Rd. Pets accepted C$20 (US$18). **Amenities:** Restaurant; spa; 24-hour room service; baby-sitting. *In room:* Coffeemaker, hair dryer, iron, steam shower, bottle of port.

WHERE TO DINE

Mom's Cafe 🎯 *Finds* CASUAL FOOD Tucked away by the community hall in downtown Sooke, Mom's Cafe is the quintessential 1950s diner, complete with juke boxes at the booths and bric-a-brac (you just know Mom never throws anything away). It serves up excellent home cooking, and is considered one of the top 10 diners in British Columbia. Mom's is always packed with locals and visitors alike. Mom's homemade dessert pies are absolute musts.

2036 Shields Rd., Sooke. ⓒ 250/642-3314. Main courses C$8–C$15 (US$7.05–US$13). MC, V. Sun–Thurs 8am–8pm; Fri–Sat 8am–9pm. Drive into Sooke on Hwy. 14; take the first right after the traffic lights at Murray Rd.

Six Mile Pub PUB FARE You'll find a good variety of brews on tap, and tasty food seasoned with fresh herbs from the pub's own garden—burgers as well as some higher end dishes such as fresh halibut with risotto, braised lamb shank, and beef tenderloin. Part of a franchise, the Six Mile Pub is one of several "mile" pubs you'll find along Highway 1A, all of them, to some degree, incorporating an oak-beamed, fireside ambience of yesteryear. Most were once mile-measured stops for stagecoaches that traveled up island from Victoria. This pub has a particularly rich history. The building dates to 1855, and was the hub for provincial bootleggers during Prohibition. Since Victoria continued the ban on booze until the early 1950s, "mile houses," as they were known, were the only places Victorians could get a tot outside of the city. Today, the Six Mile Pub has broad appeal and a loyal local following.

494 Island Hwy. ⓒ 250/478-3121. Main courses C$7–C$28 (US$6.15–US$25). MC, V. Sun–Thurs 11am–midnight; Fri–Sat 11am–1am. Follow Hwy. 14 to Six Mile Rd.

Sooke Harbour House 🎯🎯🎯 GOURMET WEST COAST The cuisine has seduced thousands of palates, and the restaurant's award-winning wine cellar is regarded as one of the best on the West Coast. Its imaginative menu focuses on local seafood and organically grown produce, much of it harvested from the over 200 edible herbs, greens, flowers and vegetables grown on premises. Their culinary transformation creates dishes such as shady lane tomato soup, garden basil puree garnished with nasturtiums and fresh tuna, and halibut baked in a crust of herbs, sunflower seeds, and Parmesan. The food is so good here that your best bet is the multi-course **tasting menu**—which allows you to sample as much as possible! These are C$99 (US$87); add C$80 (US$70) if you choose the wine pairings. The 4-course set menu is excellent value and includes a vegetarian option. Dinner is by reservation only, at least 3 days in advance (but you'd be better off calling 3 weeks in advance in the summer). Breakfast and lunch are served for hotel guests only.

In Sooke Harbour House, 1528 Whiffen Spit Rd., Sooke. ✆ **250/642-3421**. Reservations required. Main courses C$35 (US$31), set menu C$47–C$75 (US$41–US$66). DC, MC, V. Daily in summer 5:30–9:30pm; closed Tues and Wed in winter. Take Island Hwy. to the Sooke–Colwood turnoff (junction Hwy. 24); continue on Hwy. 14 to Sooke; turn left onto Whiffen Spit Rd.

3 En Route to Nanaimo: The Cowichan Valley

This blood pressure–lowering trip north along Vancouver Island's east coast to Nanaimo can take you from 1½ hours to all day, depending on how many stops you make. The **Cowichan Valley** is an ideal side trip if you're staying in Victoria, and a wonderful meander through rich, rolling countryside. The more direct route is along the Trans-Canada Highway (Hwy. 1), over the mountain hump of the **Malahat,** and down through the Cowichan Valley. The Quw'utsun' people call the valley the Warm Land, and with good reason: here, you'll find many small, family owned farms and orchards selling homemade products such as jams, candles, and soaps. You can also visit estate **vineyards** featuring award-winning wines, as well as potters' studios, craft

Totem Poles

Representing history and tradition, and full of symbolism, totem poles are some of the most fascinating examples of aboriginal art. In the Pacific Northwest, they are carved from mature cedar trees with skills that have been handed down from one generation to the next. In the past, a totem was created for a specific purpose: to tell a story, to honor a deceased elder, or to record a link to the spirit-human beings that were, and still are, so much a part of aboriginal culture. Most important, a totem is the emblem of tribal unity; through its imagery, a totem conveys a tribe's ancestry, prestige, and accomplishments. Contrary to popular belief, totem figures were not Gods, and they were never used to ward off evil spirits.

Symbols are called crests, and nearly always reflect a link between human and nature (usually an animal). For example, some Northwest Coast families claim as a crest the Thunderbird, who descended from the sky to take off his animal clothing and become their human ancestor.

Today, both Native and non-native people carve totem poles, which are a source of pride and tradition for the people in the Pacific Northwest.

Some common totem symbols:

- Bear – Strength, teaching, motherhood
- Eagle – Powerful leadership and prestige
- Frog – New life, communicator
- Hummingbird – Love, beauty, a Spirit messenger
- Killer Whale – Traveler and guardian
- Otter – Trusting, inquisitive, a loyal friend
- Owl – Wisdom
- Raven – Knowledge, bringer of the Light
- Salmon – Dependable, a good provider
- Sun – Healing energy; guardian of the Day

stores, and galleries. Many artisans work out of their homes and, other than the annual open-house tour (usually the second week of July), they may not work regular hours. Your best bet is to pick up a map from the Victoria or Duncan visitor information centers or download it from www.islandarts.ca/visions and either take your chances, or phone ahead for appointments.

One detour of interest is the city of **Duncan,** nicknamed **"City of Totem Poles"** for its impressive collection of, you guessed it, totem poles! This part of the world is famed for its residents' carving skills, yet most historic totem poles are in museums or stand in abandoned villages reclaimed by nature. In the 1980s, the mayor of Duncan commissioned local First Nations artists to carve new totem poles, and today, the city showcases one of the world's largest collections of modern totem carving. If you're just driving through Duncan, catching sight of them can be a bit hit and miss, however as many are on side streets. The best suggestions is to follow the **yellow shoeprints** on the pavement, or take a free **walking tour** that starts at the **Cowichan Valley Museum,** in the VIA Rail station, at Station Street and Caan Avenue. Call ✆ **250/ 715-1700** for information. You can also check in at the **Duncan Visitor Information Centre,** 381A Trans-Canada Hwy., Duncan, BC, V9L 3R5 (✆ **250/746-4636**).

Another worthwhile detour is the town of **Chemainus.** When the building of the Trans-Canada Highway bypassed Chemainus and the local lumber mill slowed to a virtual standstill, the town turned its declining fortunes around by painting the exteriors of its quaint buildings. Today, more than 300,000 visitors stop each year to see the 33 murals and 12 sculptures, particularly in July and August each year, when more are added. If you do decide to make a stop in Chemainus, stay in one of the heritage B&Bs (see "Where to Stay"). Spend the evening at the **Chemainus Theatre,** 9737 Chemainus Rd. (✆ **800/565/7738;** www.chemainustheatrefestival.ca). Year-round, this troupe offers professional live theater in the town's most eye-catching building, a late 19th-century opera house. Past shows have included quality productions of *She Stoops to Conquer, My Fair Lady,* and *Lost in Yonkers.* Every December, there's a seasonal family show. Tickets range from C$11 (US$9.70) for the preview to C$28 (US$25); C$44–C$54 (US$39–US$48) for the dinner-theater package. The **Visitor Information Centre** is housed in an old railroad car at 9758 Chemainus Rd., at Mill St. (✆ **250/246-3944**).

ESSENTIALS
GETTING THERE
BY CAR   Take Douglas Street north out of Victoria, which becomes Highway 1 (the Trans-Canada Highway). From here it's about 111km (67 miles) to Nanaimo.

BY BUS   **Laidlaw Coach Lines** operates between Victoria and Nanaimo, with various stops along the way. Schedules and reservations are handled by **Greyhound Canada** (✆ **800/663-8390** or 604/482-8747; www.greyhound.ca). There are six departures a day from Victoria, from 5:50am to 7:20pm. Fares are C$19 (US$17) for adults, C$17 (US$15) for seniors, C$9.40 (US$8.30) for children 5 to 11. The trip between Victoria and Nanaimo takes 2½ hours.

BY TRAIN   The **Malahat** run by VIA Rail (✆ **800/561-8630;** www.viarail.com), operates a daily service between Victoria and Courtenay. One-day sightseeing trips from Victoria include stops in Chemainus, Duncan, and Nanaimo. Trains depart from Victoria's VIA Rail station, 450 Pandora Ave. One-way fares are C$48 (US$42) adult, C$43 (US$38) senior, C$31 (US$27) student, and C$24 (US$21) children 2–11 years.

VISITOR INFORMATION

Obtain maps and information at the **Tourism Victoria Information Centre,** 812 Wharf St., Victoria, BC V8W 1T3 (© **250/953-2033;** www.tourismvictoria.com). The center is open May and June daily from 9am to 8pm; July and August daily from 9am to 9pm; September through April daily from 9am to 5pm. You can also contact **Tourism Vancouver Island,** 203–335 Wesley St., Nanaimo, BC V9R 2T5 (© **250/ 754-3500;** www.islands.bc.ca). The center is open year-round, Monday through Friday from 8:30am to 5pm.

THE TOP ATTRACTIONS

BC Forest Museum Park/BC Forest Discovery Centre *(Kids)*   An affiliate of the Royal BC Museum, this is a fabulous learning and nature experience for the entire family. Focusing on forestry practices and preservation, the museum features an exhibit on the history of logging, a miniature town, a logging camp, and a ranger station. Don't miss the 20-minute ride on a full-size steam train; it's an additional C$3 (US$2.65) per ride and a lot of fun. In winter, the train runs only at weekends. Expect to stay for an hour and a half, allowing an additional half hour for the train.

2892 Drinkwater Rd., Duncan. © 250/715-1113. www.bcforestmuseum.com. Admission C$11 (US$9.70) adults, C$9 (US$7.95) seniors and students, C$6 (US$5.30) children 5–12, free for children 4 and under; C$35 (US$31) family pass. Mid-Apr to mid-Oct daily 10am–6pm. Closed mid-Oct to mid-Apr. Take Hwy. 1 past Duncan, watching for the double-span bridge over the Cowichan River. The center is approximately 3km (2 miles) past the bridge, off the highway to the right, after the fourth set of traffic lights at Beverley St.

Quw'utsun' Cultural Centre *(Kids Kids)*   The Cowichan were the original inhabitants of the valley that now bears their name. Their culture and way of life is creatively illustrated at the Cowichan Native Village. Storytelling, dancing, and traditional feasting are some of the activities here. Go on a guided walking tour of the village, which includes several modern longhouse structures; talk to carvers as they work, or enjoy the excellent multimedia theater presentation that retells the Cowichan myth and history. A visit here will take about an hour, though you might want to stop longer to try some authentic native cuisine in the Riverwalk Café. The art gallery is the best place in the valley to buy the famous bulky, durable Cowichan sweaters, knitted with bold motifs from hand-spun raw wool.

200 Cowichan Way, Cowichan. © 877/746-8119 or 250/746-8119. Admission C$10 (US$8.80) adults, C$8 (US$7.05) seniors and students, C$6 (US$5.30) children 12 and under; C$26 (US$22) family pass. May–Sept daily 10am–5pm; Oct–Apr, Mon–Fri, 10am–4pm.

MEANDERING AMONG THE WINERIES

The wine scene in British Columbia just keeps getting better in quality and variety, and although the vineyards on Vancouver Island are young compared to those found in the province's interior, they are beginning to produce some excellent vintages. As you make your way north through the Cowichan Valley toward Nanaimo, you might want to consider a stop at any one of the worthy wineries that dot the route northward from Victoria. Touring is as easy as following the burgundy and white Wine Route signs.

The first pocket of wineries along the route is in Cobble Hill, south of Duncan. **Cherry Point Vineyards,** 840 Cherry Point Rd., RR#3, Cobble Hill (© **250/743- 1272;** www.cherrypointvineyards.com), is one of the most prominent Cowichan Valley wineries, with national awards to prove it. Cherry Point's California-like vineyards produce some of the finest Auxerrois in the country. The tasting room is a Swiss-style chalet (open year round), which opens up into a quaint bistro and patio where lunches are served mid-June to mid-October. The artwork of local artists adorns the walls. Many of the other Cowichan-area wineries are much smaller than Cherry Point, and some choose not to host formal tours. Still, visitors are welcome to drop by, and it's not uncommon to meet an owner working in the vineyard as you pull up a dusty driveway.

One example is just minutes away. As small as it is, **Glenterra Vineyards,** 3897 Cobble Hill Rd., Cobble Hill (𝒞 **250/743-2330**), produces award-winning wines. Their Vivace is exclusively from their own estate-grown grapes. Also, try their Pinot Gris and Meritage. Glenterra also has a cozy tasting room and casual eatery, Thistles, that features daily lunch specials of tapas, soups, sandwiches, and good homemade desserts.

Merridale Ciderworks, 1230 Merridale Rd., RR#1, Cobble Hill (𝒞 **800/998-9908** or 250/743-4293; www.merridalecider.com), is Canada's only orchard dedicated solely to cider and wine apples. Chat with the cider-makers, and tour the apple mills, presses, and fermentation casks. Visit in April and you'll see the orchard in magnificent bloom; turn up in October through November to watch the fragrant press. The cozy bistro, La Pommeraie, offers authentic country-style cooking, and a virtual showcase of gourmet pizzas, artisan breads, and fruit pies from its brick-oven bakery Flour Water Salt. It is open daily for lunch. **Venturi-Schulze Vineyards,** 4235 Trans-Canada Hwy., RR#1, Cobble Hill (𝒞 **250/743-5630;** www.venturischulze.com), is the smallest winery in the Cowichan Valley, and it's truly a family affair, centered on the 100-year-old farmhouse. A new winery, built partially underground, paved the way to convert the old winery into a vinegary. All wines and gourmet vinegars are grown, produced, and bottled on the property.

Another group of wineries worth visiting is found near Duncan. **Alderlea Vineyards,** 1751 Stamps Rd., TT1, Duncan (𝒞 **250/746-7122**), is located on a picturesque 4-hectare (10-acre) site. Creating wines from grapes grown only in their own vineyard, Alderlea produces an excellent Bacchus, Pinot Gris, Hearth (a port-style dessert wine), Pinot Auxerrois, and Angelique blend. **Blue Grouse Vineyards,** 4365 Blue Grouse Rd, Duncan (𝒞 **250/743-3834;** www.bluegrousevineyards.com), is one of the founding estate wineries on Vancouver Island, and is renowned for its exclusive premium wines. All are 100% estate grown and produced. Wine tastings are held in a comfortable European-style tasting room overlooking the valley. In summer, picnic tables under the arbor are perfect for a savory lunch. **Vignetti Zanatta,** 5039 Marshall Rd., RR#3, Duncan (𝒞 **250/748-2338;** www.zanatta.ca), is one of the oldest vineyards on Vancouver Island. Wines here are made by an old-world Italian method using grapes grown only on the property. Try the Ortega, a dry fruity white wine; or the Glenora Fantasia, a sparkling wine. The Pinot Grigio, Auxerrois, Muscat, Merlot, and special Damasco are all worthwhile. Plan to stop for lunch or dinner at **Vinoteca** (see

---

(Moments **Safaris**

Travel with Taste (𝒞 250/385-1527; www.travelwithtaste.com) offers a variety of culinary adventures and wine tours throughout the Saanich Peninsula and Cowichan Valley. Tours range from 6-hour meanders that include visits to working farms, cheese-makers, three wineries, and a gourmet lunch (C$500/US$440 for two people) to customized multi-day tours that are more akin to gastronomic safaris.

"Where to Dine," below), featuring many foods grown on the Zanatta's 49-hectare (120-acre) farm. Touring maps are available at most visitor centers and from www. islandwineries.ca.

WHERE TO STAY
ON THE MALAHAT
The Aerie 🟋🟋🟋   An acclaimed member of the Relais & Châteaux group of hotels, the Aerie is a magnificent Mediterranean-style mansion reminiscent of grand homes in Southern Europe. Surrounded by 4 hectares (10 acres) of meticulously kept grounds, this hotel offers a breathtaking view of the Olympic Mountains and the Gulf Islands that alone is worth the trip, especially if you arrive by helicopter (there's a helipad amid the landscaped gardens). Suites are individually designed (some are multilevel); most feature Persian and Chinese silk carpets, fireplaces, Jacuzzis, decks, and four-poster queen- or king-size beds. Inspired touches include fresh flowers, terry-cloth robes, CD/cassette players, and Bernard Callebaut chocolates hand-dipped by the renowned chocolatier based in Banff, Alberta. The Villa Cielo, set above the main building, is the Aerie's piece de resistance: offering the ultimate in luxury and space. Suites range in size from 70 to 130 sq. m (750–1,400 sq. ft.) with views that are a stunning 549m (1,800 ft.) high. The hotel's restaurant is not to be missed (see "Where to Dine," below), and the spa is also an appealing part of the Aerie experience. And birdwatchers take note: One of the hotel's best packages (especially in view of its name) is the Audubon, which includes a full day with Pacific Northwest Raptors, the only falconry/raptor educational facility of its kind in the Pacific Northwest.

600 Ebadora Lane (P.O. Box 108), Malahat, BC V0R 2L0. 🕿 **800/518-1933** or 250/743-7115. Fax 250/743-4766. www.aerie.bc.ca. 35 units. C$295–C$325 (US$260–US$286) deluxe, C$395–C$565 (US$348–US$497) suite, C$725–C$950 (US$638–US$836) villa. Rates include full breakfast. Packages available. AE, DC, MC, V. Free parking. Take Hwy. 1 to the Spectacle Lake turnoff; take the first right and follow the winding driveway. **Amenities:** 2 restaurants; bar; small heated indoor pool; outdoor tennis court; spa; Jacuzzi; sauna; concierge; 24-hr. room service; laundry; dry cleaning. *In room:* A/C, TV, dataport, minibar, coffeemaker, hair dryer, iron.

Prancing Horse   Perched on the Malahat summit, this red-roofed Gothic villa is eye-level to passing eagles. Like the Aerie across the road, it offers stupendous views up Finlayson Arm and of the snowcapped Olympic Mountains in the distance. A terraced rockery leads to a multi-tiered deck, where there's a Jacuzzi and gazebo. Trails meander through the property. Inside is all antique elegance. Guest rooms are bright, and have thoughtful touches like fresh flowers, Aveda bath products, Bernard Callebaut chocolates, and views framed by Battenberg lace drapes. The luxury suites include double soaker bathtubs, fireplaces, and private decks. A champagne breakfast is included. This is a good alternative to the pull-out-all-the-stops Aerie next door in terms of price and its less showy welcome. Besides, with the Prancing Horse being home base to Victoria's Ferrari Club, chances are good that you'll see one or two of these racy vehicles in the parking lot along with the villa's friendly owner.

573 Ebadora Lane (P.O. Box 11), Malahat, BC V0R 2L0. 🕿 **877/887-8834** or 250/743-9378. Fax 250/743-9372. www.prancinghorse.com. 7 units. May–Sept C$175–C$375 (US$154–US$330). Honeymoon package available. AE, MC, V. **Amenities:** Exercise room; Jacuzzi; laundry service. *In room:* TV, VCR, fridge, coffeemaker, hair dryer.

IN DUNCAN
Fairburn Farm Culinary Retreat & Guesthouse 🟋🟋   This one-of-a-kind inn offers guests an idealized farm experience—you can be coddled, enjoy exquisite culinary fare, and at the same time explore at your leisure this working farm, orchard, vineyard

and dairy. The farm's resident herd of water buffalo produces yogurt, ice cream, and mozzarella. Built in the 1880s, the rambling but upgraded farmhouse has high ceilings, antique moldings, tiled fireplaces, and a broad columned porch that overlooks 53 hectares (130 acres) of gardens and meadows, with mountain slopes visible in the distance. Each of the three large guest rooms is individually decorated with fine Italian linens and original art. Two have fireplaces. The two-bedroom cottage includes a fully equipped kitchen, and with its simpler furnishings, is ideal for families. Fairburn's showcase kitchen is the source of its reputation, and is where guests enjoy cooking lessons, bread-making demonstrations, and other culinary programs such as the participatory lavish Saturday dinners. Food programs reflect seasonal cycles, so call ahead of your stay to check the schedule. Breakfast, which is included in the room rate, is a homemade farm-fresh feast.

3310 Jackson Rd., Duncan, BC V9L 6N7. (✆ and fax **250/746-4637**. www.fairburnfarm.bc.ca. 3 units, cottage. C$155–C$175 (US$136–US$154) room, C$175 (US$154) cottage based on 3-night minimum stay. Extra person C$20 (US$18). MC, V. **Amenities:** Lounge. *In room:* Hair dryer, no phone.

IN CHEMAINUS
Bird Song Cottage/Castlebury Cottage   These separate bed-and-breakfasts adjoin one another, but could hardly be more different. Both have overindulged in the whimsy department, yet somehow have come out on the winning side. For example, Bird Song is filled with so much Victorian bric-a-brac that it's actually quite enchanting and theatrical. The recorded sound of birds trilling is a bit over the top; but then so is the all the architectural gingerbread. Next door, Castlebury Cottage exemplifies medieval romantic fantasy, with its vaulted ceilings, mullioned casement windows, and antique wrought-iron wall-lamp sconces. There's even a full-size suit of armor standing in one corner. The kitsch extends to the guest rooms too: oversize beds (some four-poster) are covered in satin cushions, windows are framed with lacy chiffon, and chairs are upholstered in velvet. Bathrooms are on the small side, but anything larger would detract from the Camelot-like ambience. These places might be too over the top for some people—but just think of the stories (and photos) you could take back home.

9909 Maple St., Chemainus, BC V0R 1K0. (✆ **250/246-9910**. Fax 250/246-2909. www.birdsongcottage.com. 3 units, one cottage. C$115–C$125 (US$101–US$110) Bird Song Cottage, C$140–C$280 (US$123–US$246) Castlebury Cottage. 2-night minimum stay on weekends. Rates include breakfast and afternoon tea. Extra person $25 (US$22). MC, V. **Amenities:** Lounge. *In room:* TV/VCR/DVD, hair dryer, no phone. Castlebury has TV/VCR/DVD, full-service kitchen, fireplace.

IN LADYSMITH (NEAR CHEMAINUS)
Yellow Point Lodge 🐦   Yellow Point Lodge began operating in the 1930s, and its blend of summer camp and luxury resort has remained a perennial favorite, especially with families. The main lodge has an enormous lobby, a huge fireplace, and a dining room with communal tables. Meals—good, home-style cooking such as prime rib and Yorkshire pudding, roast turkey and mashed potatoes, and a terrific seafood buffet on Friday nights—are included. There are a number of comfortable hotel-like guest rooms in the lodge, all with ocean views. Away from the lodge, self-contained cabins range from rustic, barrack-style accommodations with shared bathrooms and beach cabins with no running water, to luxurious one-, two-, and three-bedroom cottages; some are on the lodge's private beach; most are tucked in between the trees. The lodge is surrounded by 67 hectares (165 acres) of private, mostly first-growth coastal rain forest, with over a mile-and-a-half of waterfront facing the Gulf Islands.

3700 Yellow Point Rd., Ladysmith, BC V0R 2E0. *C* 250/245-7422. Fax 250/245-7411. www.yellowpointlodge.com. 53 units. May to mid-Oct and winter weekends C$185–C$196 (US$163-US$172) lodge rooms, C$102–C$198 (US$90–US$174) cabins, C$68–C$123 (US$60–US$108) barracks. Rates 15% lower mid-Oct to Apr weekdays. Rates include all meals. AE, MC, V. Children 13 and under not accepted. **Amenities:** Restaurant; 2 outdoor tennis courts; Jacuzzi; sauna; bikes; kayaks; hiking. *In room:* Fridge (some rooms), coffeemaker (some rooms), no phone.

IN COWICHAN BAY

Oceanfront Grand Resort & Marina   Every one- and two-bedroom suite faces the water and if you get one of the newly refurbished units, you're in for a treat. Furniture is handcrafted, tones are natural and woodsy, king and queen-size beds are plush and comfortable, kitchens are upgraded and contemporary. There are still a dozen or so rooms on the "to be upgraded" list, and if you don't mind tired and rather drab decor, they can scoop you some savings. Oceanfront has a good steak and seafood restaurant overlooking the marina, where you'll find kayak rentals and boat charters.

1681 Cowichan Bay Rd., Cowichan Bay, BC V0R 1N0 ((*C* **800/663-7897** or 250/701-0166. Fax 250/701-0126. www. thegrandresort.com. 57 units. C$179–C$209 (US$158–US$184). Extra person C$10 (US$8.80). Children 12 and under stay free in parent's room. AE, DISC, MC, V. Free parking. **Amenities:** Restaurant; bar; heated indoor pool; golf nearby; gym, hot tub; boat rental; bear and wine sales. *In room:* TV, coffeemaker, hair dryer, iron.

WHERE TO DINE
ON THE MALAHAT

The Aerie 𝕲𝕲𝕲 WEST COAST/FRENCH   If the entire setting of the Aerie is overwhelmingly beautiful (see "Where to Stay," above), then the restaurant takes this one step further—if that's possible—with a gold-leaf ceiling, chandeliers, gilt chairs, and faux-marble columns. Some would say it's rather exaggerated. But it sets an impressive stage for the food, which is superb. Think items such as Alberta beef tenderloin with butternut squash and hazelnut milk gratin, and a toasted hazelnut red wine sauce; or arctic char and lobster with almond cremolata gratin, stinging nettle and lobster ravioli, toasted almond oil and goat milk emulsion. The 7-course **tasting menu,** paired with exquisite wines, is highly recommended. This is a destination restaurant few Victorians miss, and you won't want to either.

600 Ebadora Lane. *C* **250/743-7115.** Reservations required. Lunch C$19 (US$17); dinner C$40 (US$35); 7-course prix fixe dinner C$110 (US$97). AE, MC, V. Mon–Sat noon–8:30pm; Sun noon–2pm. Take Hwy. 1 to the Spectacle Lake turnoff; take the first right and follow the winding driveway.

IN COWICHAN BAY

Crow & Gate PUB FARE   This classic Tudor-style pub was built in 1972, yet looks like it was plucked out of Cornwall, with its stone and timbered walls, leaded-glass windows, and low-slung ceilings. Even the hand-painted sign is just like the old pub signs you still find in England. Surrounded by a working farm, this popular watering hole offers the best of British pub fare, including roast beef and Yorkshire pudding, pasties, and shepherd's pie. There's a flower-laden patio in summer.

2313 Yellow Point Rd. *C* **250/722-3731.** Reservations recommended for dinner. Main courses C$9–C$14 (US$7.90– US$12). MC, V. Daily 11am–11pm.

Masthead Restaurant 𝕲𝕲 WEST COAST   In the late 1800s, the building was a stopover inn for those making the arduous wagon journey north from Victoria. When the railway arrived, the entire main floor became a machine shop and now, in its current incarnation, it's a bright and airy dining room that serves up some of the region's best West Coast cuisine. Much of it has local origins: the Queen Charlotte

Coho Salmon, Fanny Bay oysters, Cowichan Valley venison, chicken and pork, and Salt Spring Island mussels. Favorites include the prosciutto-wrapped red snapper stuffed with sea asparagus and Okanagan cherries, and served with roast red pepper butter sauce; and the slow-roasted venison sirloin with house-made gnocchi, sautéed mushrooms and demi-glaze. The 3-course table d'hôte is good value for taste experiences and dollars spent. Masthead has dibs on the limited editions produced annually by the Cowichan Valley Estate wineries, so you can expect to discover hard-to-find labels here like Venturi Schulze's Fear of Flying and Pinot Noir. Some of these are so in demand that they must be ordered two harvests in advance.

1705 Cowichan Bay Rd., Cowichan Bay ✆ **250/748-3714**. www.themastheadrestaurant.com. Reservations recommended. Main course C$19–C$29 (US$17–US$26); 3-course menu C$30 (US$26). MC, V. Daily from 5pm.

Rock Cod Café 🐟 FISH & CHIPS   Perched above the water, this busy cafe overlooks busy fishing docks and serves the best fish and chips in the area. After all, when the fish is pulled straight off the boats and put right into the pan, what would you expect? Check out the specials board: it's crammed with value-priced items based on whatever those boats bring in, as well as burgers, salads, and pasta dishes. This is a great place to fuel up for a stroll around the harbor.

1759 Cowichan Bay Rd. ✆ **250/746-1550**. Main courses C$7–C$15 (US$6.15–US$13). MC, V. Daily 8am–8pm.

AROUND DUNCAN

The Genoa Bay Café 🐟 PACIFIC NORTHWEST   Genoa Bay, a 20-minute drive from Duncan, was named by Giovanni Baptiste Ordano in 1858. The bay reminded him of his home in Italy, and still retains a picturesque charm. The cafe is part of the marina complex and is always busy with sea-faring folks and locals. Although the menu leans to seafood, exquisitely prepared, you'll find items such as BBQ ribs, slow roasted in apple and sun-dried cranberry BBQ sauce, and a rack of lamb with pesto and mango chutney glaze—an absolute winner. It's fish that really tops the charts—mouth-watering halibut and candied smoked salmon in white wine cream sauce, calamari with roasted red-pepper pesto dip, or sole and scallops with a mango Thai chili sauce. Foodies have rated the chocolate-pecan pie the best of the island.

5100 Genoa Bay Rd., Genoa Bay Marina, Genoa Bay. ✆ **800/572-6481** or 250/746-7621. Reservations recommended. Main courses C$19–C$29 (US$17–US$26), 3-course tasting menu C$30 (US$26). MC, V. Daily 5:30–10pm; lunch Thurs–Sun 11:30am–2:30pm.

Vinoteca 🐟🐟 LIGHT DINING   A combination wine-tasting room and tapas bar, Vinoteca is set amid the family owned and operated Vigneti Zanatta vineyards (see "Meandering Among the Wineries"). The 1903 farmhouse has been lovingly restored and is a restful place to dine or sip your afternoon away. The menu reflects the family's Italian heritage, incorporating food that is grown either on the farm or locally. A great place for a light meal, here you'll find items such as marinated vegetables, bruschetta, as well as a daily fresh pasta selection (the chicken confit cannelloni is very good), and more substantial dishes such as espresso-marinated duck breast. All are complemented by wines from their vineyards.

5039 Marshall Rd. (near Glenora south of Duncan). ✆ **250/709-2279**. Reservations recommended for dinner. Lunch C$11–C$16 (US$9.70–US$14), dinner C$14–C$30 (US$12–US$26). MC, V. Wed–Sun noon–5pm; Fri & Sat 5–10pm. Closed Mon–Tues. Closed Jan–Mar. Take Miller Rd. exit off Hwy. 1 to stop sign. Turn left onto Miller Rd., right on Koksilah Rd., and left onto Miller Rd. again. Turn left on Glenora; the vineyards are at the junction of Glenora and Marshall rds.

6

Central Vancouver Island

The central part of Vancouver Island showcases some of the best of British Columbia's natural attractions—it's a real haven for eco-adventurers. And it's so diverse that much of it is also geared to family fun. Nanaimo, the island's second largest city and the gateway to the region, is the arrival point for visitors by ferries from the mainland. Families usually head for the neighboring communities of Parksville and Qualicum Beach, where sandy beaches, warm water temperatures, tranquil lakes, and exceptional golf courses prevail. They are year-round vacation destinations, and are increasingly attractive to active retirees; few can resist the more than 2,000 hours of sunshine the townships receive each year.

Things begin to change, however, as you head inland, cutting across the island to the west coast. Here lie the deep Douglas fir forests of **Cathedral Grove,** and the mill town of **Port Alberni,** from where you can explore the region's protected inlets. And once you reach the west coast, well, the changes in scenery are dramatic. The shores are windswept and wild. Fishing villages like **Tofino** (Tough City) and **Ucluelet** (*yew-kloo-let*) are home base to kayakers, hikers, surfers, naturalists, and photographers, who flock to explore **Pacific Rim National Park,** the Broken Group Islands, and Clayoquot Sound. Here you can discover some of the most pristine and accessible coastline in the province.

1 Nanaimo

With a population close to 80,000, Nanaimo is quickly shedding its industrial roots. Once the center of vast coal-mining operations, Nanaimo developed into rather a parochial community. This image is finally beginning to change. Although its suburban environs are pretty nondescript, a small downtown nucleus is smartening up into a hip and pedestrian-friendly area where old buildings such as a century-old firehall-turned-restaurant are finding new leases on life. Around the revamped harborfront you'll find a number of galleries, intriguing shops, and quality restaurants to enjoy. An overhead walkway leads from one area to another.

ESSENTIALS
GETTING THERE
BY CAR   Nanaimo is located right off the Trans-Canada Highway (Hwy. 1), 111km (67 miles) north of Victoria.

BY PLANE   The **Nanaimo Airport** (© **250/245-2157**) is 18km (11 miles) from downtown Nanaimo. Air Canada Jazz (© **888/247-2262** or 800/661-3936) operates 7 flights daily between Nanaimo and Vancouver. There are also several harbor-to-harbor flights between Vancouver, Nanaimo, Victoria, and Seattle. These seaplane carriers include **Baxter Aviation** (© **800/661-5599** or 250/683-6525 or 250/754-1066;

www.baxterair.com), **Harbour Air** (© **800/665-0212** or 604/688-1277; www. harbourair.com), **Kenmore Air** (© **800/543-9595** or 425/486-1257; www.kenmoreair.com), and from the Sunshine Coast, **West Coast Air** (© **800/347-2222;** www.westcoastair. com).

BY BUS   Laidlaw Coach Lines/Island Coach Lines (© 800/318-0818 or 250/385-4411) operates from Victoria to Nanaimo, Tofino, and Port Hardy. **Greyhound Canada** (© **800/661-8747;** www.greyhound.ca) handles schedules and reservations. One-way fares from Victoria to Nanaimo are C$23 (US$20) for adults. Fares for seniors are 10% less; fares for children 5 to 11 are 50% less.

BY TRAIN   The **Malahat,** operated by VIA Rail (© **800/561-8630;** www.viarail. com) has daily service between Victoria and Courtenay. One-day sightseeing trips from Victoria include stops in Chemainus, Duncan, and Nanaimo.

BY FERRY   **BC Ferries** (© **888/BCFERRY** or 888/233-3779 or 250/386-3431; www.bcferries.com) runs between **Horseshoe Bay,** in West Vancouver, and **Departure Bay,** in Nanaimo, as well as between **Tsawwassen** and **Duke Point,** in Nanaimo. The latter is used primarily by trucks and commercial vehicles but if you're traveling by car (Duke Point is 16 km/9 miles south of Nanaimo and is not served by public transit), it's a good alternative to the very busy Horseshoe Bay-Departure Bay routing. Fares for either route are C$10 (US$9) adult and C$34 (US$30) per standard vehicle.

VISITOR INFORMATION

Tourism Nanaimo is located at Beban House, 2290 Bowen Rd., Nanaimo, BC V9T 3K7 (© **800/663-7337** or 250/756-0106; www.tourismnanaimo.com). A summer-only information center operates at the Pioneer Waterfront Plaza near the Bastion.

GETTING AROUND

BY CAR   Be alert to street signs; Nanaimo's roads go off at angles and change names along the way. For example, Bastion Street becomes Fitzwilliam Street (once Nanaimo's red-light district), which becomes 3rd Street, which leads to the Parkway, before becoming Jingle Pot Road, named for the time when miners walked the route to work, "jingling" their lunches in metal pails along the way. Street parking is ample and most hotels have secured underground parking.

BY PUBLIC TRANSPORTATION   Nanaimo Regional Transit System (© 250/ 390-4531; www.rdn.bc.ca) provides public transport through Nanaimo's suburbs, mainly residential areas and a couple of strip malls. From a visitor's standpoint, they're buses that go nowhere unless you're heading up to Parksville and Qualicum. Fares are C$2.25 (US$2) for adults and C$2 (US$1.75) for seniors and youths. If, for some reason, you're out in the boonies where there are few official stops, you can flag one down. **BY TAXI**   For cab service, call **AC Taxi** (© **800/753-1231** or 250/753-1231) or **Swiftsure Taxi** (© **250/753-8911**). You would be lucky to find a taxi hanging around the bus station or a downtown hotel; better to call ahead.

THE TOP ATTRACTIONS

The best thing about Nanaimo is its **Pioneer Waterfront**—refurbished with multi-level walkways, banks of flowers, marina restaurants and gift shops—some touristy, others worthwhile. On most summer days, the walkways have a mix of one-person stalls selling paintings, junk jewelry, and carvings, and come Friday, they're joined by local farm vendors selling fresh produce, homemade jams, and baked goods. The

Harbourside Walkway actually extends all the way to Departure Bay, 4km (2.5 miles) away, and is a popular route for joggers. The waterfront is anchored by the **Bastion,** Nanaimo's oldest building and the only remaining fort structure of its type in North America.

The **Old City Quarter** is also undergoing a facelift. Although only a three-block area, it's where you'll find some good restaurants, and specialty gift shops such as **Linda's Gift Gallery**, 70 Church St. (© **250/754-1021**), for hand-made crafts, jewelry, and whimsical items; **Shanghai Tea Emporium**, 13B Commerical St. (© **250/ 753-9957**); and the **Artisan's Studio**, 70 Bastion St. (© **250/753-6151**), a co-op gallery run by and featuring the work of, local artists. **Hill's Native Art**, 76 Bastion St. (© **250/755-7873**) is a reputable place for quality First Nations art. Just be aware that the "new" historic district backs onto the older area that still sports a couple of seamy clubs.

The Nanaimo Bastion   The white, fortified tower was built by the Hudson's Bay Company in 1852 to protect its Nanaimo trading post. At that time, Haida Indians traveled down from the northerly Queen Charlotte Islands and mounted a series of raids. Its three floors house a hands-on exhibit that explores early life in Nanaimo: On the first floor is The Company's Clerk's Office displaying coal-mining gear of the time; The Arsenal on the second floor (in summer, the Bastion Guards recreate the firing of the noon cannon daily at 11:45am), and the third-floor Refuge, once used in times of danger, now has displays on blacksmithing, homemaking, and farming.

> ### Know Nanaimo
>
> Pronounced *Na-nye-mo*, the city's name originated when the first white settlers tried to adapt a Coast Salish world "Snu-Ney-Muxw" meaning "The Meeting Place," into English. It was originally called Colvilletown.

Bastion & Front St., on Pioneer Waterfront Plaza. © **250/753-1821**. Admission C$1 (US90¢); May–Sept, daily 10am–4:30pm.

Nanaimo District Museum   Located in Piper's Park, which is also home to a miner's cottage and a restored 1890s locomotive, this museum is worth a visit even on a sunny day, and even though you have to climb two steep flights of stairs to reach the entrance. It offers a good overview of the region's history, depicted through intriguing dioramas featured alongside actual artifacts. The recreations of a Salish Indian village (the Snuneymuxw—the "Nanaimo people") and a mine have a very frontier feel. Make your own petroglyph rubbings for an unusual souvenir or find Snuneymuxw wooden carvings in the gift shop. The museum will relocate in 2008 to become a part of the new Nanaimo Convention Centre.

100 Cameron Rd. © **250/753-1821**; www.nanaimomuseum.ca. Admission C$2 (US$1.75) adults, C$1.75 (US$1.55) seniors, C75¢ (US65¢) children 6–12. Mid-May to Labor Day daily 10am–5pm; after Labor Day to mid-May Tues–Sat 10am–5pm.

OUTDOOR ACTIVITIES

SCUBA DIVING   Jacques Cousteau called the waters around Nanaimo "the best temperate water diving in the world, second only to the Red Sea," so suffice to say, scuba diving is big business here. Nicknamed the "Emerald Sea," its water is clear enough to see the likes of giant Pacific octopi, colorful sea anemones, and herds of marine mammals that appear to just "hang around" for entertainment. **Dodds Narrows,** between Vancouver Island and Mudge Island, is a particularly hot diving spot.

Central Vacouver Island

NANAIMO
Best Western Dorchester **1**
Coast Bastion Inn **2**
Grand Hotel Nanaimo **3**
Painted Turtle Guesthouse **4**

GABRIOLA ISLAND
Hummingbird Lodge B&B **5**
Surf Lodge **6**

PARKSVILLE &
QUALICUM BEACH
Bahari Vacation Suites **10**
Beach Acres Resort **7**
Pacific Shores Resort **8**
Tigh-Na-Mara Resort **9**

PORT ALBERNI
Best Western Barclay Hotel **12**
Hospitality Inn **11**

TOFINO & UCLUELET
Cable Cove Inn **14**
Canadian Princess Resort **21**
Clayoquot Wilderness Resort **13**
Inn at Tough City **15**
Long Beach Lodge Resort **19**
Middle Beach Lodge **17**
Pacific Sands Resort **18**
A Snug Harbour Inn **22**
Tauca Lea Coast Resort **20**
Wickaninnish Inn **16**
Woods End Landing Cottages **23**

Other areas include **Snake Island Wall** (*Tip:* even if you're not a diver, you can snorkel with the seals on nearby Snake Island), **Gabriola Passage,** and the **largest artificial upright reef in the world.** The reef is made up of a number of sunken wrecks, including the **HMCS *Saskatchewan,*** a 366-foot Canadian Naval destroyer sunk in 1997, and the **HMCS *Cape Breton.*** In 2005, *Rivtow Lion,* a retired deep-sea rescue tug, was added to the reef. The *Rivtow* rests at a manageable depth of about 15m (50 ft.) right in Departure Bay, making it a great dive for those wanting to get a bit more comfortable before heading down deeper to the Cape Breton or Saskatchewan.

A good diving operator, which offers guided dives, equipment rentals, and instruction with fast custom-dive boats, is **Ocean Explorers Diving** (1956 Zorkin Rd., near Departure Bay; ✆ **800/233-4145** or 250/753-2055; www.oceanexplorersdiving.com). Prices start at C$65 (US$57) per dive.

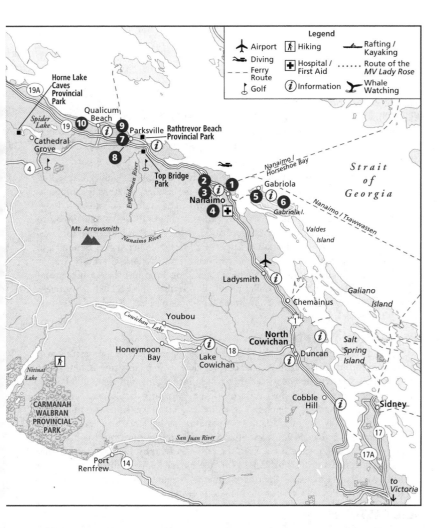

BUNGEE JUMPING Keeping your head above water delivers something quite different, if you've got the nerve. Set high over the Nanaimo River lies **Wild Play at the Bungy Zone** (© 888/668-7874 or 250/714-7874; www.wildplayparks.com), touted as the "Only Legal Bridge Bungy Jump Site in North America." If free-falling 43m (140 ft.) at speeds of up to 140 kmph (87 mph), doesn't appeal, watching the bungy bravehearts is still a thrill. An on-site gift shop sells plenty of bungy paraphernalia, so you can always pretend you dared. Jumps are C$99 (US$87) and include an I Did It! T-shirt. But that isn't all you'll find here. There's a high-elevation swing that cinches you up in a slingshot-like device (C$79/US$70) and a zip-line ride that zips you across a wooded canyon at almost 100 kmph (60 mph). The zip trips are also a part of the aerial tree obstacle course called Tree Go that's set some 3 to 15m (10–50 ft.) high in a Douglas fir forest with suspended bridges, scramble nets, and swinging logs.

Although there's a children's-only version of the course, most experiences have a minimum age limit of 12 years old. Tree Go prices range from C$19 to C$39 (US$17–US$34). Bungy Zone is a great spot for teenagers who are looking for an adrenaline rush.

GOLF   **Nanaimo Golf Club** (2800 Highland Blvd. *©* **250-758-6332;** www.nanaimo golfclub.ca) is a pretty 6,700-yard course; green fees March to September are C$66 (US$58), with reduced rates off season. **Cottonwood Golf Course** (1975 Haslam Rd.; *©* **250/245-5157;** www.cottonwoodgolfcourse.com) is an 18-hole, par-72 course with panoramic views of the coastal mountains. Green fees range from C$38–C$44 (US$33–US$39).

HIKING   One of Nanaimo's lesser known trails is the 2-km (1-mile) **Cable Bay Trail.** You hike through a serene forest to Cable Bay Bridge, where you can beach-comb or observe migrating sealions (Oct.–Apr.). The trail is an off-leash (dog-friendly) area. **Parkway Trail,** which runs alongside Hwy. 19, links Aulds Road to Chase River. The 20-km (12.5-mile) paved and tree-lined span is best suited for long-distance cyclists and joggers. It leads to Buttertubs Marsh, Colliery Dam, Bowen Park, and the Harbourfront Walkway via the Millstone Trail. Because the **E&N Trail** is paved and level, it's a magnet not only for walkers, but for in-line skaters, bikers, and skateboarders too. The 8-km (5-mile) paved trail parallels the E&N Railway tracks and the old Island Highway 19A from Rosehill Avenue to Mostar Road and is the best option for "wheels."

PROTECTION ISLAND

This island is actually a part of the City of Nanaimo, and sits like a protecting arm a kilometer offshore in Nanaimo Harbour. As close as it is, this tiny island, about 5km (3 miles) in circumference, is almost a place time forgot. With about 200 homes, and a pirate theme that runs rampant (Capt. Morgan's Boulevard, Smugglers Lake, and Pirate Lane), it has no schools, churches, post office, stores, or other busi-nesses, and virtually no cars. Island transportation is by foot, bike, or golf cart. Ferries—actually converted lifeboats—make the 10-minute run from the mainland from 7am to 10pm, on the hour. Even the pub, the **Dinghy Dock** (Canada's only floating pub/restaurant; *©* **250/753-2373**), keeps ferry hours, with last call in time for mainlanders to catch the 10pm ferry home to Nanaimo. At low tide, hikers can even wade across Pirate's Causeway to Newcastle Island.

NEWCASTLE ISLAND

Originally settled by the Coast Salish, then mined for coal and sandstone, and later a resort island for Canadian Pacific Steamship Company, **Newcastle Island Provincial Park** (*©* **250/391-2300**) has largely reverted to its natural state, though you can still

---

A Marmot Moment

The Vancouver Island marmot is rarer than even the giant panda. It is found only on Vancouver Island, and its primary habitat, just outside of Nanaimo, is protected by a special trust organization.

In the mid-1980s, the population was estimated to be over 300 animals; today the count is half that number, making them one of the rarest and most endangered mammals in the world.

(Fun Fact Tubs Ahoy!

For more than 30 years, dare-devils have raced across the Georgia Strait in one-
and two-man craft. In the early days, vessels were old clawfoot tubs fitted with
engines. Often, they sank in the harbor. In fact, these days the first racing tub
to sink now wins the prestigious Silver Plunger Award. Today, most contestants
speed across the whitecaps in sleek-looking, specially designed high-tech boats,
although there are always a handful of wildly creative vessels that hark back to
earlier times. The race is the highlight of the week-long Marine Festival held in
July, which includes a street fair, a parade, and a spirited atmosphere. For details,
visit **www.bathtubbing.com**

---

see remnants of the 1850s coal mine, sandstone, and pulp stone quarries, and two
First Nations villages. Many visitors kayak over from the mainland; others make the
10-minute crossing with **Scenic Ferries** (© **250/753-5141**), which runs trips daily
on the hour from 10am to 8pm. The round-trip fare is C$7 (US$6.20) adults; C$6
(US$5.30) seniors and children; bikes are C$2 (US$1.80). As a protected marine
park, it has a network of hiking and cycling and 18 camp sites (C$14/US$12 per
night) with toilets, showers, fire pits and wood.

Trail lengths vary, but if you're up to walking 2 to 4km (1.25–2.5 miles), the **Mallard Lake Trail,** the **Channel Trail,** and the **Shoreline Trail** are among the most
rewarding. The Mallard Lake Trail takes you through the forested heart of the island
to a freshwater lake; you can return via the Channel Trail that follows the shoreline
across from the mainland and past an old sandstone quarry. The Shoreline Trail is on
the opposite (ocean) side of the island overlooking Nanaimo, and winds itself up to
Kanaka Bay Beach. If you've the energy, continue on to viewpoints at McKay Point
and Giovando Lookout before hiking back past an old mine shaft and joining Channel Trail back to the ferry docks. The entire perimeter hike is 7.5km (4.7 miles). There
are interpretive signs along the way as well as a visitor's center, snack bar, and gift shop.

WHERE TO STAY

Best Western Dorchester Hotel   This Best Western is not only a cut above most
Best Westerns, it's the best value for the money in terms of services, quality, and central location in the Old City Quarter. The hotel stands on the site of the original Hudson's Bay Company trading post. Guest rooms may be on the small side, but they are
comfortably furnished with quality amenities and if you opt for a harbor-view room,
the vista is more than worth the C$10 (US$9) extra you'll pay. Book via the Internet
and the savings can be substantial. Check out the stunning chandeliers in the lobby
and the elaborate columns in the dining room—they came from the opera house that
also once stood on this site.

70 Church St., Nanaimo, BC V9R 5H4. © **800/661-2449** or 250/754-6835. Fax 250/754-2638. www.dorchester
nanaimo.com. 65 units. C$109–C$169 (US$96–US$149) double. Extra person C$10 (US$9). Senior, Internet, and seasonal discounts available. AE, DC, DISC, MC, V. Free parking. Pets accepted C$20 (US$18) per night. **Amenities:**
Restaurant; lounge; golf course nearby; business services; laundry service; same-day dry cleaning. *In room:* TV
w/movies, dataport, coffeemaker, hair dryer, iron.

Coast Bastion Inn ℱ   Overlooking the Strait of Georgia, right on the inner harbor,
this hotel feels geared to the business traveler. All guest rooms are (drably) comfortable

but have waterfront views. Some suites have Jacuzzis with upgraded amenities and a lot more space, especially the corner units. The extremely courteous staff seems to enjoy fulfilling every request whether it's recommending spa services or arranging for bike rentals nearby. Because the hotel is connected to the Port Theatre, which hosts plays and musical concerts from Bruce Cockburn to London Quartets, theatre packages are usually the best value in town.

11 Bastion St., Nanaimo, BC V9R 6E4. (C) **800/663-1144** or 250/753-6601. Fax 250/753-4155. www.coasthotels. com. 177 units. May–Sept C$152 (US$134) standard, C$167 (US$147) superior; Oct–Apr C$132 (US$116) standard, C$147 (US$129) superior. Extra person C$10 (US$9). Senior, AAA, off-season discounts and packages available. AE, DC, DISC, MC, V. Self-parking C$4.75 (US$4.20). Valet parking C$9.25 (US$8.15). Pets accepted C$10 (US$9). **Amenities:** Restaurant; lounge; health club; Jacuzzi; sauna; concierge; 24-hr. room service; babysitting; laundry service; same-day dry cleaning. *In room:* A/C, TV w/play movies, dataport, minibar, fridge, coffeemaker, hair dryer, iron.

Grand Hotel Nanaimo   This is Nanaimo's most luxurious full-service hotel. The facilities, especially the impressive lobby, are bright and modern. Accommodations range from standard guest rooms to spacious one-bedroom suites with jetted tubs. All have fireplaces and kitchens or kitchenettes; many have balconies. Although located on the edge of the Rutherford Golf Course, the greens have been abandoned and now only offer great views and good walks. Golfers can tee off only at the nearby Nanaimo Golf Club ((C) 250/758-6332). The Grand also has 12 fully furnished two- and three-bedroom townhouses for long-term stays.

4898 Rutherford Rd., Nanaimo, BC V9T 5P1. (C) **877/414-7263** or 250/758-3000. Fax 250/729-2808. www.thegrand hotelnanaimo.com. 72 units. May–Sept C$119–C$149 (US$105–US$131); Oct–Apr C$89–C$119 (US$78–US$105). Extra person C$10 (US$9). Senior, AAA discounts available. AE, DC, MC, V. Free parking. **Amenities:** Restaurant; lounge; small indoor heated pool; golf course nearby; health club; limited room service, laundry service; same-day dry cleaning. *In room:* A/C, TV, dataport, kitchen or kitchenette, coffeemaker, hair dryer, iron.

Painted Turtle Guesthouse *(Value*   A hybrid between an inn and a boutique hostel, this is an affordable alternative with a central location that's hard to beat. Guest rooms are simply furnished and spotlessly clean. All have queen beds; the family suites have additional bunk beds, and some rooms are set up to share, hostel-style. The share-bathroom ratio is about three rooms to one bathroom and because there are separate lavatories, lineups aren't an issue. The Great Room is bright and inviting with a large communal kitchen, an eating area, and sofas around a gas fireplace. It can get very social at night—guitars, singing, or just meeting your fellow travelers who are a mix of backpackers, families on a budget, and active retirees.

121 Bastion St., Nanaimo, BC V9R 3A2. (C) **866/309-4432** or 250/753-4432. www.paintedturtle.ca. 20 units. C$20–C$75 (US$18–US$66). MC, V. **Amenities:** Lounge; full kitchen; coin-operated laundry; complimentary-high speed-Internet. *In room:* Share bath, no phone.

Foodies' Fancy

Edible British Columbia ((C) **604/662-3644;** www.ediblebritish-columbia.com) hosts a series of two- and three-night kayaking getaways, where paddling and culinary adventure go hand in hand. Professional guides put a gourmet touch on every meal; accommodation choices include camping or intimate lodges. Prices start at C$699 (US$615) per person, inclusive of transfers from Victoria or Vancouver to launch site near Nanaimo.

WHERE TO DINE

Central Nanaimo has a surprising number of good dining spots. **Glow World Cuisine,** 7 Victoria Rd. (© **250/741-8858**), has an extensive tapas menu (tapas is very "de rigueur" in Nanaimo) and an offbeat location in a converted firehall. **Modern Food**, 221 Commerical St. (© **250/754-5022**), is a funky cafe offering over-stacked sandwiches and vegetarian fare. The **Lighthouse Bistro and Pub**, off Harbourside Walkway at 50 Anchor Way (© **250/754-3212**), serves up traditional burgers and grills alongside waterfront views of the seaplanes coming and going.

Acme Food Company *(Finds* ECLECTIC   Located on one of downtown Nanaimo's busiest corners, this triangular restaurant caters to all tastes with a range of items that leaves no choice unturned, whether you want to build your own pizza and pastas, or try one of their soups, sushi, grilled salmon, or steaks. One menu alone is dedicated to oysters from Fanny Bay, Quadra Island, Cortez, Redonda, and Prince Edward islands, each with accompaniments such as pineapple or tequila salsas. Acme is a popular hangout for locals who enjoy an unexpected, flavorful variation on standards: one of Acme's cheeseburgers features blue cheese, sun-dried tomatoes, and roasted garlic; a spicier version comes with Cajun spice and Brie. They also offer takeout.

14 Commercial St. © **250/753-0042**. www.acmefoodco.ca. Reservations recommended. Main courses C$8–C$23 (US$7–US$20) MC, V. Daily 11am–midnight.

Mahle House PACIFIC NORTHWEST   Built in 1904, Mahle (pronounced "Molly") house is a lovingly restored delight overlooking an enclosed English-style garden. This family owned restaurant has been a local favorite for almost 20 years, and the menu changes weekly. Items may include marinated duck with peanut-crusted prawns and a coconut curry sauce, a trio of tenderloins, or free-range chicken stuffed with Dungeness crab and a lemongrass sauce. Everything comes from local suppliers, while the herbs used to season these dishes come from the restaurant's own garden. Special evenings include wine tastings, "Tapas Thursdays," and "Adventurous Wednesdays," featuring a multi-course meal for C$40 (US$35). The wine list is extensive, and has been a Gold Medal winner in the Vancouver International Wine Festival.

2104 Hemer Rd. at Cedar (10 min. south of Nanaimo). © **250/722-3621**. Reservations recommended. Main courses C$16–C$32 (US$14–US$28). MC, V. Wed–Sun 5–10pm. Closed Mon–Tues.

Milanos GREEK/ITALIAN   Housed in an 1892 heritage home, Milanos is a family operated restaurant where the menu is a hybrid of dishes from Calabresian cuisine to Eastern Mediterranean specialties. Servings are on the generous side, so if you've a small appetite, consider sharing, especially if you choose the antipasti-antipasto appetizer that includes pepperoni arrostiti, marinated artichokes, olives, ratatouille, hot peppers, provolone and Italian salami, and focaccia bread. It's almost a meal in itself. Other items include a marinated rack of lamb, halibut with white wine sauce, and a fresh pear, mango and Cointreau salsa, and a range of pasta dishes from traditional spaghetti and meatballs to a wheat-free lasagna. For dessert there are homemade gelatos and a delicious chocolate-mousse cake, layered with white hazelnut cream, covered with a dark chocolate ganache and accompanied by pools of raspberry and mango sauce.

247 Milton St. © **250/740-1000**. www.milanocafe.ca. C$8–C$12 (US$7–US$11). MC, V. Mon–Sat 11am–midnight.

Nanaimo's Best Dessert, Bar None

The Nanaimo Bar—a sweet three-layered confectionery of chocolate, custard cream, and graham wafers, may be known internationally, but its origins remain a mystery. Some legends trace its roots to Nanaimo's coal-mining days when families of miners sent care packages that often included the rich custard treat. Other accounts say Duth settlers brought the recipe over in the early 1900s. Local historians figure the Nanaimo Bar was most likely inspired by a recipe in a 1952 *Woman's Auxiliary to the Nanaimo Hospital Cookbook.*

Tania's Tapas Bar & Grill TAPAS   A casual, jazz-style bistro that is a clever conversion of two side-by-side storefronts where the more light-filled front room is geared for daytime dining (breakfast and lunch) and the moody back-room, aka "The Red Room," is for romantic trysts, and live music. The tapas selection is large enough to suit every taste, with everything from chicken satay, and coconut prawns to apricot-and date-stuffed port tenderloin, all to be savored alongside imaginative martini mixes. There's jazz and blues Thursday through Saturday (get there by 7:30pm to snag a booth) and an "all jammers welcome" night on Wednesday, which is about as fun and impromptu as music gets. Remember, Nanaimo is Diana Krall's hometown, so you know the area generates talent!

1075 Front St. (℃ **250/753-5181.** www.taniasdowntown.com. Tapas C$5–C$9 (US$4.40–US$7.20); main courses C$12–C$23 (US$11–US$20). AE, MC, V. Tues–Sun 9:30am–midnight, Mon 9:30am–3pm.

Wesley Street Cafe 🎯🎯 PACIFIC NORTHWEST   This is a small, charming restaurant. Dining options progress from a casual lunch that includes gourmet soups and sandwiches, to a more sophisticated dinner menu that offers items such as roast quail with an exotic mushroom stuffing. The chef is more than willing to adapt menu items to accommodate allergies. Monday through Thursday, there's a great-value three-course dinner for C$28 (US$25) alongside an enormous wine list featuring many of the better B.C. labels. Dine inside or, in summer, opt for the flower-covered patio.

321 Wesley St., Nanaimo. ℃ **250/753-6057.** www.wesleycafe.com. Lunch C$9–C$14 (US$7.90–US$12), dinner C$17–C$28 (US$15–US$25). AE, MC, V. Mon–Fri 11:30am–2:30pm and 5:30–10pm; Sat–Sun noon–2:30pm and 5:30–10pm.

---

2 Gabriola Island

Although only a 20-minute ferry ride from Nanaimo Harbour, **Gabriola Island** feels a world away from the bustle of Vancouver Island. Known as the "Queen of the Gulf Islands," Gabriola provides a little of everything: sandy beaches, kayaking, canoeing, fine restaurants, artisan's studios and galleries, petroglyphs, and tide pools.

ESSENTIALS
GETTING THERE
BC Ferries operates a vehicle and passenger ferry between Gabriola Island and Nanaimo with crossings leaving almost every hour from 6am to 11pm. Sailing time is 20 minutes. A car passage is C$6.50 (US$5.75) per person; C$16 (US$14) per vehicle; and C$2 (US$1.75) per kayak. Bicycles are carried free of charge.

If you're getting to the island by your own boat, you can find moorage, services, and lodging at **Silva Bay Marina** (© 250/247-8931; www.silvabay.com) and **Pages Marina** (© 250/247-8931; www.pagesresort.com), where you can buy groceries, fishing licenses and tackle, as well as rent bicycles and diving gear.

GETTING AROUND

Most people bring their cars or bikes, but if you do decide to come on foot but want to tour, call Island Cabs © 250/247-0049. Gabriola is an easy island to navigate with a main circular road, appropriately called South Road and North Road depending on which side of the island you are, that leads to a number of side trips. If time is of the essence, there are some pastoral roads crossing the island's midsection. Like many of the Gulf Islands, but perhaps more so on Gabriola since its more northerly location has protected it from big city influences and people, hitch-hiking is regarded as safe and dependable, particularly among islanders themselves.

VISITOR INFORMATION

The Island has a first-rate Visitor Information Centre, located at **Folklore Village Centre** (© 250/247-9332; www.gabriolaisland.org), which is not "folksy" at all, but quite a swish shopping mall housed in the recycled Folklife Pavilion from Expo '86.

EXPLORING THE AREA

Overall, Gabriola Island has a whimsical atmosphere, which you grasp as soon as you get off the ferry. When you disembark, look up at the **White Hart Pub,** next to the terminal, and you'll see an eye-catching cyclist named Mary Ann, pedaling like fury on her recycled bike. Mary Ann, a life-size polychrome folk art carving, is an example of the tongue-in-cheek wood creations scattered all over the island by **FOGO Folk Art Studio** (3065 Commodore Way; © 250/247-8082; www.fogoart.com). The artistic center of the island, though, is at **Gabriola Artworks** (575 North Rd., © 250/247-7412; www.gabriolaartworks.com), a two-level, 279 sq. m (3,000 sq. ft.) gallery of work by local talent. Gabriola is also home to the **Silva Bay Shipyard School** (3200 Silva Bay Rd., © 250/ 247-8809), Canada's only traditional wooden boat-building school. Visitors are welcome to view works-in-progress every Friday afternoon, 2-4pm.

The island's biggest natural attraction is the **Malaspina Galleries,** an amazing series of sandstone formations carved by the surf into unusual caves and caverns. Most beaches are protected, providing excellent tidal pools and safe swimming, especially at **Drumbeg Park,** where the sun heats the sandstone rocks enough to dry your towels. Scuba divers also use this area, as it provides shore-based access to nearby **Gabriola Passage.** Other recreational activities include biking and kayaking. Helpful charter contacts include **Silver Blue Charters** (© 250/247-8807, or boat phone © 250/755-6150, www.silverbluecharters.com) for sea-fishing excursions; **The Kayak Shack**, (1956 Zorkin Rd., next to the ferry dock; © 800/529/0142 or 250/753-3234; www.thekayakshack.com) and **Jim's Kayaking** (© 250/247-8335) for rentals and guided paddles, and **Gabriola Cycle & Kayak** (© 250/247-8271) for bike rentals.

WHERE TO STAY AND DINE

Hummingbird Lodge B & B 🏵🏵   This lodge is a beautiful hand-built 465-sq.-m (5,000 sq.-ft.) home made up of the cedar and alder trees from the area. Rooms are clean and comfortable, decorated with island art. High and vaulted ceilings seem to bring the outdoors in, especially with floor-to-ceiling windows and over 2,000 sq. ft. of open and covered decks. The sunroom is especially sunny, and home to a variety of instruments—a piano, guitars, and a banjo (as well as a comprehensive musical CD library), to strike the right chord. The lodge is private and near to secluded, sandy Whalebone Beach.

RR#1 Site 55 C–54, Gabriola Island, BC V0R 1X0. (C) 877/551-9383 or 250/247-9300. www.hummingbirdlodgebb. com. 3 units. Mid-May to mid-Sept C$119–C$139 (US$105–US$122); mid-Sept to mid-May C$79–C$99 (US$70–US$87). MC, V. Nonsmoking facilities. **Amenities:** Lounge; dining room; kitchenette; fridge; hot tub; massage; microwave; BBQ; sunroom. *In-room:* Hairdryer, no phone.

Silva Bay Bar & Grill (A) CASUAL   This is really the only show on the island. Located at the Silva Bay Marina, it's the best place to savor a sunset and to nibble your way through an extensive menu. Many dishes are designed for sharing over an on-tap ale. Although it's primarily a pub-style restaurant there's also a fully licensed area where families are welcome. In summer, tables extend along the dock overlooking the marina, and there's a barbecue deck for grills and salads.

3383 South Rd., in the Silva Bay Resort and Marina. (C) 250/247-8662. Menu items from under C$10 (US$9); main courses around C$22 (US$19). MC, V. Daily 11am–midnight.

Surf Lodge   In spite of two walls of windows in the great room, the cedar siding throughout this lodge takes woodsy to the extreme, especially when set against the impressive floor-to-ceiling river-rock fireplace. Guest rooms and cabins also sport wood everywhere, making them a bit dark. Still, they're spacious and clean with crisp linens and puffy duvets. Most have ocean views, some with a window seat. There are three self-contained cabins, which are ideal for families. The pub and dining room are both rather characterless, save for the stunning views.

885 Berry Point Rd., Gabriola, BC V0R 1X1. (C) 250/247-9231. Fax 250/247-8336. www.surflodge.com. 7 rooms and 8 cabins. C$70–C$145 (US$62–US$128) double. Pets in cabins only C$20 (US$18). MC, V. **Amenities:** Lounge; pub; kitchenettes in cabins. *In room:* No phone.

3 Parksville & Qualicum Beach

There was a time when Parksville and Qualicum Beach were sleepy seaside towns that swelled with family vacationers every summer. They are still the most popular resort towns on Vancouver Island, but Oceanside, as the region is now called, is bursting with development. Waves of retirees are making this golf mecca their year-round home and young families are escaping expensive urban neighborhoods. In the past two decades, the area's population has nearly tripled, and is expected to double again by 2016.

As a consequence, much of Parksville's original park-like attributes have been overtaken by used car lots and motels that now line the highway through town, giving it a strip-mall-like air. It does redeem itself, however, with its expansive beaches and waterfront resorts. In fact, once through downtown Parksville the Oceanside shoreline along Hwy 19A opens up vistas to mountains and oceans, lush parks, formal gardens, and quaint shops and galleries. The Oceanside area extends beyond Parksville and Qualicum to include Horne Lake, Bowser, and Deep Bay, all sharing the same stretch of magnificent beach and among them offering activities such as swimming, nature hikes, golf, tennis, and spelunking.

Mark Your Calendar

April: **The Brant Festival** celebrates the arrival of thousands of migrating Brant geese. With more than 250 species of birds making their home in the coastal estuaries, the Qualicum Beach area is a premier destination for both serious ornithologists and amateur birders. Call © **866/288-7878** for information.

August: Ebbing tides can expose up to a kilometer of shore, leaving large shallow pools in the sand, perfect for sandcastle building and collecting sand dollars. In fact, the sands are so good that they host Parksville's **International Sandcastle Competition** during which competitors race—between tides—to create award-winning sculptures. Call © **250/248-4819** for information or visit www.parksvillebeachfest.ca.

September: The Qualicum Beach Harvest of Music brings together musicians from all over the world for a nine-day multicultural festival of music from Gypsy jazz to Japanese taiko drumming. Performances and workshops take place at Qualicum Beach Civic Centre, the Old School House, and other small venues. Call © **250/752-6133** or check www.theoldschoolhouse.org for information.

ESSENTIALS
GETTING THERE
BY CAR   Parksville and Qualicum Beach are located 36km (22 miles) north of Nanaimo, off Highway 19. The closest airport is in Nanaimo.

BY BUS   Laidlaw Coach Lines/Island Coach Lines (© **800/318-0818** or 250/385-4411) offers service between Nanaimo and Parksville/Qualicum Beach along the Highway 1–Highway 19 corridor. One-way fares are C$10 (US$9) for adults. Fares for seniors are 10% less; fares for children 5 to 11 are 50% less. **Greyhound Canada** (© **800/661-8747**; www.greyhound.ca) handles schedules and reservations.

BY TRAIN   VIA Rail's **Malahat** (© **800/561-8630** or 250/383-4324; www.viarail.com) stops in Parksville and Qualicum Beach on its daily trip from Victoria to Courtenay.

BY AIR   KD Air (© **800/665-4244** or 604/688-9957 or 250/752-5884; www.kdair.com) offers several daily flights from Vancouver to the Qualicum Beach Airport, for C$230 (US$202) round trip. One-way fares are C$138 (US$121) with discounts for seniors and children.

VISITOR INFORMATION
The **Parksville Visitor Information Centre** is at 1275 East Island Hwy., (P.O. Box 99), Parksville, BC V9P 2G3 (©**250/248-3613;** www.chamber.parksville.bc.ca). The **Qualicum Beach Visitor Information Centre** is at 2711 West Island Hwy., Qualicum Beach, BC V9K 2C4 (© **250/752-9532;** www.qualicum.bc.ca).

EXPLORING PARKSVILLE & QUALICUM BEACH

Of the two communities, Parksville is by far the more developed, both in terms of commercial businesses and in its destination resorts (see "Where to Stay") which have all contributed to its reputation as "Canada's Riviera." Although Parksville is a haven for fast food junkies, these are countered with a growing number of quality restaurants and specialty activities. For example, if you're a cheese aficionado, check out **Little Qualicum Cheeseworks** (403 Lowry's Rd., Parksville ℂ **250/954-3931**). From June to September, there are guided tours and hayrides around the farm, as well as a small gift shop where you can taste and purchase their artisan cheeses. Although based in Parksville, **Pacific Rainforest Adventure Tours** (215 Chestnut St.; ℂ **250/248-3667**; www.rainforestnaturehikes) provides easy walking half-day and full-day sight-seeing and nature tours (suitable for seniors) to various destinations in the region such as **Cathedral Grove, Pacific Rim National Park,** and **Green Mountain**, home to the endangered Vancouver Island marmot. This particular tour takes you by the Nanaimo River through a working forest and requires you to book a year in advance to receive a special permit.

Qualicum lies about 10 minutes north of Parksville, and although it overlooks the same stretch of beach, is far more genteel. While here, follow the Art Walk to galleries and artisan studios and browse the shops in the town center, which is actually set a few kilometers from the beach and has a garden village ambience—perhaps because Qualicum residents are passionate gardeners, having earned their community the coveted Four Blooms Award in a province-wide annual Communities in Bloom competition. Take time to visit the **Old School House** ⭐, 122 Fern Rd. W. (ℂ **250/752-6133**; www.theoldschoolhouse.org), which exhibits the works of potters, weavers, painters, and other local artists. It also holds frequent workshops, classes, and Sunday afternoon concerts as well as jazz gatherings on Tuesday evening.

Milner Gardens & Woodland ⭐⭐   Once the personal retreat of Queen Elizabeth and Prince Phillip, these princely gardens are now open to the public. After you've toured the Cotswolds-style house, put on your wellies and get set for a fabulous garden walk through a 4-hectare (10-acre) artist's garden within a 24-hectare (60-acre) old-growth Douglas-fir forest. It's a living laboratory of rare and unusual plants, combining avenues of rhododendrons (more than 500), indigenous plants, and rare and exotic species with towering Douglas firs. The ocean views are breathtaking, but then, you would expect nothing less for royals. Afternoon tea is served.

2179 W. Island Hwy., Qualicum Beach ℂ 250/752-8573 www.milnergardens.org. Admission C$10 (US$9) adult; C$6 (US$5.30) students. May–Sept daily 10am–5pm; Apr and Oct Thurs–Sun 10am–5pm. Closed Nov–Mar.

REGIONAL, PROVINCIAL & NATIONAL PARKS

Rathtrevor Beach Provincial Park ⭐⭐   is a family-oriented park that has special nature displays, interpretive walks and safe sandy beaches. The interesting sandstone formations on the beach, gentle tides, and forested campsites make this one of the

---

Fun Fact   **How Come Qualicum?**

The name Qualicum comes from *squal-li,* "chum salmon" in the language of the Pentlatch people who once fished here but were devastated by smallpox in the late 1700s.

Tips **Giving the Sun the Slip**

Leave Nanaimo in the morning to avoid afternoon sun in your eyes (and return in the afternoon so the sun is behind you in the west). In places, this is a narrow, winding, slippery, mountainous road, which you do not want to drive for the first time at night. Be sure to get gasoline in Nanaimo if you plan to drive straight through to the west coast.

---

most popular camping areas in the province (see "Where to Stay"). Located approximately 5km (3 miles) up Englishman River from Rathtrevor Provincial Park, **Top Bridge** is designated "Mountain Bike Park" and is extremely popular with bikers from all over the world for its purpose-built trails deep in the forest. Nearby **Englishman River Falls Park** is one of the prettiest parks in the region, with camping, picnic areas, swimming, and easy hiking. There are two spectacular waterfalls in the midst of the forest; during the summer a crystal clear pool at the base of the lower falls turns into one of the best swimming holes in the area. Come fall, Englishman River fills with the return of spawning salmon and throughout the year, the area serves as a protected estuary for more than 250 species of resident and migrating birds.

Just east of Parksville on Hwy. 4, the **Mt. Arrowsmith Regional Park** offers several moderate to difficult hiking trails from the **Cameron Lake** picnic area. The moderately easy hiking trail up to the 1,818m (5,963 ft.) summit follows, in part, an old logging railway. The climb passes through a series of climatic zones, each with different vegetation and forest cover. The view from the slopes and high alpine meadows of Mount Arrowsmith overlooks the entire Strait of Georgia. Allow 6 to 7 hours for the round trip. For something completely different, consider kayaking out from the Parksville-Qualicum shores to **Jedediah Marine Park**, located between Lasqueti Island and Texada Island in the Sabine Channel of the Strait of Georgia. Accessible only by boat, this recently created park was originally homesteaded in the late 1800s. The island is now inhabited by wild goats and sheep. The island has no amenities but the settlers' cabins and outbuildings are maintained in their original condition so visitors can see how people lived on the coast before roads and electricity.

If you prefer to stay on land, **Spider Lake Park** is a smaller day-use park on the lake located just off the Horne Lake Road. Stocked with small mouthed bass and trout, the lake has excellent fishing and a warm safe sandy beach to launch kayaks and canoes. No motorized watercraft are allowed, so it attracts swimmers as well as anglers. Many visitors bypass Spider Lake, however, in favor of Horne Lake Regional Park that sits at the west end of Horne Lake, adjacent to Horne Lakes Caves Provincial Park, (see below). This 105-hectacre (260-acre) regional park includes about 3km (2 miles) of lakefront and another 2km (1 mile) of riverfront along the Qualicum River. Offering both wooded (C\$17/US\$15) and lakefront (C\$22/US\$19) campsites, it's an excellent base for family camping with day-use picnicking and swimming, canoeing, rock climbing, and spelunking activities, as well as evening and daily nature programs. Call ⓒ **250/927-0053** for camping reservations.

Note: To reach the Horne Lake area from Hwy. 19, take the Horne Lake Road exit (#75) and follow the signs. It's about a 13km (8-mile) drive on a mainly gravel road, which can get deeply rutted after a rainfall. Also, logging trucks use this road seven days a week so drive carefully—there are some narrow blind corners.

Teeing Up

There are six golf courses in the Parksville–Qualicum Beach area, and over a dozen within an hour's drive.

The **Eaglecrest Golf Club,** 2035 Island Hwy., Qualicum Beach (℃ **800/567-1320** or 250/752-9744; www.eaglecrest.bc.ca), is an 18-hole, par-71 course with an emphasis on shot-making and accuracy.

Fairwinds, 3730 Fairwinds Dr., just east of Parksville at Nanoose Bay (℃ **250/468-7666;** www.fairwinds.bc.ca), is a challenging 18-hole, par-71 course with ocean views and lots of trees.

Pheasant Glen Golf Resort, 1025 Qualicum Rd., Qualicum Beach (℃ **877/407-4653** or 250/752-8786; www.pheasantglen.com), has 18 holes, 9 of which are links-style.

The long established **Qualicum Beach Memorial,** 115 West Crescent Rd., Qualicum Beach (℃ **250/752-6312**), has 9 holes, stunning ocean views, a pro shop, and a restaurant.

Morningstar Golf Club, 525 Lowry's Rd., Parksville (℃ **800/567-1320** or 250/248-2244; www.morningstar.bc.ca), is an 18-hole, par-72 championship course with seaside links and fairways running in and out of the woods.

Arrowsmith Golf and Country Club, 2250 Fowler Rd., north of Qualicum Beach (℃ **250/752-9727;** www.golfarrowsmith.com), is a family oriented course with 18 holes and a par-61 rating. All have a driving range, clubhouse, and pro shop. From April to October, green fees average C$65 (US$57) for adults; from November to March, they average C$35 (US$31) for adults. Twilight rates and discounts for children 18 and under are offered year round.

HORNE LAKE CAVES PROVINCIAL PARK 😊😊😊

This is one of Vancouver Island's best outdoor adventure destinations. Nestled in the mountains of the Beaufort Range, beside a lakeside park with camping and canoeing, Horne Lake Caves attracts spelunkers for half- or full-day adventures. Getting to the park is a bit of an adventure in itself. Take the **Horne Lake exit** off **Highway 19** (the Island Highway) or **19A,** and follow the signs for 12km (7 miles). Drive with your headlights on and watch out for logging trucks.

Two caves are open year round for self-guided tours, although you must bring at least two sources of light, and helmets are recommended. In summer, you can rent these from the **park office.** The park also offers a number of guided tours, catering to everything from easygoing family fun to extreme experiences. The 1½-hour **Family Cavern Tour** is the easiest of these tours, and most popular. It starts with a short uphill hike through the forest to the cave entrance, which leads to a haven of beautiful crystal formations and ancient fossils. This tour costs C$17 (US$15) for adults, C$15 (US$13) for children 12 and under. The 3-hour **Spelunking Adventure** is a shade more challenging, involving some tight passages and lots of cave scrambling. It costs C$49 (US$43) per adults, C$42 (US$37) for children 12 and under. The minimum age for this is 8 years old. For real diehards, there's a 5-hour Extreme Rappel tour.

It includes instruction in basic rock climbing and roping, which you'll need to rappel down a seven-story waterfall known as the "Rainbarrel." Sturdy footwear and warm clothing is a must, although previous climbing experience is not. The tour costs C$139 (US$122) per person. Two-hour **Outdoor Rappel** clinics are available, and strongly recommended for those without recent rappel experience. The clinic cost is C$38 (US$33). *Note:* You must be 15 years or older and sign a liability waiver form to participate in the more extreme tours. Although you might get lucky and find space on one of the many daily family cavern tours; advance reservations are required for all tours, year round. Call ✆ **250/248-7829** for reservations; ✆ 250/757-8687 for recorded information or visit www.hornelake.com.

CAMPING

Located next to 2km (1 mile) of sandy shore, Rathtrevor Beach Provincial Park offers 200 tent and RV forested sites, with showers, firewood, a sani-station, and interpretive programs. Reservations are a must; beachfront sites are obviously the hot favorites, but all sites are really well maintained with a natural, surprisingly private, landscape. Most folks are just grateful to be in. There's a one-week-stay limit and usually a lineup of tenters and RVs in front of the park gate as early as 8am, waiting for cancellations. The early birds are often successful in securing a spot. Alternative camping space is at Englishman River Falls Provincial Park (13km/8 miles) and Little Qualicum Falls Provincial Park (24km/15 miles). All these parks accept reservations. Rates are C$14 to C$17 (US$12–US$15) per night. Contact Discover Camping (✆ **800/689-9025** (reservations) or ✆ 250/954-4600 (information); www. discovercamping.ca). Also, see "Horne Lake Caves Provincial Park" earlier.

WHERE TO STAY

Bahari Vacation Apartments ✿   Perched on the forested shoreline near Qualicum Beach, Bahari offers guests West Coast luxury with a Japanese ambience. A blend of raku pottery, Ikebana (a stylized Japanese floral arrangement), and modern Canadian work offsets other objets d'art. An embroidered wedding kimono that hangs in the atrium stairwell is a stunning centerpiece. Each of the self-contained two-bedroom apartments has custom-designed drapes, bedspreads, and accessories, with finishing touches that will relegate most domestic divas to the sidelines. The kitchens and bathrooms also contain one-of-a-kind fixtures such as hand-painted basins. Relax in the garden, wander the trails down to the beach, or take in the sweeping views of the Georgia Strait from the cliffside Jacuzzi.

5101 Island Hwy., Qualicum Beach, BC V9K 1Z1. ✆ **877/752-9278** or 250/752-9278. Fax 250/752-9038. www. baharibandb.com. 2 units. June–Sept C$225–C$235 (US$198–US$207). Oct–May C$125–C$145 (US$110–US$128). 2-night minimum stay in high season. Weekly rates and seasonal packages available. AE, MC, V. **Amenities:** Jacuzzi; coin-op washers and dryers. *In room:* TV/DVD, kitchen, hair dryer.

Beach Acres Resort ✿ *Kids*   Reminiscent of the great family resorts of days gone by, this resort entices families to return summer after summer to catch up with old friends and to make new ones. Located on Parksville's Rathtrevor Beach, the resort offers 9 hectares (23 acres) of family fun with a carefree, summer-camp atmosphere. Children's programs include everything from scavenger hunts to sandcastle contests, and there's a supervised indoor swimming pool. While the children have fun, Mom and Dad can relax in the Jacuzzi, or challenge each other to a tennis match. Accommodations-wise, guests can choose among cottages in a forest setting with country-style furniture, one-and two-bedroom Tudor-style cottages on the beach, or oceanview townhouses which sleep up to 6 people. All have full kitchens and either gas or wood-burning fireplaces. The resort has a roster of rentals such as high chairs, playpens, and BBQs.

25-1015 East Island Hwy., Parksville, BC V9P 2E4. ℂ 800/663-7309 or 250/248-3424. Fax 250/248-6145. www. beachacresresort.com. 55 units. June–Sept and holidays C$$244–C$325 (US$215–US$286). Oct–May C$129–C$199 (US$114–US$175). Weekly rates available. 7-night minimum stay Jul–Aug. AE, DC, DISC, MC, V. **Amenities:** Large heated indoor pool; 3 tennis courts; 1 outdoor basketball court; 1 outdoor volleyball court; Jacuzzi; sauna; children's programs; coin-op washers and dryers. In room: TV, kitchen, fridge, coffeemaker, iron, fireplace.

Pacific Shores Resort and Spa　Adjacent to The Nature Trust Bird sanctuary, part of the Englishman River Estuary, the resort is set on a landscaped 5.5 hectares (14 acres). There are 76 two-bedroom suites that become studios or one-bedroom suites on demand, creating quite a mix accommodation. Studio suites are like a contemporary hotel room; when configured into one- and two-bedroom units, they offer full kitchens, fireplaces, washers/dryers and all the home-away-from-home amenities you need. The resort is popular with families in summer, which is good if you're traveling with children and looking to keep involved with their peer group, but disastrous if you're seeking a romantic getaway. Family areas include a thermally heated outdoor pool, a picnic and BBQ area, and an outdoor playground. **The Aquaterre Spa** provides respite for harried adults; **The Landing Restaurant** (see "Where to Dine") is worth a visit. Because this complex is a part of the Avia West Vacation Group (ℂ 866/986-2222; www.aviawest.com), you may want to ignore some of the Internet discounts and make your reservations direct with the resort. The discounts often have strings attached, like having to listen to the sales pitch for timeshare.

1600 Stroulger Rd., Nanoose Bay, BC V9P 9B7 ℂ 866/986-2222 or 250/468-7121. Fax 250/468-2001. www.pacific-shores.com. 76 units. June–early Sept C$255–C$350 (US$224–US$308) 1- & 2-bedroom condo; C$115 (US$101) studio. Mar–May and Oct C$190–C$265 (US$167–US$233) 1- & 2-bedroom condo; C$105 (US$92) studio. Nov–Feb C$160–C$200 (US$141–US$176) 1- & 2-bedroom condo; C$85 (US$75) studio. AE, DISC, MC, V. Free parking. **Amenities:** Restaurant; large indoor pool; health club; spa; Jacuzzis; sauna; free kayaks; babysitting; laundry service; Internet access; convenience store and deli; outdoor children's play area. In room: TV/VCR/DVD, dataport, kitchen, fridge, coffeemaker, iron.

Tigh-Na-Mara Seaside Resort & Spa 𝖪𝖪 Kids　Romantic family getaways might sound like an oxymoron, but not here at Tigh-Na-Mara, Gaelic for "the house by the sea." Established in the 1940s on an 11-hectare (26-acre) forested waterfront beach near Rathtrevor Beach Provincial Park, this time-honored resort just keeps getting better. Romantics gravitate here for the Grotto Spa; it's the largest spa in British Columbia and offers a mineral pool and exceptional spa services such as massages, and hair and skin care. Tigh-Na-Mara also has a diverse range of quality accommodation; guests can stay in intimate one- or two-bedroom log cottages in a forest setting, luxuriate in special spa-suites, splurge on the lavish oceanview condominiums (many with Jacuzzis), or enjoy lodge-style standard rooms. All guest accommodations have fireplaces and some have kitchen facilities. The three- and four-room cottages can sleep up to 8. Families flock to Tigh-Na-Mara for its supervised child-friendly programs as much as for its stunning location. Activities are numerous and even include "parents' nights out" every Tuesday and Thursday when children are entertained with movies and the like. The lodge has a sushi and jazz lounge, and a welcoming cedar-paneled **Cedar Restaurant** featuring Northwest cuisine alongside barbecues in summer, and a children's menu.

1155 Resort Dr., Parksville, BC V9P 2E5. © 800/663-7373 or 250/248-2072. Fax 250/248-4140. www.tigh-na-mara.com. 210 units, some with fireplace. July–Aug C$159–C$199 (US$140–US$175) lodge rooms; C$179–C$299 (US$158–US$263) oceanview studios and suites; C$239–C$359 (US$210–US$154) cottages and spa bungalows. May, Jun & Sept C$149–C$189 (US$131–US$166) lodge rooms; C$159–C$259 (US$140–US$228) oceanview studios & suites; C$189–C$309 (US$166–US$272) cottages and spa bungalows. Oct–Apr C$119–C$159 (US$105–US$140) lodge rooms; C$129–C$209 (US$114–US$184) oceanview studios & suites; C$169–C$289 (US$149–US$254) cottages & spa bungalows. 3–7-night minimum stay July–Aug. Seasonal and spa packages available. AE, DC, MC, V. Pets accepted Sept–May. **Amenities:** Restaurant; lounge; large heated indoor pool; 1 outdoor tennis court; exercise room; Jacuzzi; sauna; paddleboat rentals; mountain bike rentals; business center; babysitting. *In room:* TV, kitchen, fridge, coffeemaker.

WHERE TO DINE

Beach House Cafe WEST COAST   Located right at the water's edge, the fully licensed Beach House Cafe is a local favorite, serving good food without a lot of frills. Its bistro-style atmosphere carries through from an easy soup-and-sandwich lunch to a casual, intimate dinner. Some lunch items are repeated at dinner, although in the evening, you'll be treated to house specialties, such as a bouillabaisse loaded with local seafood. Homemade pies, whether savory steak-and-mushroom or sweet rhubarb-and-strawberry, are a must. It's a tiny place that fills up quickly, so if you make reservations, be on time.

2775 West Island Hwy., Qualicum Beach. © 250/752-9626. Reservations recommended on weekends. Main courses C$10–C$20 (US$9–US$18). MC, V. Daily 11am–2:30pm and 5–10pm.

Kalvas EUROPEAN   Inside the rustic-looking log cabin is an intimate dining room that locals favor as a special-occasion restaurant. The menu specializes in seafood and traditional German dishes. Consequently, you can't go wrong with sole amandine, the salmon Oscar (poached, topped with shrimp and hollandaise sauce) and wiener schnitzel, which is just about as good as it gets. The menu also has a wide range of steaks and pastas, and an excellent oyster and live crab bar—the latter is simply steamed and served with drawn butter. Be sure to ask for the house-made spaetzles.

180 Molliet St., Parksville © 250/248-6933. Reservations recommended. Main courses C$12–C$69 (US$11–US$61). MC, V. Daily 5–10pm.

The Landing West Coast Grill WEST COAST   With so many seaside resorts lining these expansive beaches, it's hard to know which ones, if any, have decent restaurants that are open to the public. This is one of them. Despite an outdoor heated patio, wine bar, and terrific ocean views, it's the 6,000-gallon curvaceous saltwater aquarium wall that will really catch your eye. Food focuses on seafood and local produce such as milk-poached smoked sablefish, smoked duck breast with cucumber linguine and blackberry port syrup, or baby back ribs with lashings of Jack Daniel's BBQ sauce. There's a good vegetarian selection. An exceptional value is the Chef's Showcase on Thursday night: a five-course meal for C$40 to C$45 (US$35–US$40). Lovers of live jazz should stake out a table on Monday nights when local ensembles are featured.

At Pacific Shores, 1600 Stroulger Rd., Nanoose Bay. © 888/640-7799 or 250/468-2400. www.landinggrill.com. Main courses C$15–C$35 (US$13–US$31). AE, MC, V. Mon–Fri 11am–9pm; Sat–Sun 10am–10pm.

Shady Rest Waterfront Pub & Restaurant CANADIAN   With skylights, and a wall of windows fronting the beach, this restaurant offers a view to every seat in the house, although in warmer weather you'll probably prefer a spot on the deck. Open for breakfast, lunch, and dinner, its menu items are no-frill classics such as steak and prawns, fish and chips, stir fries, schnitzels, pasta, and pizzas. It does these well for lunch and dinner, but the evening menu's fancier items are a bit hit and miss. Ask your waitress to be honest about the specials to avoid disappointment.

3109 W. Island Hwy., Qualicum Beach. ⓒ 250/752-9111. Reservations recommended for restaurant dinner. Main courses C$10–C$20 (US$9–US$18) MC, V. Restaurant daily 8am–9pm; pub-food service Sun–Thurs 11am–9pm; Fri–Sat 11am–10pm. Pub open Fri & Sat to 1am.

Triskell Restaurant & Creperie FRENCH   When Triskell's husband-and-wife team closed up their Victoria creperie and relocated here, they brought with them a loyal following that makes the trip up to Parksville worth it just for the crepes. The small dining room with white linens, and whitewashed walls with prints of the French countryside, hints at the French-influenced menu. In addition to savory and sweet crepes, there's a range of local fresh fish, game, beef, and lamb dishes. Specialties include a mussels pate, a tasty rabbit, braised in a Beaujolais and apricot sauce, and a Callebaut chocolate mousse. As might be expected from a French restaurant, the wine list includes an excellent selection from France as well as from Australia, Chile, and British Columbia.

220 West Island Hwy. ⓒ 250/248-2011. Main courses C$18–C$25 (US$16–US$22). MC, V. Tues–Sat 5–10pm.

4 Heading West: Port Alberni & Bamfield

Jump into your vehicle, hit the accelerator, and begin a memorable voyage from the east to west side of central Vancouver Island. The trip is about 200km (125 miles) and takes about 3 hours to drive. En route, you'll pass through **Coombs,** a farming community with a good selection of country crafts boutiques. The **Old Country Market** (2310 Alberni Hwy. ⓒ **250/248-3349**), complete with goats on the roof, is a Kodak moment, and a chance to stretch your legs, buy a delicious ice cream, or pick up picnic supplies. There's also an intriguing gift-for-yourself emporium with teapots, marmalades, imported clothes, and baskets. If you can put up with the squawking, drop by the **World Parrot Refuge** (2116 Alberni Hwy. ⓒ **250/248-5194** or 250/951-1166; www.worldparrotrefuge.org), and its sanctuary for more than 400 previously owned parrots. Admission is by donation.

As you near the west coast, you pass waterfalls beneath a canopy of rain forest. **Port Alberni** is another stopover that's an interesting detour for a quick lunch and wander, but unless you're taking a trip on the **MV** *Lady Rose* to Bamfield, there's no draw to stay overnight. **Bamfield,** on the other hand, is a delightful diversion that's worth at least a day trip, if not an overnight stay. Reached only by boat, this village is built on boardwalks, with lovely coves, homes, and B&Bs tucked into the surrounding inlets.

ESSENTIALS
GETTING THERE
BY CAR   From Nanaimo, take the Island Highway (Hwy. 19) 52km (31 miles) north toward Parksville. Just before you hit Parksville, take the turnoff for Highway 4, which leads west to Port Alberni and on to the coastal towns of Tofino and Ucluelet. It's a good idea to leave Nanaimo in the morning to avoid having the afternoon sun in your eyes as you drive west (and to return in the afternoon so that the sun is behind you as you head east). A secondary highway, Highway 4, is narrow in places, as well as winding, slippery, and mountainous. Night driving isn't recommended. If you plan to drive straight through to Tofino or Ucluelet, gas up in Nanaimo. Gas stations are scarce along Highway 4.

BY BUS   Island Coach Lines (℃ **800/318-0818** or 250/385-4411; www. greyhound.ca) operates regular daily service between Victoria and Tofino–Ucluelet, departing at 5:30am and arriving in Tofino about 1pm. The bus stops in Nanaimo to pick up passengers arriving on the Vancouver ferry (the bus station is a 10-minute cab ride from the ferry docks). Fares from Victoria to Tofino are C$55 (US$48); from Nanaimo to Tofino are C$13 (US$11); and from Nanaimo to Port Alberni are C$16 (US$14). **The Tofino Bus Company** (℃ **866/986-3466**; www.tofinobus.com) also runs a daily service from Vancouver and Victoria to Tofino–Ucluelet. From Vancouver the one-way (hotel-to-hotel) adult fare is C$85 (US$68); from Victoria, C$53 (US$47); from Nanaimo, C$35 (US$31). Nanaimo to Port Alberni is also C$35 (US$31). Discounts of about 5% apply to seniors and youths; children are half price.

BY TRAIN   VIA Rail's **Malahat** (℃ **800/561-8630** or 250/383-4324; www. viarail.com) stops in Parksville and Qualicum Beach on its daily trip from Victoria to Courtenay.

BY AIR   KD Air (℃ **800/665-4244** or 604/688-9957 or 250/752-4495; www. kdair.com) offers several daily flights from Vancouver to Port Alberni via Qualicum Airport and then bus transportation, for C$280 (US$246) round trip. One-way fares are C$165 (US$145), with discounts for seniors and children.

BY FERRY   Although a somewhat unconventional ferry, Lady Rose Marine Services (℃ **800/663-7192** or 250/723-8313), runs two packet freighters from Port Alberni to different points on the island's west coast, including a trip to Ucluelet. Call for seasonal sailing times and costs.

VISITOR INFORMATION
For more information on Port Alberni, the Alberni Valley Chamber of Commerce runs a **Visitor Information Centre** at 2533 Port Alberni Hwy., Port Alberni, BC V9Y 7L6 (℃ **250/724-6535;** www.avcoc.com).

EXPLORING THE AREA
Located midway between Parksville and Port Alberni in MacMillan Provincial Park is the world-renowned **Cathedral Grove.** If you've time, don't simply drive through; take an hour or two to follow the winding interpretive trail system through the 1,000-year-old forest of Douglas fir, western hemlock, grand fir, and western red cedar. The trees stand so tall, you'll feel like you're standing inside of a cathedral, hence the name. This day park gives you a sense of what Vancouver Island and the West Coast looked like before the arrival of European settlers. To see where many trees like these end up, you need look no farther than Port Alberni.

   Port Alberni is a hard-working little town of nearly 20,000. Along the waterfront, logs are milled into lumber, pulp, and paper. Smoke from the mills spews up into the low-lying clouds that cling to the surrounding mountains. On a dull day, the entire town is grey with nary a hint of the fabulous views that a sunny day brings. Port Alberni is currently trying to revitalize its rather industrial facade, but it's an uphill effort despite the self-professed nickname "Positive Port Alberni."

   If you need to break the drive to the coast, head down to the redeveloped **Harbour Quay** area at the foot of **Argyle Street,** and you'll find restaurants and gift shops amid the cackle of seagulls and the full-throated honk of ship's horns. There's a **Maritime Discovery Centre** (℃ **250/723-2181**; www.alberniheritage.com) housed in a lighthouse replica at the end of the pier; it tells the story of Port Alberni's seafaring past.

Alberni's land-based history is shown at **The Alberni Valley Museum** (4255 Wallace St.; © 250/ 723-2181; www.alberniheritage.com) which displays local Nuu Chah Nulth art and pioneer artifacts. Admission to both museums is by donation. Garden enthusiasts can head for **Rollins Art Centre and Gardens** (3061 8th Ave.; © **250/ 724-3412**), a combination fine-arts gallery and gardens, including a traditional Japanese garden that was a gift from Abashiri, Port Alberni's sister city. Aviation fans might want to stop at the **Home of the Mars Water Bombers,** the largest water-bombing plane in the world, headquartered at lovely **Sproat Lake** nearby.

In summer, you can head over to the restored Port Alberni **railway station** (built around 1912) and board an antique locomotive for the 35-minute ride up to the McLean Mill National Historic Site. The train also makes a stop at the **Case and Warren Winery** (6253 Drinkwater Rd.; © **250/724-4906**) for a tour and tasting). Originally used by The Esquimalt and Nanaimo (E&N) Railway to transport logs and lumber between the mills and the harbor, the fully restored steam train now carries passengers. It operates two rides a day, Thursday through Monday. Call © **250/723-2181** for fares, which include admission to the McLean Mill (see listing below) and schedules. For marine-oriented activities, **Six Gill Adventures** (7935 Beaver Creek Rd.; © **800/761-5661** or 250/720-7386) offers a range of half-day and full-day Zodiac diving and eco-tours in the Strait of Georgia and Barkley Sound, and to hiking destinations such as Della Falls.

A truly unique way to experience the area is a day trip with **Lady Rose Marine Services** (© **800/663-7192** April to September; or © 250/723-8313; www.ladyrose marine.com), which operates MV *Lady Rose,* and MV *Frances Barkley* ⊛⊛⊛, packet freighters that transport supplies to some of British Columbia's far-flung coastal communities along Barkley Sound and the Alberni Inlet. Passengers observe life aboard a coastal freighter first-hand as it delivers all manner of cargo: from newspapers and groceries bound for general stores, to equipment for logging camps—even laundry. For some residents scattered along this coast, the MV *Lady Rose* and the MV *Frances Barkley* are their only links to civilization. The scenery, of course, is spectacular. Kayakers and canoeists en route to the **Broken Group Islands** take the MV *Lady Rose* to a base camp at Sechart. Hikers bound for the **West Coast Trail,** and day trippers, can catch a ride to **Bamfield**, a picturesque fishing village just north of the trailhead (see "A Side Trip to Bamfield"). In summer, there are also day trips through the Broken Groups Islands to Ucluelet. Wear sensible shoes and bring warm, windproof clothing because the decks are open and weather on the coastal waters can be temperamental. Basic food such as egg and bacon sandwiches is available on board in a tiny galley-restaurant. The freighters depart at 8am, year round, from **Harbour Quay** on Tuesday, Thursday, and Saturday, returning to Port Alberni at about 5:30pm. From June through September, there are additional 8am sailings to Ucluelet, via Sechart near the Broken Group Islands, on Monday, Wednesday, and Friday, returning to Port

World's Largest Flying Boat

The Mars are known as the world's largest flying boat, capable of scooping up 27 tons of water at any one time beneath their 61-m (200-ft.) wingspan. There are only two active Mars Tankers left in the world; both are based in Port Alberni.

Alberni at about 7pm, as well as an extra sailing on Sunday to Bamfield, again via Sechart to drop off/pick up kayakers.

Adult fares to Bamfield are C$28 (US$25), return C$55 (US$48); one-way to Ucluelet C$30 (US$26), return C$60 (US$53); and one-way to Sechart C$28 (US$25), return C$55 (US$48). Fares are half price for children 8 to 15. Children 7 and under ride free. Reservations are required.

Butterfly World and Gardens   It's not quite to the standard of Butterfly Gardens near Victoria, but it's still a worthwhile detour. Outside, the gardens are planted to attract wild native butterflies while inside are more exotic varieties, as well as a display of creepy crawly bugs (a kid's dream), and an aviary of exotic birds, including multi-colored finches. An Orchid Garden featuring hundreds of orchids from around the world opens in 2007 as the largest indoor exhibit of its kind in Canada. Thirty minutes should be sufficient for a visit; longer if you love orchids or have bug-crazy children in tow.

1080 Winchester Rd. ✆ **250/248-7026.** www.nature-world.com. Daily 10am–5pm. Admission C$9 (US$7.90) adult, C$8 (US$7.05) senior, C$5 (US$4.40) student, $3.75 (US$3.30) children 4–12 years.

McLean Mill National Historic Site   Built in 1926, this is the only family run steam-driven sawmill in Canada and is a township all on its own. More than 30 buildings include an operational mill, bunkhouse accommodations for the 20-odd mill-workers who once worked there, and a schoolhouse for the workers' children, as well as a steam donkey (an antiquated steam engine that powered winches), logging trucks, and lumber carriers. Although only operational in summer, it's a place where visitors are welcome to wander year round. Located on Smith Road, off Beaver Creek Road, west of Port Alberni, the site is easiest to reach by train(see above). Allow 3½ hours for the entire experience—more if you're a hiker or mountain biker. The Mill happens to be the hub for a network of hiking trails for hikers and mountain bikers alike. The best trail is the Log Train Trail, an easy to moderate 26-km (16-mile) linear trail that travels alongside the historic site.

⌐**Fun Fact** **Smart, Eh?**

Bamfield is reputed to have the highest per-capita education of any town in Canada. The reason? Most of the populace are marine biologists and other scientists.

5633 Smith Rd. ✆ **250/723-1376.** www.alberniheritage.com. Mid-June to Labor Day C$29 (US$26) adults, C$22 (US$19) seniors and youth, C$9.95 (US$8.75) child, C$75 (US$66) family pass.

WHERE TO STAY

There are a lot of seedy dives in Port Alberni, so if you're staying overnight here, most likely because you're catching an 8am sailing aboard *Lady Rose,* you want to stick to tried-and-true hotels. These two recommendations are standard, each with downtown locations and offering a comfortable night's rest.

Best Western Barclay Hotel   This is as close to the waterfront as you can get, and within walking distance of all its activities. Guest rooms are on the small side, but pleasantly furnished with appealing blue-toned fabrics and warm woods. Suites have fridges, microwaves, and coffeemakers. The **Stamps Cafe** serves casual fare. If you're looking for something more lively, there are no fewer than 22 TV screens in **Pastimes Sports Bar and Grill.**

A Side Trip to Bamfield ⭐⭐

With its flowing high street, **Bamfield** (© 250/728-3006; www.bamfield chamber.com) is the Venice of Vancouver Island, and although this isolated community can be reached from Port Alberni via a 102-km (63-mile) unpaved road, most people arrive by boat or floatplane (see "Exploring the Area"). Bamfield's high street is lined with marine suppliers and quirky boardwalks that join weather-beaten houses, stores, and resorts. Crossing the street means hitching a ride with a local boat owner or hailing a water taxi. Day-trippers off the MV *Lady Rose* have just enough time to meander the boardwalks, buy a carving from a soapstone studio, and maybe enjoy a drink at the historic **Bamfield** Inn (Customs House Lane; © 250/728-3354), before the return trip to Port Alberni.

Outdoor enthusiasts tend to linger, using Bamfield as a base for fishing, diving, or kayaking. **Broken Island Adventures** (© 888/728-6200 or 250/728-3500) offers customized diving excursions in Barkley Sound, kayak rentals, and kayak and wildlife-viewing tours. Check out the **Bamfield Marine Sciences Centre** (100 Pachena Rd.; © 250/728-3301; www.bms.b.ca), a stellar local attraction with programs and hands-on displays. There are scenic hiking trails to Brady's Beach, Cape Beale, Pachena Lighthouse, Keeha Beach, and Tapaltos Beach. Hikers heading for the West Coast Trail use Bamfield as a pit stop before or after a week in the rugged coastal wilderness (see "Pacific Rim National Park," later in the chapter). **The Hook and Web Pub** (© 250/728-3422) is a good place to eavesdrop on their harrowing stories of survival. If you just want to get away from it all, **Woods End Landing Cottages,** 168 Wild Duck Rd., Bamfield, BC V0R 1B0 (© 877/828-3383 or 250/728-3383; www.woodsend.travel.bc.ca), offers comfort and character. **The Great Canadian Adventure Company** (© 888/285-1676; www.adventures.ca) offers an easy hiking tour on remote Tapaltos Beach. It starts with a 2-hour drive along the logging road to Bamfield before you hit the trail for an hour's hike through rainforest to the beach, where you can enjoy a picnic lunch and some beachcombing.

4277 Stamp Ave., Port Alberni, BC V9Y 7X8. © **800/563-6590** or 250/724-7171. Fax 250/724-9691. www.best westernbarclay.com. 86 units. May–Sept C$129–C$199 (US$114–US$175). Oct–Apr C$99–C$179 (US$87–US$158). Off-season discounts available. Extra person C$10 (US$9). Children 17 and under stay free in parent's room. Free parking. AE, DC, DISC, MC, V. Free parking. **Amenities:** Restaurant; pub; sports bar; small heated outdoor pool; exercise room; Jacuzzi; sauna; Internet. *In room:* A/C, TV, coffeemaker, hair dryer, iron.

Hospitality Inn   A cozy fireplace in the lobby welcomes guests to this modern Tudor-style inn that is set away from the waterfront, a few minutes' drive down the hill. There's an upbeat, executive feel to the chocolate-brown and beige decor, and services include all the standard amenities such as fair sized rooms, comfortable beds, and nothing-to-write-home-about bathroom toiletries. The **Harvest Restaurant** specializes in home-style cooking, while **Polly's Pub** serves a lighter menu and traditional pub fare.

3835 Redford St., Port Alberni, BC V9Y 3S2. ℂ 800/663-1144 or 250/723-8111. Fax 250/723-0088. www.hospitality innportalberni.com. 50 units. June–Sept C$159–C$169 (US$140–US$149). Oct–May C$155–C$165 (US$136–US$145). Family plan, AAA and seniors discounts, and off-season discounts available. AE, DC, MC, V. Free parking. **Amenities:** Restaurant, pub; limited room service; babysitting; laundry service; dry cleaning. *In room:* A/C, TV, dataport, coffeemaker, hair dryer, iron.

5 Tofino, Ucluelet & Pacific Rim National Park

The scenic drive through the center of Vancouver Island is only a taste of what's to come once you reach the wild coast of Western Canada. Here, the Pacific Ocean rollers crash against the shore, beaches stretch for miles, and the mist clings to the rainforest like cobwebs. Most of what you'll see is part of **Pacific Rim National Park.** In winter, you'll witness some of the best storms in the world—as dramatic and angry as a Turner landscape. In summer, families play alongside surfers, kayakers, and others enjoying this Valhalla for outdoor activities. **Tofino** has long been the commercial center of the region and as such, has many more services to offer visitors, including a sushi restaurant and decent, albeit small, shops and galleries. Tofino is the gateway to **Clayoquot Sound,** North America's largest remaining expanse of low-elevation old-growth temperate rain forest and a UNESCO World Biosphere Reserve. It's a "living laboratory," where you'll find isolated resorts and cabins clinging to the edge of the wilderness, and bears scavenging the shoreline for tasty delicacies, flipping rocks like flapjacks. Unfortunately, Tofino becomes so busy in summer that its popularity is eroding its charm.

For many, the town of **Ucluelet,** 42km (27 miles) away, is a quieter haven. Although a little rougher around the edges, here you can link up with the Wild Pacific Trail, and find B&Bs that are truly away from the madding crowd—although judging from new developments, it's only a matter of time until eco-adventurers and urban escapees start to influence the wilderness here too. Wherever you decide to stay, getting from A to B you really do need a set of wheels, or strong legs, to explore the area more fully. If driving, be careful. Black bear and deer are common, and at times, the roads can be windy and unexpectedly foggy.

ESSENTIALS
GETTING THERE
BY CAR   From Port Alberni, continue west on Highway 4 for about 145km (90 miles) to a T-junction. Turn north to Tofino (34km/21 miles), or south to Ucluelet (8km/5 miles).

BY PLANE   Sonic Blue Airways (ℂ **800/228-6608** or 604/278-1608; www. noniclbueair.com) operates twin-engine, turbo-prop planes year round between Vancouver and Tofino; return fares are about C$350 (US$308) per adult with discounts offered on advanced bookings. Craig Air (ℂ **877/866-3466** or 250/266-0267; www. craigair.com) offers year-round air service from Vancouver to Tofino; fares are priced per flight, at C$169 (US$149) per adult, with an additional Victoria–Tofino routing in the summer. **Sound Flight** (ℂ **866/921-3474** or 425/254-8064; www.sound flight.net) provides regular floatplane service between Seattle and Tofino from mid-June to late September. One-way fares are about C$425 (US$374) for adults. For all carriers, discounts for seniors and children are 5% to 10% off listed price.

BY BUS   Island Coach Lines (ℂ **800/318-0818** or 250/385-4411; www.greyhound. ca) operates regular daily service between Victoria and Tofino–Ucluelet, departing at

5:30am and arriving in Tofino about 1pm. The bus stops in Nanaimo and will drop off/pick up at Port Alberni. Fares from Port Alberni to Tofino are C$23 (US$20) per adult. **The Tofino Bus Company** (© **866/986-3466**; www.tofinobus.com) also runs a daily service from Vancouver and Victoria to Tofino–Ucluelet (see earlier). From Port Alberni to Tofino–Ucluelet, single adult fare is C$20 (US$18).

VISITOR INFORMATION

The **Tofino–Long Beach Chamber of Commerce** is located at 1426 Pacific Rim Hwy. (© **250/725-3414**; www.tourismtofino.com); opening hours are March through September, weekdays 11am to 5pm. The **Ucluelet Chamber of Commerce** is at the foot of Main St. (© **250/726-4641**; www.uclueletinfo.com or www.ucluelet. com), and open July to September, Monday through Friday, 11am to 5pm.

EXPLORING TOFINO

Picturesque Tofino, or "Tough City," is an intriguing combination of old-growth forests, white sand beaches, and the ever-churning Pacific Ocean. It got its name from a Spanish hydrographer who had a reputation for fights and wild living. But don't let the name's origins scare you. For most of the year, Tofino is a sleepy community, though in the summer it's frenzied. As visitors flock toward the Clayoquot Sound Biosphere Reserve, boat charters, whale-watching companies, fishing boats, and sea-planes create a hubbub of activity in the harbor.

The small high street has a number of junk souvenir shops as well as several galleries showcasing aboriginal art. If you've time for only one stop, it must be Roy Henry Vickers's **Eagle Aerie Gallery** ✸✸, 350 Campbell St. (© **250/725-3235**). As the first First Nations artist with his own gallery in British Columbia, Vickers and his work both inspire and dominate. The carved wooden door makes an impressive entrance and the entire gallery feels like a life-revering chapel. First Nations artists carved all woodwork within the gallery, including the rails, canoes, and eagles. A percentage of sales of certain works is given to First Peoples recovery programs. **The Tofino Botanical Gardens** (1084 Pacific Rim Hwy.; © **250/725-1220**; www.tofinobotanical gardens.com) is a 10-minute drive from downtown Tofino. Wander past garden sculptures on boardwalks and trails that take you through the rainforest to themed clearings such as a kitchen garden (much of which is used by the on-site **SoBo Restaurant**—see "Where to Dine"), and beds filled with native plants, medicinal herbs, and English and Japanese imports that were introduced to the region by early homesteaders. The gardens are an excellent resource for finding out more about the Clayoquot Sound biosphere. On site there's a hostel-style field station for up to 34 guests, mostly as shared accommodation, for those who want to immerse themselves in the eco-experience. Private rooms are C$49 (US$43) per person or C$32 (US$28) per bunk bed, sharing four to a room.

Fun Fact Sandpiper Stopover

In late April, many of the world's 2 to 5 million western sandpipers stop to feed on B.C.'s coastal mudflats, including the Tofino mudflats, en route to Arctic breeding grounds. Single flocks of 100,000 are not uncommon at peak migration.

About Clayoquot

Clayoquot Sound contains the largest remnant of ancient temperate rainforest in the world. With its fjord-like inlets, protected archipelagos, and shores, the rainforest has a complex ecosystem of intertidal zones, extensive mudflats, giant kelp and eelgrass beds, and strong tidal currents. The rich diversity of its habitat serves an equally diverse population of both marine and terrestrial species such as migrating whales and shorebirds, basking sharks, Dungeness crabs, various shellfish, wild salmon, herring, ground fish, otters and sea lions, as well as black bears, Roosevelt elk, marbled murrelets, cougars, wolves, bald eages, and red legged frogs.

The Nuu-chah-nulth people have occupied Clayoquot Sound and much of the west coast of Vancouver Island for the past several millennia. Of the Nuu-chah-nulth Nation, the Ahousaht, Tla-o-qui-aht, and Hesquiaht tribes live in Clayoquot Sound. First Nations make up approximately 50% of the population, primarily residing in the communities of Hot Springs, Opitsaht, Esowista, and Marktosis.

SIDE TRIPS FROM TOFINO

An hour's boat ride north of Tofino (even faster by seaplane), **Hot Springs Cove** is the only all-natural thermal hot springs on Vancouver Island. A beautifully maintained, 2-km (1-mile) boardwalk winds through lush rainforest to the sulfur-scented springs. Wisps of steam rise from water that is 122°F (50°C) at its source and cools as it cascades through a series of pools to the sea. It's a busy place in summer, so if you want to experience the tranquility of the place, get there before 10am.

Just 30 minutes north of Tofino, **Flores Island** is where to find the 32-km (20-mile) **Ahousaht Wildside Heritage Trail,** an easy hike through rainforests and along beaches. Nearby **Meares Island,** a 15-minute water-taxi ride from Tofino, is worth seeing both for its beauty and its devastation from clear-cutting. It's the site of many a tree-hugger-versus-logging-company conflict. **The Big Cedar Trail** is a 3-km (2-mile) boardwalked path through the forest with a long staircase leading up to the Hanging Garden Tree, said to be 1,500 years old. On **Vargas Island, The Ahous Trail** (5-km/3-mile return) is an old telegraph trail that bisects the island from one magnificent beach to another, taking you through salal, tussocky bog, and hummocks of peat. Many Tofino outfitters offer tours and boat transportation to the islands (see "Outdoor Activities" for some recommendations).

EXPLORING UCLUELET

Smaller and less sophisticated than Tofino, Ucluelet (*yew-kloo-let*) is waking up to the extraordinary magnetism of the surrounding area. It used to be that Ucluelet was Tofino's "ugly little stepsister," but that's changing quickly. It's becoming a year-round resort and tourist destination in its own right. New developments such as Whiskey Landing Resort (opening late 2007) are sprucing up the downtown core, and in its harbor, you'll now find the masts of classic fishing boats bobbing alongside moneyed, modern yachts.

The village has a couple of **folk art galleries,** and there are numerous picnic areas along the beaches and rocky coast offering spectacular views. These views are best experienced on the **Wild Pacific Trail** ⍟, which is reason alone to visit Ucluelet. If you're not hardy enough to take on the West Coast Trail, then this is a good bet. The 14-km (8.5-mile) trail is being developed in phases, and will eventually run along the outer coast to Long Beach at Florencia Bay. The first 2.5km (1.5 miles) is a loop that leads along the coastline from **Amphitrite Point** and its **lighthouse** overlooking Barkley Sound to the Broken Group Islands. In winter, storm watchers come to this headland to see it pounded by 30-m waves, and in March, this is *the* place to gather to watch the annual migration of the grey whales. Boardwalks lead you through rainforest to bluffs high above the ocean, where trees, beaten back by the wind, grow at 90-degree angles. It's an easy path that gets you close to the fury of winter waves or the splendor of summer sunsets. Another section (6km/3.7 miles) has been completed from Big Beach Park to the bike path just outside of Ucluelet. It's a mix of boardwalks, stairs, and gravel paths that follow the edge of the forest.

> ### A Whale of a Festival
> The annual **Pacific Rim Whale Festival** (ⓒ 250/726-7742) celebrates the annual migration of 20,000 Pacific grey whales through the region. Held in Tofino and Ucluelet in March, activities include whale-watching hikes; First Nations storytelling, programs for children, music, dancing, and art exhibits.

OUTDOOR ACTIVITIES

FISHING   Tofino and Ucluelet are at the heart of the region's commercial fishing industry and you'll find a number of sport-fishing charters in both marinas. The big draws are salmon, steelhead, rainbow trout, Dolly Varden char, halibut, snapper, and cod. **Jay's Clayoquot Ventures** (564 Campbell St.; ⓒ 888/534-7422 or 250/725-2700; www.tofinofishing.com) is an experienced and reputable company that organizes fishing charters throughout Clayoquot Sound—deep-sea and freshwater excursions. Saltwater fly-fishing trips start at C$85 (US$75) per hour for a 5-hour minimum and include equipment and flies; all inclusive, fly-in freshwater fishing trips, overnighting at a remote camp, start at C$2,495 (US$2,196) for 1 or 2 people. **Lance's Sportfishing Adventures** (120 Fourth St.; ⓒ 888/725-6125 or 250/725-2569; www.fish tofino.com) combines fishing trips aboard 24-foot offshore vessels with a visit to Hot Springs—the advantage being you'll enjoy the springs before the crowds. Rates are C$105 (US$92) per hour for a 6-hour minimum and include all gear.

GOLFING   At press time, a Jack Nicklaus signature golf course is set to open in 2008, as part of a new 150-hectare (370-acre) oceanfront luxury resort under development in Ucluelet. For information check out www.golfvancouverisland.ca or www.marinedriveproperties.com (ⓒ 250/726 8406).

HIKING   Naturalist, biologist, author, and ecologist Bill McIntyre was such a sought-after guide that he now runs a full program of guided beach and rainforest walks, land-based whale-watching tours, and storm-watching hikes through **Oceans Edge** (855 Barkley Cres., Ucluelet; ⓒ 250-726-7099). All excursions are 3 to 6 hours over moderate terrain and prices vary according to activity. Book well in advance or just hope he has a cancellation when you arrive. Other star hikes include the 3.5-km/ 2-mile **Gold Mine Trail** near Florencia Bay, so called for its gold-mining heritage; the partially boardwalked **South Beach Trail** (about1.5km/1 mile), and the even shorter **Schooner Beach Trail**, both of which take you through rainforest before opening up onto sandy beaches.

KAYAKING   Kayaking through Clayoquot Sound is one of the most intimate ways to experience its history, serenity, and natural beauty. The trick is to find an outfitter who can enrich the experience beyond just a paddle. The owners of **Rainforest Kayak Adventures** (316 Main St.; ✆ **877/422-WILD** or 250/725-3117; www.rainforest kayak.com) helped set the benchmark for sea-kayak instruction in B.C. more than 20 years ago and have been guiding the area for almost as long. Group paddles are maxed out at 8 participants, plus two guides, so involvement in experiential learning about kayaking and the region is laced with contagious enthusiasm. Multi-day wilderness camping and overnight trips to Vargas Island and others around Calyoquot Sound start at C$245 (US$216) per person. The **Tofino Sea-Kayaking Company** (320 Main St.; ✆ **800/863-4664** or 250/725-4222; www.tofino-kayaking.com) also offers guided tours, including all-day excursions at C$155 (US$136). **Jamie's** has 4-hour tours including about a 1½ hour guided hike through the Big Tree Trail on Meares Island at C$68 (US$60) per person and provides kayak rentals at C$40 (US$35) single and C$65 (US$57) double per day. If you're based in Ucluelet, **Majestic Ocean Kayaking** (✆ **800/889-7644** or 250/726-2868; www.oceankayaking.com) might be more convenient. They have a range of ecotourism adventures to Barkley Sound, Pacific Rim National Park, and Deer Group Islands. Prices start at C$60 (US$53) for a 3-hour paddle around Ucluelet Harbour to a full-day trip to Broken Group Islands (including cruiser transport there) at C$225 (US$198) per person.

SURFING   The heavy, constant rollers of the Pacific Ocean against wide expanses of beach have made this one of the world's hot spots for surfing. Whether beginner or experienced, you'll find outfitters to help you catch the wave, year round. **Live to Surf** (1180 Pacific Rim Hwy.; ✆ **250/725-4463**; www.livetosurf.com) is Tofino's original surf shop and offers rentals of boards and wetsuits as well as daily surf lessons through its Westside Surf School (✆ **250/725-2404**). Two-hour lessons include all the gear (wetsuit, booties, gloves, and board) and cost C$75 (US$66) per person; 5-hour surf camps (recommended only if you're experienced or very fit) are C$150 (US$132) per person. **Pacific Surf School** (440 Campbell St.; ✆ **888/777-9961** or 250/725-2155) holds 3-hour lessons (C$79/US$70) and provides private tutoring (C$135/US$119), and **Surf Sister** (625 Campbell St.; ✆ **877/724-SURF** or 250/725-4456; www.surfsister.com) is, as the name suggests, geared to women, with it mother–daughter camps and yoga surf retreats.

WHALE   WATCHING   Operating out of Tofino and Ucluelet, **Jamie's Whaling Station** (606 Campell St., Tofino; ✆ **800/667-9913** or 250/725-3919; and 168 Fraser Lane; ✆ **877/726-7444** or 250/726-7444; www.jamies.com) is a pioneer of the adventure business.

> (*Fun Fact* **A Lot of Lions**
>
> More than 2,400 Stellars and California Sea Lions congregate in Barkley Sound.

It's been around since 1982 and has evolved a full roster of whale-watching, bear-watching, and other wildlife tours. There's a choice of venturing out in 12-passenger Zodiacs—C$79/US$70 per adult or C$50/US$44 per child—or in the comfort of a 65-foot vessel—C$89/US$78 per adult, C$50/US$44 per child—complete with snack bar, inside heated seating, and washrooms. A C$2 (US$1.75) surcharge is added, contributing to local wildlife research and rescue programs, and the local bird hospital. *Note:* Jamie's also has a 35-foot cabin cruiser for the 1¼–hour boat ride up to Hot Springs Cove where you can soak up the waters for a couple of hours before the return trip either by boat, or by seaplane. The boat has space for sea kayaks.

PACIFIC RIM NATIONAL PARK ⨀⨀⨀

Designated a national park in 1970 to protect the significant coastal environment, Pacific Rim National Park presents outstanding examples of coastal rainforest, surf-swept beaches, marine life, and the cultural history of the area's settlement. Composed of three "units," or sections, the **West Coast Trail Unit, the Long Beach Unit,** and **the Broken Group Islands,** the park spans 130km (82 miles) of shoreline. You access each unit via a different route. The variety of activities and level of services offered in each unit varies. The Long Beach Unit is the most accessible—a good choice for families and visitors who want to take it a little easier, whereas the West Coast Trail Unit is for no-nonsense hikers with nothing but trekking in mind. Contact the **Pacific Rim National Park Reserve,** P.O. Box 280, Ucluelet, BC V0R 3A0 (© **250/726-7721**) for information.

WEST COAST TRAIL UNIT

The West Coast Trail is billed as one of the most grueling treks in North America. And when you see experienced backpackers stagger out of its wilderness, muddy, bedraggled, and exhausted, you might think even that is an understatement. This once-in-a-lifetime wilderness adventure attracts 8,000 hikers each year to do battle with the 77-km (48-mile) trail between **Port Renfrew** and **Bamfield** along the southwestern coast of Vancouver Island, known as the "graveyard of the Pacific" because of the numerous shipwrecks along the coast. The trail was originally cleared at the start of the 20th century as a lifesaving rail for shipwrecked mariners. It was upgraded in the 1970s, but trekking it still requires much experience, stamina, and strength. At any point on the trail, you may need to balance yourself on a fallen log to cross a deep gully, negotiate steep slopes, climb and descend ladders 25m (92 ft.) at a time, or wade thigh-deep across a river. In fact, hell on the WCT corresponds directly to rain, which can drop 15 centimeters (6 in.) in just 12 hours, turning the trail to mud. More than 100 people are evacuated from the trail every year; one of the main reasons is hypothermia. Bring painkillers and guards for ankle sprains and be prepared to take a *minimum* of 5 days to complete the trail end to end.

Tip: If you're not up to the entire challenge, consider taking on the far more accessible 11-km (6.8-mile) oceanfront stretch at the trail head near Bamfield. You'll still need your wits (and survival gear) about you, but at least you'll be able to wear the West Coast Trail badge of honor—or part of it, anyway! For peace of mind, such as is possible on this trail, you may prefer to spend the extra money and go with an experienced outfitter such as **Sea to Sky Expeditions** (© **800/900-8735** or 604/594-770l), which offers 9-day guides through the West Coast Trail, starting from C$1,395 (US$1,228), and an 8-day hike exploring a part of the Clayoquot region where, from a remote clearing in the rainforest, Annie Rae-Arthur ran a nursery garden and shipped plants across Canada. She was nicknamed Cougar Annie for her handiness with a rifle in defending her lonely lifestyle from hungry cougars.

BOOKING YOUR HIKE The West Coast Trail is open to hikers from May 1 to September 30. You should reserve up to 3 months ahead, since only 52 hikers are allowed to enter the trail a day: 26 from Bamfield, 26 from Port Renfrew. To reserve, call © **800/HELLOBC** or 800/435-5622 or 250/387-1642 (international callers) or 604/435-5622. There is a nonrefundable booking fee of C$25 (US$22) per hiker, and a C$108 (US$95) hiking fee, both payable at time of booking. You also need to register at the park office before you set out, and be at the trailhead by noon, or lose your spot. For more information on weather conditions and last minute options only, call the park's offices © **250/647-5434** (for hikers departing from Port Renfrew) or © **250/728-3234** (for hikers departing from Bamfield www.pc.gc.ca). *Note:* In high season, you may have to wait for up to 3 days, but there are six standby slots per day, filled on a first-come, first-served basis. Wait-list openings are at each trail head— Gordon River at the south end and Pachena Bay at the north end.

BROKEN GROUP ISLANDS

Made up of more than 100 rocky islands and islets in **Barkley Sound,** the Broken Group Islands can only be reached by boat. Amidst this pristine archipelago, eagles, sea lions, and marine life abound, and tide pools and dozens of sandy cove beaches lure nature enthusiasts, photographers, and boating sightseers. Chartered boats, guided tours, and transport for campers and kayakers can be booked in Bamfield, Tofino, and Ucluelet, or, you can arrive via the MV *Lady Rose* (see "Exploring the Area," in "Heading West: Port Alberni & Bamfield," earlier in the chapter).

Only experienced boaters, canoeists, and kayakers should consider an expedition to this unit. Waters are studded with reefs, and visibility is often obscured by heavy fog. The weather in the channels that separate the islands can also be extremely variable. The most popular islands include Turtle and Effingham islands as well as those eight islands designated for camping: Gibralter, Hand, Turret, Dodd, Willis, Clark, Benson, and Gilbert islands. In July and August, you can expect to share these sites with many other campers, all seeking the authentic back-country wilderness experience. Other than pit toilets, there are no facilities. Bring your own water. Call the **Pacific Rim National Park** offices for details and reservations at © **877/737-3783** or 905/426-4648; www.pccamping.ca.

LONG BEACH UNIT

Located between Tofino and Ucluelet, the Long Beach Unit is the most accessible and most developed component of the park. Named for its 20-km (12-mile) stretch of surf-swept sand, Long Beach offers outstanding beaches, surfing, and more. Open year-round, the area offers nine hiking trails, each between 1 and 3.5km (.5–2 miles) long, and most of them boardwalk-surfaced and wheelchair accessible. Star hikes include the 2.8-km (1.7-mile) round-trip **Willowbrae Trail**, just south of Tofino at the Ucluelet junction. It leads down some very steep stairs and ramps to either **Half Moon Bay** (the most romantic cove on the Long Beach stretch) or Florencia Bay. The partially boardwalked **South Beach Trail** (about a 1.5-km/1-mile round trip), and the shorter **Schooner Beach Trail** both take you through rainforest before opening up onto sandy beaches. **Radar Hill**, formerly cellared for a radar installation during World War II, is the only elevated hike from which to see panoramas of Clayoquot Sound. It claims to be the wettest spot on Vancouver Island. *Note:* Storm action can wash trails out, or render them temporarily inaccessible, so it's always best to check with **The Wickaninnish Beach & Interpretive Centre, (© 250/726-4212)** at the south end of Long Beach. It has a marine interpretive center, and provides information on park programs, activities, and events.

> **Tips** **Camping in Pacific Rim National Park**
>
> The only place you can camp on Long Beach is the forested bluff at **Green Point** (© **877/737-3783** or 905/426-4648; www.pccamping.ca), which has 94 drive-through and 20 walk-in campsites. Access down to the beach is quite steep. There's an indoor theater with nightly interpretive programs, and a real sense of camaraderie between campers. This is a busy family spot in high season; it you're looking for quieter times, book in June or September. The campsite is open mid-March to mid-October; walk-in sites cost C$10 (US$9) per night, drive-in sites cost C$21 (US$18). There are flush toilets, but no showers or hookups. Expect to be wait-listed for up to 2 days in July and August.

WHERE TO STAY
IN TOFINO/CLAYOQUOT SOUND

Cable Cove Inn 𝒜 Where do you look first when entering this inn? At the wild oceanfront vistas outside, or at the beautiful selection of Robert Davidson and Roy Vickers prints, and First Nations masks on the inside? It all blends together for an authentic West Coast ambience and membership in the Small Elegant Hotels of the World. Each of the seven romantic suites provides more than just creature comforts; each boasts contemporary decor featuring fireplaces, goose-down duvets draped over queen-size four-poster beds, and decks with ocean views. Two suites have private outdoor Jacuzzis; the others have marble indoor Jacuzzis. Shared areas include a small TV lounge and a fully stocked kitchen. Cable Cove is located within a 5-minute walk of downtown Tofino.

201 Main St. (P.O. Box 339), Tofino, BC V0R 2Z0. © 800/663-6449 or 259/725-4236. Fax 250/725-2857. www. cablecoveinn.com. 7 units. June to mid-Oct C$160–C$235 (US$141–US$207)). Mid-Oct to Feb C$110–C$175 (US$97–US$154). Mar–May C$140–C$190 (US$123–US$167). Rates include breakfast. AE, MC, V. Pets not accepted. Children not accepted. **Amenities:** Lounge; coin-op washers and dryers. *In room:* Hair dryer, Jacuzzi, no phone.

Clayoquot Wilderness Resort 𝒜𝒜𝒜 The name says it all: splendid, luxurious isolation, in the heart of Clayoquot Sound, and reached either by floatplane or 25-minute boat ride out of Tofino. At night, the darkness is blacker than ebony, the stars, brighter than diamonds, and the silence, deliciously deafening. The floating lodge, restaurant, and spa, which has been a fixture at Quait Bay for a number of years, is closed for extensive renovations and will likely reopen in 2008. The resort's wilderness outposts are still operating, and are the most unique destinations you will find. Based at Sky Lake, Orca Beach, and River Valley, these luxurious camps are geared to tender-footed eco-adventurers, and give sleeping under canvas a new twist. Fashioned after turn-of-the-century Rockefeller safari campsites, they have opulently furnished prospector-style tents raised on wooden platforms with antiques, handmade furniture, Persian rugs, four-poster beds topped with down duvets, and freestanding propane and wood stoves. Stays are sold only as multi-night packages. The resort has created a number of trails through the surrounding virgin forest, suitable for mountain biking and horseback riding. Other activities include a trip to Hot Springs Cove as well as kayaking and wildlife-viewing excursions.

P.O. Box 728, Tofino, BC V0R 2Z0. © 888/333-5405 or 250/725-2688. Fax 250/725-2689. www.wildertreat.com. 20 outpost tents. May–Sept 3–7 night stays C$4,750–C$9,450 (US$4,180–US$8,316). Rates include 3 meals/day plus transport to and from Tofino. Fishing packages available. AE, MC, V. Parking in Tofino. Closed Nov–Feb. **Amenities:**

Kayak rentals; free canoes; bike rental; sailing; whale-watching; fishing; hiking; horseback riding. *In room:* TV, hair dryer, no phone.

Inn at Tough City *(Finds)*   Take a close look and you'll see this inn for what it is— a recycled treasure, and one of the quirkiest, small inns in downtown Tofino. Constructed with over 45,000 recycled bricks, refurbished hardwood floors, and original stained-glass windows from as far away as Scotland, the Inn at Tough City is a find. You've got to love the vintage collection of advertising signs and old tins. All guest rooms have their own color scheme, accented with stained glass and antique furniture. They also have decks or balconies with water views, though rooms 3 and 6 have only peekaboo ones. The upstairs guest rooms have fireplaces. All have custom-made bed linens in soft, environment-friendly, unbleached cotton. The inn doesn't provide breakfast, but does have the only authentic sushi restaurant in town (see "Where to Dine").

350 Main St., (P.O. Box 8), Tofino, BC V0R 2Z0. ℂ **250/725-2021**. Fax 250/725-2088. www.toughcity.com. 8 units. Jun–Sept C$169–C$229 (US$149–US$202). Oct & Mar–May C$99 (US$87). Closed Nov–Feb. AE, MC, V. **Amenities:** Restaurant; library-lounge. *In room:* TV, coffeemaker.

Long Beach Lodge Resort *(❋❋)*   This upscale resort lies on the beach at Cox Bay, between Pacific Rim National Park and Clayoquot Sound. Set among towering trees and taking full advantage of the rugged coastline and sandy beach, the cedar-shingled lodge rivals the Wickaninnish Inn (reviewed below in this section). The welcoming Great Room, with its dramatic First Nations art, oversize granite fireplace and deep armchairs, is an ideal spot to relax overlooking the bay, and sample the chef's daily creations that feature fresh, organic ingredients for lunch and dinner, as well as shared plates of hors d'oeuvres. Accommodation includes 41 beachfront lodge rooms with oversize beds, fireplaces, Jacuzzis or extra-deep-soaker bathtubs, and private balconies, as well as 20 two-bedroom cottages nestled in the rainforest. Surfers opt for the ground floor, beachfront rooms that literally puts the rollers on their doorstep. Rain gear is provided to guests who want to venture forth into the storms. Rates include a buffet breakfast.

1441 Pacific Rim Hwy., Tofino, BC V0R 2Z0. ℂ **877/844-7873** or 250/725-2442. Fax 250/725-24662402. www.longbeachlodgeresort.com. 61 units, cottages with hot tubs. June–Sept C$279 (US$246) forest room; C$369–C$399 (US$325–US$351) oceanview room. Oct–May C$179 (US$158) forest room; C$239–C$279 (US$210–US$246) oceanview room. Rates include continental breakfast buffet. **Amenities:** Restaurant; lounge; oceanfront health club. *In room:* Coffeemaker, hair dryer, fireplace.

Middle Beach Lodge   Set among tall hemlocks with a steep slope down to a kilometer of private beach, the rustic ambience of Middle Beach makes it less pretentious than some of the area's other resorts. Perhaps it's because much of the complex was built with recycled lumber so it has a weathered appeal. There are various accommodation styles including standard lodge rooms, suites and self-contained cabins, one of which can sleep 6. Of the entire complex, only two cabins are geared for families. Rooms are priced accordingly to what they offer: some have no phones and great ocean views; others have TVs, balconies, and fireplaces, and still others have full kitchens and Jacuzzis. Room 26 is the most romantic with its king-size bed, kitchenette, and oceanfront location. The high-beamed restaurant and lounge overlook the ocean, serving up a menu of tasty standards such as salmon, steak, and pasta. Although it's open daily for breakfast and dinner during high season, opening hours are sporadic in the winter. Some cabins close in winter.

400 MacKenzie Beach Rd., (PO Box 100), Tofino, BC V0R 2Z0 ℂ 866/725-2900 or 250/725-2900. Fax 250/725-2901. www.middlebeach.com. 45 units, 19 cabins. Mid-June to Sept C$140–C$230 (US$123–US$202) lodge rooms; C$165–C$450 (US$145–US$396) suites and cabins. Oct to mid-June C$110–C$170 (US$97–US$150) lodge rooms. 2-night minimum stay Apr–Sept. Spa packages and off-season discounts available. AE, MC, V. **Amenities:** Restaurant; lounge; exercise room; tour desk; laundry service. *In room:* TV/VCR/DVD (suites and cabins), kitchenette, fridge, coffeemaker, no phone.

Pacific Sands Resort 🐟🐟 This resort nudges against Pacific Rim National Park; white sand beaches, islands, and old-growth rainforests are at your doorstep. In fact, the sound of the surf, although sometimes tumultuous, sets a tranquil, metronome-like quality for sleep. Accommodation ranges from one- and two-bedroom suites to oceanfront cottages, all with kitchens, fireplaces, balconies, and spectacular views. Some have Jacuzzis. The new two- and three-bedroom villas are especially spacious with an open floorplan and West Coast modern decor including heated slate floors and deeper soaker tubs. They're especially suited for families, or couples traveling together. Complimentary rain gear lets guests ignore the weather and ocean spray and get outside.

Cox Bay, Tofino, BC V0R 2Z0. ℂ 800/565-2322 or 250/725-2322. Fax 250/725-3155. www.pacificsands.com. 77 units. July–Sept C$235–C$535 (US$207–US$471). Oct–Jun C$160–C$395 (US$141–US$348). Seasonal discounts available. AE, MC, V. **Amenities:** Bike rental; children's programs; concierge. *In room:* TV.

Wickaninnish Inn 🐟🐟🐟 Perched on a rocky promontory overlooking Chesterman Beach, between old-growth forest and the Pacific Ocean, this member of the renowned Relais & Châteaux network of hotels sets the standard by which other fine hoteliers seem to judge themselves. It describes itself as rustically elegant, which translates into handmade driftwood furniture, local artwork in every room alongside fireplaces, large-screen TVs, richly textured linens and furnishings, en suites with double soakers, and all with breathtaking views of the ocean. The corner suites have an additional wall of windows that seem to beckon the outside in. Adjacent to the original lodge is the **Wickaninnish On the Beach** with 30 even more luxurious two-level guest suites and a health club.

Camping in Tofino

Crystal Cove Beach Resort (Mackenzie Beach, Box 559, Tofino BC V0R 2Z0 (ℂ 250/725-4213; www.crystalcove.cc) has 76 RV and campsites all with fire pits and a picnic table. Flush toilets, free hot showers, and laundry facilities are in a clean, modern building. Full and partial hookups, sewer and water outlets, sani-station are also available. There are also 34 private, modern log cabins with full kitchen, wood-burning fireplace, deck with barbecues, and some with private hot tub. Open year round. Rates based on double occupancy: C$41 (US$36); serviced C$51 (US$45). Cabins range from C$290 to C$410 (US$255–US$361) in high season. Off-season rates are available.

For information on other campsites in the region, check out www.camping.bc.ca. Reservations can be made March to September at www.discovercamping.bc, ℂ 800/689-9025 or 604/689-9025.

In summer, the sprawling sands of Chesterman Beach are littered with sandcastles, tidal pools, and sun worshippers. In winter, it's quite a different story. As thundering waves, howling winds, and sheets of rain lash up against the inn's cedar siding, storm watching becomes an art. Every guest room provides grandstand views through triple-glazed, floor-to-ceiling windows. The result is a surreal feeling of being enveloped by a storm in virtual silence, especially when snuggled up in front of the fire. Rain gear is provided for those brave souls who want to take on the elements first-hand. The **Ancient Cedars Spa** will mellow your mood, especially since every treatment begins with an aromatic footbath. The best treatment room is the new one out on the rocks. Cuisine is another one of the inn's draws. Reservations at the **Pointe Restaurant** are sought-after, so be sure to make them when you book your room (see "Where to Dine").

Osprey Lane at Chesterman Beach (P.O. Box 250), Tofino, BC V0R 2Z0. ℂ 800/ 333-4604 or 250/725-3300. Fax 250/ 725-3110. www.wickinn.com. 75 units. Mid-June to Sept C$460–C$1,500 (US$405–US$1,320). Oct C$300–C$975 (US$264–US$858). Nov to mid-June C$260–C$$975 (US$229–US$858). Rates may vary over holiday periods. Storm-watching, spa, and other packages available. AE, MC, V. **Amenities:** Restaurant; bar; lounge; health club; spa; concierge; in-room massage; babysitting; non smoking facilities. In room: TV/DVD, dataport, minibar, coffeemaker, hair dryer, iron.

IN UCLUELET

Canadian Princess Resort   This former hydrographic survey ship, moored in Ucluelet's central harbor and completely refurbished, sails to nowhere but offers no-nonsense, nautical-style accommodations. Small guest cabins, brightly decorated, offer basic bunk-style beds with washbasins; showers and bathroom facilities are shared. Standard, more comfortable onshore accommodations are also available. These guest rooms have two double beds and private bathrooms. Larger rooms sleep up to 4. The vessel's dining and lounge areas are cozy and add to the seafaring atmosphere. Remember, this was once a working ship, which is a great part of its charm, and is probably why it seems to attract the fishing crowd. It's also a great find for families traveling on a budget.

Ucluelet Harbour, Ucluelet, BC V0R 3A0. ℂ 800/663-7090 or 250/726-7771. Fax 250/726-7121. www.canadian princess.com. 76 units. Mar to mid-Sept C$69–C$109 (US$61–US$96) stateroom; C$145–C$285 (US$128–US$251) on-shore room; C$119–C$139 (US$105–US$122) Captain's Cabin. Extra person C$15 (US$13). Fishing packages available. AE, MC, V. Closed mid-Sept to Feb. **Amenities:** Restaurant; 2 lounges; tour desk. In room: A/C, TV in on-shore rooms, coffeemaker, hair dryer.

A Snug Harbour Inn   Set on a 26-m (85-ft.) cliff overlooking the pounding Pacific, A Snug Harbour Inn is a romantic oasis that takes the credit for at least 75 wedding engagements. Each guest room is decorated a little differently: one has an Atlantic nautical theme; a three-level Lighthouse Suite boasts the best views; and the Sawadee tops the list for snuggly comfort. One suite was built for wheelchair accessibility, including a large, walk-in shower; and another is pet friendly. All have fireplaces, down duvets over queen- or king-size beds, double jet bathtubs, and private decks boasting vast ocean views. For a nominal extra charge, you can order up items such as roses, champagne, and other gifts to add a special touch to your stay. There's a powerful telescope in the Great Room, through which you can watch sea lions on the rocks below. Outside, there's a trail of steps down to the beach, appropriately called "Stairway from the Stars." It's worth the descent, but it's a bit of a hike back up—take it in the morning to whet your appetite for a terrific breakfast.

460 Marine Dr. (P.O. Box 367), Ucluelet, BC V0R 3A0. ℂ 888/936-5222 or 250/726-2686. Fax 250/726-2685. www. awesomview.com. 6 units. June–Sept C$295–C$325 (US$260–US$286). Oct & Mar–May C$225–C$255 (US$198–US$224). Nov–Feb C$185–C$205 (US$163–US$180). MC, V. Pets accepted. **Amenities:** Lounge; Jacuzzi; Internet. *In room:* Hair dryer, no phone.

Tauca Lea Coast Resort ✸✸✸ Overlooking the fishing boats, commercial trollers, and yachts moored in Ucluelet's inner harbor, Tauca Lea exudes a rustic, West Coast style. Its cathedral windows seem to beckon the outdoors in. The resort includes one- and two-bedroom suites, each solidly constructed and beautifully finished with a designer's eye for texture and detail. Furnishings include items such as leather La-Z-Boys in front of gas fireplaces, original artwork, kitchens with designer kitchenware, luxury linens, and all the amenities you would expect in a fine hotel. Some have two-person hot tubs on private decks. The Rainforest Spa and Boat Basin Restaurant (see "Where to Dine") has helped establish this resort as a sought-after romantic getaway.

1971 Harbour Dr., Ucluelet, BC V0R 3A0. ℂ 800/979-9303 or 250/726-4625. Fax 250/726-4663. www.taucalearesort. com. 32 units, some with hot tub. July–Aug C$269–C$369 (US$237–US$298). Sept–Oct & Apr–June C$189–C$299 (US$166–US$263). Nov–Mar C$169–C$259 (US$149–US$228). AE, DC, MC, V. **Amenities:** Restaurant; lounge; spa; concierge; gift shop; coin laundry. *In room:* TV/VCR, CD player, kitchen, fridge, coffeemaker, hair dryer, iron.

WHERE TO DINE
IN TOFINO/CLAYOQUOT SOUND

Pointe Restaurant ✸✸✸ WEST COAST If the 240-degree view of the Pacific Ocean pounding at your feet doesn't inspire, then the food and award-winning wine list certainly will. The menu is an imaginative showcase of fresh coastal food and seafood that's caught within a stone's throw of the inn. Chanterelles, boletus, angel wings, and pine mushrooms are brought in from neighboring forests. Gooseneck barnacles come off the rocks on the beach, and Indian Candy, made from salmon marinated and smoked for six days, comes from Tofino. A chef's four-course Tasting Menu showcases the best of the season; C$115 (US$101) with wine pairings; C$75 (US$66) without. And if the tempest outside is brewing over your meal, take note. The restaurant has special surround-sound to make it feel as if you're eating in the eye of a storm.

At Wickaninnish Inn, Osprey Lane at Chesterman Beach. ℂ 800/333-4604 or 250/725-3100.. www.wickinn.com. Reservations required. Main courses C$22–C$45 (US$19–US$40) AE, MC, V. Daily 8am–9:30pm.

The Schooner on Second ✸ PACIFIC NORTHWEST Originally constructed as the hospital for the WWII RCAF Squadron Unit at Long Beach, it was towed to its present location when the war ended and has had various food incarnations, from coffee shop to crab shack. One of the former chefs, Morris, is even said to be its resident ghost. These days, however, the shack is the place for a romantic or special-occasion dinner. Menu items include beef tenderloin, a succulent lamb roast (and a rack) as well as a range of creatively prepared seafood, often with an ethnic touch as in the West Coast Seafood Hot Pot—halibut, prawns, and scallops sautéed in a spicy red Thai-inspired curry-coconut cream and served with lime-leaf scented basmati rice.

331 Campbell St. ℂ 250/725-3444. Reservations recommended. Main courses C$24–C$$38 (US$21–US$33) MC, V. Daily 9am–3pm and 5–9:30pm.

Shelter ✸✸ PACIFIC NORTHWEST Polished wood dominates the decor of this cozy spot, which also features a large stone fireplace. Although there's meat on the menu, fish is the house specialty, and it's done to perfection, whether crisp albacore tuna rolls, steamed mussels with caramelized onion and roasted garlic, or the clam linguine with smoked bacon. Don't leave without at least trying the bouillabaisse (tasters are by request). It's the signature dish crammed with local fish from sable and Chinook salmon, to prawns, clams, and mussels that have simmered away in a fire-roasted tomato sauce. As expected for a quality fish-focused restaurant, most wines are award-winning whites from B.C. vineyards.

601 Campbell St. ⓒ 250/725-3353. www.shelterrestaurant.com. Reservations recommended. Main courses C$20–C$32 (US$18–US$28). MC, V. Daily 5–10pm.

SoBo *(Finds* ECLECTIC   For an inland location in this area, you can't get much prettier than at the Tofino Botanical Gardens. The chefs have a long pedigree of cooking at high-end lodges, but this is a far cry from froufrou cooking. SoBo is actually short for Sophisticated Bohemian, which describes the decor: a hodgepodge of tables, chairs, and colorful art, as well as the imaginative cuisine that consists mainly of hand-held eats such as "gringo" soft chicken tacos, and crispy shrimp cakes, or a fish taco filled with local wild fish and topped with a fresh fruit salsa. Items are priced tapas-style, so you can order one as a snack or three if you're starving.

Tofino Botanical Gardens, 1084 Pacific Rim Hwy. ⓒ 250/725-2341 or 250/725-4265. www.sobo.ca. Main courses C$5–C$10 (US$4.40–US$9). MC, V. Daily 11am–9pm. Closed Monday in off season.

Sushi Bar at Tough City *⚓* SUSHI   This restaurant has earned such a reputation for authenticity that it's grown from a small bar to the entire main floor of this popular B&B, and in warmer weather even spills over onto the outdoor patio. The menu has all the traditional favorites: sushi rolls, tempura rolls, nigiri, and sashimi as well as other Japanese dishes such as teriyaki salmon, chicken, and beef. If you're not a fan of sushi, but love crab, the Dungeness crab dinner (C$34/US$30) is one of the best, in part because it's so simply prepared—steamed and served cold with melted garlic butter and a fresh Caesar salad. In July and August, the bar opens for lunch as well as dinner.

350 Main St., (P.O. Box 8), Tofino, BC V0R 2Z0. ⓒ 250/725-2021. www.toughcity.com. Main courses C$10–C$24 (US$9–US$21). AE, MC, V. Year round daily 5:30–9pm; July–Aug 11:30am–9pm.

IN UCLUELET
Boat Basin Lounge and Restaurant BISTRO   This marina-side bistro serves a seasonal West Coast menu that focuses on fish, free-range poultry, and local produce. One night this might be pan-roasted halibut with red curry, Arborio rice, and a papaya chutney, cedar plank salmon with an olive tapinade, or spatchcok quail warm-spinach salad with port-wine-poached pear. The Alberta Black Angus filet is a menu staple, as are the selection of Agassiz specialty cheeses which, with the selection of B.C. wines, are a savory conclusion to any meal.

Storm Watching
From November through February, the world's largest ocean unleashes its winter fury with epic proportions so don your rain gear and get set for a dynamic and exhilarating experience. Breakers roll in as much as 15m (50 ft.) high, and crash against the craggy shore with awesome force. Favorite storm watching spots are along the Wild Pacific Trail, Big Beach, at the Amphitrite Point Lighthouse located at the Canadian Coast Guard Station, the Wickanninish Centre, and Chesterman Beach.

Know the Names

In the Nuu-Chah-Nulth language, *Wickaninnish* means "roaring waters;" *Ucluelet* means "safe harbor."

At Tauca Lea Resort, 1971 Harbour Dr. © 800/979-9303 or 250/726-4625. www.taucalearesort.com. Main courses C$15–C$36 (US$13–US$32) AE, DC, MC, V. Daily 5:30–8:30pm.

Matterson House CANADIAN   From the outside, this tiny 1931 cottage is very non-descript, yet once inside you're in for a treat in terms of good food and warm service. By day, there are generous breakfasts and lunches of traditional favorites: burgers, pasta, salads, and homemade breads. By dusk, the menu turns to ocean and from-the-garden cuisine with filling standards such as prime rib; fancier items such as venison with blueberry sauce, or almond-crusted chicken with raspberry sauce, and excellent seafood dishes that include shrimp and scallop skewers and a tasty seafood chowder. The wine list features mostly B.C. labels, some of them special order. With only 7 tables, plus an outside patio of another 7 tables, reservations are recommended. While the food is consistently good, the service is not. The restaurant opens daily year round, although in winter, call first because hours are determined by staff availability and what's happening in town.

1682 Peninsula Rd. © 250/726-2200. Main courses C$13–C$26 (US$11–US$23). MC, V. Daily 9am–9pm (call ahead to confirm).

The Wickaninnish Restaurant CANADIAN   Not to be confused with the restaurant at the Wickaninnish Inn up the road, this dining room sits right on, and above, one of the prettiest parts of Long Beach. There isn't a better spot to savor the area's expansive sands, either inside from behind humongous windows or on heated ocean-front sun deck. Menu items can sometimes be overly ambitious, so if a lofty description takes your fancy, probe your waiter for an honest assessment. Lunches lean to excellent soups, sandwiches, crepes and quiches; dinners include pasta, seafood, and standards such as New York steak. The crowd is a mix of upscale hikers and urban escapees (in other words, you don't see many gloriously muddy hiking boots—they've likely been changed in the car). This is one of the most romantic spots to view a West Coast sunset. **Note:** There's a regular shuttle that runs from the Canadian Princess Resort to the restaurant; if you're driving, be sure to ask your waiter for a complimentary parking pass.

Wickaninnish Interpretive Centre, Long Beach. © 250/726-7706. Reservations recommended. Main courses C$17–C$33 (US$15–US$29). AE, MC, V. Mid-Mar to mid-Sept 11:30am–9:30pm.

7

Northern Vancouver Island

The differences between the North Island and the South are profound. The farther north you drive, the wilder Vancouver Island becomes, and as urban sophistication falls to the wayside, you'll start to discover the diversity of the region. Fewer than 3% of the island's residents live in the northern part, with its vast forests of deep green, its crystal-clear rivers and its inviting beaches. It's a paradise for eco-adventurers and nature photographers—a mecca for anyone looking for Canadian wilderness. Some communities, such as Kyoquot, are accessible only by chartered floatplane or boat, and to reach them you travel through country that is quintessential West Coast Canada. Travel inland is also an adventure, usually via logging roads toward off-the-beaten-track destinations. If you drive these routes, remember to use caution. Logging is a primary industry in this part of the world; logging trucks are numerous, and have the right of way.

Natural resources have long been the economic backbone of Vancouver Island, and as those resources diminish, towns are looking to alternative investments. In **Courtenay–Comox,** the fastest-growing region on the island, and fish-happy **Campbell River,** resorts are springing up alongside entire retirement communities. Far-flung mining hamlets like **Zeballos,** which once made its fortune in gold, and **Holberg,** are becoming bases for eco-adventurers, and picturesque places like **Telegraph Cove,** are succumbing to 21st-century development. Despite these changes, you'll still come across communities, such as **Port McNeill** and **Port Hardy,** that are pretty rough-and-ready, as well as places like **Alert Bay,** whose isolation has protected its rich First Nations culture.

This great diversity is the region's primary appeal. If you're a culture buff, stay in Victoria. If you're traveling with very young children, again, stay south, unless you're heading for **Mount Washington** to ski, or to **Miracle Beach,** one of the province's most popular provincial parks. But if you're hankering to experience nature with no boundaries, you won't get much better than North Vancouver Island.

1 Courtenay & the Comox Valley

If you drive 62km (39 miles) north of Parksville–Qualicum Beach on Highway 19, you'll come upon Vancouver Island's other set of twin towns, Courtenay–Comox. Unlike their neighbors to the south, Courtenay and Comox are refreshingly untouristy, and so close together that you can hop from one to the other in a matter of minutes. Courtenay, with a population of 20,000, is a center of lumber milling on Vancouver Island, and basks in a wide agricultural valley, while its sister community, Comox, with a population of 12,000, lies on the peninsula just east of Comox Harbour. Originally known as Port Augusta, it was once the only harbor from which supply ships could reach mid-island communities such as Gold River.

Today, the Comox Valley is one of the fastest-growing regions on Vancouver Island. Retirees are attracted to its rural ambience and urban amenities. For travelers—particularly outdoorsy types—it is the gateway to wilderness adventure. The Beaufort Mountains, **Mount Washington Alpine Resort,** and **Strathcona Provincial Park** are within easy reach, and the promise of alpine lakes, glacial basins, and craggy peaks brings with it abundant opportunity to view wildlife, as well as to hike, ski, kayak, and much more. If you've time, spend a day or two touring **Denman and Hornby islands,** a 10-minute ferry trip from Buckley Bay, just north of Fanny Bay.

ESSENTIALS
GETTING THERE
By Car
The driving distance from Victoria to Courtenay, along Highway 19, due north, is 220km (137 miles). From Nanaimo, the distance is 113km (70 miles). From Parksville, it is 73km (45 miles). Highway 19 becomes Cliffe Avenue as it enters Courtenay.

By Plane
Air Canada Jazz (✆ 888/247-2262; www.flyjazz.ca) and **Pacific Coastal Airlines** (✆800/663-2872; www.pacificcoastal.com) operate daily flights between Victoria, Port Hardy, and Campbell River to the **Comox Valley Regional Airport** (✆ 250/897-3123; www.comoxairport.com). **WestJet Airlines** (✆ 888/937-8538 or 800/538-5696; www.westjet.com) operates nonstop flights between Comox and Calgary. Small aircraft and floatplanes can land at the **Courtenay Airpark** (✆ 250/334-8545).

By Bus
Laidlaw Coach Lines (✆ 250/385-4411) operates between Victoria and Port Hardy, with various stops along the way. **Greyhound Canada** (✆ 800/663-8390 or 604/482-8747; www.greyhound.ca) handles schedules and reservations. The one-way fare from Victoria to Courtenay is C$39 (US$34) for adults. From Nanaimo to Courtenay, it's C$21 (US$19) for adults. Fares for seniors are 10% less; fares for children 5 to 11 are 50% less. The trip from Victoria to Courtenay takes 4½ hours; from Nanaimo, it's 2 hours.

By Train
Courtenay is the termination point of the daily service offered by the **Malahat,** run by **VIA Rail** (✆ 800/561-8630; www.viarail.com) between Victoria and Courtenay.

By Ferry
BC Ferries (✆ 888/223-3779; www.bcferries.com) operates two daily crossings from **Powell River,** on the BC Sunshine Coast, to **Little River,** in Comox, a 10-minute drive from Courtenay. One-way fares are C$8.65 (US$7.60) for adults, C$4.35 (US$3.80) for children 5 to 11, C$30 (US$26) for a standard-size vehicle. The crossing takes 1¼ hours.

VISITOR INFORMATION
The **Comox Valley Information Centre** is at 2040 Cliffe Ave., Courtenay, BC V9N 2L3 (✆ 888/357-4471 or 250/334-3234; www.tourism-comox-valley.bc.ca). If you'd like to find out more about the Comox Valley beforehand, you can contact the **Tourism Association of Vancouver Island,** Suite 203, 335 Wesley St., Nanaimo, BC V9R 2T5 (✆ 250/754-3500; www.islands.bc.ca).

Tips **Circle Pac Savings**

BC Ferries offers a special circle tour, enabling passengers to follow routes between the Mainland and Vancouver Island. You can choose to circle in any direction, between Victoria, Nanaimo, and Comox on the island, across to Powell River, Horseshoe Bay, and Tsawwassen on the mainland. Whichever direction you choose, this special four-route travel package gives you up to 15% off regular, one-way fares.

GETTING AROUND

The Comox Valley Transit System (© 250/339-5453) operates local bus service in and between Courtenay, Comox, and Cumberland, a smaller community about 8km (5 miles) south of Courtenay. **United Cabs** (© 250/339-7955) provides taxi service in these same communities.

EXPLORING THE AREA
COMOX

The tallest building in **Comox** belongs to the Logger's Union, and bears testimony to the backbone of the region's economy. The center of town bustles around a new **harborside promenade,** where fishing boats are so plentiful, you can often buy fish or prawns straight from the vessel.

The Filberg Lodge and Park   Once a private residence, the estate was first cleared in 1929 and today covers some 3.6 hectares (9 acres) of wooded and landscaped gardens. The handsome stone and timbered lodge rests on piles driven into an old salt marsh and Native shell midden (a refuse heap) and exudes old-world craftsmanship inside and out. Examples include hand-milled beams, a yew-tree handrail on the staircase, and a stone fireplace featuring a Native petroglyph. Outside, the waterfront gardens are filled with rare and exotic trees, hundreds of rhododendrons, and numerous flower beds. There's even a four-figure totem pole. Filberg appeals to all ages, and if you're traveling with kids, be sure to visit the hands-on petting farm (open mid-June to mid-August). Take the morning or afternoon to explore Filberg; the teahouse serves lunch as well as traditional afternoon tea with cucumber sandwiches, scones, and Devonshire cream, so either way, you need not go hungry. Over the first weekend of August, the park is the site of the four-day Filberg Festival (© **250/334-9242;** www.filbergfestival.com), an outdoor art exhibition showcasing the work of more than 150 of British Columbia's top craftspeople.

61 Filberg Rd. Comox, BC V9M 2S7 © **250/339-2715.** www.filberg.com. Admission C$10 (US$9) adults, free for children under 16. May–Sept daily 8am–dusk. No pets.

Kitty Coleman Woodland Gardens   Named after a First Nations woman who set up residence in the area in the late 1800s, the gardens are a loving and extraordinary creation of one man, Bryan Zimmerman, without the help of heavy equipment that might have destroyed the land. These spectacular, half-wild gardens must be seen to be believed—for the 3,000 rhododendrons alone! There are 9.7 hectares (24 acres) to explore, so bring along shoes with good treads; the bark-mulch trails can be slippery.

6183 Whittaker Rd. (just north of Seal Bay Park), Courtenay, BC V9J 1V7 © **250/338-6901.** www.woodland gardens.ca. Admission C$6 (US$5.30) adults, C$2 (US$1.75) children 5–12. Year-round daily 9am–dusk.

Northern Vancouver Island

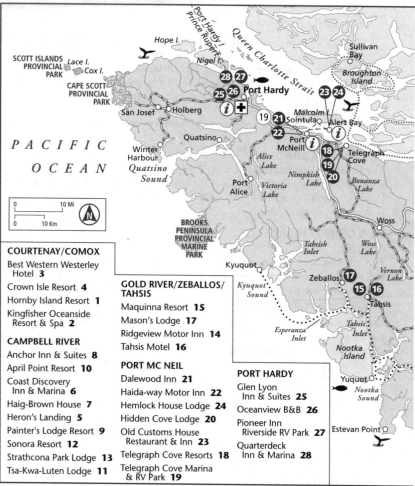

COURTENAY/COMOX

Best Western Westerley Hotel **3**

Crown Isle Resort **4**

Hornby Island Resort **1**

Kingfisher Oceanside Resort & Spa **2**

CAMPBELL RIVER

Anchor Inn & Suites **8**

April Point Resort **10**

Coast Discovery Inn & Marina **6**

Haig-Brown House **7**

Heron's Landing **5**

Painter's Lodge Resort **9**

Sonora Resort **12**

Strathcona Park Lodge **13**

Tsa-Kwa-Luten Lodge **11**

GOLD RIVER/ZEBALLOS/ TAHSIS

Maquinna Resort **15**

Mason's Lodge **17**

Ridgeview Motor Inn **14**

Tahsis Motel **16**

PORT MC NEIL

Dalewood Inn **21**

Haida-way Motor Inn **22**

Hemlock House Lodge **24**

Hidden Cove Lodge **20**

Old Customs House Restaurant & Inn **23**

Telegraph Cove Resorts **18**

Telegraph Cove Marina & RV Park **19**

PORT HARDY

Glen Lyon Inn & Suites **25**

Oceanview B&B **26**

Pioneer Inn Riverside RV Park **27**

Quarterdeck Inn & Marina **28**

COURTENAY

Courtenay's sexiest claim to fame is that it's the hometown of Kim Cattrall, from the TV show *Sex and the City*. But it just about stops there. Sure, Courtenay is a pleasant enough community, but it doesn't have a particular hub of activity, except for a few galleries and shops around 4th, 5th, and 6th streets, including the **Comox Valley Art Gallery,** 580 Duncan St. at 6th (✆ **250/338-6211**), opposite the library. There's also quite an enclave of local artists at **The Artisans Courtyard,** (180B 5th St. ✆ **250/ 338-6564**) as well as at the **Potter's Place** (180A 5th St. ✆ **250/334-4613**).

The **Kingfisher Oceanside Resort & Spa** and the **Crown Isle Resort** (see "Where to Stay") are doing their part to change all that, however. More than a place to stay, Crown Isle is an entire complex of lavish condominiums, restaurants, and lounges centered on an 18-hole links-style **championship golf course** that offers sweeping views of the Comox Glacier and Beaufort Mountains. The course is open year-round.

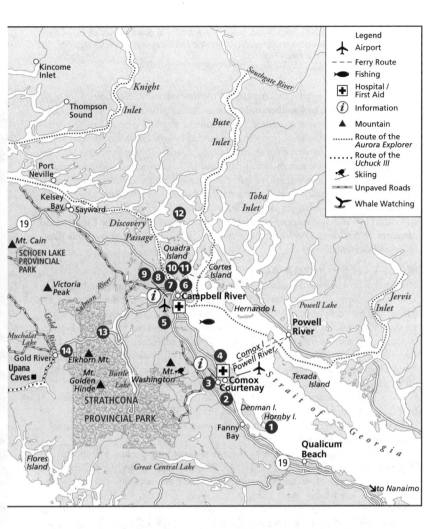

From June to September, nonmember green fees are C$75 (US$66); from October to March, C$40 (US$35); in April, C$50 (US$44), and in May, C$60 (US$53). While you're there, be sure to see the **Classic Car Museum,** featuring a collection of predominantly fifties and sixties Chevrolets and Fords, some of which were previously owned by the likes of Sylvester Stallone and Mary Hart.

The Courtenay Museum & Paleontology Centre ⦅ Housed in the town's old post office, the center holds a collection of First Nations masks and basketry, pioneer artifacts, and a 12-m (40-ft.) cast skeleton of an elasmosaur, a crocodile-like Cretaceous-era reptile. Half-day tours are offered year-round, and run the gamut from exploring the paleontology lab to digging in the riverbed. A tropical sea once covered the Comox Valley, so there's a wealth of marine fossils to be found. Open year-round, admission is by donation. To make the most of the experience, a tour is the way to go. Great for kids.

360 Cliffe Ave. (© **250/334-3611.** www.courtenaymuseum.ca. Admission by donation. Tours are C$20 (US$18) adults, C$18 (US$15) students and seniors, C$13 (US$11) children under 12. May–Sept. Mon to Sat 10am–5pm, Sun noon–4pm; winter hours Tues–Sat 10am– 5pm.

CUMBERLAND

Just 16km (10 miles) south of Courtenay, in the foothills of the Beaufort Mountains, the coal-mining town of **Cumberland** still stirs the imagination with pretty heritage homes and storefronts—as evidenced by the piles of slag and sheets of rusted corrugated iron scattered around old buildings. Founded by coal baron Robert Dunsmuir, and named after the famous English coal-mining district, Cumberland was once the second largest coal producer in North America. In 1912, one mine alone produced some 2,580 kilograms (5,688 lbs.) of coal a day. Back then, the town's population was five times what it is today, made up of some 13,000 workers from around the world. Cumberland once claimed the largest Chinatown north of San Francisco. The mine was closed in 1966, but you can get a feel for Cumberland's story at the **Cumberland Museum & Archives,** 2680 Dunsmuir Ave. (© **250/336-2445;** www.cumberland. museum.bc.ca/cma).

MOUNT WASHINGTON ALPINE RESORT 🦌🦌

Drive north on Highway 19 and take Exit 130 to the Mount Washington exit, about a 30-minute drive from Courtenay–Comox. Then it's an ear-popping climb to the base of the resort. (The road is in excellent condition.) Mount Washington is hardly a resort in the upscale, four-season Whistler sense of the word but you will find mountain bikers, alpine fly-fishing enthusiasts, and hikers adventuring through the landscape. Many trails, such as those leading off the 2-km (1.2 miles) **Paradise Meadows Loop Trail,** connect to Strathcona Provincial Park (see below.) Take the scenic chairlift to the summit and you'll find a number of easy bark-mulch, interpretive trails to explore. In winter, skiing is the mountain's raison d'être. With a 488-m (1,600-ft.) vertical drop, and more than 50 groomed runs, most above 1,200m (3,937 ft.), serviced by four lifts and a beginners' tow, Mount Washington has become British Columbia's third largest ski and snowboard area.

As for other winter sports, there's a 0-Zone **snow-tubing park,** a 250-m (820-ft.) **luge run,** and 30km (19 miles) of track-set **Nordic trails** connecting to Strathcona Provincial Park. To avoid crowds and lift lineups, plan to go on a weekday—the mountain is remarkably quiet. This is something that can never be said about Whistler. From December to March, day passes for skiing are C$54 (US$48) for adults, C$44 (US$39) for seniors and children 13 to 18, C$29 (US$26) for children 7 to 12, free for children 6 and under. The Alpine and Raven Lodges have restaurants, rentals, and some shops, and there are about 200 condominium units for rent on the mountain. For details on lift passes, snow school programs, equipment, and condominium rentals, call the central information and reservations number, (© **888/231-1499** or 250/338-1386, or log on to **www.mtwashington.ca.**

STRATHCONA PROVINCIAL PARK 🦌🦌🦌

Located almost in the center of Vancouver Island, Strathcona Provincial Park is a rugged wilderness of more than 250,000 hectares (617,000 acres). In the summer it can be accessed via several moderately easy trails from Mount Washington Alpine Resort (see above), and year-round by driving to Campbell River on Highway 19 and taking the Highway 28 exit to Gold River.

Strathcona was British Columbia's first designated wilderness and recreation area (created in 1911), and is managed by the **Ministry of Environment, Lands, and Parks** (© 250/337-2400; www.elp.gov.bc.ca/bcparks). The park brims with treasures: snow-capped mountain peaks, lakes set in amphitheaters of ice, valleys filled with pristine rain forest, alpine meadows painted with heather, as well as rivers and waterfalls—including Canada's tallest waterfall, **Della Falls,** at 440m (1,445 ft.). Wildlife is plentiful, and because of Vancouver Island's separation from the mainland, there are no chipmunks, porcupines, coyotes, or grizzly bears, and species such as Roosevelt elk, black-tailed deer, marmot, and wolf here are slightly smaller than their mainland cousins. Birds are also numerous, and include the chestnut-backed chickadee, redbreasted nuthatch, winter wren, ruffed grouse, and a limited number of unique Vancouver Island white-tailed ptarmigan.

But Strathcona's greatest treasures aren't exactly on display so if you really want to explore this diverse park, you'll need to hike or backpack into the alpine wilderness. Getting to Della Falls, for example, requires a boat ride to reach the trailhead and a multi-day hike that follows the old railway grade up the Drinkwater Valley.

In addition to Paradise Meadows (Mount Washington), **Forbidden Plateau** and **Buttle Lake** are good access points to the park, largely because they can be reached by car, and both have information centers. The Forbidden Plateau offers views to the horizon of glaciers, forests, and pastoral landscapes, and, starting at the former ski lodge, a fairly steep 4.8-km (3-mile) trail up Mount Becher. The views of the valley and the Strait of Georgia make the effort worthwhile. At Buttle Lake, you'll find camping facilities (for reservations call Discover Camping, © **800-689-9025**), a honey-hole for rainbow trout and Dolly Varden, and several trails. Three notable hikes are the easy 20-minute walk to Lady Falls, the 6.5-km (4-mile) hike along Marble Meadows Trail, and the 3.2-km (2-mile) Upper Myra Falls Trail through old-growth forests and past waterfalls.

Because of the diversity of this park, I suggest you check out the Strathcona Park Lodge (see "Where to Stay"), if not to stay, at least to get the lowdown on their many programs, which are geared as much to wilderness neophytes as to experienced outdoor adventurers.

WHERE TO STAY

Best Western Westerley Hotel   You can't miss it. The Westerley looks like an angular three-story greenhouse, right on Highway 19, the main route into Courtenay. Once you're past the uninviting glass facade, though, you'll find a comfortable spot to rest your road-weary bones. Guest rooms are clean, spacious, and comfortably furnished. The building is divided into two wings; the rear one is the better bet, offering rooms with balconies and views of the Courtenay River. The hotel has an indoor pool and health club as well as a casual restaurant, a pool lounge, and a lively sports pub which is a lot more savory than some of the other drinking establishments you'll find down the street.

1590 Cliffe Ave., Courtenay, BC V9N 2K4. © **800/668-7797** or 250/338-7741. Fax 250/338-5442. www.coasthotels. com. 108 units. C$154–C$164 (US$136–US$144) regular and deluxe room; C$209 (US$184) suite. Extra person C$10 (US$9). Lower rates off season. Children 18 and under stay free in parent's room. AE, MC, V. Pets accepted. **Amenities:** Restaurant; sports pub; large heated indoor pool; health club & spa; limited room service; liquor store. *In room:* TV w/pay movies, dataport, minibar, coffeemaker, hair dryer, iron.

Crown Isle Resort 🎄🎄🎄   This resort breathes golf at every turn, and little wonder. Its 72-par, Platinum-rated course is suitable for golfers at all levels, and is the centerpiece of the entire development. You don't have to be a member to play, and you don't have to be a golf nut to stay. The villas, which come in a variety of configurations, are lavish and are more like small townhouses. Finishing touches include two-sided gas fireplaces with marble surrounds and deep soaker Jacuzzis, over which there's a starlit ceiling that twinkles from blue to yellow. Most have fully equipped kitchens; some have wet bars and separate dining areas. A newer building offers equally sumptuous hotel-style rooms, though slightly set back from the fairway. All guests have access to the resort's fitness center in the upscale clubhouse. There's a cozy pub, and if you're a steak connoisseur, the Silverado Steak House (see "Where to Dine") is a must.

399 Clubhouse Dr., Courtenay, BC V9N 9G3. ⓒ 888/338-8439 or 250/703-5050. Fax 250/703-5051. www.crown isle.com. 90 units. June–Sept C$139 (US$122) standard; C$249–C$335 (US$219–US$295) villa/loft. Oct & May C$119 (US$105) standard; C$189–C$289 (US$166–US$254) villa/loft. Nov–Apr C$109 (US$96) standard; C$159–C$259 (US$140–US$228) villa/loft. Golf and ski packages available. Extra person C$15 (US$13). Children 17 and under stay free in parent's room. AE, MC, V. Free parking. **Amenities:** Two restaurants; pub; golf course; health club; business center; limited room service; laundry service; same-day dry cleaning. *In room:* TV/DVD, dataport, coffeemaker, hair dryer, Jacuzzi.

Kingfisher Oceanside Resort & Spa *☆☆*   Located 7km (4½ miles) south of Courtenay, this adult-oriented resort still hints as to its Best Western origins: the rooms tend to be extra large and sport balconies or patios with ocean views. The decor, however, is more like an upscale Holiday Inn with pine furniture and brightly colored linens. The beachfront suites are particularly deluxe and come with kitchenettes, and heated bathroom floors; most have Jacuzzis. The suites are worth the extra money for the extra comfort and ability to do your own thing meal-wise. The impressive spa, of course, is why most people come here. Facilities include a heated outdoor pool with shoulder-massaging waterfall, a cave steam-room and sauna, as well as a broad range of spa services (at an additional cost) such as thalassotherapy wraps, hot stone massages, Reiki, reflexology, and facials. There's also a small and elegant yoga studio with various drop-in stretch classes. A complimentary shuttle run between the resort and downtown, and to the Comox Valley Regional Airport, as well as to Mount Washington Alpine Resort (see "Mount Washington Alpine Resort," above). The Kingfisher Oceanside Restaurant is one of the better places to dine in the area (see "Where to Dine" below).

4330 Island Hwy. S., Courtenay, BC V9N 9R9. ⓒ 800/663-7929 or 250/338-1323. Fax 250/338-0058. www.kingfisher spa.com. 64 units. C$165 (US$145) oceanview room; C$179–C$325 (US$158–US$286) beachfront suite; C$450 (US$396) deluxe suite. Low-season discounts; spa, ski and golf packages available. Extra person C$15 (US$13). AE, DC, DISC, MC, V. **Amenities:** Restaurant; lounge; golf nearby; unlit outdoor tennis court; health club & spa; canoe and kayak rentals; activities desk; business center; 24-hr. room service; laundry service; dry cleaning. *In room:* TV, (VCR/DVD in beachfront suites), dataport, coffeemaker, hair dryer.

Strathcona Park Lodge & Outdoor Education Centre *☆☆*   Perched on the shores of Upper Campbell Lake, just outside the park's eastern boundary, this privately owned lodge provides not only a comfortable place to stay, from lodge rooms and cabins to chalet-type accommodation, but also a variety of opportunities for exploring the surrounding wilderness. Staying here has been described as a cross between Outward Bound and Club Med. Everyone from hard-core outdoor types to parents with young children can find an educational and adventure program to fit their niche, experiencing activities such as sailing, wilderness survival, rock climbing, backcountry hiking, fishing, swimming, canoeing, and kayaking. Special packages are available, and guides and instructors can be hired by the hour. Unless you know the park well, or are comfortably at ease trekking through backcountry, then the lodge is definitely worth checking out.

25 miles west of Campbell River on Hwy. 28. Mailing address: Box 2160, Campbell River, BC V9W 5C5 (⟨C⟩ **250/ 286-3122.** Fax 250/286-6010. www.strathcona.bc.ca. 39 units. C$50–C$88 (US$44–US$77) chalet double with shared bathroom; C$88–C$159 (US$77–US$140) double with private bathroom; C$169–C$325 (US$149–US$286) cabin. 2–3 night minimum stay in cabins. Adventure packages and off-season discounts available. MC, V. **Amenities:** Restaurant; exercise room; sauna; canoe and kayak rentals; children's programs; massage; babysitting; coin-op laundry; nonsmoking. *In room:* No phone.

WHERE TO DINE

Atlas Cafe *(Finds) (Value)* INTERNATIONAL   From this small restaurant in downtown Courtenay, you can travel the world food-wise with large portions of Mexican quesadillas, Greek spanakopitas, Thai satays, Italian-style sandwiches on focaccia as well as a good selection of vegetarian dishes. Dinner adds more substantial dishes such as stir-fries, noodle creations, fish, and roast beef. The cafe is busy from the moment it opens—locals know where to come for breakfast, and has specialty coffees that put Starbucks on the back burner. Weekends, breakfast is served until 2pm. Although the wine list is limited, the bar is making quite a name for itself on the martini circuit.

250 6th St., Courtenay. ⟨C⟩ **250/338-9838.** www.comoxvalleyrestaurants.ca/atlas.htm. Reservations accepted for parties of 6 or more. Lunch C$7–C$15 (US$6–US$13); dinner C$15–C$20 (US$13–US$18). MC, V. Mon 8:30am– 3:30pm; Tues–Sat 8:30am–10pm; Sun 8:30am–9pm.

Black Fin Pub *(Finds)(Finds)* PUB/CANADIAN   The view is splendid, stretching from a logstrewn beach, across the water, and on to the distant Beaufort Mountains. The atmosphere is what you want in a stylish pub: dark wood trim complemented by deep blue upholstery with nautical accents. There's a sunken dining area and plenty of chairs against the bar, and the menu includes quality pub dishes like burgers, sandwiches, wraps, fish and chips, as well as grazing options such as crab and shrimp cakes (they're really worth the trip), a spicy beef satay and chicken wings.

132 Port Augusta St., Comox. ⟨C⟩ **250/339-5030.** Reservations accepted for parties of 4 or more in early evening. Main courses C$10–C$23 (US$9–US$20). AE, MC, V. Sun–Thurs 11am–10pm; Fri–Sat 11am–11pm.

Kingfisher Oceanside Restaurant SEAFOOD/CONTINENTAL   Although the food doesn't always match the hype of the lavish menu descriptions, it is good enough to make this one of the region's better eateries. And the waterfront views are terrific. Because of its proximity to the spa, the menu includes a number of low-fat, lowcalorie options. The poached halibut jardinière with salad of grilled fruit, roasted nuts, crumbled Stilton cheese and more is a popular choice. If lean cuisine's not your thing, there are steaks, schnitzels, and lamb dishes as well as vegetarian choices such as porcini-mushroom homemade ravioli served with fresh tomato and chipotle-pepper coulis with a fresh Asiago crisp.

4330 Island Hwy. S., 7km (4½ miles) south of Courtenay. ⟨C⟩ **250/338-1323.** www.kingfisherspa.com. Reservations advised. Main courses C$15–C$25 (US$13–US$22). AE, DC, DISC, MC, V. Weekdays 7am–9pm; weekends 7am–10pm.

Monte Christo on the River *(Value) (Kids)* WEST COAST   This rambling period home is full of rooms, each of which has been converted into an individual dining area, including a room for two that's about the size of a broom closet! It's a rather bizarre yet beguiling feeling: at any one time, you're never aware of how large the place really is, or how many others are breaking bread with you. A patio opens in summer right on the river's edge. The menu's broad, offering everything from hearty soups and salads for lunch to prime beef, lamb, seafood and pasta for dinner. Monte Christo is a favorite for families and seniors. A bonus for modest eaters is that most choices are available in smaller portions.

975 Comox Rd., Courtenay. ℂ **250/338-1468**. Reservations recommended. Lunch C$7–C$13 (US$6-US$11); dinner C$9–C$20 (US$8–US$18). AE, MC, V. Sun–Thurs 11:30am–10pm; Fri and Sat 4–11pm.

Silverado Steak House ℱ   The atrium-style fine-dining restaurant specializes in AAA-grade steak from Alberta, and serves it up alongside some spectacular views of the Beaufort Mountains as well as the 18th hole. Big eaters can opt for the 20-oz. Delmonico rib steak chop while for more modest appetites there's a 6-oz. filet mignon. Both are exceptionally good with either a red wine garlic or blue cheese cream demi. There's also a good selection of local seafood such as oysters from nearby Talbot Cove, trout, halibut, and salmon.

399 Clubhouse Dr., Courtenay. ℂ **888/338-8439** or 250/703-5000. Reservations recommended. Main courses C$20–C$35 (US$18–US$31). AE, MC, V. Daily 5–10pm.

Tomato Tomato ℱℱ WEST COAST   Now part of a development (www.oldhouse village.com) that includes chic rental suites, shops, a spa, and other amenities under construction, Tomato Tomato is a significant updo of the former Old House Restaurant. Traces of the original restaurant remain—you'll still find rough-hewn timbers crossing the open ceiling, four fireplaces, and picturesque wooden windows inside, and flower-filled gardens edging the Courtenay River outside. The menu is typical West Coast cuisine, offering steak and local seafood. The grilled Sooke trout sounds ordinary but the pine-nut butter makes it outstanding. There's a very good herb-crusted halibut with Thai red curry sauce that manages to complement, not overwhelm, the fish, and the rack of lamb with blackcurrant is a popular choice. This is the place to celebrate family gatherings and romantic notions.

1760 Riverside Lane, Courtenay. ℂ **250/338-5406**. www.tomatotomato.ca. Reservations recommended. Lunch C$12 (US$11); dinner C$22 (US$19). AE, MC, V. Mon–Thurs 11:30am–9:30pm; Fri–Sun11:30am–10pm.

Toscanos Trattoria ℱℱ ITALIAN   This casual, convivial licensed bistro is filled with cheerful colors—oranges, yellows, and reds—and wonderfully aromatic smells. The menu includes huge panini, excellent pastas, and specialty entrees such as chicken breast filled with ricotta, sundried tomatoes, and spinach, and served in a basil sauce. Save room for Italian classics such as tiramisu, and the mmm, so delicious, Mario Gelato. Toscanos Trattoria is where the trendies on a budget dine.

140 Port Augusta, Comox. ℂ **250/890-7575**. Reservations required. Main courses C$12–C$24 (US$11–US$21). MC, V. Mon–Sat 11am–2pm and 5–9pm.

2 Hornby & Denman Islands

A haven for aging flower children and Vietnam draft dodgers who stayed north of the 49th parallel after amnesty, Hornby and Denman islands are an inspiration. Their distinct bohemian charm is a throwback to 1960s creativity, and their beautiful landscapes have made them one of British Columbia's most popular beach vacation destinations. If you really want to appreciate the rural isolation of these islands, visit in low season; Hornby's year-round population of 1,000 swells to as many as 10,000 in summer.

GETTING THERE

To get there, canoe or kayak across the narrow channel, or hop onto the ferry at Buckley Bay, just north of Fanny Bay. To get to Hornby Island, you must first cross Denman. The dozen daily trips to each island take 10 minutes one-way and each leg of the journey costs C$5.75 (US$5.10) adult, C$2.90 (US$2.55) child, and C$14 (US$12) regular vehicle.

VISITOR INFORMATION

On Denman Island, the Denman General Store, 1069 Northwest Rd., Denman Island, BC V0R 1T0 (© 250-335-2293) acts as the Denman/Hornby Visitor Services. It offers a free island guide, information on the small one and two-bedroom B&Bs, as well as a brochure listing the *many* small arts and crafts galleries. You can also get information at www.denmanisland.com and www.hornbyisland.com.

GETTING AROUND

The islands are great for bicycling. Bring bikes on the ferry or contact Denman Island Cycles & Repairs (© 250/335-1759) for rentals; they can meet you at the ferry or wherever you may be staying.

EXPLORING THE ISLANDS

DENMAN

On Denman, beautiful sandstone and gravel shores are full of life: oysters, rock crabs, clams, eagles, and seabirds. There's good salmon fishing, particularly off the south end. Off the north shores, you can kayak across to **Sandy Island Provincial Marine Park**, a group of beautiful wooded islands with limited camping (© 250/334-4600). **Denman Hornby Canoes & Kayaks**, 4005 East Rd. (© 250/335-0079), offers rentals (half-day C$45/US$40; full-day C$65/US$57) and custom-guided excursions ranging from 2½ hrs (C$70/US$62) to a full day (C$110/US$97). These folks also offer a modest B&B, geared for paddlers.

HORNBY

You need no other excuse to visit Hornby than **Tribune Bay Provincial Park**. Here, the sea has beaten the soft rock faces into dramatic cave and hoodoo formations. **Helliwell Bay Provincial Park** is worth exploring, both for the trails along the bluff and to see the thousands of nesting birds tucked into the side of the cliffs. Hornby's two claims to fame are as the only spot in Canada where you'll fine certain types of butterflies, including the Taylor's Checkerspot, and the only place in the world where divers will find primitive deep-sea six-gill shark swimming in shallow waters.

WHERE TO STAY & DINE

Because of the islands' popularity, accommodation can be hard to come by, so even if you're sleeping under canvas, book at least three months in advance. There are also few places to eat. On Hornby, check out some of the tiny eateries at Ringside Market, or head for the **Thatch Neighbourhead Pub**, 4305 Shingle Spit Rd. © 250/335-0136, open daily, offering casual pub fare. It's the only waterside watering hole on the island, and is a popular local nightspot with live music Friday and Saturday. Notice the tabletops; they represent the work of 22 local artists. Look further, and you'll notice imaginative art throughout. There's a tiny licensed bistro with very limited opening hours at the Denman Island Hostel (© 250/335-2688) in "downtown." The guesthouse, a 1912 heritage farmhouse, has a mix of accommodations with shared bathrooms alongside caravans and rather odd-looking tree spheres that are accessed by rope ladders. From a distance they look like giant eyeballs hanging in the trees. Rates range from C$20 to C$40 (US$18–US$35) a night depending on where you hang your shingle.

Hornby Island Resort   Book months in advance if you want to get a spot at this popular waterfront resort, largely because it's the only show in town. The rustic cottage rooms are plainly furnished and come with small bathrooms and full kitchen; the campsites are fairly private, separated by roses and honeysuckle plants, and well-maintained. Each has a picnic table, a fire pit, and optional electrical plug-ins. Campground facilities include hot showers and laundry.

4305 Shingle Spit Rd. (next to the ferry terminal), Hornby Island BC V0R 1Z0. © **250/335-0136.** Fax 250/335-9136. hornbyislandresort@hornbyisland.com. 2 units, 2 cottages, 10 campsites. C$75 (US$66) double; C$19 (US$17) campsite; C$1 (US$88¢) electric hookup. C$950 (US$836) weekly (only in summer) cabin, C$100 (US$88 per night off season cabin. MC, V **Amenities:** Restaurant, pub, laundry, tennis, boat moorage. *In-room:* TV.

3 Campbell River, Gold River & Tahsis, Nootka & Kyoquot Sounds

Once you hit mid island, the entire topography starts to shift. Campbell River is the last major town you come across, and is the gateway to Vancouver Island's wilder nature. Head towards Gold River, and you start to see how important the island's inner waterways are to its economy. Go farther to Tahsis, Nootka, and Kyoquot Sounds, and you're in some of the most beautiful coastal waters in the world—the places where the Spanish and Captain Cook first explored, and that are now opening up to varied eco-tourism activities.

CAMPBELL RIVER

Although you could take the fast inland highway, Highway 19, north from Courtenay for the 48-km (30-mile) drive to Campbell River, I suggest you take the scenic and more leisurely route along Highway 19A, also called the **Oceanside Route.** Exit Highway 19 at **Miracle Beach,** and head north on Highway 19A. Follow the Starfish signs past scenic coves and through small, picturesque communities, many of which have small galleries and art studios to browse through. Bring your camera and enjoy weaving along the water's edge. Check out **www.oceansideroute.com** for details.

Fun Fact **Tyee Chiefs**

The Tyee Club reflects the community's obsession with fishing. Founded in 1924 by Ted Painter, first owner of Painter's Lodge (see "Where to Stay"), the Tyee Club boasts an elite roster of sports fishing enthusiasts. Although also the Native word for "chief," in angling jargon, "tyee" is the name given to any Chinook salmon weighing 13.5kg (30 lb.) or more. Hence, Club membership is open to anyone who can land a Tyee, but in accordance with club rules. Requirements include fishing from a guided rowboat in a small, designated area, using a single hook and only certain types of poles and line weights. Between mid-July and mid-September, many try and few succeed. John Wayne, Bob Hope, and Bing Crosby all tried, and failed, to become Tyee members. A Texan named Walter Shutts holds the all-time Tyee record for a 32-kg (71½-lb.) Chinook, caught in 1968.

Once in Campbell River, you'll be in a true North Island community with roots deep in lumber and fishing. The town center is marked by the high rigger *Big Mike,* a carved wooden lumberjack swinging from a harness at the top of a spar pole. The renowned **Tyee Club** attracts fishing enthusiasts from around the world in their pursuit of landing excessively large Chinook salmon. Every year between July and September, the Campbell River, which in 2000 was designated a British Columbia Heritage River, swells with both visitors and fish, as salmon pass through the mile-wide passage, known as the **Discovery Channel,** en route to spawning grounds in northerly rivers. The area has historically produced vast hauls of incredibly large fish; thus Campbell River has become known as the "Salmon Fishing Capital of the World."

But today, as salmon numbers diminish, catch and release programs are in force, and those leading fishing expeditions are billing them more as wildlife adventures in an attempt to diversify. Some local operators have already been successful in this regard. Day trips aboard the **MV *Uchuck III,*** from Gold River to the Tahsis, Nootka, and Kyoquot sounds, are great family fun, and mini cruises to Bute Inlet or Kingcome Inlet aboard the **MV *Aurora Explorer*** reveal parts of British Columbia many visitors never get to see.

ESSENTIALS
Getting There
BY CAR   Driving distances up the center of Vancouver Island are fast and easy with the new inland highway (Hwy. 19) between Nanaimo and Campbell River. Campbell River is 264km (164 miles) north of Victoria (about 2½ hours' worth of driving); 153km (95 miles) north of Nanaimo (about 1½ hours); and 48km (29 miles) north of Courtenay (about half an hour).

BY PLANE   Commercial airlines fly into the Campbell River and District Regional Airport (✆ 250/923-5012; www.campbellriver.ca/city_services/cr_airport/index. html). **Air Canada Jazz** (✆ **888/247-2262;** www.flyjazz.ca), **Pacific Coastal Airlines** (✆ **800/663-2872;** www.pacific-coastal. com), and **WestJet** (✆ **888-937-8538;** www. westjet.com) operate daily scheduled flights from Vancouver, Calgary, Victoria, and Seattle. Car-rental companies at the airport include **Budget** (✆ **800/668-3233** or 250/923-4283; www.budget.com) and **National Car Rental** (✆ **888/669-9922** or 250/923-7278; www.nationalcarvictoria.com). Smaller carriers, such as **Coril Air** (✆ **888/287-8366** or 250/287-8371; www.corilair.com), provide harbor-to-harbor service between Port Hardy, Campbell River, and several small island communities. **Kenmore Air** (✆ **800/543-9595;** www.kenmoreair.com) flies from Seattle Harbor on a seasonal basis.

BY BUS   **Island Coach Lines,** operated by **Laidlaw Coach Lines,** (✆ **800/318-0818** or 250/385-4411; www.victoriatours.com) runs daily service from Victoria to Port Hardy, stopping in Nanaimo, Campbell River, and other towns along the way. **Greyhound Canada** (✆ **800/661-8747;** www.greyhound.ca) handles reservations. The one-way fare from Victoria to Campbell River is C$49 (US$43) for adults. From Nanaimo to Campbell River, it's C$25 (US$22) for adults. Fares for seniors are 10% less; fares for children 5 to 11 are 50% less. The trip from Victoria takes 5½ hours, while the trip from Nanaimo takes 3½ hours.

Visitor Information
The **Campbell River Visitor Information Centre** is located at 1235 Shoppers Row (P.O. Box 44), Campbell River, BC V9W 5B6 (✆ **800/463-4386** or 250/287-4636; www.campbellrivertourism.bc.ca).

Cruising the Queen Charlotte Strait

A rather unique option exists if you want to explore the island's coastal communities. Book a trip aboard the MV *Aurora Explorer*, a 41-m (135-ft.) landing craft that plies the western waterways on 5-day excursions to the remote inlets of the Queen Charlotte Strait. The MV *Aurora Explorer* is the only overnight passenger-freight vessel of its kind, sailing on an itinerary that is set by the tidal currents and the cargo she carries on her open deck. This might include supplies for solitary island retreats, refrigerators for First Nations villages, heavy equipment for a logging outpost, or mail and newspapers for a floating post office.

Passenger quarters, housed just below the main lounge and galley, sleep 12 in cramped but hospitable bunk-style cabins. The crew is friendly, and food is hearty and constant, with a daily supply of fresh-baked cookies and bread. Most passengers are active retirees or 40-something soft adventurers who come from all walks of life so entertainment relies on conversation, a good book, the awesome scenery, unexpected wildlife, and being part of a working vessel in action, watching the crew on the deck below hoist that winch and tote that bale—sometimes at four in the morning. Usually, the schedule includes stops at heritage sites, abandoned villages, or even a pebbly beach for an impromptu barbecue (if trolling for supper has proved successful). So in addition to a seafaring adventure, there are opportunities for shore explorations.

From May to mid-September, all-inclusive fares start at C$2,100 (US$1,848) a person; from mid-September through October and from the end of March through April, all-inclusive fares are C$1,575 to C$1,840 (US$1,386–US$1,619). The MV *Aurora Explorer* does not sail November through February. For information, contact Marine Link Tours, P.O. Box 451, Campbell River, BC V9W 5C1 (© **250/286-3347;** www.marinelinktours.com).

Getting Around

In Campbell River itself, **Campbell River Airporter & Taxi Service** (© **250/286-3000**) offers door-to-door service anywhere. As well, **Campbell River Transit** (© **250/287-7433**) operates regular bus service.

FABULOUS FISHING

Campbell River is an excellent home base for numerous sport-fishing excursions, and there are several quality outfitters and charter boat companies. These include **Coastal Island Fishing Adventures,** 663 Glenalan Rd. (© **888/225-9776** or 250/923-5831; www.coastalislandfishing.com). Rates are from C$90 (US$79) an hour (not per person), inclusive of gear and tackle and your choice of a Grady White or Trophy vessel.

Profish Adventures, 507 Grayson Rd. (© **250/923-6335;** www.profish.bc.ca), offers all-inclusive saltwater fishing trips at C$95 (US$84) an hour for up to two people, minimum 4 hours, and freshwater fishing excursions at C$600 (US$528) a day, for one person; C$500 (US$440) a day, for two people. Virtually every hotel and inn has a recommendation or package to do with fishing so ask when you make your reservation, and the Info Centre has a comprehensive directory to fishing guides.

Charter companies will handle licensing requirements, but if you decide to fish independently, **nonresident fishing licenses** are available at outdoor recreation stores throughout Campbell River, including **Painter's Lodge Holiday & Fishing Resort,** where you can also watch all the action from beautiful decks (see "Where to Stay," below). Saltwater licenses cost C$7.42 (US$6.55) per day; C$20 (US$18) for 3 days and C$33 (US$29) for 5 days. Freshwater licenses cost C$20 (US$18) per day or C$50 (US$44) for 8 days. Fees are reduced for BC and Canadian residents.

If private charters are still your preference, be aware that most are geared for fishing. That said, **Rippingale's Fishing,** 2330 Steelhead Rd., Campbell River (✆ **800/988-8242** or 250/286-7290; www.rippingalesfishing. com), offers 3-night packages ranging from C$489 (US$430) per person, per day, as well as half-day and full-day excursions.

WHERE TO STAY

Anchor Inn & Suites *Kids*   If you're looking for the extraordinary, the inn's five themed suites will satiate the most whimsical dreams with decor that runs from exotic Arabian and wild African to an Arctic-inspired room with igloo-style bed canopy. The English is twee; the Western is great for kids as they have bunk beds hidden in a "jail cell." More standard rooms are available, each sporting ocean views and comfortably furnished with a choice of queen and king-size beds. The restaurant serves all three meals, and in the evening adds a sushi dimension to tried-and-true regular fare of pasta, chicken, and steak.

261 Island Hwy., Campbell River, BC V9W 2B3. ✆ **800/663-7227** or 250/286-1131. Fax 250/287-4055. www. anchorinn.ca. 76 units. C$139 (US$122) double; C$249–C$289 (US$219–US$254) theme room double. Extra person C$10 (US$9). Theme, honeymoon, golf and fishing packages available. AE, MC, V. Free parking. **Amenities:** Restaurant; lounge; indoor pool; golf course nearby; exercise room; Jacuzzi; business center; coin-op laundry; laundry service; dry cleaning. *In room:* TV w/pay movies, wireless Internet, fridge, coffeemaker, hair dryer, iron.

Coast Discovery Inn & Marina   Adjacent to a busy shopping plaza right on the main drag, this is the only deluxe hotel you'll find downtown. As you might expect, it's a bit noisy by day, but since nothing much happens in Campbell River post-10pm, the location doesn't affect a quiet night's sleep. Guest rooms and suites are nondescript, though roomy enough and comfortable. All guest rooms have views of the harbor, and suites have welcome extras like Jacuzzis. The marina can accommodate 70 yachts up to 46m (150 ft.), as well as smaller pleasure crafts. Moorage can be arranged through the marina. Guided fishing tours are also available. There's a restaurant, and a pub that features live evening entertainment Thursday through Saturday.

975 Shoppers Row, Campbell River, BC V9W 2C4. ✆ **800/663-1144** or 250/287-7155. Fax 250/287-2213. www. coasthotels.com. 90 units. May–Sept C$138 (US$121) standard; C$154 (US$136) superior; C$174 (US$153) suite. Oct–Apr C$105 (US$92) standard; C$120 (US$106) superior; C$140 (US$123) suite. Extra person C$10 (US$9). MC, V. Free parking. Pets accepted C$10 (US$9). **Amenities:** Restaurant; pub; golf course nearby; exercise room; Jacuzzi; 24-hour room service; same-day dry cleaning. *In room:* AC, TV w/pay movies, dataport, Wi-Fi, minibar, coffeemaker, hair dryer.

Haig-Brown House   Prolific writer, avid outdoorsman, and respected judge, Roderick Haig-Brown was also one of British Columbia's most spirited conservationists. It was largely because of his efforts that the Fraser River, which runs down through the

BC Interior to Vancouver, was never dammed. From his 1923 farmhouse, set amidst 8 hectares (20 acres) of gardens beside the Campbell River, he wrote ardently about fly-fishing, resource management, and preserving BC's natural environment. Fully restored as a BC Heritage Property, Haig-Brown's home is a delightful B&B where you can enjoy big country breakfasts while looking out over the orchard and garden to the river. Guest rooms are decorated with comfy furnishings, although nothing too palatial. Guests share bathroom facilities.

2250 Campbell River Rd., Campbell River, BC V9W 4N7. © 250/286-6646. 3 units. May–end Oct C$75–C$95 (US$66–US$84). Extra person C$20 (US$18). Closed in winter. MC, V. Young children not accepted. **Amenities:** Lounge. *In room:* No phone.

Heron's Landing *(Finds* This lovely Bavarian-style hotel, formerly known as the Bachmair, has been refurbished and updated to create a European boutique ambience. All rooms and one-bedroom suites, while standardized in terms of amenities, are decorated with tasteful antiques, hardwood floors, oriental rugs, co-ordinated linens and drapes. Many have cozy living areas and full kitchens, making Heron's Landing a good choice for longer stays. Guests have access to the restaurant, pub, and other facilities across the street at the Best Western Austrian Chalet Village (© **800/667-7207** or 250/923-4231), a first-class second choice if Heron's Landing is full.

492 South Island Hwy., Campbell River, BC V9W 1A5. © **888/923-2849** or 250/923-2848. Fax 250/923-2849. www.heronslandinghotel.com. 30 units. C$139 (US$122) standard; C$159 (US$140) 1-bedroom; C$300–C$500 (US$264–US$440) penthouse. AE, MC, V. Indoor parking. Small pets accepted C$25 (US$22). **Amenities:** Restaurant; bar next door; golf course nearby; coin-op washers and dryers; nonsmoking. *In room:* TV, dataport, wireless Internet, kitchen, fridge, coffeemaker, hair dryer, iron.

Painter's Lodge Holiday & Fishing Resort *(* An international favorite of avid fishermen and celebrities, Painter's Lodge has welcomed the likes of Bob Hope, Julie Andrews, Goldie Hawn, and the Prince of Luxembourg. Its location overlooking Discovery Passage is awesome, and its rustic grandeur has a terrific West Coast ambience, with comfortable lounges, large decks, and spacious guest rooms and suites decorated in natural wood and pastels. Wrapped in windows, the lodge's restaurant, **Legends,** boasts a view of the Passage from every table (see "Where to Dine"). One of the neatest dining experiences is to take the speedboat trip (10 minutes in each direction) over to **April Point Lodge on Quadra Island** (see "Where to Stay," Quadra Island) for a pre-dinner martini at their sushi bar before returning to Legends for the catch of the day. The trip is included in hotel rates.

Kids Camping

Miracle Beach Provincial Park (© **250/954-4600**) is one of BC's best parks. Native legend speaks to a supernatural stranger who appeared on the beach and miraculously transformed a Native princess into Mitlenatch Island. True or not, the beach itself is appropriately named with countless tidal pools, warm sand and soft, undulating waves. Add to this: roomy campsites beneath tall, sun-dappled trees, forested trails down to the beach, hot showers and playgrounds, and you've got the makings of a great family camping holiday. A seasonal visitor center has nature displays and park interpreters. For reservations, call Discover Camping © **800/689-9025** or 604/689-9025.

1625 MacDonald Rd. (P.O. Box 460, Dept 2), Campbell River, BC V9W 4S5. © **800/663-7090** or 250/286-1102. Fax 250/286-1102. www.obmg.com. 94 units. Apr–Oct C$189 (US$166) gardenside room; C$229 (US$202) oceanside room; C$429 (US$378) suite. AE, DC, MC, V. Closed mid-Oct to early Apr. **Amenities:** Restaurant; pub; lounge; large heated outdoor pool; golf course nearby; 2 outdoor tennis courts; health club; 2 Jacuzzis; children's center; activities desk; babysitting; laundry service; same-day dry cleaning; nonsmoking facility. *In room:* TV, coffeemaker, hair dryer.

Sonora Resort ✹✹✹ *Finds*   Once known only as an upscale fishing lodge, Sonora Resort has undergone a multi-million-dollar uplift to become one of the region's most sought-after retreats. Fishing is still a primary activity—the resort has a fleet of well-equipped Grady Whites, but with an indoor tennis court, 12-seat movie theater, virtual golf, a luxurious spa, hiking trails, and zodiac eco-tours, Sonora has high-end appeal. Lodges offer a variety of differently themed accommodations from luxurious multi-roomed cottages to hotel-like suites and guest rooms. Bedding is plush, bathrooms feature quality amenities, and furnishings are warm and inviting. The all-inclusive rates cover use of all resort facilities, all meals, and even alcohol. Spa treatments, fishing trips, and tours are extra, as are its private transfers to the island. Sonora can provide a boat shuttle from Campbell River, as well as direct flights from Vancouver and Seattle via its private, state-of-the-art Agusta Bell helicopter. Kenmore Air and SeaAir Seaplanes can also get you there from Seattle and Vancouver respectively. Kids are welcome. *Tip:* Be sure to be dockside when the boats return after a day's fishing; the discards after cleaning the fish attract a gathering of harbor seals all playing and vying for these easy-to-get delicacies.

Sonora Resort, Sonora Island (mail: 105–5360 Airport Rd. S., Richmond, BC V7B 1B4); © **888/576-6672** or 604/233-0460. Fax 604/233-0465. www.sonoraresort.com. 83 units. May–Sept C$525–C$675 (US$462–US$594) per couple; C$394–C$506 (US$347–US$445) children aged 2–19. Closed Oct–Apr. **Amenities:** Restaurant; outdoor pool; golf nearby; tennis; gym; spa; Jacuzzi; sauna; games room; concierge; 24-hr. room service; laundry; yoga/pilates; fishing; kayaks; hiking; fly fishing pond; movie theater; eco-tours. *In room:* A/C, TV/DVD, fridge.

WHERE TO DINE

Baan Thai ✹✹ THAI CUISINE   It's so refreshing to find a great ethnic eatery away from the big city lights, and this one is as good as it gets. In fact, the menu is so popular it hasn't changed much in seven years. You can always judge a quality thai restaurant by its pad thai, and this one is extremely flavorful, as are the curries. If your palette isn't up for the fire of Thai spices, all dishes can be modified to suit. The 40-seat saffron-colored restaurant is located over a storefront on Shoppers Row (Campbell River's main drag). The entrance is easy to miss but let the aromatic smells be your guide. Tables are on the small side, but close quarters simply adds to the intimate atmosphere of this eatery.

1090 B Shoppers Row. © **250/286-4853**. Reservations recommended. Main courses C$12–C$15 (US$11–US$13). MC, V. Mon–Fri. 11:30am–2pm and 5–9pm; Sat 5–9pm; closed Sunday.

Harbour Grill ✹✹ STEAK & SEAFOOD   You wouldn't expect to find the best restaurant in town in a shopping mall, but that's exactly where Harbour Grill set up shop. Thankfully, the restaurant faces the waterside Discovery Harbour Marina, rather that a hoard of retail outlets, so the mall experience doesn't touch on the dining experience one iota—except for always being able to find a parking spot! Grab a window seat and you're likely to see cruise ships pass by on their way to the Inside Passage. Food-wise, Harbour Grill is classic fine dining with crisp white linens, attentive staff, and traditional French-influenced dishes such as veal Oscar and Duck a l'orange. Steaks (Alberta grain-fed AAA beef only) are the house specialty: peppered, bearnaised, *la Wellington*—you name it—and then there's its gi-normous Chateaubriand, done to perfection. The wine list features many VQA wines from BC as well as a selection from France, Australia, and California.

In the Discovery Harbour Centre, 112–1334 Island Hwy. ⓒ 250/287-4143. www.harbourgrill.com. Reservations recommended. Main courses C$27–C$38 (US$24–US$33). AE, DC, MC, V. Daily 5:30–10pm.

Legends Dining Room ⚐ WESTCOAST/CONTINENTAL   Located at Painter's Lodge, this restaurant's only open in season, which is a shame. Floor-to-ceiling windows afford terrific views of the comings and goings across Discovery Passage and an intimate fine-dining area. The menu is varied, and, not surprisingly, includes many fish and seafood specialties. This is, after all, a fishing lodge. The perennial favorite? The crab and salmon cakes, with chipotle garlic aioli and sweetcorn vinaigrette. You can't go wrong with the halibut, which always has a different twist, whether it's with purple mustard or sautéed tandoori-spiced almonds. If you've just come off the water and are looking for something more casual, The Tyee Pub is an informal option with an oversize deck offering ringside seats to the water. *Note:* The restaurant often opens at 5am to get fishing enthusiasts off to a good start.

Painter's Lodge, 1625 Mcdonald Rd. ⓒ 250/286-1102. Reservations recommended. Main courses C$10–C$17 (US$9–US$15) lunch; C$19–C$33 (US$17–US$29) dinner. AE, DC, MC, V. Daily 7am–10pm. Closed mid-Oct to early Apr.

Riptide Marine Pub & Grill PUB/WEST COAST   If you're exploring the Discovery Harbour Shopping Plaza, this is a great pit stop for lunch, snacks, and dinner, or just a drink over appies. There's nothing unexpected here; traditional burgers, salads and pizza go alongside more substantial meals like rack of lamb, filet mignon, and salmon. But its smart-casual style, and its location next to the bustling marina attracts boaters, walkers, and folks in transit to another island via water taxi or seaplane. Showers, laundry facilities, and a liquor store are part of the complex.

1340 Island Hwy., Discovering Harbour Shopping Plaza. ⓒ 250/830-0044. Dinner C$17–C$20 (US$15–US$18). AE, MC, V. Tues–Sat 11am–1am; Sun–Mon 11am–midnight.

GOLD RIVER

The traditional territory of the Mowachaht and Muchalaht peoples, it wasn't until the 1860s, when the Chinese started pulling gold from the river, that Gold River started to find its way onto maps and into public awareness. Even then, when the gold ran out, it would take almost a hundred years for lumberjacks to arrive and start harvesting the forested hills. When a pulp mill opened here in 1965, **Gold River** ⚐ was literally built out of the wilderness—a British Columbia "instant community," whose existence was predicated on forestry and economic need. Gold River was Canada's first all-electric town and the first to have underground wiring. Since the pulp mill closed in 1998, however, Gold River has been forced to reinvent itself in order to survive. Looking to its natural resources once again, the community now is creating an eco-tourism industry that includes salt water and fresh water fishing, and the opportunities that abound in the surrounding wilderness.

ESSENTIALS
Getting There

Aside from Tofino and Ucluelet (see chapter 6), Gold River is the only community on Vancouver Island's west coast reachable by a well-maintained paved road. It's 92km (57 miles) west of Campbell River along **Highway 28,** driving there takes about

1½ hours. You pass through spectacular **Strathcona Provincial Park** and on to the remote **Muchalaht Inlet.**

Visitor Information

For more information and maps on Gold River and the surrounding area, visit the **Gold River Visitor Information Centre** at 499 Muchalat Dr., Gold River, BC V0P 1G0 (✆ **250/283-2418** [mid-May to Labor Day] or 250/283-2202 [Labor Day to mid-May]; www.village.goldriver.bc.ca).

EXPLORING GOLD RIVER

Sport fishing, rugged scenery, and abundant wildlife have always been the region's trademarks, and since the pulp mill closed in 1998, these natural attractions are becoming the center of a tourist-based local economy. One of the area's larger and most reliable fishing outfitters, particularly for saltwater salmon, halibut, and cod, is **Nootka Charters** (✆ **250/202-5922;** www.nootkacharters.com). Trips start at C$80 (US$70) per hour for up to 2 people; 5-hour minimum. Additional passengers incur a nominal extra charge.

If fishing's not your thing, there's kayaking, hiking, and wildlife viewing, as well as spelunking in the **Upana Caves** ✸, 27km (17 miles) northwest of Gold River. A well-marked trail connects the five caves, which include the two-chambered Main Cave with a waterfall at the end of one passage, the marble-smooth Resurgence Cave, with its toothy outcrops, and the spiraling Corner Cave. There are a number of modest restaurants, B&Bs, and motels, which makes Gold River a good base from which to explore places like **Nootka Sound,** especially if you opt to experience the *Uchuck III,* a working passenger and freight vessel offering scenic tours (see below). Local helicopters (Vancouver Island Helicopters ✆ **250/283-7616**) and floatplanes (Air Nootka ✆ **250/283-2255**) provide the closest air access to popular Hot Springs Cove.

WHERE TO STAY & DINE

Ridgeview Motor Inn   Clean, simply furnished, and comfortable, this motor inn is pretty standard fare and while it may not win any awards for style, the folks who run it are friendly and knowledgeable about the area. This is the first choice for most visitors, especially fishing enthusiasts; the inn has a fish-cleaning station. Rates include continental breakfast and some rooms have microwaves, kitchenettes, and valley views. The Ridge Neighbourhood pub/restaurant (✆ **250/283-2461**) is next door.

395 Donner Court, Gold River, BC V0P 1G0 ✆ **800/989-3393** or 250/283-2277. Fax 250/283-7611. 44 units. C$89–C$99 (US$78–US$87) standard; C$125 (US$110) suite. Extra person C$10 (US$9). AE, MC. **Amenities:** Dining area; golf nearby; activity desk. *In room:* TV, fridge, coffeemaker, some w/microwaves.

TAHSIS, NOOTKA & KYOQUOT SOUNDS

If you decide to venture farther west from Gold River, you'll explore the coastal communities in and around **Tahsis, Nootka, and Kyoquot sounds** ✸✸✸—some of the most beautiful coastal scenery in the world. Kyoquot is the ancestral home of the Mowachaht/Muchalaht people of the Nuu-chah-nulth (formerly Nootka) nation. A little farther along, the almost uninhabited First Nations village of historic Yuquot (Friendly Cove) is where British explorer Captain James Cook first came ashore in 1778, making this area, in effect, the birthplace of British Columbia.

Tahsis is the only community that's accessible by a well-maintained gravel road, affectionately dubbed the Tree to Sea Drive. Take this road to the Upana Caves that lie just before Bull Lake Summit. As you near Tahsis, you'll find the Leiner River Bouldering

Trail, a short loop trail along the narrow valley of Leiner River, as well as a longer (4-hour) trail to The Lookout over Tahsis Inlet. Typical of those in rugged coastal communities, most visitor services are geared to wilderness tourism. Hiking the rain forests and coastline is big business here, as is fishing and wildlife viewing.

ESSENTIALS
Getting There
Although Tahsis can also be reached by gravel road, the best way to visit Tahsis, or explore Nootka and Kyoquot sounds is aboard the *Uchuck III* (see below) or via seaplane (AIR NOOTKA; *C* **250/283-2255**). Both operate out of Gold River.

Visitor Information
For maps and information, contact Gold River Information Centre (499 Muchalat Dr., Gold River, BC V0P 1G0 (*C* **250/283-2418** [mid-May to Labor Day] or 250/283-2202 [Labor Day to mid-May]; www.village.goldriver.bc.ca), or the **Tahsis Chamber of Commerce** (36 Rugged Mountain Rd., Box 278, Tahsis BC V0P 1X0; *C* **250/934-6344**).

EXPLORING THE AREA
Uchuck III *GGG*   Exploring this coastline aboard the workboat MV *Uchuck III* is not only a treat for the whole family, but good value for money. It's a much more cost-effective option than chartering a private boat, and you'll see, hear, taste, and smell more along the way than you will in the more "sanitized" environment of a private vessel. A converted WWII minesweeper, the MV *Uchuck III* sails year-round on day-long and overnight stays. Depending on the day and time of year, your destination might be **Tahsis, Zeballos, Kyoquot, or Yuquot** (Friendly Cove). As the workhorse of the sounds, and the lifeline of many of these isolated communities, the MV *Uchuck III* also puts in at remote logging camps and fishing ports, picking up passengers and offloading anything from stoves to Oh Henry! bars.

Nootka Sound Services, P.O. Box 57, Gold River, BC V0P 1G0 (*C* **250/283-2325**. www.mvuchuck.com. Year-round day-trip rates are C$60 (US$53) for adults, $C55 (US$48) seniors, C$25 (US$22) children 7 to 12. Children 6 and under sail for free. Overnight trip rates range from C$215 to 260 (US$189–US$229) for adults, C$65–C$100 (US$57–US$88) for children 7 to 12. Children 6 and under sail for free. There are no seniors' rates on overnight trips.

WHERE TO STAY & DINE
Most of the lodges in Nootka Sound have a definite fishing bent, either floating in protected coves, operating as part home/part one- and two-bedroom inns, or as small executive-styled homes for high rollers. Many close in winter.

Maquinna Resort   Located next door to the Maquinna Mall, this resort offers the conveniences of a tackle and bait store, postal services, a small gallery, and a bakery. It also offers well-maintained, quality hotel rooms, well furnished with comfortable beds as well as a selection of self-catering one- and two-bedroom condos. The hotel corner rooms are the most spacious and have great ocean views. The resort has a lively pub (*C* **250/934-5522**), and a licensed bistro-style restaurant serving seafood dishes, steaks, chicken, pasta, and burgers. **Nootka Sound Charters** (*C* **250/934-5558**) and **Tahtsa Dive Charters** (*C* **866/934-6365** or 250/934-6365) operate diving and fishing trips out of here.

1400 S. Maquinna Dr., (Box 400), Tahsis, BC V0P 1X0. *C* **250/934-6367**. Fax 250/934-7884. 24 units. June–Labor Day C$115–C$125 (US$101–US$110) standard room; C$155–C$200 (US$136–US$176) condos w/ kitchen. MC, V. Free parking. **Amenities:** Restaurant; pub; laundry; marina. *In room:* TV.

Moments Nootka Trail

Hugging the west coast of Nootka Island, the Nootka Trail is world famous for its wilderness hiking experience featuring long beaches, secluded bays, and spectacular headlands jutting into the Pacific Ocean. Unlike its tough cousin, The West Coast Trail (see Chapter 6), this is a relatively easy hike that never rises more than 50m (164 ft.) above sea level. Along the way, you're likely to see whales and old native middens. Hikers can take a water taxi to either trailhead (Louie Bay or Friendly Cove) from Tahsis or can arrive by floatplane from Gold River. Purchasing a tide guide before your trip is mandatory as you can use low tides to follow the beach flats. Most people take 4 days or longer to complete the hike.

Tahsis Motel   Very basic but at least clean, this motel is up to date and provides creature comforts that will probably feel luxurious after a day on the water or trekking through rain forest. The Spar Tree pub/restaurant serves pub fare for lunch and dinner and will provide bag lunches by request.

187 Head Bay Rd., Tahsis, BC V0P 1X0; ✆ **250/934-6318**. Fax 250/934-7808. 11 units. C$78 (US$69). Extra person C$20 (US$18). Pets C$5 (US$4.40). MC, V. **Amenities:** Pub/restaurant; liquor store; convenience store. *In room:* TV.

4 Quadra & Cortes Islands

Affectionately called the Discovery Islands, Quadra and Cortes islands march to the beat of a different drummer. Both are richly pastoral with stretches of sandy beaches to explore and meandering roads that lead to hidden coves, artist studios, and sudden dead-ends that may or may not have an overgrown path to the beach. Quadra is more mainstream, probably because of its proximity to Campbell River, while Cortes is a haven for those walking the talk of living a holistic, alternative lifestyle.

ESSENTIALS
Getting There
The islands are accessible only by water. To reach Cortes by public transit, you'll need to cross to Quadra Island.

BC Ferries (✆ **250-386-3431**) operates year-round between these islands with 18 sailings from Campbell River and Quadra Island. The crossing takes 10 minutes and costs C$5.75 (US$5.10) adult, C$2.90 (US$2.55) child, and C$14 (US$12) standard-size vehicle. To get to Cortes Island, you need to travel to Quadra Island for the connector to Cortes. There are half a dozen daily trips both ways between Quadra and Cortes islands. This crossing takes 45 minutes and costs C$6.80 (US$6) adult, C$3.40 (US$3) child, and C$17 (US$15) standard vehicle. All fares are return.

Note: The Ship's crew collects fares, so either pay via credit card for a through fare from Campbell River to Cortes Island, or have enough cash on you to bunny-hop from Quadra Island to Cortes Island.

Visitor Information
There is no visitor centre on Quadra; though you can check out www.quadraisland.ca, or the **Campbell River Visitor Information Centre** (✆ **800/463-4386** or 250/287-4636).

EXPLORING THE ISLANDS
QUADRA ISLAND

Touring Quadra Island by car, bike, or scooter (rent the latter from April Point Lodge) is a delight, with plenty of stop-off points at parks and beaches to enjoy. There are over 20 studio locations to visit potters, carvers, painters, and sculptors; visit www.quadra islandarts.com for more information. One of the most rewarding destinations is the **Kwagiulth Museum and Cultural Centre** ☆—if it's open. Located in Cape Mudge Village, the museum drifts from one season to the other—sometimes opening at odd hours; sometimes not at all. Islanders will have the latest scoop.

CORTES ISLAND

Located at the entrance to Desolation Sound, one of BC's most celebrated cruising areas, Cortes Island (www.cortesisland.com) is a beautiful wilderness hideaway. It is a lovely island to wander through, with breathtaking vignettes: Gorge Harbour Marina, Von Donop Provincial Marine Park, Squirrel Cove with an anchorage facing Desolation Sound, and 100-hectare Manson's Landing Provincial Marine Park. Here's where you find excellent sandy beaches—the park (as well as Smelt Bay and Squirrel Cove) is one of the few places where you can collect shellfish legally. An easy 15-minute walk south from the government float at Manson's Landing leads to Hague Lake which has a 1km perimeter trail to the sandspit. Watch your step, it's steep in places. Most walks around Cortes aren't this formal; so if you decide to explore, say, the wilderness of Von Donop Provincial Marine Park, you would do well to create your own marking system. Just be sure to retrieve them all—islanders don't take kindly to eco-unfriendly practices.

WHERE TO STAY & DINE
QUADRA ISLAND

Tsa-Kwa-Luten Lodge & RV Park   This establishment is owned and operated by the Laichwiltach (the Cape Mudge Band); you can enjoy the Native experience with a luxurious twist (hence the Canada Select four-star rating). This modern resort resembles a native Big House, offering guests suites and waterfront cabins, as well as an excellent (primarily) seafood restaurant that often stages Native dancing; reservations are recommended. All rooms have an ocean view and either a balcony or patio; décor is contemporary with earth-tones co-ordinating floors, bedspreads and walls. Tsa-Kwa-Luten translates as "gathering place" in the Kwak'wala language of the Laichwiltach people, and is located on the site of the band's original village. The lodge is usually open early April to mid-October, but starting 2007/08 may be extending its season through the winter. There are also 13 RV sites with full hookups.

Kwagiulth Museum and Cultural Centre

This museum is one of the few places where you can explore the area's Native heritage. On display is one of the world's best collections of potlatch artifacts, ceremonial masks, and tribal costumes, once used by the Cape Mudge Band. Behind the museum is K'Ik'Ik G'Illas, or "The House of Eagles," a longhouse-like structure used to teach carving, dancing, and other traditional skills. There's also an opportunity to make petroglyph rubbings from fiberglass castings of ancient stone carvings.

WeiWai Road, Cape Mudge Village. ☏ 250/285-3733.

Tracking the Wild Side

As you travel through the northern regions of Vancouver Island, the richness of the aboriginal heritage becomes evident. Two outfitters, both owned and operated by different First Nations peoples, offer wildlife and bear tours of their traditional territories, alongside stories, history, and cultural insights. **Aboriginal Journeys** (398–1434 Island Hwy., Campbell River ✆ **888/455-8101** or 250/850-1101; www.aboriginaljourneys.com) operates wildlife viewing and adventure tours within the traditional territory of the Laichwiltach peoples. This extends from Cape Mudge to the mouth of Bute Inlet, to Smith Inlet and around northern Vancouver Island. Tours include whale watching, grizzly and black bear viewing, and other wildlife sightings from a 24-foot Zodiac or a 55-foot classic wooden fishing vessel. **Homalco Wildlife Tours** (1218 Bute Crescent Campbell River ✆ **866/234-2327** or 250/923-0758; www.bearsofbute.com), operated by the Homalco First Nations people, offer tours aboard the 32-foot M.V. *Chinook Spirit* to the Orford River, one of the last pristine watersheds in Bute Inlet and home to the largest concentration of grizzly bears in British Columbia. With both companies, prices and tour length varies depending on the tour and destination selected. For example, a 3-hour Eagle tour is C$79 (US$70) per person; a 7-hour grizzly bear tour is C$225 (US$198) per person.

1 Lighthouse Rd. Box 460, Quathiaski Cove, Quadra Island, BC V0P 1N0. ✆ **800/665-7745** or 250/598-3366. Fax 250/285-2532. www.capemudgeresort.com. 35 units. C$125 (US$110) lodge suite; C$180 (US$158) cottage. RV C$30 (US$26) oceanview; C$35 (US$31) beachfront. Open early Apr to mid-Oct. Meal plans available. AE, DC, MC, V. Free parking. Small pets allowed in cabins for C$10 (US$9). **Amenities:** Restaurant; lounge; lit tennis courts nearby; exercise room; Jacuzzi; sauna; free bikes; massage; laundry service. *In room:* Coffeemaker, hair dryer, iron.

April Point Lodge & Marina   The sister resort to Painter's Lodge, April Point caters to a slightly less fish-oriented crowd with its kayak, bike, and scooter rentals as well as its Aveda concept spa at the water's edge. Accommodation ranges from deluxe suites with Jacuzzi tubs to comfortable 1- to 4-bedroom "woodsy' cabins," all of which have ocean views and decks. The spacious restaurant has floor-to-ceiling windows with views, and serves quality West Coast cuisine from early morning breakfast to fine dining at night, but the sushi bar sometimes steals the show, especially as a prelude to dinner. A free water taxi shuttles guests between April Point and Painter's Lodge.

April Point Rd., Quadra Island, c/o Box 1, Campbell River, BC V9W 4Z9. ✆ **800/663-7090** or 250/285-2222. www.aprilpoint.com. 36 units, some w/Jacuzzi. C$229–C$425 (US$202–US$374). Extra person C$20 (US$18). Closed mid-Oct to early Apr. AE, DC, MC, V. **Amenities:** Restaurant; sushi bar; lounge; spa; bike, scooter, and kayak rentals; tour/activities desk; babysitting; laundry service; same-day dry cleaning; nonsmoking facility. *In room:* TV, coffeemaker, hair dryer.

CORTES ISLAND

Cortes is small, so it's a good idea to reserve accommodation. The New Age set tend to head for **Hollyhock** (Box 127, Manson's Landing, ✆ **800/933-6339,** www.hollyhock.ca), a holistic and spiritual retreat center. The back-to-the-wilderness, kayaking crowd favor **T'ai Li Lodge** (Box 16, Cortes Bay ✆ **800/939-6644** or

250/935-6749; www.island.net/~taili/). **Cortes Island Vacation Rentals** has access to several privately owned beach cabins and family homes with rates from C$500 to C$1,500 (US$440–US$1,320) a week.

5 En Route to Port Hardy

Trees, trees, and more trees line either side of Highway 19 heading north from Campbell River. The livelihood of the communities along this stretch are still mine- and timber-based economies, and every now and then, the stands of trees break to reveal mountainsides scalded by machinery or fields of blackened stumps, left to rot before replanting. The destinations that follow are listed geographically, heading north from Campbell River along Highway 19.

While logging is still the mainstay for communities such as **Port McNeill,** smaller hamlets such as **Holberg, Woss, Zeballos,** and picturesque **Telegraph Cove** seem to co-exist in their lumber-industry environment more peacefully. As a result, they have developed distinct personalities, whether from the Finnish influence still holding court in **Sointula,** or the richness of First Nations culture in **Alert Bay.**

ESSENTIALS
GETTING THERE
By Car

Although the road north is a well-maintained two-lane highway, this is the only drivable route, and it's used by logging trucks as well as local traffic. Getting stuck behind one of these lumbering vehicles can slow you down, since they aren't always easy to pass. Give yourself extra time, and avoid frustration by taking detours. In summer, the road gets particularly busy with ferry travelers heading to and from Port Hardy. The distance from Campbell River to Port Hardy is 238km (148 miles), which could take up to 3½ hours to drive. From Nanaimo to Port Hardy it's 391km (243 miles)—allow at least 5 hours. For the long haul from Victoria to Port Hardy, it's a whopping 502km (312 miles). For this killer road trip, set aside 7 hours.

By Plane

Air Canada Jazz (✆ **888/247-2262;** www.flyjazz.ca) operates daily flights between Vancouver, Victoria, Port Hardy, Comox, and Campbell River, as does **Pacific Coastal Airlines** (✆ **800/663-2872;** www.pacific-coastal.com). **Kenmore Air** (✆ **800/543-9595** or 425-486-1257; www.kenmoreair.com) flies from Seattle Harbor to Port Hardy, Port McNeill, and Quadra Island.

By Bus

Island Coach Lines, operated by **Laidlaw Coach Lines** (✆ **800/318-0818** or 250/385-4411; www.victoriatours.com), runs daily service from Victoria to Port Hardy, stopping in Campbell River. The one-way fare from Victoria to Port Hardy is C$74 (US$65) for adults (be aware it's a 5:30am departure). From Nanaimo to Port Hardy, it's C$64 (US$56) for adults. Fares for seniors are 10% less; fares for children 5 to 11 are 50% less. The trip from Victoria to Port Hardy is just under 10 hours. From Nanaimo to Port Hardy, it's approximately 7 hours. Contact **Greyhound Canada** (✆ **800/661-8747;** www.greyhound.ca) for reservations.

By Ferry

BC Ferries (✆ **888/223-3779;** www.bcferries.com) operates nine crossings daily between Port McNeill and the community of **Alert Bay,** on Cormorant Island, and between Port McNeill and **Sointula,** on Malcolm Island. One-way fares are C$6.80 (US$6) for adults, C$3.40 (US$2.70) for children 5 to 11. Crossing time is 45 minutes. BC Ferries also operates service between Port Hardy and Prince Rupert, a 15-hour journey via the famed **Inside Passage.**

VISITOR INFORMATION

There are visitor information centers in several of the communities along the route to Port Hardy, such as **Port McNeill Visitor Information** at 351 Shelley Cres. (P.O. Box 129), Port McNeill, BC V0N 2R0 (℃ **250/956-3131;** www.portmcneill.net) and **Alert Bay Visitor Information** at 116 Fir St. Alert Bay, BC V0N 1A0 (℃ **250/974-5024;** www.alertbay.net). Once in Port Hardy, head to the **Port Hardy Visitor Information Centre,** 7250 Market St. (P.O. Box 249), Port Hardy, BC V0N 2P0 (℃ **250/ 949-7622;** www.ph-chamber.bc.ca). Open daily during normal office hours, these folks also provide an **accommodation reservations service** for Port Hardy and Prince Rupert (for those going to Prince Rupert with BC Ferries). For more information on the north region of Vancouver Island, contact Vancouver Island North Visitors' Association (℃ **800/903-6606** or 250/949-9094; www.vinva.bc.ca).

ZEBALLOS

Located 191km (118 miles) north of Campbell River, at the end of a 40-km (25-mile) gravel road off Highway 19, historic **Zeballos** once produced more than C$13 million (US$11.5 million) worth of gold. Tailings from the mines were used to build up the roads and led to a local legend that the streets were literally "paved with gold." But when Zeballos lost its Midas touch, logging, fish farming, and tourism became its mainstays. Although still fairly rough and ready, some of the false-fronted historic gold rush buildings have been spruced up, including the old hospital downtown and the old Privateer gold mine a few minutes up the Zeballos River. Today, this pretty village is also the jumping off point to an eco-adventurer's dream—everything from kayaking and fishing to diving. Recreational cavers and experienced spelunkers will head to **Little Hustan Caves** for its sinkholes, canyons, and fast-moving river that disappears and reappears in the rock formations. Hikers will find any number of trails including the old logging road down to Little Zeballos and a fairly strenuous climb up Sugarloaf Mountain for amazing views of Little Espinoza Inlet. If you decide to check in with a local outfitter, be sure to ask about the tidal fall change on this inlet. You need a boat to get up close to the swirling waters, and an experienced hand at the wheel.

    Zeballos Village Museum (℃ **250/761-4070** May–Sept; 250/761-4229 Sept–Apr) doubles as a **Visitors Information Centre** and is your best bet for arranging excursions since many outfitters are seasonal or seemingly come and go with the tide. The center can also help you reserve accommodations and campsites, both of which are fairly limited, and one of the 30 RV sites. The museum part of the centre is filled with old mining equipment, photos of 'old' Zeballos, and is a good starting point to learn about this community that's survived a history of hard knocks, including a tsunami in 1964.

⌐Fun Fact Woss's Claim to Fame

Woss only changed its status from logging camp to an official community in 1999, and it operates a 122-km (76-mile) logging railway—the longest still-working logging railway in North America.

WHERE TO STAY & DINE

Mason's Lodge   Built in 1936, during the height of the gold rush, owners Daniel O'Connor and Cristina Lepore have done a good job in maintaining its heritage ambience while providing creature comforts. Rooms are bright with touches of cedar paneling, and spacious enough to have sitting areas although the public lounge has nice leather bound chairs to sink into. All rooms have views of the Zeballos River and mountains. All have private bath; some have kitchenettes. **The Blue Heron Restaurant** offers hearty breakfasts (this meal is not included in the room rate), lunches that feature sandwiches, salads, homemade soups and fruit pies, and a dinner selection that changes frequently depending on the catch, and the season. True to the multitasking nature of those on the Zeballos tourism scene, you'll find here kayak rentals, fishing charters, and water taxi services.

203 Pandora Ave. (P.O.Box 10), Zeballos, BC V0P 2A0 © **866/222-2235** or 250/761-4137. www.masonslodge. zeballos.bc.ca. 15 units. C$85–C$130 (US$75–US$114). Extra person C$20 (US$18). AE, MC, V. Free parking. **Amenities:** Restaurant; lounge. *In room:* Satellite TV, Wi-Fi, fridge, hair dryer.

TELEGRAPH COVE

A highlight of your trip north must be Telegraph Cove, a picture-perfect village located 239km (180 miles) north of Campbell River. Overlooking Johnstone Strait, it epitomizes the West Coast, and is one of the few remaining **elevated-boardwalk villages** on Vancouver Island. This historic community got its start in 1912 as a one-room telegraph station that marked the end of a cable, strung tree to tree, all the way from Victoria. When messages were received, the operator hopped into a boat and rowed to the community of **Alert Bay,** on Cormorant Island, to deliver the news.

Part of the cove's charm is that many of the original buildings still stand, including the telegraph station, an army mess hall, picturesque residences, and cozy cabins perched on stilts over the water's edge and joined by boardwalks. Walk to the end and you'll find the **Johnstone Strait Whale Interpretive Centre,** dubbed the Bones Project, where they are piecing together the skeleton of a fin whale. You'll also find hands-on displays of the numerous species of marine life populating the area.

OUTDOOR ACTIVITIES

Because of its proximity to Robson Bight Ecological Reserve, whale-watching is big business, though any trip along Johnstone Strait will include sightings of dolphins, seals, porpoises, and eagles. At the end of the boardwalk lies **Stubbs Island Charters** (© **800/665-3066** or 250/928-3185; www. stubbs-island.com), BC's first orca- and wildlife-watching company. The 60-foot boats are equipped with hydrophones so you can listen to the whales' underwater conversations. The 3½-hour cruises run May through late October and cost C$69 to C$79 (US$61–US$70) for adults.

For those who want to stay on land, **Tide Rip Tours,** 28 Boardwalk (© **888/643-9319** or 250/339-5320; www.tiderip.com), runs various wildlife viewing excursions from black bear photo safaris (C$145/US$128) to pricier expeditions to see grizzly bears (from C$233/US$205).

For kayak rentals and guided multi-day kayaking trips into Telegraph Cove and Johnstone Strait, contact **Telegraph Cove Sea Kayaking** (© **888/756-0099** or 250/756-0094; www.tckayaks.com). Rentals are C$25 (US$22) a day, single; C$35 (US$31) double. A 3-day trip runs C$399 (US$351) per person, and includes all camping gear. **Discovery Expeditions** is the company's more adventurous arm, and focuses on 4–7 day trips, using Sophia Island (across from Robson Bight) as a base camp. A 4-day trip is C$850 (US$748) per person; a 6-day adventure is C$1,250 (US$1,100) per person.

WHERE TO STAY & DINE

Hidden Cove Lodge   Located 6.5km (4 miles) from Telegraph Cove, this 557 sq. m (6,000 sq. ft.) retreat lodge was once only accessible by water. It exudes an easy going, West Coast charm, with cedar beams throughout, floor-to-ceiling windows to take advantage of the terrific waterfront views, and comfortable furnishings. There are eight lodge rooms, and three private self-contained cottages. All accommodations are clean and simply decorated; children are welcome in the cottages only. The licensed dining room, which serves quality international dishes, is open to non-guests by reservation only. Numerous eco-tours, including heli-fishing, can be arranged.

Lewis Point, 1 Hidden Cove Rd., Telegraph Cove, BC V0N 2R0. ⓒ/fax **250/956-3916.** www.bcbbonly.com/1263.php. 8 units with private bathroom, 3 cottages. C$155 (US$136) lodge double; C$199 (US$175) 1-bedroom cottage; C$299 (US$263) 2-bedroom cottage. Extra person C$25 (US$22). Lodge rates include full breakfast. 2-night minimum stay. Off-season rates available. MC, V. Free parking and moorage for boaters. **Amenities:** Restaurant; golf course nearby; Jacuzzi; in-room massage; babysitting; coin-op laundry; nonsmoking facility. *In room:* No phone.

Telegraph Cove Marina & RV Park   The "old" Telegraph Cove still holds its charm of antiquity; the same can't be said of the cove's other side, which is dominated by an unsightly 48-space full hookup RV park. It's part of a larger development program that includes cliff-clinging lots of real estate for sale, a 130-slip marina, and Dockside 29, a hotel offering a comparatively luxurious alternative to the 1930s-style structures across the water. Open year-round, the over-the-water rooms and suites are well furnished, clean and bright with hardwood floors, small kitchens and "perfect reception" satellite TV.

Box 2–8,Telegraph Cove, BC V0N 3J0, ⓒ **877/835-2683** or 250/928-3161. Fax 250/928-3162. www.telegraph cove.ca. 29 units, 48 RV sites. C$115–C$175 (US$101–US$154) double. Off-season rates available. RV sites C$30 (US$26) per day. MC, V. **Amenities:** Marina; coin-op laundry. *In room:* Kitchen.

Telegraph Cove Resorts   The accommodations here are refurbished, self-contained homes from the 1920s and 1930s, and include everything from a converted floating hospital on the boardwalk to a fisherman's cottage. Each has a story to share, and upgrades in decor have managed to combine simplicity with heritage charm. Some homes are cozy enough for 2, while others sleep 4, 6 and even up to 9 people. Wastell Manor, a two-level family home built in 1929, is a bit fancier. Because the manor is perched on a bluff, it offers exceptional views of the cove. Some 120 campsites set back from the village, among the trees; all have water hookups; some also have

---

Moments Tummy Rubs

Robson Bight Ecological Reserve, near Telegraph Cove, provides some of the most fascinating whale-watching in the province. Orcas regularly beach themselves in the shallow waters of the Bight's pebbly beaches, to rub their stomachs free of barnacles. Boaters, including kayakers and tour operators, are not allowed to enter the reserve, but can visit nearby areas. Whale fans anywhere within 15km (9 miles) of the Bight can tune in to CJKW 88.5 to hear the orcas sing.

electrical access; some have full hookups. Telegraph Cove Resorts also run the Old Saltery Pub (a converted saltery) and the Killer Whale Café (© 250/928-3131). Both are good eateries, which is fortunate as they really are the only shows in town.

Box 1, Telegraph Cove, BC V0N 3J0. © **800/200-HOOK** or 250/928-3131. Fax 250/928-3105. www.telegraphcove resorts.com. 24 units. Jun–Sept. C$99–C$275 (US$87–US$242) cabins/suites. Extra person C$10 (US$9). C$21–C$26 (US$18–US$23) campsites. Lower rates May and October. Packages available. MC, V. Closed mid-Oct to Apr. Pets allowed in some cabins for C$5 (US$4.40) per night. **Amenities**: Restaurant; pub; kayak rentals; coin-op laundry. *In room*: Coffeemaker, no phone.

PORT MCNEILL, ALERT BAY & SOINTULA

From Telegraph Cove, it's approximately 40km (25 miles) to **Port McNeill,** a hard-working, hard-edged township founded on logging and fishing. To wit, one of the main attractions is a record-breaking, 500-year-old burl (a dome-shaped tree growth) that weighs in at 24 tons, making it the world's largest, and an old steam donkey engine, circa 1938.

Besides those dubious attractions, Port McNeill offers visitors the chance to embark upon whale-watching expeditions. **Mackay Whale Watching,** P.O. Box 66, Port McNeill, BC V0N 2R0 © **877/663-6277** or 250/956-9865; www.whaletime.com), which uses 55-foot aluminum vessels, has been around for more than 25 years and was instrumental in helping to establish the Robson Bight whale reserve nearby. Tours run about 4½ hours, cost C$80 (US$70) per person, and include a light lunch. **Sea Orca Whale Watching,** Government Dock, P.O. Box 483, Alert Bay, BC V0N 1A0 (© **800/668-6722** or 250/974-5225; www.seaorca.com) offers 5- to 8-hour sail-with-the-whales excursions aboard S.V. *Tuan,* a 40-foot craft, for C$79 to C$170 (US$70–US$150) per adult.

From Port McNeill, BC Ferries runs 9 daily crossings to the 1,800-strong community of **Alert Bay** on Cormorant Island or to **Sointula** on Malcolm Island. One-way fares are C$6.50 (US$5.70) for adults, C$3.40 (US$3) for children 5 to 11. The crossing time is 45 minutes. Alternatively, North Island Air (© **250/956-2020**) runs charters and daily scenic flights out of Port McNeill. Prices vary according to destination and time in the air.

A Kwagiulth tribal village for thousands of years, Alert Bay exudes its rich, cultural heritage, and is most proud of the 53-m (173-ft.) cedar totem pole featuring 22 hand-carved figures of bears, orcas, and ravens. It stands outside the Big House at the top of the hill. The modern building is modeled after a Kwakwaka'wakw Big House, and in July and August hosts performances by 'Na'Nakwala dancers, usually Wednesday through Saturday. The cost is C$12 (US$11) for adults and C$5 (US$4.40) for children under 12. Near the ferry dock at Alert Bay, at the **U'Mista Cultural Centre** ✸✸ (© **250/974-5403;** www.umista.org), you'll find an extraordinary collection of carved-wood ceremonial masks, cedar baskets, copper jewelry, and other potlatch artifacts that were confiscated by the Canadian government in 1922, and repatriated in 1980. Although the displays are self-explanatory, try to take a guided tour to really appreciate the stories and folklore that the exhibits represent. Admission is C$5.30 (US$4.70) for adults, C$4.24 (US$3.70) for seniors and students, and C$1 (US88¢) for children 12 and under. The museum is open in summer daily 9am to 5:30pm, and in winter Monday through Friday 9am to 5pm.

At the other end of town—about a 15-minute stroll along the waterfront—is the ancient 'Namgis burial ground. It's sacred territory, so don't step over the wall to take photos of the many colorful and unusual totem poles. En route, keep an eye open for the **Anglican Church** with graveyard which reflects the arrival of Scottish immigrants into the area at the turn of the 20th century. Erected in 1881, the church's stained-glass windows are an interesting blend of Native Kwagiulth and Scottish design motifs. Also, check out the Ecological Park, a natural wonder that resembles the Florida Everglades without the alligators. An extensive system of trails for hiking and mountain biking criss-cross the island. Maps are available at the information centre.

Founded by Finnish settlers in 1901, the community of **Sointula,** on Malcolm Island, was to be a Utopian society, "a place of harmony." Although the concept collapsed, you can still feel the peaceful atmosphere of that dream. Finnish was the island's principal language until as recently as 30 years ago. But today, less than half of the 1,000-strong population is Finn. Sointula is a charming fishing village. There's a local gallery, store, and the **Sointula Museum** (© **250/973-6764**), next to the tennis courts by the ferry terminal, which tells the Finnish story. Six kilometers of gravel road takes you to **Bere Point Regional Park,** a known killer whale rubbing beach. The park offers two hiking trails of note: The 3.2km (2-mile) Matejeo Heritage Trail is a short walk from the ferry terminal and takes you through bogs, forest and beside pretty lakes; the 2.5-km (1.5-mile) Beautiful Bay Trail is more challenging. It starts at Bere Point and follows the bay to Malcolm Point.

WHERE TO STAY & DINE

Although tourists visit for the fishing, First Nations culture, and outdoor pursuits, Port McNeill, Alert Bay, and Sointula aren't geared for visitors. Accommodations are basic and restaurants cater to local tastes with burgers, fish and chips, and pasta.

In Port McNeill, **Haida-Way Motor Inn** (1817 Campbell Way; © **800/ 956-3373** or 250/956-3373; www.pmhotels.com) and **Dalewood Inn** (1703 Broughton Blvd.; © **877/956-3304** or 250/956-3304; www.dalewoodinn.com) are two motels with decent rooms as well as on-site pubs, and restaurants that add good (but nothing to write home about) steaks and chicken dishes to their dinner menu. Both inns have comparable rates, ranging from C$85 to C$109 (US$75–US$96).

In Alert Bay, one of your best bets is the **Old Customs House Restaurant & Inn,** (19 Fir St.; © **250/974-2282**), a 1918 historic building that has three rooms, kitchen facilities, and a great deck overlooking Johnstone Strait. **Alert Bay Lodge** (549 Fir St.; © **800/255-5057** or 250/974-2026) is more upscale and certainly roomier, in large part because it was once the United church for Alert Bay. The great room and library features high arched cedar beams, the cedar adds a warmth to its five simply furnished guest rooms—that means no TVs or radios. Rates range from C$45 to C$75 (US$40–US$66) per person.

Hemlock House Lodge (© **866/392-8377** or 250/974-7146; fax 250/824-8877; www.hemlockhouse.ca) is a hidden jewel on nearby Swanson Island. A renovated 1920's lodge, it has three double-occupancy rooms, a private beach, and quiet retreat areas. Open June to September, it specializes in kayaking adventures and photo safaris for wildlife in the Broughton Archipelago, Blackfish Sound, and Johnstone Strait. Rates, inclusive of all meals, are C$1,295 (US$1,492) for 3 nights/4 days and C$1,695 (US$1,492) for 4 nights/5 days.

On Malcolm Island, **Sund's Lodge,** 445 Kaleva Rd., Box 10, Sointula, BC V0N 3E0 (© **800/663-2872** or 250/902-1400 Oct–May; 250/973-6381 June–Sept; www.sundslodge.com) is a fully inclusive "adventure or do nothing" luxury resort located on 16 hectares (40 acres) of unspoiled wilderness on Blackfish Sound. Open

Kayaking Adventures with a Twist

Paddling softly through some of the hundreds of islands in the Broughton Inlet must be one of the most magical kayaking experiences available, especially when eagles, sea lions, and whales join in the fun. Your "base camp" is a beautifully restored heritage vessel called **MV Columbia III** that, 50 years ago, served as a missionary, hospital, and overall life-line vessel to BC's coastal communities. Today, outfitted with half a dozen quality kayaks, the ship travels between different dropoff and pickup paddling points which you could never hope to reach from an on-shore origin. Passenger accommodations comprise five tiny staterooms with extremely comfortable, queen-size bunk beds, a cozy lounge/dining area, and a sheltered deck.

The Campbell family, who own and operate this venture, has pooled its talents to provide expert naturalist and guiding tips, scrumptious food, and informal hospitality that might include an impromptu recital of Irish music after dinner. Passengers range from older teenagers to active retirees and schedules often include shore stops to explore First Nations communities, a hike through the rain forest, or a beachside picnic of just-caught crab. If ever you get paddle weary, the ship's zodiac will quickly take you back to the boat. The *Columbia* runs out of Port McNeil June through September; all inclusive 7-day trips are C$1,900 to C$3,000 (US$1,672–US$2,640) per person. Mothership Adventures, PO Box 30, Heriot Bay, BC V0 1H0; ℭ **888/833-8887** or 250/202-3229; www.mothershipadventures.com.

mid-June until the end of September, the family-run, luxury lodge accommodates up to 20 guests in cabins furnished with overstuffed log chairs and cozy beds with thick down comforters. Food is equally inviting, with an emphasis on local fare with spicy marinades, homemade sauces, and fresh herbs. A 3-night/4-day stay starts at C$2,400 (US$2,112) per person inclusive of accommodation, meals, guided fishing, hiking, and kayaking.

6 Port Hardy & Cape Scott Provincial Park ★★★

Port Hardy is 44km (27 miles) north of Port McNeill and the final stop on Island Highway. Many visitors, however, come via ferry, en route either to or from **Prince Rupert.** Port Hardy is also the departure point for the Discovery Coast Passage trip to the First Nations communities of Bella Bella, Shearwater, Ocean Falls, and Klemtu, among others. In summer, this tiny town gets so busy with ferry travelers that decent accommodation gets full fast, leaving a motley assortment of tired motels to choose from.

Until recently, the town's prosperity was fueled by forestry, mining, and commercial fishing, but the refurbished seaside promenade, and the fresh coat of paint here and there, are evidence of Port Hardy's efforts to diversify its economic base through tourism. Is this why the timbered **Port Hardy Visitor Information Centre,** 7250 Market St. (P.O. Box 294), Port Hardy, BC V0N 2P0 (ℭ **250/949-7622**), is the nicest building downtown? If you have an hour to spare, drop into the **Port Hardy Museum,** 7110 Market St. (ℭ **250/949-8143**), which has some interesting relics from early Danish settlers, plus a collection of stone tools, found nearby, which date from about 8,000 BC.

When you make it to **Port Hardy,** you may feel like you've reached the edge of the world, but in fact, Port Hardy is the jumping-off point for exhilarating, year-round outdoor activities, such as **hiking in Cape Scott Provincial Park** (see below), fishing, kayaking, and diving, as well as to several very remote, very exclusive fishing lodges further north.

North Island Daytrippers (© **800/956-2411** or 250/956-2411; www.islandday trippers.com) is a good option for hikers who would rather not go it alone in these wilderness areas. Based in Port McNeill, these savvy guides offer year-round half-day and full-day hikes to San Josef Bay and Ronning Gardens, Raft Cove, and many of the beaches and coves in between. Fees include lunch and start at C$120 (US$106) per person for a full day and decrease according to the number of people in the party.

OUTDOOR ACTIVITIES

The northern region epitomizes Vancouver Island's wildest (and wettest) coastal country. Although a lot of it can be enjoyed by visitors who just want a look-see, you'll learn that the deeper you explore, the greater the rewards. But to do that, be sure that you go with an experienced outfitter or that you are completely at ease when left to your own devices in the great outdoors.

DIVING   Water clarity and tidal action have made this one of the best dive locations in the world. There are more than two dozen outfitters in the area, some of which will provide fully equipped dive boats. A good resource is **North Island Dive & Charters,** 8665 Hastings St. (© **250/949-2664;** www.northislanddiver.com), a full-service dive store that also offers rentals and instruction. Pricing varies depending on the type of dive you're looking for, and whether or not equipment is required, but as a guideline, a two-tank dive involving about 6 hours on the water is C$135 (US$119) per person.

FISHING   Fishing nirvana awaits, as do several of the local outfitters. Charter trips and self-skippered boat rentals abound. **Catala Charters** (© **800/515-5511** or 250/949-7560; www.catalacharters.net) offers guided fishing trips, and **Codfather Charters** (© **250/949-6696;** www.codfathercharters.com) offers year-round fishing as well as accommodations in a waterfront lodge. If you just want to rent a boat, contact **Hardy Bay Boat Rental,** Quarterdeck Marina, 6555 Hardy Bay Rd. (© **250/949-7048** or 250/949-0155; www.hardybayfishing.com). Rates start at C$22/ US$19 per hour and C$190/US$168 per day.

Port Hardy is the gateway for trips to remote fishing camps, many of which cater to the heavy wallet brigade with upscale exclusivity. These include **King Pacific Lodge** (www.kingpacificlodge.com), and **Nimmo Bay Resort** (www.nimmobay.com), where access is by floatplane or boat, and all-inclusive prices start at about C$5,000 (US$4,400) for 3 days.

Duval Point Lodge (© **250/949-6667;** www.duvalpointlodge.com) is an affordable alternative where you can do your own thing without frou-frou frills. Located 8km (5 miles) north of Port Hardy (accessed by boat), the lodge has both a floating lodge and land-based log cabins, all of which share a full kitchen (guests do their own cooking) and living area. Some rooms share bathrooms too. Open May through October, the outfitter provides fishing tackle, bait, and boat for multi-day packages that start from C$510 (US$449) per person for 3 nights; and less (from US$320) if you bring your own boat. All guests can use the lodge's kayaks at no extra charge.

HIKING   Heavy rainfalls (nearly 504 centimeters [200 in.] per year) and violent windstorms predominate in this wild landscape, turning hiking trails into muddy quagmires. But if you thrive on doing things off the beaten track, these trails deliver. The easiest and most popular hike is the 2.5-km (1.5-mile) **San Josef Bay Trail,** a fairly easy walk through marshy ferns, skunk cabbage, and along the San Josef River to San Josef Bay, where there's an expanse of sandy beach, and the ruins of a Danish settlement.

More experienced and well-equipped hikers can opt for the challenging 24-km (15-mile) **Cape Scott Trail.** This grueling trek starts in mud, but once you're on your way, the scenery is pure wilderness: ocean bay beauty, weathered grass, high-rise canopies of Sitka spruce, and vast stretches of natural beach. Stops along the way include **Eric Lake,** an ideal spot for fishing and warm water swimming, and **Hansen Lagoon,** once a Danish settlement, and now a stopping place for Canada geese and a variety of waterfowl traveling the Pacific Flyway. Allow 3 days of heavy hiking, and a good week if you want to explore all the offshoot trails. Other than Eric Lake, where there are 11 designated camp pads, camping is unrestricted. You'll find food caches and pit toilets here and at Guise Bay, Nels Bight, San Josef, and Nissen Bight. There's an honor-system backcountry fee (C$5/US$4.40 per person) for overnight camping operative May to September. Self-registration vaults are located at the San Josef River boat launch and trailhead. South of Cape Scott lies Raft Cove Provincial Park, 405 hectares (1,001 acres) of rugged wilderness and wind-swept beaches that make for a good full day's excursion or longer. Campers will find the cove extremely exposed to the Pacific so even in summer, you can expect temperamental weather systems to dampen your canvas so prepare accordingly. Access to the park by road is on Ronning Main, off the Cape Scott road out of Holberg. Experienced sea kayakers paddle to Raft Cove down the San Josef River and out to the Pacific through San Josef Bay.

KAYAKING   The shores of Hardy Bay are scattered with coves, inlets, and islands to explore and stop along the way. The major islands are Deer, Peel, Cattle, Round, and Shell Island, all of which you can make into a leisurely day trip or single over-nighter. **Odyssey Kayaking** (© 888/792-3366 or 250/902-0565; www.odyssey kayaking.com) offers day-long guided paddles from C$99 (US$87) per person as well as longer, customized trips. Kayak rentals are from C$40 (US$35) per day.

CAPE SCOTT PROVINCIAL PARK ✦✦✦

Clinging to the northwest tip of Vancouver Island, Cape Scott Provincial Park is 21,840 hectares (53,967 acres) of untamed raincoast wilderness, where the wild Pacific Ocean pounds wide, windswept beaches and crashes against rocky headlands. In the late 1890s, enterprising Danish colonists from the American Midwest carved the tortuous route to Cape Scott itself out of the tangled bush. They hoped to build a community there. But the land was too isolated, and the weather too inhospitable to let the settlement grow. Today, their wagon roads are now hiking trails, and heritage markers along the way point out the remains of their endeavors: tumbledown cabins, sun-bleached driftwood fence posts, a dilapidated cougar trap, and cedar planked "corduroy roads."

Getting there is a 2-hour, 67-km (42-mile) drive west from Port Hardy down a heavily used gravel logging road toward the tiny town of **Holberg,** a good place to break the journey, especially if you stop in at the **Scarlet Ibis Pub** (© 250/288-3386). On the outskirts of Holberg, you'll find **Ronning Gardens.** Established in

1910 by Bernt Ronning, a Norwegian settler, the gardens are an extraordinary anomaly of exotic trees and plants from all over the world, including a pair of enormous Chilean Araucario araucana—also known as monkey-puzzle trees. These were grown from seedlings, male and female, and have been the starting point of several hundred of the monkey puzzle trees in North America.

Then continue on until the Cape Scott parking lot, where you'll find the trailheads to the rugged 23.5-km (15-mile) **Cape Scott Trail** with its stunning coastal scenery and some 30km (17 miles) of sandy beach. There's also a more accessible, 45-minute, 2.5km (1.5-mile) hike that leads to scenic San Josef Bay.

WHERE TO STAY

Glen Lyon Inn & Suites 🎖🎖   Once you make it past the rather daunting stuffed eagle showcased in the lobby, you'll find a clean, modern motel. All rooms have an ocean view, decent furnishings and come in a mix of configurations to match your needs, whether it's a family suite with bunk beds for the kids, an executive-style room, or the honeymoon suite, with Jacuzzi and wet bar. The family-style restaurant is bright and welcoming (see "Where to Dine") and the Glen Lyon pub opens for lunch and is a popular spot until last orders at around midnight.

6435 Hardy Bay Rd. (P.O. Box 103), Port Hardy, BC V0N 2P0. ✆ **877/949-7115** or 250/949-7115. Fax 250/949-7415. www.glenlyoninn.com. 44 units. May to mid-Oct C$85–C$120 (US$75–US$106) double; C$125–C$170 (US$110–US$150) suite. Mid-Oct to Apr C$62–C$69 (US$55–US$61) double; C$95–C$125 (US$84–US$110) suite. AE, MC, V. Small pets accepted C$10 (US$9). **Amenities:** Restaurant; pub; exercise room; laundry service. *In room:* TV, dataport, fridge, coffeemaker, hair dryer.

Oceanview B&B 🎖🎖   Although it has rather a grandiose exterior, this lovely home extends a warm welcome to weary travelers. Guest rooms are spacious—they have small sitting areas—and quaintly decorated, with brass or wrought-iron beds. Two of the rooms share a bathroom, and the third has a private ensuite bathroom. Thoughtful touches such as fresh-cut flowers, pillow chocolates, and a plate of homemade chocolate chip cookies greet you in your room. A European-style breakfast, with plenty of cold cuts and assorted cheeses, is served up in a bright and spacious kitchen. The sitting room is decorated with wicker furniture, and offers various reading materials, a piano, and a fireplace. The house has wonderful views of Hardy Bay and the snow-covered mountains on the mainland. An unexpected bonus is free parking for guests who wish to leave their vehicles while they take the ferry to Prince Rupert or to Discovery Passage.

7735 Cedar Place (P.O. Box 183), Port Hardy, BC V0N 2P0. ✆ and fax **250/949-8302.** www.island.net/~oceanvue. 3 units, 2 w/shared bathroom. C$85–C$100 (US$75–US$88). Rates include breakfast. Extra person C$15 (US$13). MC, V. Free parking. **Amenities:** Lounge. *In room:* TV/VCR, hair dryer, no phone.

Pioneer Inn Riverside RV Park   Located in a park-like setting of the Quatse River, the inn is located only minutes away from the ferry terminal, and is a great choice for travelers taking the Inside Passage cruise to Prince Rupert. Rooms aren't fancy, but they're bright, clean, and some contain kitchens. One room is wheelchair-accessible. The RV park is one of the nicest in the area. Rates include full electrical, sewer, and water hookups; cable TV and telephone are extra.

4965 Byng Rd., Box 699, Port Hardy, BC V0N 2P0. ✆ **800/663-8744** or 250/949-7271. Fax 250/949-7334. 36 units. Mid-May to mid-Oct C$85–C$95 (US$75–US$84); mid-Oct to mid-May C$46–C$54 (US$41–US$48). 25 RV sites C$20 (US$18) per vehicle. AE, MC, V. Free parking. Pets allowed for C$10 (US$9) **Amenities:** Restaurant; coffee shop; golf course nearby; coin-op laundry; playground; miniature golf. *In room:* TV, kitchen, coffeemaker.

Quarterdeck Inn & Marina Resort 🦀🦀 A smart, if generic-looking hotel, the Quarterdeck opened in 1999 and still feels very new. Peppermint-green corridors (a favorite color of many Port Hardy buildings) lead to spacious, pastel-colored rooms, with comfortable beds, quality furniture, and ocean views from every window. Some have kitchenettes and DVD players. The hotel is surrounded by a working boatyard and marina, so there's always something to see. The friendly staff can arrange a variety of outdoor activities such as charter fishing, whale-watching, and kayaking.

6555 Hardy Bay Rd. (P.O. Box 910), Port Hardy, BC V0N 2P0. © **877/902-0459** or 250/902-0455. Fax 250/902-0454. www.quarterdeckresort.net. 40 units. May–Sept C$105–C$135 (US$92–US$119); Oct–Apr C$75–C$85 (US$66–US$75). Rates include continental breakfast. AE, DC, DISC, MC, V. Free parking. Small pets allowed for C$10 (US$9). **Amenities:** Restaurant; pub; golf course nearby; Jacuzzi; tour/activities desk; coin-op laundry. *In room:* TV, DVD, kitchenette, coffeemaker, hair dryer.

WHERE TO DINE

IV's Quarterdeck Pub PUB/CANADIAN This nautical-style pub-restaurant, situated on the marina, serves great fresh halibut and chips, sandwiches, burgers, and other traditional pub fare as well as standards like steaks and chicken. It's really the only decent eatery in town with evening specials and to-go items, making it a local favorite for both working fisherman and visitors.

6555 Hardy Bay Rd. © **250/949-6922.** www.quarterdeckresort.net. Reservations not accepted. Main courses C$7–C$20 (US$6–US$18). AE, MC, V. Daily 11am–midnight.

Glen Lyon Restaurant CANADIAN Bright and airy, the restaurant bustles with activity from breakfast in the early morning through to dinner. The extensive menu covers all bases with great salads and burgers by day and dishes such as barbecued ribs, steak and a very good seafood platter by night. Families are especially welcome (kids portions are available) and all the desserts, whether apple crumble or the surprisingly good tiramisu, are homemade.

6435 Hardy Bay Rd. © **250/949-7115.** www.glenlyoninn.com. Main courses C$7–C$18 (US$6–US$16). AE, MC, V. Daily 6:30am–9pm.

8

The Gulf Islands

Snuggled between Vancouver Island and the mainland, the Gulf Islands are pastoral havens. Their protected waterways provide some of the finest cruising in the world, and their semi-Mediterranean climate is enviable, even by West Coast standards. Add to this, sweeping scenes of woods and water, pebble and shell beaches, and placid lakes stocked with bass and rainbow trout ideal for fly-fishing, and you can understand why the Gulf Islands have been described as "fragments of paradise."

The raggedly beautiful archipelago, the northern extension of Washington's San Juan Islands, is made up of more than 200 islands. Although most are small, uninhabited, and accessible only by private boat, the five larger islands, off the southeastern tip of Vancouver Island—Salt Spring Island, the Pender islands, Galiano, Mayne, and Saturna islands—are home to about 15,000 permanent residents and are served by a regularly scheduled ferry service.

From the beginning, the islands have attracted a polyglot of individuals: writers and artists, poets and cooks, ecologists and escapists. So, far from being an unsophisticated backwater, the region offers the visitor first-class restaurants, as well as heritage B&Bs, galleries, farmhouses, and artisans' studios. In recent years, relocated urbanites have started to gentrify the islands, resulting in an uneasy mix with the existing counterculture. Land values have skyrocketed and petty crime is on the rise. Only the self-governing Islands Trust holds development in check. One example of the fallout from this concerns the islands' water supply. As more and more city folk migrate to the islands (prompting a population increase of almost 30% in the past decade), resources must stretch to accommodate their city habits. With the onslaught of multi-bathroom homes, dishwashers, and Jacuzzis, fresh water has become a precious commodity. Today, homesteaders must dig twice as deep for water as they did 20 years ago. Boiling and filtering is becoming a way of life, and summer often means water shortages.

That said, the Gulf Islands are still a heavenly place to hike, kayak, and canoe, or simply enjoy a glass of wine from the deck of a cottage. Families usually resort to the latter because many of the islands' inns and B&Bs are geared to adults. When a hotel welcomes children, this information is included in the review in this guide. Refer to the "Where to Stay" sections for individual islands. The islands may lack many urban amenities such as ATMs and Laundromats, but they do have a wealth of quirky features that will make your visit memorable. One example is the "honesty stands" that dot the roadsides. You drop your money in the box provided, and walk away with honey, flowers, veggies, jams, and whatever else local folk have for sale. Deer are another feature. With no natural predators on the islands, they are free to roam roads, gardens, and forests, so be sure to drive carefully, especially at night.

Of all the islands, Salt Spring is the most dynamic, and the easiest to get to from Vancouver Island, especially if you have only a day to spare. Once on a Gulf Island, it is easy to hop to another, arriving in the early morning and departing late afternoon. You're best to incorporate at least one night on each island—it's the only way to experience the very different personality of each, although you might be tempted to stay far longer. After all, they are fragments of paradise.

1 Essentials

GETTING THERE

BY PLANE

Seaplanes crisscross the skies above the Gulf Islands at regular intervals, between Vancouver Island, Vancouver on the mainland, and Seattle. **Seair Seaplanes** (© 800/447-3247 or 604/273-8900; www.seairseaplanes.com) and **Harbour Air** (© 800/665-0212 or 604/274-1277; www.harbour-air.com) offer daily flights. One-way fares range from C$79 to $87 (US$70–US$77). **Kenmore Air** (© 800/543-9595; www.kenmore air.com) flies from Seattle May through September. One-way fares are C$188 (US$165); round-trip fares are C$339 (US$297). There are no areas on the islands that accommodate commercial flights, although some islands have small, grassy airstrips for private aircraft.

BY FERRY

Juggling your schedule with ferry departures is an art that requires patience, if not a master's degree in reading timetables. **BC Ferries** (© 888/223-3779 or 250/386-3431; www.bcferries.com) provides good basic service to the Gulf Islands, with at least two sailings a day from **Tsawwassen,** a 22-km (14-mile) drive south of Vancouver on the mainland, and from **Swartz Bay,** 32km (20 miles) north of Victoria on Vancouver Island. Ferries also run frequently between islands. Schedules are available from **BC Ferries.** One-way fares from Tsawwassen to the Gulf Islands average C$11 (US$10) per person; C$42 (US$37) for a standard-size vehicle. One-way fares from Swartz Bay to the islands average C$7 (US$6.15) per person; C$23 (US$20) for a standard-size vehicle. Return fares to Tsawwassen are less, and vary according to which island you are returning from. Return fares to **Swartz Bay** are free. Inter-island trips average C$4 (US$3.50) per person; C$8 (US$7) for a standard-size vehicle.

Note: Ferry travel can be costly if you're taking a vehicle, and long boarding waits are not uncommon. Ticket prices vary seasonally; mid-week travel is slightly less expensive than that on weekends and holidays, when reservations are essential. During these peak periods, book at least 3 weeks in advance to avoid disappointment. Reservations can be made with BC Ferries by phone or online. **Washington State Ferries** (© 800/843-3779 in Washington, or 888/808-7977 in Canada, or 206/464-6400; www.wsdot.wa. gov/ferries) provides daily service from **Anacortes to Sidney,** a short distance from Swartz Bay (see "The Saanich Peninsula" in chapter 4). From Swartz Bay, you can transfer to a BC Ferries ferry to the Gulf Islands. There is only one Anacortes–Sidney crossing daily; two in summer, during which vehicle reservations are strongly recommended. Reservations must be made by 5:30pm the day prior to travel. From May to early October, one-way fares are C$16 (US$14) for adults, C$8.90 (US$7.80) for seniors, C$12 (US$11) for children 6 to 18, C$59 (US$52) for a standard-size vehicle and driver. From mid-October to April, fares remain the same for adults, seniors, and children, but reduce to C$48 (US$42) for a standard-size vehicle and driver. Crossing time is 3 hours.

A local **inter-island water taxi** (© 250/537-2510; www.salt spring.com/watertaxi) operates June through August on Wednesdays and Saturdays. When school is in session, September through June, it operates as a weekday school boat, and adults often hitch a ride for day excursions. The one-way fare between any two points is C$15 (US$13) per person. Round trips are C$25 (US$22). People often transport kayaks for C$5 (US$4.40). Transporting bicycles is free.

VISITOR INFORMATION

Services operate through the local chamber of commerce or general store on individual islands (see "Essentials," below, for the island in question). You can also check out **www.gulfislands.net** for general information. Tourism Vancouver Island (© **250/ 754-3500;** www.islands.bc.ca) is another good resource. Not all islands have public campgrounds, and moorage facilities for pleasure craft vary in size and amenities considerably.

2 Salt Spring Island

Named for the briny springs on the island, Salt Spring Island is the largest and most accessible of the Gulf Islands. Lying just north of Vancouver Island's Swartz Bay, this thriving community is made up of almost 10,500 commuters, retirees, farmers, and artistic free-spirits. You'll come across a number of home-based entrepreneurs: everything from potters and weavers, to llama farms and cheese-makers! And make no mistake, Salt Spring is filled with characters whether dreadlocked or salt-and-peppered, who are as likely to hold a PhD in Comparative Literature as to be a self-professed expert in UFO technology. Much of the island is considered sacred by the local Coast Salish people. Mount Tuam, the site of a Buddhist Retreat Centre, contains quartz crystal that purportedly infuses those who visit with calm and well-being.

Salt Spring has two golf courses, a small movie theater that substitutes ads and trailers with slides of local people and places, an ice rink, lots of restaurants, and a scattering of hotly debated condominium developments, mostly in the **Ganges** area. Tour Salt Spring's pastoral landscape and you'll quickly see why sheep are Salt Spring's insignia—they're everywhere. You'll also discover any number of lakes (many are good fishing spots) and hiking trails, such as those in **Mount Maxwell Provincial Park,** which includes a 1.5-km (1-mile) trek up to **Baynes Peak.** Rising 595m (1,952 ft.),

---

⸤Tips⸥ Collect Island Dollars

Although they're not worth a pinch of salt off the island, Salt Spring Island Dollars are a valued commodity when you're there. They are accepted by most island businesses, some of which have bills on hand to give as change, or they can be purchased dollar-for-dollar at the tourist Information Centre in Ganges. The goal of the local currency is to raise funds for worthwhile community projects while promoting local commerce and good will. Art featured on the back of limited editions of the notes help to make them collectible after the two-year expiry date. Legally considered gift certificates, the Salt Spring Island Dollar is Canada's only local legal-tender currency in circulation.

The Gulf Islands

Legend

- ☂ Beach
- – – – Ferry Route
- 🐟 Fishing
- ⓘ Information
- ▲ Mountain
- 🏭 Winery

Reid Island

Alcala Point

DIONISIO POINT PROVINCIAL PARK

Hall I.

Norway I.

Secretary Islands

Kuper Island

Devina Dr.

Porlier Pass Rd.

36

Bodega Beach Dr.

Vineyard Way

Bodega Ridge

Houston Passage

Wallace Island

Retreat Cove

Porlier Pass Road

GALIANO

Strait of Georgia

Tent Island

1

North End Rd.

Sunset Dr.

2

N. Beach Rd.

Walker's Hook Rd.

Fernwood

3

4

ISLAND

35

Wise I.

Charles I.

Trincomali

Parminter Point

Saint Mary Lake

Vesuvius Bay

Vesuvius

Crofton

Channel Ridge

Stark Rd.

5

Vesuvius Bay Rd.

Bullock Lake

Robinson Rd.

Mansell Rd.

Channel

Sturdies Bay Rd.

32

31 31

Montague Rd.

33

Georgeson Bay Rd.

Parker Island

Montague Harbour

34

Morgan Bluff Rd.

BLUFFS PARK

Stuart Channel

Vesuvius Bay Rd.

Long Harbour Rd.

6

7

8   10

9

ⓘ 11

Ganges

Ganges Harbour

Long Harbour

Julia I.

Mt. Galiano ▲

Georgeson Bay

Tsawwassen

MAPLE MOUNTAIN PARK

▲ Maple Mt.

Fulford-Ganges Rd.

12

SISTER ISLANDS

Captain Passage

Prevost Island

Village Bay

Maple Bay

Sansom Narrows

Cranberry Rd.

Maxwell Rd.

Blackburn Lake

13

Bedis Rd.

Maple Bay

Maxwell Lake

S A L T

Cusheon Lake

14

Cusheon-Stewart Road

MT. MAXWELL PROVINCIAL PARK

Fulford-Ganges Rd.

Burgoyne Bay

S P R I N G

Stowell Lake

Beaver Pt. Rd.

Weston Lake

RUCKLE PROVINCIAL PARK

Vancouver

Island

Mt. Sulivan ▲

Mt. Bruce ▲

Fulford-Ganges Rd.

Isabella Pt. Rd.

Fulford Harbour

Beaver Pt. Road

Cowichan Bay

Cowichan Bay

Separation Point

I S L A N D

Musgrave Rd.

Satellite Channel

Mt. Tuam ▲

ECOLOGICAL RESERVE

16

Swartz Bay

Swartz Bay / Tsawwassen

PRINCESS MARGARET PROVINCIAL MARINE PARK

Portland Island

Piers Island

1

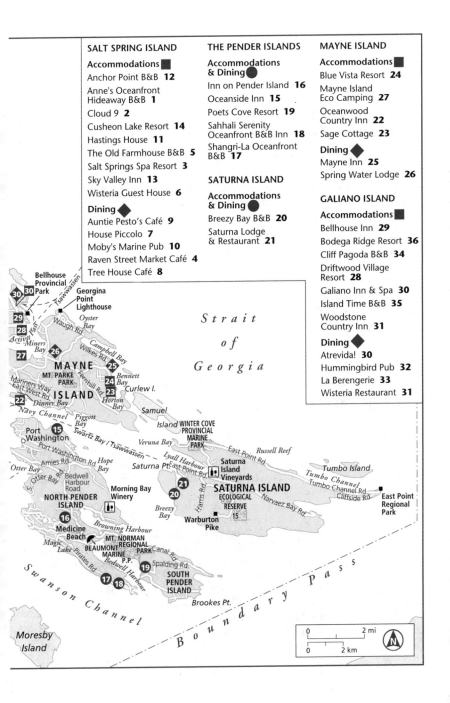

SALT SPRING ISLAND

Accommodations ■
Anchor Point B&B **12**
Anne's Oceanfront Hideaway B&B **1**
Cloud 9 **2**
Cusheon Lake Resort **14**
Hastings House **11**
The Old Farmhouse B&B **5**
Salt Springs Spa Resort **3**
Sky Valley Inn **13**
Wisteria Guest House **6**

Dining ◆
Auntie Pesto's Café **9**
House Piccolo **7**
Moby's Marine Pub **10**
Raven Street Market Café **4**
Tree House Café **8**

THE PENDER ISLANDS

Accommodations & Dining ●
Inn on Pender Island **16**
Oceanside Inn **15**
Poets Cove Resort **19**
Sahhali Serenity Oceanfront B&B Inn **18**
Shangri-La Oceanfront B&B **17**

SATURNA ISLAND

Accommodations & Dining ●
Breezy Bay B&B **20**
Saturna Lodge & Restaurant **21**

MAYNE ISLAND

Accommodations ■
Blue Vista Resort **24**
Mayne Island Eco Camping **27**
Oceanwood Country Inn **22**
Sage Cottage **23**

Dining ◆
Mayne Inn **25**
Spring Water Lodge **26**

GALIANO ISLAND

Accommodations ■
Bellhouse Inn **29**
Bodega Ridge Resort **36**
Cliff Pagoda B&B **34**
Driftwood Village Resort **28**
Galiano Inn & Spa **30**
Island Time B&B **35**
Woodstone Country Inn **31**

Dining ◆
Atrevida! **30**
Hummingbird Pub **32**
La Berengerie **33**
Wisteria Restaurant **31**

Strait of Georgia

Bellhouse Provincial Park
Georgina Point Lighthouse
Oyster Bay
Waugh Rd
Campbell Bay
Wilkes Rd
MAYNE
MT. PARKE PARK
Miners Bay
Active Pass
Tsawwassen
Fernhill Rd
Bennett Bay
Curlew I.
Mariners Way
East West Rd
ISLAND
Horton Bay
Navy Channel
Dinner Bay
Piggott Bay
Samuel
Island
Port Washington
Swartz Bay / Tsawwassen
Veruna Bay
Hope Bay
Amies Rd.
Port Washington Rd.
Otter Bay
Bedwell Harbour Road
NORTH PENDER ISLAND
Morning Bay Winery
Breezy Bay
Warburton Pike
Medicine Beach
Magic Lake
Pirates Rd
BEAUMONT MARINE P.P.
MT. NORMAN REGIONAL PARK
Bedwell Harbour
Browning Harbour
Canal Rd.
Spalding Rd.
SOUTH PENDER ISLAND
WINTER COVE PROVINCIAL MARINE PARK
Lyall Harbour
Saturna Pt.
East Point Rd
Saturna Island Vineyards
East Point Rd
Russell Reef
Tumbo Island
Tumbo Channel
Tumbo Channel Rd.
Cliffside Rd.
East Point Regional Park
Harris Rd.
SATURNA ISLAND
ECOLOGICAL RESERVE 15
Narvaez Bay Rd.
Brookes Pt.
Swanson Channel
Moresby Island
Boundary Pass

0   2 mi
0   2 km

it is the third highest mountain on the Gulf Islands. You can drive to the trailhead, but go easy, the paved road becomes a narrow, gravel surface that's too rough for RVs to negotiate.

ESSENTIALS
GETTING THERE

BC Ferries sails to **Fulford Harbour,** in the southern part of Salt Spring, or **Long Harbour,** toward the north. Seaplanes land in **Ganges Harbour,** in the center of the island. See "Getting There," above, for information about fares and schedules.

If you're arriving via ferry to Fulford Harbour, look out for **St. Paul's Church** (best seen from the water). Founded by a Roman Catholic missionary in 1878, this picturesque tiny stone church was built by immigrants from Hawaii who worked for the Hudson's Bay Company, descendants of whom still live on the island.

VISITOR INFORMATION

Head to the **Salt Spring Island Chamber of Commerce,** 121 Lower Ganges Rd., Salt Spring Island, BC V8K 2T1 (✆ **866/216-2936** or 250/537-5252; www.saltspring island.bc.ca), in the village of Ganges. Open daily, year-round, 11am–3pm. Another good online resource is **www.saltspringtourism.com.**

GETTING AROUND

Silver Shadow Taxi (✆ **250/537-3030**) services the island. If you want to rent a car, there's **Little Beaver Car Rental,** 161 Lower Ganges Rd. (✆ **250/537-9600**). Rental for a mid-range vehicle is about C$46 (US$40) a day. **Salt Spring Kayaks,** 2933 Fulford-Ganges Rd., Fulford Harbour (✆ **866/341-0007** or 250/653-4222), rents both bikes (C$30/US$26 a day) and kayaks (C$50–C$85/US$44–US$75 a day), and will deliver them to anywhere on Salt Spring Island for a nominal charge.

EXPLORING SALT SPRING ISLAND
GANGES

The bustling seaside village of **Ganges** ☆☆☆ belies the notion that the Gulf Islands are sleepy hideaways. The sheer number of Realtors is a gauge of Salt Spring's "love-at-first-sight" appeal. Historic buildings and bright new commercial structures harbor banks and shopping malls, liquor stores, cafes, bakeries, and a busy marina. In this cultural center of the island, you'll also find several quality galleries of locally crafted goods. In spring, this showcase expands into **Artcraft,** an exhibition of more than 250 Gulf Island artisans. Housed at Mahon Hall, Artcraft runs May through September daily from 10am to 5pm (✆ **250/537-0899**). A **Studio Tour** (www.saltspringstudio tour.com) explores all manner of studios scattered among nooks and crannies on the island, letting you chat with the artists, view their work, and watch them create. Although officially tour season is from mid-May to the end of September, many spots are open year-round. Keep a lookout for the blue "sheep" signs for participating studios. Be warned, it can take about a week to visit them all!

Salt Spring's Saturday **farmers' market,** held in Centennial Park in the heart of Ganges, is another summer must-see. This weekly gathering is a glorious melee of islanders and visitors, dogs and children, craftspeople, food vendors, jugglers, and musicians. Everything for sale must be handmade or homegrown, so it's as much a feast for the eyes as for the stomach. If you're looking to snatch up some of the freshly baked goods, be sure to arrive before 10am, as they're often sold out within an hour or so of opening. Otherwise, be prepared to stroll through the crowds, right up until late afternoon, when fresh-produce vendors, having sold their lot, start to drift away. And be prepared to find a few items that are unexpected, whether it's an alpaca throw, hand-painted Wellington boots, a pottery apple-baker, or whimsical jewelry. It's *the* place to shop if you're heading out for a weekend picnic or sail. Go to **www.salt springmarket.com** for more information.

As good as it is, the farmers' market pales in comparison to the **Salt Spring Island Fall Fair,** an annual weekend event held toward the end of September at the Farmers' Institute fairgrounds (351 Rainbow Rd.). Filled with all the sights, sounds, tastes, and smells of a good old-fashioned country fair, it showcases award-winning livestock and home-baked pies, alongside rides and classic games like balloon darts. The sheepdog trials are superb, with hardworking collies maneuvering bundles of sheep from one corner of the field to another, all to the command of a whistle. A shuttle runs from Ganges to the fairgrounds; call ℰ **250/537-4448** for fair information.

Inspired to explore Ganges further? **Salt Spring Marina** at Harbour's End (124 Upper Ganges Rd. ℰ **800/334-6629** or 250/537-5810) rents **scooters** (C$50/US$44 for 4 hours) and 15-foot aluminum **motorboats** (C$25/US$22 per hour) and can arrange for fishing charters.

RUCKLE PROVINCIAL PARK 𝒜𝒜

This 433-hectare (1,070-acre) park starts out along 8km (5 miles) of shoreline around **Beaver Point,** and sweeps up to an expanse of open and grassy meadow. Once owned by the Ruckle family, Irish immigrants in the late 1800s, part of the park is still operated as a sheep farm by the Ruckle family. Several of the original buildings, including a barn and an old residence, still stand. Ruckle Park is by far the easiest hiking ground on Salt Spring Island, offering more than 15km (9 miles) of trails, the favorite being a shoreline trail than runs 4,400m (14,436 ft.) from the heritage farm area right through to Yeo Point. Another trail, about the same distance but with some hills to climb, leaves from the park headquarters and heads inland in a loop around Merganser Pond. Trail maps are available at the park's visitor center. Be sure to remember your binoculars so that you can enjoy the abundance of wildlife. You're also likely to see scuba divers in the waters off Ruckle Park, where castle-like underwater caves and a profusion of marine life create intriguing dives.

The park has 70 walk-in campsites with fire pits (firewood is provided in the summer), plus some group sites, a picnic area, a large kitchen shelter, drinking water, several pit toilets, and a security patrol for the entire camping area. The park attracts eco-adventurers and families alike, though for young children you would be better off heading for **Cusheon Lake.** Ruckle Park has no designated swimming and playground areas, and no interpretive programs. From mid-March to October, a camping fee of C$14 (US$12) per night applies, and you must reserve your campsite in advance. Camping is free from November to mid-March, on a first-come, first-served basis. No firewood is supplied November through mid-March. Call **Discover Camping** (ℰ **877/559-2115** or 250/539-2115) for reservations and information, or log on to **www.discovercamping.ca**.

VESUVIUS

Located at the western edge of Salt Spring Island, the village, which consists of old seaside cottages knitted together by winding lanes, was named for its wonderful sunsets, made all the more dramatic by the clouds of smoke that spew forth across the Stuart Channel, from a pulp mill in Crofton on Vancouver Island. Unfortunately, this

---

Palatable Diversions

Treats for your taste buds, here are some of Salt Springs' top culinary diversions:

- **Big Foot Organic Herb Farm** (104 Eagle Ridge Dr. ⓒ 250/537-4466): Unusual varieties of fresh and dried herbs along with salsas, jams, jellies, chutney, flavored vinegars, honeys, and mustards.
- **Salt Spring Cheese Company** (285 Reynolds Rd. ⓒ 250/653-2300) and **Moonstruck Organic Cheese** (1306 Beddis Rd. ⓒ 250/537-4987; www.moonstruckcheese.com) Artisan goat cheeses, and a gourmet selection of blues, savory, and ash-ripened Camembert cheeses.
- **Salt Spring Vineyards & Winery** (151 Lee Rd. ⓒ 250/653-9463; www.saltspringvineyards.com), and **Oaks Vineyard** (1880 Fulford-Ganges Rd. ⓒ 250/653-4687): Cottage wineries with wine tasting and retail sales of Pinot Gris, Pinot Noir, Blackberry port, and Gewürztraminer.
- **Sacred Mountain Lavender Farm** (401 Musgrave Rd. ⓒ 250/653-2315; www.sacredmountainlavender.com): A boutique lavender farm with specialty and custom-made products from lavender salts and scrubs to lavender coffee and chocolates.
- **Gulf Islands Brewery** (270 Furness Rd. ⓒ 250/653-2383; www.gulfisland brewery.com): Producer of golden ales and an Irish-style extra stout; it's the only brewery in the Gulf Islands.

And for those who would rather not go it alone, **Island Gourmet Safaris** (ⓒ 250/537-4118) hosts year-round tours to discover Salt Spring through its art and cuisine. Tours are 6 hours long and start at C$500 (US$440) for 1 to 4 people, including lunch, which features only Salt Spring Island produce.

---

artistry also carries an off-putting pulpy odor, though that's not putting off a remake of the area that has started with the closure of one of the island's time-honored watering holes, The Vesuvius Inn, and is continuing with a substantial development of soon-to-be condominiums and vacation cottages. **BC Ferries** (ⓒ 888/223-3777 or 250/386-3432; www.bcferries.com) runs a regular service—almost every hour—across the Stuart Channel to Crofton. Return fares are C$7 (US$6.15) for adults, C$4 (US$3.50) for children, and C$23(US$20) for a standard-size vehicle. The crossing takes 20 minutes.

WHERE TO STAY

Anchor Point B&B   Surrounded by a courtyard garden and terraces, Anchor Point is a traditional Cape Cod–style B&B with a homey atmosphere. Guests can use a comfortable lounge and dining area with lovely water views, as well as a TV/VCR den where the movie library comprises more than 800 titles. The two guest rooms are sparkling clean, with fireplaces, designer linens, and quality amenities, including robes and slippers—pretty handy for scuttling to the outside Jacuzzi. Turndown service is a pampering touch, as is the never-ending supply of freshly baked cookies. Breakfasts offer unusual and tasty twists such as pecan-stuffed nectarines, and savory French toasts with tomato and rosemary.

150 Beddis Rd., Salt Spring Island, BC V8K 2J2. ℂ **800/648-2560** or 250/538-0110. Fax 250/538-0120. www.anchorpointbb.com. 2 units. Mid-May to mid-Sept C$165 (US$145). Mid-Sept to mid-May C$145 (US$128). Rates include breakfast. MC, V. **Amenities:** Jacuzzi; laundry service. *In room:* TV/VCR/DVD, Wi-Fi, hair dryer.

Anne's Oceanfront Hideaway B&B

This oceanfront inn offers cozy lounges (one a library with a TV/DVD/VCR, the other with a coffee/cookie counter) and comfortable furnishings. A central staircase leads upstairs to guest rooms that are well appointed and individually decorated, and include a fireplace. Décor ranges from French country styling to Queen Anne elegance and tend to appeal to the older crowd on a romantic getaway. Situated on the edge of a cliff, Anne's provides sweeping views of the island and sea. Thoughtful touches include free soft drinks in the guest-room fridge upon arrival, slippers and robe for when you want to head outside to the Jacuzzi, and evening turndown service. An elevator makes the four upstairs guest rooms wheelchair accessible, as well as the lower level, where, with advance notice, you can enjoy an aromatherapy massage. Breakfasts are elegantly served and include items such as a salmon scramble wrap, a portobello benedict, and an artichoke and pimento frittata.

168 Simson Rd., Salt Spring Island, BC V8K 1E2. ℂ **888/474-2663** or 250/537-0851. Fax 250/537-0861. www.annesoceanfront.com. 4 units. May–Sept C$210–C$275 (US$185–US$242). Oct–Apr C$195–C$225 (US$172–US$198). Rates include breakfast. AE, MC, V. Children not accepted. **Amenities:** Lounges; Jacuzzi; massage; high-speed Internet. *In room:* Fridge, hair dryer, no phone.

Cloud 9 🎿🎿

Perched atop one of Salt Spring Island's highest hills, Cloud 9 lives up to its name, with unobstructed 180-degree views of the ocean and neighboring islands. With vaulted ceilings, scores of large windows, and more than 46 sq. m (500 sq. ft.) of decks, the views are spectacular. The Morningstar Suite, in the main house, boasts almost two walls of windows (magical only if you're early risers), while the remaining two suites are past a Japanese-style garden in a separate cedar-sided cottage. All guest rooms have private entrances and French doors leading to a spacious private patio, and feature enough pampering touches to encourage cocooning and romance. Of special note are the individually controlled heated floors, fireplaces, down duvets and pillows, satellite TV, and genuine Persian rugs that complement the overall modern West Coast decor. Enormous bathrooms have deep double-soaker or jetted bathtubs. You even get two pairs of slippers: one for inside, the other for outside (to get to the cliff-side Jacuzzi), as well as a pair of binoculars. If you choose to have breakfast in your suite, it's included in the rate. If you choose the more formal option of dining in the main house, there's a surcharge of C$20 (US$18). The first is a very good continental breakfast; the latter includes a hot selection.

238 Sun Eagle Dr., Salt Spring Island, BC V8K 1E5. ℂ **877/722-8233** or 250/537-2776. Fax 250/537-2776. www.cloud9oceanview.com. 3 units. Mid-Jun to Sept C$180–C$200 (US$158–US$176). Oct & May to mid-Jun C$155–C$175 (US$136–US$154). Nov–Apr C$135–C$155 (US$119–US$136). Extra person C$50 (US$44). MC, V. Pets accepted with prior approval. Children 12 and under not accepted. **Amenities:** 2 lounges; Jacuzzi; bike rental; laundry service. *In room:* TV/VCR, Wi-Fi, dataport, hair dryer.

Cusheon Lake Resort 🄺ids

With its location right on the shores of Cusheon Lake, this family oriented resort has a holiday camp feel. The one- and two-bedroom log cabins and A-frame chalets are spotlessly clean and furnished in a no nonsense style that suits families and people who want a self-catering, un-froufrou getaway. The kitchen is well stocked with all the essentials, including coffee filters. Beach towels are also part of the deal because there's so much to do in and around the lake: canoeing, swimming, rowing, picnicking, and lawn games.

171 Natalie Lane, Salt Spring Island, BC V8K 2C6. ℂ **250/537-9629.** www.cusheonlake.com. 16 units. Mid-May to mid-Oct C$135–C$202 (US$119–US$178). Mid-Oct to mid-May C$105–C$165 (US$92–US$145). C$20 (US$18) additional person. 2-night minimum stay Jul and Aug. Weekly rates available. MC, V. Pets not accepted (kennel nearby). **Amenities:** Canoes; rowboats; lake swimming; picnic tables; outdoor hot tub; BBQ. *In room:* Kitchen, fridge, coffeemaker, microwave, no phone.

Hastings House ✦✦✦ A member of the exclusive French hotel network Relais & Châteaux, this upscale inn lies an olive pip's throw from the village of Ganges, in a magnificent garden and orchard overlooking Ganges Harbour. First a Hudson's Bay Company trading post, and then a farm, the homestead was bought in the 1930s by Barbara Wedgwood, the British pottery heiress, who turned the site into a replica of a 16th-century Sussex estate (all the while driving around Salt Spring's country roads in a Rolls-Royce). Since then, the Tudor-style manor house, farmhouse, barn, and trading post have been renovated into cottages and suites, each charged with character and filled with original art and antiques, and all the modern luxuries of a first-class hotel (including bathrooms large enough for deep soaking tubs), save for TVs, DVD players, and VCRs, which are provided only on request. Its restaurant is equally impressive (see "Where to Dine"). Reserve 6 months in advance for summer visits. Rates include a morning hamper (a lavish continental breakfast); if you're still hungry, breakfast is offered at a la carte prices.

160 Upper Ganges Rd., Ganges, Salt Spring Island, BC V8K 2S8. ℂ **800/661-9255** or 250/537-2362. Fax 250/537-5333. www.hastingshouse.com. 18 units. June–Sept C$360–C$910 (US$317–US$801). Mid-Mar to May and Oct–mid-Nov C$295–C$800 (US$260–US$704). Rates include wake-up hamper, and afternoon tea. Extra person C$85 (US$75). AE, DC, MC, V. Closed mid-Nov to mid-Mar. Children 16 and under not accepted. **Amenities:** Restaurant; lounge with honor bar; media room with Internet. *In room:* No phone.

The Old Farmhouse B&B ✦ The driveway is flanked by meadows and ancient orchards, and is a fitting prelude to this heritage B&B. The original white clapboard farmhouse has been lovingly renovated to retain much of its yesteryear charm, but with modern conveniences such as private bathrooms, a private entrance, and a sophisticated European ambience. Geraniums cascade from porches and private patios, and guest rooms are spacious with appealing country decor. A separate cottage—actually a chicken house transformed into a cozy one-bedroom suite nicknamed Château de Poulet—is especially romantic. The multi-course breakfasts also have a country appeal, and from the warm and inviting, farm-style open kitchen comes freshly baked cinnamon rolls, crepes, omelettes, and platters of sliced fruit. The home site was staked in 1860 by black American settlers from Kentucky, who had been recruited north in return for their vote that British Columbia join Canada rather than the U.S.

1077 North End Rd., Salt Spring Island, BC V8K 1L9. ℂ **250/537-4113.** Fax 250/537-4969. www.oldfarmhouse.ca. 5 units. May–Sept & Dec C$185 (US$163). Jan–Apr and Oct–Nov C$155 (US$136). Rates include breakfast. Extra person C$30 (US$26). MC, V. Children not accepted. **Amenities:** Lounge. *In room:* No phone.

Salt Springs Spa Resort This spa resort is the only spot where the island's salty spring waters can be enjoyed. The day spa offers a variety of facials, body wraps, and massages, and even if spa-ing isn't your thing, Salt Springs is a great getaway; choose from several one-, two-, and three-bedroom A-frame chalets. A handful are in the forest, but most sport an ocean view, looking across Trincomali Channel to Wallace Island, a marine park. All chalets have full kitchen, wood-burning fireplace, wide porch with barbecue, and an oversize, two-person mineral tub in addition to a regular bathtub. Clamming gear and crab traps are available for those wanting to try their luck on the beach across the road.

1460 North Beach Rd., Salt Spring Island, BC V8K 1J4. © **800/665-0039** or 250/537-4111. Fax 250/537-2939. www.saltspringspa.com. 13 chalets. Late Jun–Aug C$199–C$299 (US$175–US$263). Mar–late Jun and Sept–Oct C$135–C$219 (US$119–US$193). Nov–Feb C$109–C$199 (US$96–US$175). 2-night minimum stay in summer. Weekly rates and packages available. Extra person C$20 (US$18). AE, MC, V. Free parking. Children not accepted. **Amenities:** Spa; free bikes and rowboats; games room; coin-op washer and dryer. *In room:* iKtchen, fridge, coffeemaker, hair dryer, fireplace, no phone.

Sky Valley Inn *(Finds* With a touch of Provence in every renovated corner, Sky Valley is more like an old French country retreat nestled in 4.5 hectares (11 acres), with outstanding views to neighboring islands. Each of the three guest rooms is distinctly decorated with hardwood floors, French toile wallpaper, wainscoting and hardwood floors. The king- and queen-size down-feather mattresses are topped with down duvets and crisp white linens for a luxurious feel. Each room has a private entrance; the Garden Room is completely separate from the main house. Gourmet breakfasts are served in an open French-style country kitchen and will likely include cheese blintz crepes, and a frittata or soufflé, as well as lavender scones, and peach and lavender jams that have won first prizes in the Salt Spring Island Fall Fair.

421 Sky Valley Rd., Salt Spring Island, BC V8K 2C3 © **866/537-1028** or 250/537-9800. www.skyvalleyinn.com. 3 units. C$170–C$220 (US$150–US$194) year-round. 2-night minimum stay in summer. Pets not accepted. Children not accepted. MC, V. **Amenities:** Outdoor swimming pool; lounge with TV/DVD; Wi-Fi. *In room:* No phone.

Wisteria Guest House *∂* Located within a 10-minute stroll of Ganges, this charming inn is so full of color and character, it's hard to believe that it was once a nursing home. Its renaissance has certainly created something for everyone. The main guest house has six vibrantly decorated rooms: two with en suites, and four that share two bathrooms making them a good choice for friends and family traveling together. The two studios are the most romantic. Each has a private entrance and French doors leading onto a sunny patio, and a well-equipped kitchenette. One has a king, the other a queen-size bed. If you want to be totally independent and able to prepare your own meals, the private cottage, with twin beds, has a fully equipped kitchen, cable TV, and private patio. In winter, only a cold breakfast is served, though that might not be the drawback it sounds. One of the owners was a pastry chef at the Westin New York, so breakfast is still a pretty lavish affair of home-made Swiss-style muesli and almond croissants. In summer, you can enjoy additional items such as savory egg strudels or baked eggs.

268 Park Dr., Salt Spring Island, BC V8K 2S1 © **250/537-5899**. Fax 250/537-5644. www.wisteriaguesthouse.com. 9 units. Mid-May to mid-Oct C$139–C$169 (US$122–US$149); C$99–C$129 (US$87–US$114) shared bath. Mid-Oct to Feb C$109–C$129 (US$96–US$114); C$89–C$99 (US$78–US$87) shared bath. Mar to mid-May C$129–C$149 (US$114–US$131); C$99–C$129 (US$87–US$114) shared bath. Extra person C$10–C$15 (US$9–US$13). Pets accepted. AE, MC, V. **Amenities:** Common room w/TV and fireplace; nonsmoking facility. *In room:* No phone.

WHERE TO DINE

Auntie Pesto's Café ECLECTIC WESTCOAST With a lovely view of Ganges Harbour and a waterfront patio, this tiny eatery is busy all day long, whether because of its hearty soups and over-stuffed sandwiches on fresh-baked breads, or its excellent pasta dishes (including wheat-free) that come with a choice of toppings such as marinated tofu, prawns, meatballs, and home-made sauces. The dinner menu features steak and seafood specials that may include Thai-prawn stir-fry or grilled halibut with salsa topping. The deli counter lists 21 different cheeses as well as an orgy of olives and meats such as chouriço, Genoa salami, and Filicetti prosciutto.

2104–115 Fulford-Ganges Rd., Grace Point Sq. (C) 250/537-4181. www.auntiepestos.com. Reservations recommended (and only accepted) for dinner Jul–Aug. Main courses C$8–C$12 (US$7–US$11) lunch; C$10–C$20 (US$9–US$18) dinner. MC, V. Daily 8am–9pm.

Hastings House ✿✿ PACIFIC NORTHWEST Impeccable cuisine, attentive service, and a gracious setting have helped make Hastings House one of the most sought-after destination restaurants—and inns—in the Pacific Northwest (see "Where to Stay"). In addition to a la carte selections, there's a superb, multi-course menu that changes daily; many of the ingredients come from the estate's gardens and orchards. Dinner can be a sophisticated, evening-long affair with an excellent wine list. The choice of entrees nearly always features Salt Spring lamb, the house specialty (try it grilled with rosemary spaetzle and a grainy mustard jus), local salmon (perhaps a paprika-crusted white spring), as well as other selections such as a popular duck breast with wild mushroom risotto and port wine jus. The Snug Lounge, a cozy retreat away from the main room, offers less formal dining. There was a time when attire demanded jackets; thankfully, dress is now the much easier "smart casual." Get there early to secure a spot by the fire for pre-dinner cocktails.

160 Upper Ganges Rd. (C) 250/537-2362. Reservations required. 4-course prix fixe dinner C$95 (US$84); entrees C$12–C$48 (US$11–US$42). AE, DC, MC, V. Mid-Mar to mid-Nov daily 6–10pm. Closed mid-Nov to mid-Mar.

House Piccolo ✿ SCANDINAVIAN CONTINENTAL This small blue-and-white heritage farmhouse-turned-restaurant is wonderfully intimate. Two-person tables are scattered through two connecting country-style dining rooms accented with copper kettles set high on shelves. Everything on the Scandinavian-style menu is enticing, particularly the fresh bread, broiled sea scallop brochettes, and roasted British Columbia venison with juniper berries. You might even want to open your wallet up for the caviar (at C$125/US$110 per oz.) and buckwheat blinis—it's that good. Save room for homemade ice cream or the signature chocolate terrine. House Piccolo is a member of Chaine des Rôtisseurs, an international gastronomic society dedicated to the promotion of fine dining around the world.

108 Hereford Ave. (C) 250/537-1844. www.housepiccolo.com. Reservations recommended July–Sept. Main courses C$25–C$32 (US$22–US$28). AE, DC, MC, V. May–Sept daily 5–10pm; Oct–Apr 5–8pm.

Moby's Marine Pub PUB FARE This is a contemporary multilevel marine pub with big beams, wood floors, and great views of Ganges Harbour from cathedral-size windows. It's a local favorite, especially on live entertainment nights when an eclectic mix of R&B, folk, jazz, and rock takes to the stage. If it's a local headliner, such as Valdy, performing, get there early to grab a table. The menu includes burgers and fajitas alongside savory entrees like Caribbean fish pot (to die for) and Louisiana lamb curry. Jazz on Sunday nights is a dinner tradition. Ten beers are on tap. Moby's deck hangs over the water, within inches of bullwhip kelp and minnows. It's a great place to catch some summer rays over a cold one. The entire complex is destined for redevelopment before the decade's out, so enjoy it while you can.

124 Upper Ganges Rd. (C) 250/537-5559. Main courses C$8–C$17 (US$7–US$15). MC, V. Sun–Thurs 10am–midnight; Fri–Sat 10am–1am.

Raven Street Market Café PIZZA The thin-crust, wood-fired pizzas here are among the best and most creative you'll find anywhere. Made in the traditional Neopolitan way, they include combinations such as roasted pepper chicken, basil, cilantro, and fresh tomatoes; herbed lamb and artichoke pesto; and "the Canadianne":

Resort Development Opening 2007

Salt Spring is the largest and most populated of the Gulf Islands, and it's little wonder the developers are moving in on its quieter pockets and making their mark. One of the largest arrivals, opening 2007, is the Salt Spring Island Village Resort (𝒞 **888/538-6246;** www.saltspringvillage.com), an impressive complex involving a three-story West Coast–style lodge, spa, restaurant, and series of vacation cottages, all on the edge of Bullock Lake.

---

real back bacon, chorizo sausage, mushroom, white mozzarella, black olives, and green pepper. Other dishes include a delicious seafood and sausage gumbo, a very good chicken paella, as well as focaccia sandwiches, burgers, and salads. This is a grocery and deli market as much as it is an eatery, which makes the atmosphere convivial and a tad busy; so the waitstaff may not be as attentive as you might like.

321 Fernwood Rd. 𝒞 250/537-2273. www.ravenstreet.ca. Main courses C$10–C$17 (US$9–US$15). Tues–Sun 9am–8pm; Mon 9am–5pm.

Tree House Cafe CAFE   Set in the heart of Ganges, this 12-seat cafe spills over onto a larger patio that stakes its claim around and beneath a sprawling old plum tree. In summer, the place is jammed, in part because of the folksy musical entertainment, but also because of the great food that includes everything from Thai peanut tofu and vegetarian chili, to burgers and BLTs. The organic Salt Spring coffee sidelines Starbucks.

In the heart of Ganges, under the plum tree. 𝒞 250/537-5379. Main courses C$5–C$7 (US$4.40–US$6.15). MC, V. Oct–May daily 8am–3pm; June–Sep daily 8am–11pm.

3 The Pender Islands

Known for their secluded coves, beautiful beaches, and islets, the Penders are a tranquil escape, and a boater's nirvana. With a population of barely 2,000, they remain small enough that, as one resident says, "The sight of another human being still conjures up a smile!"

The Penders are actually two islands, linked by a short wooden bridge that spans a canal between **Bedwell and Browning harbors.** Until 1903, when the canal was dug, island pioneers were forced to haul their boats laboriously over a wide neck of land known as "Indian Portant." Centuries before, the Coast Salish, a local First Nations group, used to set up seasonal camps in the area, and several shell middens (refuse heaps), some dating from 4500 B.C., have revealed thousands of artifacts, including carved spoons and lip ornaments. With several parks, picnic areas, and overnight camping facilities, the Penders are threaded with meandering, illogical roads that are a delight to tour by car or bicycle. Picturesque cottages, orchards, and a dozen or so artisans' home galleries add to the idyllic setting. The nine-hole golf course is a pleasant diversion, as is the golf Frisbee–throwing park, where the "tees" are metal poles tucked in between trees. The real trick is to keep your Frisbee from ricocheting off the trees on its flight to the target.

ESSENTIALS

GETTING THERE

BC Ferries sails to **Otter Bay,** on the northwest side of North Pender Island. Pleasure boats can dock at **Bedwell Harbour,** on the southern cove where North and South

Pender meet. See "Getting There," at the beginning of the chapter, for information on ferry fares and schedules.

VISITOR INFORMATION

There is no formal visitor information center on Pender Island, although you can pick up brochures at the "mall," **The Driftwood Centre** (4605 Bedwell Harbour Rd. *(C)* **250/629-6555**). Or contact the **Pender Island Chamber of Commerce** (*(C)* **866/ 468-7924**; www.penderislandchamber.com).

GETTING AROUND

Pender Island Taxi & Tours (*(C)* **250/629-3555**; www.pendercab.com) provides service to various points around the islands. For a water taxi to other islands, contact **Sound Passage Adventures** (*(C)* **877/629-3930**; www.soundpassageadventures.com); they also rent kayaks (C$20/US$18 per hour) and paddleboats (C$15/US$13) per hour. Bike rentals are available in season at **Otter Bay Marina** (*(C)* **250/629-3579**) at C$8 (US$7) per day.

EXPLORING THE PENDERS
NORTH PENDER

The larger of the two islands, **North Pender** is more populated and more developed than its southerly neighbor. Surprisingly, there's no real town center in the traditional sense on North Pender, so the modern **Driftwood Centre** (4605 Bedwell Harbour Rd. near Razor Point Road) in the center of the island, is the nucleus of island life. The **Saturday Market** (May through October, 9:30am–12:30pm) is a fine place for mixing with the locals, sampling island-grown produce, and browsing through artisan stalls. Continue on along Razor Point Road toward Browning Harbour and you'll find one of the island's newest additions: **Morning Bay Vineyard,** 6621 Harbour Hill Dr. (*(C)* **250/629-8352**; www.morningbay.ca). Overlooking Plumber Sound and with a main building designed to look like a barn, it features 20 terraces that climb up the south side of Mount Menzies. In 2007, the vineyard is promising to deliver its first estate wines: Pinot Noir, Pinot Gris, Gerwürztraminer, Riesling, Maréchal Foch, and Schonberger. Tastings are Wednesday through Saturday, 10am to 5pm.

Away from The Driftwood, most activity happens around **Otter Bay,** where the ferries arrive, and **Port Browning.** At **Port Washington,** northwest of Otter Bay, you'll find orchards and charming old cottages reminiscent of a turn-of-the-century coastal village. Nearby, **Otter Bay Marina** (*(C)* **250/629-3579**) is a good place to rent boats, kayaks, and bikes. Check out **Kayak Pender Island,** at the Otter Bay Marina

---

⌒ Fun Fact Nature Preserved

Established in 2003, the Gulf Islands National Park Reserve now safeguards park lands and waters spread out over more than 15 islands and numerous smaller islets and reefs. Some are unforested and highly valued as marine mammal haulouts (for seals and sea lions) and nesting sites for Black Oystercatcher, Glaucous-winged gulls, and Pigeon Guillemot. Other areas are peninsulas of old-growth, arbutus, and Garry oak forests.

(© **250/629-6939;** www.kayakpenderisland.com), for guided kayaking tours and lessons in and around island coves and to neighboring Mayne and Saturna islands. Beginners to advanced kayakers are welcome. Two-hour guided tours are C$39 (US$34) for adults, C$25 (US$22) for children 11 and under; 3-hour tours are C$49 (US$43) per person; and all-day paddles are C$95 (US$84). *Tip:* Mondays are geared for family outings: pay for your first child and the second paddles for free. **Port Browning Marina,** 4605 Oak Rd. (© **250/629-3493**), on the northern cove where North and South Pender meet, is an inviting "watering hole," with First Nations decor, including a totem pole. This marina is cheerfully downscale from Bedwell Harbour on the other side of the narrow neck of land that separates the two islands, where Poets Cove Resort has made its mark. (see "Where to Stay"). North Pender parks include **Medicine Beach,** one of the last wetlands in the Gulf Islands, and home to many native plants once used for food and medicine. The beach is within walking distance of **Prior Centennial Provincial Park,** a forest of cedar, maple, fir and alder trees. Located 6km (4 miles) from the ferry terminal, Prior Centennial can also be reached off Canal Road. **Roesland** is a 230-hectare (568-acre) park that includes a headland, Roe Lake, a freshwater lake, beaches, and lots of forest. The site was once a summer cottage resort, and has an original farmhouse dating back to 1908. Take the trail past the Davidson home to the headland, to see the rotting remains of a 220-year-old Indian canoe that lies 6km (4 miles) from the Otter Bay ferry terminal off Canal Road.

SOUTH PENDER

This remote part of the island has always attracted independent, sometimes eccentric, fun-loving spirits who don't mind the isolation. Although the only services to be found are at the **Poets Cove Marina,** 9801 Spalding Rd. (© **250/629-3212**), there are lots of beaches, parks, and trails to enjoy. Hikers should head for Mount Norman Regional Park (www.crd.bc.ca/parks/mount_norman). At 244m (800 ft.), Mount Norman is the highest point on the Penders.

The gravel access road up to Mount Norman is uninteresting, but the 1-km (.5-mile) hike to the summit is well worth the effort. It starts at the Ainslie Point Road trailhead, and as the trail begins to climb, the landscape changes from wetlands to forests of Douglas fir and western red cedar and ends with lichen-covered bedrock up top, where the panoramas are stunning. From Mount Norman Regional Park, you can access **Beaumont Marine Provincial Park** ✸✸✸, without a doubt the prettiest marine park in the Gulf Islands, its picturesque coastal wilderness seemingly tamed by gentle waters, moss-covered rocks, and grassy verges. It's now a part of the Gulf Islands National Park Reserve (© **250/654-4000;** www.pc.gc.ca/pn-np/bc/gulf), and is a moderate, 40-minute hike from Mount Norman.

Unlike the limited facilities of most of these parks, nearby Prior Centennial (also a part of the Reserve) includes 17 vehicle/tent sites, pit toilets, water, fire pits, and picnic tables. Call © **800/689-9025** for reservations. Sites are C$14 (US$12) per night. Another favorite recreation area, **Brookes Point,** is one of the last undeveloped headlands in the Gulf Islands. The coastal bluff is ecologically important as it hosts rare types of native grass, and more than 100 bird species, some of which are endangered. Large pods of **killer whales** sometimes swim right under the point in the nearby kelp beds, as do mink, seal, otter, and Dall's porpoises. Tidal pools contain abalone, sea anemones, and coral.

WHERE TO STAY

Inn on Pender Island ☆ *Value*   Situated next to Prior Centennial Provincial Park, this unpretentious inn offers a choice of nine motel-style lodge rooms or three studio log cabins, many with ocean-views and some with private Jacuzzis. Lodge rooms are clean and spacious; cabins have fireplaces and deck swings. Children and pets are welcome. **Memories at the Inn** is a fully licensed restaurant, and although the decor's a bit plain, it's a popular choice for affordable dining. The homemade pizza is exceptionally good.

4709 Canal Rd. (P.O. Box 72), Pender Island, BC V0N 2M0. ☎ **800/550-0172** or 250/629-3353. Fax 250/629-3167. www.innonpender.com. 12 units. May–Sept C$79–C$99 (US$70–US$87) lodge room; C$149 (US$131) cabin. Oct–Apr C$69–C$89 (US$61–US$78) lodge room; C$139 (US$122) cabin. MC, V. Small pets accepted. **Amenities:** Restaurant; Jacuzzi. *In room:* TV/VCR, fridge, coffeemaker.

Oceanside Inn ☆   You can't beat the location: minutes from the ferry terminal and nestled amid arbutus trees on a secluded oceanfront. The name of each room describes its best attribute: Ocean View, with its modern, chocolate-toned decor; Garden View, with country wicker furniture; and the largest and most romantic suite, The Channel View. These are the only two rooms with fireplaces, though all rooms have private decks and outdoor hot tubs. Rates include a breakfast such as eggs benedict, orange French toast, or seafood omelette alongside fresh fruit and home-baked scones.

4230 Armadale Rd. (P.O. Box 50), Pender Island, BC V0N 2M0. ☎ **250/629-6691.** www.penderisland.com. 3 units. C$159–C$239 (US$140–US$210) double. Closed mid-Oct to early Apr. V. Children not accepted. **Amenities:** Lounge; private hot tub; tour/activities information; in-room massage; beach access from property; Internet. *In room:* Fridge, hair dryer, iron, no phone.

Poets Cove Resort & Spa ☆☆ *Kids*   This seaside resort has undergone a metamorphosis in recent years to become one of the most upscale, year-round destinations in the Gulf Islands, offering so much to do that you never have to leave the resort. Accommodation ranges from 22 modern lodge rooms (they all face west to catch terrific sunsets) to deluxe two- and three-bedroom cottages (best for romantic getaways) and spacious and family oriented villas complete with kitchens, dining rooms, living rooms with fireplaces, balconies, and BBQs. Most have private hot tubs. Children's programs and a 110-slip marina make it a popular spot for families and boaters. The bright, airy Aurora Restaurant (see "Where to Dine") features French-influenced fine dining, and Syrens Lounge & Bistro offers casual dining inside or on the enormous deck. The menu includes kid-friendly burgers and pint portions of other selections for smaller appetites. If you're staying in a cottage or villa, you can order items from the "raw menu" to BBQ yourself. The Susurrus Spa is a destination unto itself, with six large treatment rooms, a steam cave, and oceanfront Jacuzzi.

Tip: The "Poets Cruise" is an excellent 3-hour island hop and eco-adventure (C$94/US$83) that includes stopovers at historic Hope Bay on Pender and the vineyard on Saturna Island.

9801 Spalding Rd., South Pender Island, BC V0N 2M3. ☎ **888/512-7638** or 250/629-2100. Fax 250/629-2105. www.poetscove.com. 22 rooms, 15 cottages, 9 villas. C$179–C$299 (US$158–US$263) lodge room; C$359–C$599 (US$316–US$527) cottage; C$339–C$589 (US$298–US$518) villa. Children 17 and under stay free in parent's room. AE, MC, V. **Amenities:** Restaurant; pub; large heated outdoor pool; 2 outdoor tennis courts; spa; extensive water-sports rentals; children's programs; activity center; marina; Wi-Fi. *In-room:* TV/DVD, dataport, fridge, coffeemaker, hair dryer.

Sahhali Serenity Oceanfront B&B Inn ☆☆ *Finds*   Sitting atop a high and majestic bluff with incomparable vistas, this Timberlok coastal manor puts you eye-to-eye with eagles, and not many places give you that. Be careful wending your way up the

.5-km (⅓-mile) gravel road to get there. Guest rooms are exceptionally large (one is 70sq. m/750 sq. ft) and so pampering, there's virtually no need (and even less desire) to leave the premises. Features include vaulted ceilings, wood-burning fireplaces, wet bars, private outdoor Jacuzzis, and double marble showers. Decor includes antiques and original watercolors and Bombay-style furnishings. The Bonsai and Overlook suites boast up to 13m (42 ft.) and 11m (35 ft.) of continuous windows respectively, overlooking 27 islands. With no blinds, however, the moonlight across the water may be bright enough to encourage you to don the eye-mask provided. The Turnpoint Suite is the inn's "allergy-free" room. Made-to-order breakfasts are delivered to your suite to be savored by the fireplace or on deck in the morning sun. *Note:* There is a C$50 (US$44) surcharge for one-night stays.

5915 Pirates Rd. (P.O. Box 83), Pender Island, BC V0N 2M0. © 877/625-2583 or 250/629-3664. www.sahhali serenity.com. 4 units. Mar–Sep C$285–C$295 (US$251–US$260). Oct–Feb C$125–C$235 (US$110–US$207). Rates include full breakfast. Extra person C$20 (US$18). MC, V. Pets accepted w/prior approval. **Amenities:** Canoe rental; Internet. *In room:* TV/VCR, fridge, coffeemaker.

Shangri-La Oceanfront B&B   Perched on Pender's Oaks Bluff with 4 hectares (10 acres) of wilderness at its feet, this sprawling house has views across Swanson Channel to Washington State's Mount Baker and the Olympic Range, plus 511sq. m (5,500 sq. ft.) of wraparound balconies from which to drink it all in. Staying here is like nesting in your own deluxe aerie, complete with private deck and Jacuzzi. Guest rooms have fireplaces, hot tubs, covered decks with furnishings of pale earth tones and muted floral fabrics. Beds include down duvets, and queen-size mattresses have foam toppers for extra comfort. The Lost in Space Suite even has glow-in-the-dark planetary wallpaper, and, because of its extra size and amenities such as a BBQ, microwave, and private hot tub, it's good for longer stays.

5909 Pirate's Rd., Pender Island, BC V0N 2M2. © 877/629-2800 or 250/629-3808. Fax 250/629-3018. www. penderislandsshangrila.com. 3 units. May–Oct C$170–C$195 (US$150–US$172). Nov–Apr C$130–C$175 (US$114–US$154). Extra person C$35 (US$31). Rates include full breakfast. MC, V. Pets accepted C$20 (US$18). **Amenities:** Jacuzzi; complimentary bikes; games room; massage. *In room:* TV, fridge, coffeemaker, no phone.

WHERE TO DINE

Aurora ⍟ PACIFIC NORTHWEST   By far the most sophisticated dining room you'll find anywhere on the Penders, Aurora serves food to match the great marine views. There's a French influence to the menu items, which lean to local produce. Standouts include the Salt Spring goat-cheese tart and herb salad, an herb-crusted halibut (the catch of the day is always a good choice), and Pender Island lamb. For dessert, try the excellent crème brûlée. The restaurant is a romantic spot, whether you sit by the huge stone fireplace that dominates one wall or beside the floor-to-ceiling windows. If you're an oenophile you'll probably prefer a table near the wall of wine bottles—the wine list is extensive.

In Poets Cove Resort & Spa, 9801 Spalding Rd. © 250/629-2100. Reservations recommended. Main courses C$26–C$32 (US$23–US$28). AE, MC, V. Daily 5:30–10pm.

Hope Bay Café ⍟ *Finds*   At first blush, you wouldn't expect this casual, light-filled bistro to have such a gourmet attitude to food. But you're in for a treat. It's the only on-the-water restaurant on the island and virtually every table has a view of the ocean only feet away. Everything is prepared in an open kitchen, which adds to the bustle. It starts in the morning as a coffee-and scone-place in the morning and at lunch serves dishes ranging from fish and chips, to burgers and quesadillas, to soups and salads.

Dinners feature unusual combinations such as grilled salmon with red Thai curry and lentils, or pork tenderloin crusted with hazelnuts and served with a wild mushroom sauce. The wine list has about 20 red and white selections, including some from the local Pender winery, Morning Bay. Hot breakfast–brunch is served only on Sundays. The deck is a favorite spot for alfresco dining.

4301 Bedwell Harbour Rd. ℭ 250/629-6668. Main courses C$15–C$22 (US$13–US$19). MC, V. Wed–Sun 9am–8pm.

The Islander   From The Islander, a cozy, 40-seat casual bistro overlooking Swanson Channel, a few minutes from the ferry docks, there's a good chance you'll see whales passing by. And even if whale-sighting isn't on the menu, the food will not disappoint. Although there's a nice twist to traditional Caesar salad, with seared romaine leaves, most starters are fish, such as a pound of mussels in a Sambuca cream sauce or an appetizer plank with variations of Indian candy (dried salmon) and fresh oysters, perhaps splashed with tequila and pesto. You'll also find fish specialties among the entrees, though you're as likely to find meat and vegetarian options. These include a tasty lemon-glazed duck breast with cranberry, a pound of pork spareribs with Hermann's dark lager and chipotle sauce, New York steak, as well as a selection of pastas and crepes. The wine list isn't extensive, but does feature several island labels such as Saturna Vineyard's Late Harvest Semillon. Off-season special events include a Guest Chef Night, cooking classes, and an annual pajamas-only dinner!

1325 MacKinnon Rd. ℭ 250/629-3929. Reservations recommended. Main courses C$17–C$25 (US$15–US$22). MC, V. Jul–Aug daily 5:30–8:30pm; Sept–June Thurs–Mon 5–9pm.

4 Galiano Island

Galiano Island is a magnet for outdoor enthusiasts. It's a long, skinny island that stretches more than 26km (16 miles) from top to bottom, and is no more than 2km (1½ miles) across. Two harbors and several parks provide abundant opportunity to hike, camp, fish, boat, and bird-watch—activities that have, in fact, been hard won. Until recently, logging was Galiano's biggest industry, and one that was changing the landscape dramatically. Determined that clear-cutting should cease, the community rallied, and has managed to purchase key tracts of land with the intention that it return to, and remain, as wilderness. Remnants of lumber operations are still evident in parts, including a shoreline strewn with salt-laden, sun-bleached logs. In spite of their activism, the folks on Galiano are actually very laid back. It's as if they've not quite outgrown their obsession with growing marijuana back in the seventies. For boomers, this may be strangely comforting.

Most of the 1,100 or so permanent residents live on the southern part of the island, close to **Sturdies Bay,** which, for all intents and purposes, is the island's downtown. So it's here that you'll find accommodations, restaurants, and stores, as well as in the surrounding areas of **Georgeson Bay, Montague Harbour,** and **Spotlight Cove.** North Galiano is much wilder, and although you'll find pockets of housing, the country is dense with cedar and fir trees, maple and alder stands.

ESSENTIALS
GETTING THERE
BC Ferries sails to **Sturdies Bay** on the southern tip of the island. Boaters and floatplanes dock at **Montague Harbour,** on the west coast, about a 20-minute drive from Sturdies Bay.

VISITOR INFORMATION

Contact the **Galiano Chamber of Commerce,** 2590 Sturdies Bay Rd. (P.O. Box 73), Galiano Island, BC V0N 1P0 (© **250/539-2233;** www.galianoisland.com). Open in July and August daily, 9am–5pm; September to June on occasional weekends, 9am–5pm.

GETTING AROUND

The **Go Galiano Island Shuttle** (© **250/539-0202**) provides year-round land-based taxi service, and the **Galiano Water Taxi** (© **250/537-2510**) runs a service between Galiano, Mayne, and Salt Spring islands. You can also rent mopeds from **Galiano Mopeds,** at Montague Harbour (© **250/539-3443**), and bicycles from **Galiano Bicycle,** 36 Burrill Rd., Sturdies Bay (© **250/539-9906**). Mopeds are available from May to September and cost C$18 (US$16) per hour. Bike rentals are C$28 (US$25) for a 24-hour period.

EXPLORING GALIANO ISLAND

In and around **Sturdies Bay,** you'll find picturesque B&Bs, a few galleries, and a handful of shops. Nearby, **Bellhouse Provincial Park** ⚐ is one of prettiest spots on the island, with a rocky, moss-covered peninsula, sculpted sandstone, and magnificent groves of copper-red arbutus trees. Situated at the entrance to **Active Pass,** it's an ideal place to picnic and to linger for an hour or two, watching the myriad kinds of wildlife. Tides run up to 5 knots here and the shoreline drops sharply into deep water, making it an excellent point to spin-cast for salmon.

    Galiano Bluffs Park ⚐, another favorite area, is also at the entrance to Active Pass but sits 120m (394 ft.) above it. The views from the bluffs deserve rave reviews. Watch BC Ferries' largest ships rumble past, and grab your binoculars to see eagles catching the updrafts, as well as seals, sea lions, and other marine life. Seasonal wildflowers are an equal delight. Go easy on the approach road; it has some serious potholes. **Montague Harbour Marina** (© **250/539-5733**) is a fun place to visit, if only to yacht watch or grab a light meal in the marina restaurant. While there, check out **Galiano Island Kayaking** (© **250/539-2442;** www.seakayak.bc.ca/tour). The 3-hour rentals are C$38 (US$25) a person; full-day paddles are from C$83 (US$73) a person. You can also rent canoes. If you would rather have someone else do the skippering, **Sporades Tours** (© **250/539-2278**) offers wildlife tours and fishing excursions in a 37-foot classic motorized fishing boat. The cost is C$120 (US$106) per hour (for a 3-hour minimum) for up to 10 people.

MONTAGUE HARBOUR PROVINCIAL MARINE PARK ⚐⚐

One of the Gulf Islands' most popular provincial parks, Montague Harbour is a great place from which to watch giant American yachts arriving, and chattering kingfishers diving for salmon. Swim and beachcomb to your heart's content along gorgeous shell and gravel beaches, enjoy a picnic on the bluff, and search through shell middens dating back 3,000 years. The protected waters are perfect for beginner rowers, and hiking trails include an easy 3-km (2-mile) forest and beach walk that loops around Gray Peninsula, originally inhabited by First Nations peoples. Along the northwest edge of the peninsula are spectacular rippled rock ledges as well as white shell beaches, and along the southern shore are two caves that can be reached by foot at low tide, or by boat.

    If you want to stay a while, the park has two year-round campgrounds: one with 15 walk-in sites for boaters and cyclists, another with 25 drive-in sites for motorists.

Note: There are no RV hookups. There's a boat ramp, 35 mooring buoys, and a store. Free interpretive talks are offered during July and August. Check the **Nature House** for schedules. Buoys are C$10 (US$9) per vessel; campsites are C$17 (US$15) each. Call **Discover Camping** at ☎ **800/689-9025** or 250/391-2300 for information and reservations, or go online to **www.discovercamping.ca**. For a more rustic camping experience, head up to the northern tip of Galiano, where you'll find Dionisio Point Provincial Park. Sitting at the entrance to Porlier Pass, it is accessed only by water. Be sure to approach it at slack tide, as the currents can be unruly. There are 30 first-come, first-served walk-in campsites. Even if you're not overnighting here, the park's beaches are strewn with shell middens to comb, making them a good pit stop for day-tripping kayakers.

WHERE TO STAY

Bellhouse Inn 🏠🏠   Built in the 1880s, this scenic waterfront farmhouse is surrounded by meadows, grazing sheep, and orchards. Views of Active Pass are up close and personal, whether you're playing croquet on the lawn, lazing on the sandy beach, or sprawling in a hammock. Guest rooms are small, and decorated with hardwood floors, wicker furniture, and quilted country-style bedspreads. Rooms have lovely bathrooms and private balconies. Thankfully, the main lounge is large and extremely comfortable (think sink-into sofas and deep chairs). The owners will arrange an in-room massage, just in case lazing around hasn't worked out all the muscle knots. This inn even provides guests with hot water bottles—not because the rooms are cold, but because the owners are English and therefore have a natural predisposition to these homey comforts. In summer you'll probably spend most of your time on the expansive decks, unless you're tempted to go sailing; the owners also charter a 43-foot yacht.

29 Farmhouse Rd. (P.O. Box 16), Site 4 Galiano Island, BC V0N 1P0. ☎ 800/970-7464 or 250/539-5667. Fax 250/539-5316. www.bellhouseinn.com. 3 units. June–Sep C$135–C$195 (US$119-US$172). Oct–May C$85–C$135 (US$75–US$119). 2-night minimum stay in cabin. Rates include full breakfast. MC, V. Children not accepted. **Amenities:** Lounge; in-room massage; library. *In room:* Hair dryer, no phone.

Bodega Ridge Resort 🏠 (Kids) (Value)   Located near Spanish Hills, at the island's northern end, this hilltop resort and sheep farm is a rambling collection of hand-hewn cottages, offering majestic views and basic comforts. The immaculate two-level log chalets are simply decorated and have full kitchens, making them ideal for families. They feature stained-glass doors and tasteful wood furnishings. Kiwi and grape vines clamber over the main farmhouse, and landscaped gardens are sprinkled with Celtic standing stones, ponds, and kilometers of hiking trails. The resort offers mountain bike rentals and exclusive guided tours through the network of private trails.

120 Manastee Rd. (P.O. Box 115), Galiano Island, BC V0N 1P0. ☎ 250/539-2677. Fax 250/539-2677. www.bodega ridge.com. 7 units. Apr to mid-Oct C$125–C$150 (US$110–US$132). Mid-Oct to Mar C$125 (US$110). Extra person C$25 (US$22). MC, V. Pets accepted C$15 (US$13). **Amenities:** Lounge; mountain bike rentals; Wi-Fi; TV/DVD upon request. *In room:* Kitchen, BBQ, no phone.

Cliff Pagoda   The purpose-built B&B looks like a pagoda, and sets the tone for the whimsical décor you'll find inside. The multicultural theme of this B&B is immediately apparent with its pagoda-style architecture. Every bedroom features colorful fabrics from India, local art, canopied beds, and spectacular views over Montague Harbour. The Maharaja Suite has a bathtub set into the rock and is the most opulent, although the Meditation Room is hard to beat—perched at the top of the Pagoda, it feels more like an exotic tree house with a private deck.

2851 Montague Rd., Galiano Island, BC V0N 1P0. ② **250/539-2260.** www.galiano.gulfislands.com/cliff_pagoda. 5 units. C$75–C$125 (US$66–US$110) year-round, double. Extra person C$45 (US$40). Rates include continental breakfast. MC, V. **Amenities:** Lounge; hot tub; sauna; meditation garden. *In room:* Private patio or deck, no phone.

Driftwood Village Resort ☆ *(Kids* ✓*Value* Set in a delightful garden filled with fruit trees, the Driftwood Village Resort's studio, one- and two-bedroom cottages are charming, cozy, and decorated with original artwork. While various bed-linen combinations give each cabin a different feel, all cottages have oceanfront views, private bathrooms, well-equipped kitchens, and private decks with barbecues. All but one of the cottages have wood-burning fireplaces. There's a Jacuzzi in the center of the garden—a great spot from which to stargaze. A footpath leads down to a sandy beach on Matthews Point, one of Galiano's many bird-watching spots.

205 Bluff Rd. E., Galiano Island, BC V0N 1P0. ② **888/240-1466** or 250/539-5457. www.driftwoodcottages.com. 10 units. Mid-June to mid-Sept C$110–C$165 (US$97–US$145). Mid-Sept to mid-June C$70–C$120 (US$62–US$106). Extra person C$10 (US$9). Children 12 and under stay free in parent's cottage. MC, V. Pets accepted. **Amenities:** Jacuzzi; massage; free ferry pickup/dropoff. *In room:* TV, kitchen, no phone.

Galiano Inn & Spa ☆☆☆ Recent renovations have transformed a great resort into a boutique spa where every room is its own tranquil, eco-conscious retreat. Rooms are invitingly uncluttered with open-beam ceilings, and decor that includes chocolate-brown cork floors and a ledge-rock wood-burning fireplace that conceals a TV/DVD player. At a push of a button, a hidden table emerges from the cherry-wood wall for intimate, in-suite dining. A push of another button reveals a massage table for in-room spa services. All beds have silk stuffed duvets (versus allergenic down duvets). All rooms overlook Active Pass and have private balconies or terraces. En suite bathrooms feature heated floors, air-jetted Jacuzzis or soaker tubs, separate showers—and 24-karat gold fixtures! The Atrevida! restaurant is an island favorite (see "Where to Dine") and the Madrona del Mar Spa has made this a popular destination getaway for urbanites from Victoria and Vancouver. Rates are consistent year-round. In winter, however, they include several value-items such as certificates to the spa. *Tip:* The inn is located only two blocks from the ferry terminal, so save yourself some dollars and travel to the island as a foot passenger.

134 Madrona Dr., Galiano Island, BC V0N 1P0. ② **877/530-3939** or 250/539-3388. Fax 250/539-3338. www.galianoinn.com. 10 units. Year-round C$249–C$299 (US$219–US$263). Rates include breakfast. Extra person C$25 (US$22). MC, V. **Amenities:** Restaurant; lounge; spa; hot tub; activities desk; laundry service; wine shop. *In room:* TV/DVD, hair dryer, iron, massage.

Island Time B&B The amazing view makes standing in the living room feel like being on the prow of a ship heading out to sea. If you look through the telescope, focused due north to Grouse Mountain above Vancouver, you can actually see skiers slaloming down the slopes. Add deep-seated sofas and crackling fireplaces to the picture. Guest rooms are exceptional. All have fireplaces; one has two marble bathrooms as well as a double Jacuzzi. Shared guest areas include a movie-viewing lounge and library. Recreational facilities such as tennis, table tennis, and a universal gym, make this bed-and-breakfast more like a mini resort.

952 Sticks Allison Rd., Galiano Island, BC V0N 1P0. ② **877/588-3506** or 250/ 539-3506. Fax 250/539-3507. www.islandtimebc.com. 3 units. Mid-May to mid-Oct C$185–C$215. Mid-Oct to mid-May C$125–C$215 (US$110–US$189). 2-night minimum July–September. Rates include full breakfast. AE, MC, V. Pets accepted w/prior approval. **Amenities:** 1 night-lit outdoor tennis court; Jacuzzi; TV/DVD lounge; Internet; free ferry pickup/dropoff. *In room:* TV/DVD, hair dryer.

Woodstone Country Inn ★★★   This inn is set amid towering fir trees overlooking an expanse of meadow and cultivated gardens. In summer, both meadow and garden overflow with flowers, and birds are everywhere. Inside, the inn is graciously decorated with quality antiques, folk art, and exotic sculptures, all garnered during the owner's travels around the world. Guest rooms are named for meadow flowers, and are exceptionally spacious and bright, with bathrooms that positively sparkle. Pampering touches include luxury Lord & Mayfair toiletries. All main-floor guest rooms have private patios. The inn's restaurant is one of the finest in the Gulf Islands (see "Where to Dine," below).

743 Georgeson Bay Rd., RR 1, Galiano Island, BC V0N 1P0. © 888/339-2022 or 250/539-2022. Fax 250/539-5198. www.woodstoneinn.com. 13 units. May–Sept C$129–C$209 (US$114–US$184) 2 nights. Oct–Apr C$129–C$199 (US$114–US$175) 2 nights. 2-night minimum. Rates include breakfast, afternoon tea. AE, MC, V. Closed Dec–Jan. Children not accepted. **Amenities:** Restaurant; lounge. *In room:* Hair dryer, no phone.

WHERE TO DINE

Atrevida! ★ PACIFIC NORTHWEST   Galiano Island's only oceanfront restaurant is a treat. Watch the ferries ply through Active Pass as you enjoy smoked duck ravioli with goat cheese and rosemary garlic white-wine sauce, or island rack of lamb with blackberry port reduction and lemon-mint risotto. The vegetarian Indian thali plate is exceptional: saag, mung dal, potato cauliflower curry, and coriander flatbread. The wine list focuses on special orders from British Columbia, some of which you can purchase from the wine store. If you've a ferry wait, park your car in the lineup and head over to the outdoor patio to chill out over a cold drink.

In the Galiano Inn, 134 Madrona Dr. © 250/539-3388. Reservations required. Main courses C$18–C$29 (US$16–US$26). MC, V. Daily 5:30–9:30pm.

Hummingbird Pub PUB FARE   Serving hearty pub grub (burgers, fish and chips, steaks, and pasta) at reasonable prices, the Hummingbird is *the* local watering hole, and tempts with ales on tap from the Gulf Islands brewery on Salt Spring Island. The classic west coast cedar-and-beam architecture creates a warm atmosphere for playing pool and darts, and although there's no water view, the decor and perennial garden more than makes up for it. From mid-May to October, this resourceful pub runs its own shuttle bus to the ferry at Sturdies Bay, and from the Montague Park Marina. The pub could be of particular interest to boaters seeking some liquid libations on dry land.

47 Sturdies Bay Rd. © 250/539-5472. Main courses C$7–C$17 (US$6.15–US$15). MC, V. Sun–Thurs 11am–midnight; Fri–Sat 11am–1am.

La Berengerie ★ FRENCH   Shrouded by evergreen clematis, this tiny log cabin is a jewel in the forest. Floral linen tablecloths, soft classical music, and watercolor paintings by local artists set a romantic tone. The food rarely disappoints. Described as French-Algerian, the cuisine uses herbs to brings Middle Eastern flavor to classics such as duck à l'orange, coq qu vin, and red snapper with gingered tomato sauce. La Berengerie also does an excellent bouillabaisse. A four-course menu features a choice of appetizers, entrees, and desserts. The homemade breads and comfort desserts are delicious. In July and August, the vegetarian sundeck opens up, as does a garden patio. The drawback is that it closes in winter.

Montague Harbour Rd. © 250/539-5392. Reservations recommended on weekends. 4-course prix fixe dinner C$30 (US$26). MC, V. July–Aug daily 5–9pm. Apr–June & Sept–Oct Fri–Sun only, call ahead for hours. Closed Nov–Mar.

Finds **Have Meals Will Travel**

The Max and Moritz truck at Sturdies Bay ferry terminal (📞 **250/539-5888**) serves up an excellent combination of Indonesian noodles, German bratwurst, North American burgers, and Italian gelati. Try it to believe it.

Wisteria Restaurant 🕊🕊 FRENCH/INTERNATIONAL   This enchanting restaurant is one of the best on the Gulf Islands and certainly the place of choice to celebrate something special. Service is impeccable and the cuisine is a blend of classic French and vivid international flavors such as in the yellow fin tuna with sweet peppers, artichokes, olives, and roasted garlic aioli, and the seared duck breast prepared with sweet-and-sour braised pearl onions and an orange demi-glace sauce. Each day's menu offers a choice of three entrees (which determines what you'll pay) and also includes homemade bread, soup, and salad. Desserts are decadent, and the wine list is an interesting mix of Okanagan, Californian, and French vintages. There are no additional a la carte items.

At the Woodstone Country Inn, 743 Georgeson Bay Rd. 📞 **250/539-2022.** Reservations required. 4-course dinner C$24–C$33 (US$21–US$29). AE, DC, MC, V. Feb–Nov nightly from 5pm. Closed Dec–Jan.

5 Mayne Island

Mayne has always been a transfer point between islands. This began in the 1860s, when prospectors rested up in Miners Bay before crossing the Georgia Strait on their way to the gold mines in the Fraser Valley and the Cariboo. But as gold fever faded, so did Mayne's importance, and today, stopovers are somewhat tamer. The 900 or so permanent residents like it this way, as it's enabled the island to retain much of its charm and heritage.

Because most of Mayne Island is privately owned, there are few public trails, so walkers and cyclists take to the network of hilly roads, traveling past 19th-century buildings, farms, beaches, and home studios. Avid cyclists could complete Mayne's 25-km (15½-mile) circuit in a day. There are numerous sheltered bays, including **Village Bay, Miners Bay,** and **Horton Bay,** all with docking facilities and accommodations that run the gamut from bare bones to luxurious.

ESSENTIALS
GETTING THERE
BC Ferries sails to **Village Bay,** on the northwest side of the island. Pleasure boaters dock at **Horton Bay,** at the southwest corner of the island. Floatplanes arrive at the docks at Miners Bay.

VISITOR INFORMATION
Mayne Island Community Chamber of Commerce (📞 **877/535-2424**) doesn't have a bricks-and-mortar headquarters but does maintain a resource site at www.mayneislandchamber.ca. Useful maps and event information are usually posted on bulletin boards in the windows of the gas station (which doubles as a video-movie rental place), and the grocery store. This is where you can also purchase a copy of *The Mayneliner* (C$1/US88¢), a monthly publication of gossip, happenings, and island issues.

GETTING AROUND

M.I.D.A.S. taxi company (℃ **250/539-3132** or 250/539-5756) offers pickup and dropoff service to the ferry, as well as island tours. The Dodge Caravan seats 6 and can carry bikes, pets, oversize luggage, and camping or fishing gear.

EXPLORING MAYNE ISLAND

Miners Bay is the hub of Mayne, housing a surprisingly well-stocked supermarket, a small library, and a bakery-cafe. The liquor store, which is actually only a counter with a separate till, is part of a store that has sold goods and groceries since World War I. On summer Saturdays, a small farmer's market is held outside the **Agricultural Hall,** which on other days doubles as a theater, bingo hall, and exhibition center. On the lawns opposite the Spring Water Lodge (see "Where to Dine"), you'll find kayaks for rent from **Mayne Kayaks & Canoes,** 411 Fernhill Rd. (℃ **250/539-5599;** www.maynekayak.com). Rates range from C$32 (US$28) per person for a 2-hour rental, to C$58 (US$51) per person for a 24-hour rental of a fiberglass kayak, with an option to extend the rental. Guided tours include a 5-hour paddle to Saturna's winery for a tasting (C$90/US$79), and the company also offers bike rentals at C$18 (US$16) for 4 hours or C$25 (US$22) per day. The **Mayne Island Museum** is in a former one-room jail dating from 1896, and displays all manner of local artifacts from the early 1900s. Located on Fernhill Road, just up from the Springwater, it usually opens on July and August weekends, as well as holiday weekends, from 10am to 3pm. Admission is by donation; C$2 (US$1.75) is suggested.

The road from Miners Bay to **Georgina Point** and the **Active Pass Lighthouse** is the most picturesque on Mayne Island. En route, you'll pass **St. Mary Magdalene Anglican Church,** built in 1898, on a hill amid a grove of red arbutus trees. The steeple of the church overlooking Active Pass has been a landmark for sailors for more than a century. Many of the headstones in the mossy graveyard are silent testament to Mayne Island's pioneers, whose names are also reflected in the names of the coves and streets of the island. Established in 1885, the lighthouse marks the entrance to Active Pass and, now automated, is open daily, from 9am to 3pm, with free admission. This is a great spot from which to see seals, seabirds, and the occasional whale.

Because most of Mayne Island is privately owned, there are few public parks in which to hike. **Mount Parke Park** ⟨⟩, however, is an exception. Although many islanders have "back routes" to the top of Mount Parke itself, officially there's only one

---

Tips The Cob Wave

Mayne Island is cob-house central in the Gulf Islands, in large part because an enterprising islander helped put earth houses back on the map. Using only unprocessed, natural products such as sand, clay, straw, and recycled materials, these are the ultimate in eco-friendly, earthquake-resilient dwellings that are surprisingly modern in design and functionality. Cob is a mixture of sand, clay, and straw that is applied wet and molded into curved walls, arches, and creative niches. Workshops in building earth houses, as well as tours of existing homes, are available year-round. Contact ℃ **250/386-7790** or www.cobworks.com for details.

Fun Fact   Respites from Bully Birds

The nest boxes you'll see mounted on pilings in the water in Bennett Bay, beside the Mayne Inn's dock and in front of the Springwater Lodge are all part of a stewardship and recovery program for the Purple Martin. Muscled out of their traditional nesting areas by House Sparrows and Starlings, the Western Purple Martin is at risk in British Columbia. Placing these boxes over water minimizes competition from the "bully birds" and is working. In 2006, Mayne Island welcomed their first nesting Purple Martin pairs.

---

public hiking trail up, and it's a fairly strenuous 30- to 40-minute uphill hike. (Cyclists must leave their bikes at the trailhead rack.) At 255m (836 ft.), the end of the trail is the highest point on Mayne, and if you can forgive the obligatory antennae towers, you'll be rewarded with wonderful views and maybe an air show of soaring eagles and turkey vultures. Six beaches on the island are open to the public, but since a distinct lack of signs to access points makes them easy to miss, keep your eyes peeled for road markers that lead down to the shoreline—and avoid tromping on private land. Two of the best beaches for picnics are at **Georgina Point,** and at **Dinner Bay,** so-called because it once teemed with fish and shellfish. "When the tide goes out," the old prospector's slogan goes, "the table is laid for breakfast." A **Japanese Garden** is a part of Dinner Bay, and commemorates the Japanese who settled and worked on the island between 1900 and 1942. Admission is free. **Bennett Bay,** now a part of the Gulf Islands National Park Reserve, has an undisturbed waterfront that is home to herons, kingfishers, and unusual pink seashells. When the tide goes out far enough (which doesn't seem to happen often), the pebbly beach eventually gives way to fine sand. **Oyster Bay, Piggott Bay,** and **Campbell Bay** are good for swimming. The latter has eye-catching rock formations that served as models for the artificial rocks around the killer whale pool in the Vancouver Aquarium.

WHERE TO STAY

Blue Vista Resort *(Value* Blue Vista's value-for-money one- and two-bedroom cabins are ideal for family vacations. Comfortable, but not fancy, each of the blue-painted wood-framed units comes with a fully equipped kitchen, private bathroom, fireplace, deck, and barbecue. The resort's open, park-like setting encourages children to play with newfound friends. Bikes are available for rental by guests. If you're staying over a weekend, be sure to catch the resort's Saturday Sundaes, for which they provide all the fixings for personalized and delicious ice-cream treats. Each session becomes a sundae-creating contest among guests.

563 Arbutus Dr., Mayne Island, BC V0N 2J0. (C) **877/535-2424** or 250/539-2463. Fax 250/539-2463. www.blue vistaresort.com. 8 units. May–Sept C$85–C$120 (US$75–US$106). Oct–Apr C$65–$90 (US$57–US$79). Kayaking packages and weekly rates available. MC, V. Closed mid-Jan to mid-Feb. Pets accepted w/prior approval. **Amenities:** Bike and kayak rentals; coin-op washers and dryers; free ferry pickup/dropoff. *In room:* Kitchen, no phone.

Mayne Island Eco Camping Of the two campgrounds on Mayne, this is by far the superior, with waterfront sites, outdoor hot and cold showers amid the trees, outhouses, a communal fire pit, and even a hot tub. Many kayakers choose to paddle right up to the beach—a pretty but pebbly cove near Miners Bay—or take advantage of the free pickup and delivery service to and from other islands.

359 Maple Dr., Mayne Island, BC V0N 2J0. ℂ 250/539-2667. Fax: 250/539-3187. www.mayneisle.com. May–Sept C$12 (US$11). Oct–Apr C$10 (US$9). Children 13 years and under half price. **Amenities:** Hot tub; kayak rentals.

Oceanwood Country Inn 🐾 This waterfront English country inn is as upscale as you can get on Mayne. It's a gated property, so the deer haven't ravaged the gardens of tulips, irises, and other tasty morsels, as they have most Mayne gardens. Every guest suite is decorated in a floral or bird theme, with names like Kingfisher, Daffodil, and Rose. Most are romantic, with deep-soaker bathtubs and private balconies. Many have fireplaces. The Wisteria Suite even has a sunken living room and private outdoor soaking tub—perfect for a moonlit soak *àdeux*. The Geranium is particularly large, and also has a private outdoor soaking tub—on a rooftop deck, no less. The living room in the main lodge features a crackling fireplace, full bookshelves, board games, and good listening music. Enjoying dinner at Oceanwood's gourmet restaurant is a highlight of most people's stays (see "Where to Dine," below).

630 Dinner Bay Rd., Mayne Island, BC V0N 2J0. ℂ 250/539-5074. Fax 250/539-3002. www.oceanwood.com. 12 units. Mid-June to mid-Sept C$179–C$349 (US$158–US$307). Mid-Mar to mid-June & mid-Sept to Oct C$139–C$259 (US$122–US$228). 2-night stay required if staying over Sat. Rates include breakfast and afternoon tea. MC, V. Closed Nov–mid-Mar. Children not accepted. **Amenities:** Restaurant; lounge; Jacuzzi; sauna; complimentary bikes; library. *In room:* Hair dryer, no phone.

Sage Cottage The two oceanfront bedrooms are sumptuous, decorated in neutral earth tones of sand and sage, and with all the trimmings of luxurious bathrobes, toiletries, duvets, a satellite TV and DVD player with a growing title list to choose from. A shared deck overlooks a picturesque beach and boat launch. Rates include a gourmet breakfast that includes Brie-stuffed French toast or an herb-flavored egg soufflé. Scones and jams are homemade. Custom-made picnic lunches can be ordered, too, for a nominal additional charge. If you would like to eat dinner in, you're welcome to join the family. The cost is a reasonable C$25 (US$22) and includes a full three-course meal such as a mixed green salad, BBQ pork tenderloin, and a lemon cheesecake pie.

782 Steward Dr., Mayne Island, BC V0N 2J0. ℂ 250/539-2859. www.sageonmayne.com. Dec–Apr C$90–$110 (US$79–US$97). May to mid-Jun & Oct to mid-Nov C$100–C$120 (US$88–US$106). Mid-Jun to Sept C$120–C$135 (US$106–US$119). V. **Amenities:** Deck; Internet and phone access. *In room:* TV/DVD, no phone.

WHERE TO DINE

Mayne Inn PACIFIC NORTHWEST Within the next year or so, this historic inn will be at the epicenter of an impressive development project (www.mayneislandresort.com) involving vacation cottages, a spa, a marina, and an upgraded inn. Until then, it makes do with a fairly decent restaurant, eight simply furnished guest rooms, and a small, licensed TV lounge that gets particularly crowded when a hockey game is on. By day, the menu offers burgers, clubhouse sandwiches, and wraps, and toward evening, expands to include good, albeit predictable, pastas such as fettuccine alfredo, steak, chicken, and a catch of the day, usually grilled salmon or halibut. The restaurant is far more family friendly that the Spring Water (see below).

494 Arbutus Dr. ℂ 250/539-3122. Breakfast C$7 (US$6.15); lunch C$9 (US$7.90); dinner C$15 (US$13). MC, V. Apr–Sept daily 7am–8:30pm.

Oceanwood Country Inn 🐾🐾 PACIFIC NORTHWEST Opening onto a terrace overlooking the water, Oceanwood's restaurant has a romantic, Mediterranean ambience in which it dishes up extravagant daily creations. Set, four-course menus change nightly, but are posted a week in advance on notice boards throughout the island so that diners can plan a visit according to their taste buds. Cuisine highlights fresh local ingredients, as imaginative to read as they are to experience. Try the Oceanwood day lilies stuffed with smoked salmon mousse, fennel snap bread, and nasturtium flower oil; or the white wine and rosemary-marinated black cod with cauliflower puree, served with a zucchini-thyme sauce; or the roast venison strip loin with blueberry-fennel sauce. It's these sorts of culinary creations that have earned Oceanwood multiple Gold Medals at the Vancouver Food & Restaurant Show. The wine list, too, is an award-winner for its focus on West Coast labels, especially those from British Columbia. This is the only place on the island where you'll want to doff your Reeboks for something a little smarter (though clean jeans are fine).

In the Oceanwood Country Inn, 630 Dinner Bay Rd. (℃) 250/539-5074. Reservations required. 4-course prix fixe dinner C$55–C$65 (US$48–US$57). MC, V. Daily 6-9:30pm.

Spring Water Lodge PUB FARE/PACIFIC NORTHWEST   Built in the 1890s, this pub and restaurant is the heart of the Mayne Island community. In summer, people crowd the flower-brightened outdoor decks to watch the boats thread through Active Pass. In winter, the pub overflows with boisterous gossip. Live bands are often featured on Saturday nights. On the whole, food is good, though sometimes the restaurant specials are overly ambitious and don't live up to their promise. The fish and chips are great, and the onion rings are the best. Despite service that's rather offhand, it's a great place to kick back and grab a meal. Unfortunately, this good review doesn't extend to the guest rooms. Despite what you might hear, they are nothing to write home about, and the beach cabins are even less appealing.

400 Fernhill Rd. (℃) 250/539-5521. Pub main courses C$8.50 (US$7.50); restaurant main courses C$19 (US$17). MC, V. Mid-May to mid-Sept daily 9am–9pm. Mid-Sept to mid-May Mon–Thurs 11am–8:30pm; Fri–Sun 9am–8:30pm. Pub open until 1am.

6 Saturna Island

Time seems to have bypassed Saturna Island, making remote tranquility the island's star attraction. Home to approximately 325 permanent residents, Saturna is still fairly primitive. There are no banks or cash machines, no pharmacies or drug stores; the library's located in the church basement and the general store doubles as a tiny coffee shop. In fact, Jose Maria Narvaez would probably still recognize the forests and shorelines of the island named after his ship, *Santa Saturnina,* even though his last visit was in 1791. The Gulf Islands National Park Reserve protects some 44% of Saturna's 49sq. km (19 sq. miles), making the island great for hiking, boating, and communing with nature. Of all the Gulf Islands, Saturna is the most ecologically vigilant. It also boasts British Columbia's largest estate winery, **Saturna Island Vineyards,** which alone is worth the ferry trip.

Visitors may quickly note the island's drawbridge mentality, but Saturna people aren't unfriendly—they just prefer to keep their own company.

Laced with trails through mixed forest and marshland, the island is ideal for hikers, who usually head for **Winter Cove Marine Park,** a sanctuary to eagles, shorebirds, kingfishers, seals, and otters; or up to the summit of Mount Warburton. Kayakers will prefer **Thomson Park,** or **Cabbage Island Marine Park,** near **Tumbo Island,** and **Veruna Bay** and **Russell Reef** are the hot spots for family swimming. What commerce

---

Finds **Saturna Island Vineyards**

The location is idyllic, and offers visitors more than just a taste of wine. Nestled among the Pacific Ocean, a soaring granite cliff face, and picturesque Campbell farm, these south-facing vineyards—making up the largest estate winery in British Columbia—are a pleasure to explore. The first wines from the 1998 harvest were released to critical acclaim, and no wonder: Saturna has managed to lasso one of BC's finest winemakers, Eric Von Krosigk. Look for good Chardonnays, Pinot Noirs, Pinot Gris, and Gewürztraminers for less than C$20 (US$18) per bottle in the wine shop, as well as other merchandise, and a small bistro. The vineyards are at 8 Quarry Rd. (P.O. Box 54), Saturna Island, BC V0N 2Y0 (© **877/918-3388** or 250/539-5139; www.saturnavineyards.com). They are open May through October from 11:00am to 4:30pm, and through the winter by appointment. Tours and tastings are free. Take East Point Road from Lyall Harbour, and then Harris Road for 2.5km (1½ miles).

---

there is happens around the community center at **Lyall Harbour,** where the ferry docks. Here you'll find a grocery store, pub, gas station, kayak rentals, and a gallery, as well as a couple of B&Bs. *Note:* There are no public campgrounds.

ESSENTIALS
GETTING THERE
BC Ferries sails to **Lyall Harbour.** Most trips involve a transfer at Mayne Island. Boaters dock at **Winter Cove Marine Park,** north of Lyall Harbour. Seaplanes can dock at Lyall Harbour.

VISITOR INFORMATION
Head to the **Saturna Island General Store,** 101 Narvaez Bay Rd., Saturna Island, BC V0N 2Y0 (© **250/539-2936;** www.saturnatourism.com).

GETTING AROUND
At time of printing, the island has no pickup or touring service, although your B&B may step in to fill this need on an as-required basis. Bring your own bike (there are no rentals) or come to kayak. Saturna Sea Kayaking (© **250/539-5553**) is located in the village and can fit you out with single and double fiberglass kayaks from C$30–C$65 (US$26–US$57) for 3 hours. Multiple-day rates are available.

EXPLORING SATURNA ISLAND
East Point Regional Park 🛇🛇, on the island's southeastern tip, is a naturalist's delight. It starts with the ocean views from the sculptured sandstone headlands and just gets better. Strong tides curl around the point to create back eddies where salmon and small fish congregate; rocks, honeycombed by wind and waves, form tidal pools filled with starfish, limpets, spider crabs, and more; and waving kelp beds attract cormorants, oystercatchers, eagles, seals, and even whales. Take the very short trail down to the **East Point Lighthouse,** built in 1888, and you'll be standing at the easternmost edge of the Gulf Islands, looking over to **Patos Island Lighthouse,** on the U.S. side of the border. Together, the lighthouses guide large vessels through the channel's surging waters. Some of the area is on private land; be careful not to trespass off the

trails. A longer trail (300m/328 yards) leaves the parking lot and heads north to a viewpoint of Tumbo Channel and the Strait of Georgia.

If you've time, make the 4.5-km (3-mile) drive or hike up to the 497-m (1,630-ft.) summit of **Warburton Pike** ✚. If you can disregard the unbecoming sprawl of TV towers, the sweeping vistas from the top are nothing short of fantastic. The way up is via a winding gravel road that's narrow and sometimes slippery in wet weather, but the beautiful Douglas fir forest more than makes up for the occasional rough patch of road. Look out for feral goats, wild descendants of domestic goats imported here in the early 1900s, along the paths at the edge of the bluff.

WHERE TO STAY & DINE

Breezy Bay B&B ✚ *Kids*   This charming 1890s heritage house lies at the heart of a 20-hectare (50-acre) farm approximately 2km (1 mile) from the ferry dock. You enter beneath a canopy of century-old Lombardy poplars that gives way to gardens filled with trees: walnut, maple, scented linden, and hawthorne. Inside, you'll find architectural details such as Victorian wainscoting and period wood paneling. The guest library is full of assorted titles, from nature books to historical novels, while the spacious piano lounge is comfortable without being pretentious. The four guest rooms are small, simply furnished, but inviting; they share two bathrooms. On the first floor, an outside veranda runs the length of the house and overlooks the orchard, waterfowl pond, and pastures of sheep and llama. The beach at the end of the garden is ideal for swimming and launching kayaks. The kids will love it.

131 Payne Rd., Saturna Island, BC V0N 2Y0. © **250/539-5957** or 250/539-3339. www.saturnacan.net/breezy. 4 units. Apr–Sept C$85–C$95 (US$75–US$84). Rates include full breakfast. No credit cards. Closed Oct–Mar. **Amenities:** Lounge; library. *In room:* No phone.

Saturna Lodge & Restaurant *Kids*   Set amid the rustic, rural charms of the island, a stone's throw from the **Saturna Island Vineyards,** this casual country inn comes as an unexpected delight. Guest rooms are named after wine grapes, and are comfortably appointed with duvet-covered queen-size beds and private en suites (twin beds in the

---

Fun Fact **Island Legend: Warburton Pike**

Mount Warburton Pike is named for the legendary English "gentleman adventurer," the biggest property owner on Saturna at the turn of the century. A member of the British gentry and an Oxford graduate, Pike was temperamentally better suited to life in the great outdoors and much preferred to sleep under a large maple tree in the yard than in his pretty, well-furnished bungalow. During his life, Pike was a big-game hunter, a Wyoming cowboy, an Arctic and Icelandic explorer, a businessman and community benefactor, a mining and railroad promoter, a Yukon gold prospector, a sheep rancher, and author of two books on the North. Among many stories about this elusive adventurer is the one tale about how Pike used the ocean as his washtub. He just tied his clothes to a long rope and trailed them behind his sailboat *Fleetwing* while he stretched out and relaxed on the gunwale.

Ambrosia Suite). This and the Napa Suite share a bathroom and can be joined for family accommodation. All have views of Plumber Sound (though some are pretty peekaboo); some have private decks, and while most guests might choose the larger Sauterne Suite for its deluxe soaker tub, the private patio and bay windows in the Reisling Suite are more inviting. TV-hungry urbanites can cozy up in front of the fireplace in the downstairs lounge, or pick a VCR title from the lodge's small library. To encourage longer stays, the lodge discounts its nightly rate by a progressive C$20 (US$18) per night. The other surprise is the quality of its small restaurant, where an ever-changing prix fixe menu features superb Pacific Northwest cuisine (Saturna Island lamb, organic produce, and local seafood). The extensive wine list features many award-winning labels; on midsummer evenings, there's nothing better than enjoying a chilled chardonnay on the outdoor deck overlooking the cove. At time of publication, this lodge, although still in operation, was up for sale; call ahead to avoid disappointment.

130 Payne Rd. (P.O. Box 54), Saturna Island, BC V0N 2Y0. (©) **888/539-8800** or 250/539-2254. Fax 250/539-3091. www.saturna.ca. 7 units. Mid-May to mid-Oct C$130 (US$114). Discounts for longer stays. Rates include full breakfast. Children 12 and under stay free in parent's room. MC, V. Closed mid-Oct to mid-May. Pets accepted w/prior approval. **Amenities:** Restaurant; lounge; Jacuzzi; complimentary bikes; library; free shuttle to and from vineyard and ferries. *In room:* DVD, no phone.

The San Juan Islands

Beckoning just off the coast of Vancouver Island, south of the Gulf Islands, the San Juan Islands are a mostly blue-sky oasis in a region better known for its clouds. Like their island neighbors, they provide mariners with spectacular waters, hundreds of small, protected coves, and a landscape where stands of coastal trees give way to grassy meadows and gardens. The ferry trip between the San Juan Islands and Sidney, on Vancouver Island, is a delightful 1½-hour mini-cruise, and provides the opportunity to create a really diverse islands adventure. From Sidney, you can choose to explore Vancouver Island, or take a ferry to the Gulf Islands, creating an itinerary that can stretch from a few days to a few weeks.

Although many of the 700 or so islands in the archipelago disappear at high tide, there are still about 400 or so to explore. Some are no more than a raised tuft of land; others are wildlife sanctuaries or privately owned paradises. For years the San Juans' pastoral tranquility was a favorite getaway for Washingtonians, but this is now taking its toll. Today, land deals for would-be homeowners are long gone. There are nearly 30 different real estate dealers on the San Juans—that's one for every 40 residents; and assessed property values are almost three times the state average. Although development is controlled somewhat by the San Juan Preservation Trust, monumental homes are appearing in what was once humble rock and farmland.

In the 1800s, because of their proximity to British Columbia (San Juan Island lies only 26km [16 miles] from Sidney), many British settlers moved to the islands alongside their American counterparts. Remnants of those pioneering years are seen throughout the islands, and many landmarks are listed in the National Register of Historic Places. On San Juan Island, in particular, you'll find the Anglo–American rivalry especially well documented in the American and English camps.

The three largest islands, San Juan, Orcas, and Lopez, are home to about 12,000 people. For much of the year, the residents' easygoing lifestyle is quite solitary, but when summer arrives, the population triples, with the arrival of eco-adventurers and vacationers. *Note:* If you're traveling with children, be aware that family fun is derived mainly from beachcombing, kayaking, and hiking, with the larger resorts providing children's programs and supervised swimming. (Consult the individual hotel reviews to see whether an establishment offers these programs.) Also note that despite the annual influx of visitors, accommodations on the San Juans are limited, and prearranged accommodation is highly recommended. Touring all three islands can be done in 3 or 4 days, but chances are that you'll acclimatize to "island time," slow down, and wish you had set aside a day or two longer. But leave your jet skis at home. When locals complained that the incessant buzzing of city folk zipping around their waterfront was disrupting the serenity and marine habitat of the islands, San Juan County promptly outlawed the noisy watercraft. The only wild time you'll find on the San Juan Islands is pretty much what nature provides.

1 Essentials

GETTING THERE

BY PLANE

Kenmore Air Seaplanes (© **800/543-9595** or 425/486-1257; www.kenmoreair.com) provides daily flights from **Seattle** to the three major San Juan Islands. One-way fares are C$147 (US$129) for adults, C$124 (US$109) for children 3 to 11, free for children 2 and under. Kenmore Air also offers daily departures from Seattle to Victoria. Fares are C$179 (US$149) one-way and C$178 (US$156) return for adults, C$147 (US$129) one-way and C$155 (US$136) return for children 3 to 11, free for children 2 and under. The return fares include a C$8 (US$7) immigration fee. **San Juan Airlines** (© **800/874-4434** or 360/293-4691; www.sanjuanairlines.com) has daily land plane flights from **Anacortes** at C$50 (US$44) per person, and **Bellingham** at C$50 (US$44) per person, to Orcas, San Juan, and Lopez islands. Private plane arrivals can be accommodated at small public airstrips on San Juan, Orcas, and Lopez islands.

BY FERRY

Washington State Ferries, Column Dock/Pier 52, Seattle, WA 98104 (© **888/808-7977** or 206/464-6400; www.wsdot.wa.gov/ferries), offers multiple daily sailings between **Anacortes** and the San Juan Islands, and limited service from **Sidney,** on Vancouver Island. From Anacortes, loading is on a first-come, first-served basis. It's a good idea to get in line about 30 minutes in advance of the scheduled sailing. If you bring a vehicle, allow for at least an hour's wait—up to 3 hours at peak travel times on summer and holiday weekends. Also, be sure to fill your tank in Anacortes. Gas stations on the islands charge at least 30% more for gas than on the mainland. Some food service and a picnic area are available near the terminal. Check out **www.ferrycam.net** to see live images of the ferry lanes.

One-way passenger fares during the high season, from May 3 to October 1, are C$15 (US$13) for adults, C$12 (US$10) for children 6 to 18 years, C$7.30 (US$6.40) for seniors, C$56 (US$49) for a driver and standard-size vehicle. Inter-island travel is C$22 (US$19) for a driver and standard-size vehicle; passengers and bicycles are free.

⌒Tips Makes Cents

Ferry foot-passengers are charged only in the westbound direction; eastbound travel within the San Juan Islands or from the San Juan Islands to Anacortes is free (the only exception to this is for travelers leaving from Sidney, BC). If you're planning to visit all the San Juan Islands, save money by heading straight to Friday Harbor on San Juan Island, the most westerly of the islands, and work your way back through the others at no additional charge.

San Juan Islands

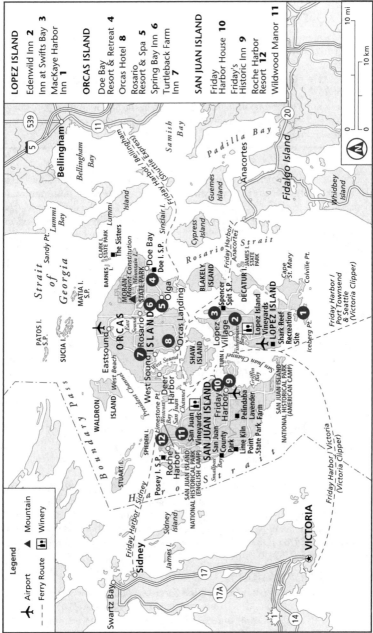

Fun Fact   San Juan Trivia

- There are no traffic lights anywhere in the islands. People don't even honk.
- San Juan county has more miles of marine shoreline (408) than any other county.
- There are no rivers in the islands, but there are several waterfalls on Orcas Island.
- There are 83 National Wildlife Refuge sites in the San Juan Islands. A number are clustered along the southern coast of Lopez Island, and near Spieden and Waldron islands.

Twice a day in summer (once a day in winter), the ferry continues to Sidney, 26km (16 miles) north of Victoria, and returns. Summer vehicle reservations are recommended to and from Canada, and must be made by 5:30pm the day prior to travel, at least 24 hours in advance. One-way passenger fares from May 1 to mid-October are C$18 (US$16) for adults, C$9 (US$7.80) for seniors, C$14 (US$13) for children 6 to 18 years, C$60 (US$52) for a driver and standard-size vehicle. From mid-October to April 30, fares remain the same for adults, seniors, and children, but reduce to C$48 (US$42) for driver and standard-size vehicle. Crossing time is 3 hours. From the San Juan Islands to Sidney, one-way fares are C$6.70 (US$5.85) for adults, C$3.30 (US$2.90) for seniors, C$5.35 (US$4.70) for children, C$31 (US$27) for a standard-size vehicle and driver. Fares are lower October 2 through May 2.

Victoria Clipper (© **800/888-2535** or 206/448-5000; www. victoriaclipper.com) is a popular way to reach the San Juan Islands from either **Seattle or Victoria.** This passenger-only boat departs from Seattle's **Pier 69** daily from May 1 to September 8. Fares from Seattle to Friday Harbor, on San Juan Island, are C$86 (US$75) return and C$48 (US$43) single for adults, C$43 (US$38) return and C$34 (US$30) single for children 1 to 11. Advance purchase discounts and an add-on whale-watching feature are also offered. Reservations originating in Victoria should call © 250/382-8100. **Puget Sound Express** (© **360/385-5288**) offers passenger-only service between **Port Townsend,** northwest of Seattle, and Friday Harbor, May through September. The captain takes the 3-hour scenic route. Round-trip fare is about C$82 (US$72) per person. The **San Juan Island Island Express** (© **877/473-9777** or 360/299-2875) runs a year-round passenger taxi from downtown Anacortes to the three major San Juan Islands, and many of the smaller ones, too, that are so popular for kayakers. Fares are based on the number of passengers sharing a common destination and generally range from C$47 to C$138 (US$41–US$112) per person. Bicycles are C$6.85 (US$6) and kayaks are C$15 (US$13) extra.

VISITOR INFORMATION

The **San Juan Islands Visitor Information Services,** 640 Mullis St., Building A, Suite 210, Friday Harbor, San Juan Island, WA 98250 (© **888/468-3701** or 360/378-6822; www.visitsanjuans.com), offers a range of maps and information throughout the islands. For live images of the San Juan Islands, check out **www.islandcam.com**. San Juan, Lopez, and Orcas islands also operate visitor services through their local Chambers of Commerce (see "Essentials," in separate sections devoted to each island).

2 San Juan Island

Compared to sleepier Orcas and Lopez islands, San Juan Island is "downtown central." Home to about 7,000 people, most of whom prefer this island's quicker pace, and covering over 142sq. km (55 sq. mi.), San Juan is a popular holiday destination, offering visitors the most in terms of urban amenities, relaxing hideaways, and wilderness hikes. For those who like to fill their days with different types of activities, San Juan is your best bet. It is also the most practical destination in the San Juan Islands if you're traveling without a car, since restaurants, shops, and museums are within walking distance of the ferry landing. Car and moped rentals are available all the same. The island even has a small winery, the **San Juan Vineyards** (3136 Roche Harbor Rd., ✆ **360/378-9463;** www.sanjuanvineyards.com), housed in a century-old schoolhouse near **Roche Harbor.**

San Juan Island has historic appeal, too. Its colorful past stems from a boundary dispute between the U.S. and Great Britain when, from 1860 to 1872, both countries occupied the island. In one of the stranger pieces of history, the killing of a British homesteader's pig by an American settler nearly sent the two countries to the battlefield. Ill will quickly escalated, but fortunately cooler heads prevailed, so that what is now referred to as the Pig War of 1869 only resulted in one casualty: the pig. The San Juan Islands were eventually declared American territory.

The history of this little-known war is chronicled through the interpretive centers in **San Juan Island National Historical Park,** divided into **English Camp** and **American Camp** (see "Exploring the Area," below). The Pig War was the last time that Great Britain and the U.S. opposed each other in war. General George Pickett, of the famed "Pickett's Charge" at the Civil War's Battle of Gettysburg, was commander of U.S. forces during the Pig War.

ESSENTIALS

GETTING THERE

Washington State Ferries arrive at **Friday Harbor** on the island's eastern coast. See "Getting There," at the beginning of the chapter, for information about fares and schedules.

VISITOR INFORMATION

The **San Juan Island Chamber of Commerce,** 135 Spring St. (P.O. Box 98), Friday Harbor, WA 98250 (✆ **360/378-5240;** www. sanjuanisland.org), will be happy to tell you what you need to know about the island.

GETTING AROUND

There are two island taxi services, **Bob's Taxi & Tours** (✆ **360/378-6777**) and **San Juan Taxi** (✆ **360/378-3550**). In summer months, **San Juan Transit** (✆ **800/887-8387** or 360/378-8887) provides bus transportation. Rental cars are available year-round from **M&W Auto,** 725 Spring St., Friday Harbor (✆ **800/323-6037** or 360/378-2886; www.sanjuanauto.com). Rates for a mid-size car are C$63 (US$55) per day mid-May through September; C$9 (US$10) less per day October through mid-May. Touring the island via bicycle, scooter, or moped is great fun. Rent bikes at **Island Bicycles,** 380 Argyle Ave., Friday Harbor (✆ **360/378-4941;** www. islandbicycles.com). Rates for mountain and hybrid bikes are C$40 (US$35) per day. Hourly and multiple-day rates are available. Rent mopeds at **Susie's Mopeds**

(© **800/532-0087** or 360/378-5244; 125 Nichols St., www.susiesmopeds.com), located two blocks up from the ferry landing at Friday Harbor. Susie's is the only place to find "scootcars," an inventive composite of a car and scooter. Moped rentals are C$29 (US$25) per hour; scootcars are C$57 (US$50) per hour. Per-day rates are available.

EXPLORING THE AREA
FRIDAY HARBOR

The busy fishing village of **Friday Harbor** was first populated by a feisty bunch of scalawags in the mid-1800s, and only gained respectability when it became the county seat in 1873. Today it encompasses 259 hectares (640 acres) and is the business center of the San Juan Islands: its harbor teems with commercial fishing boats and pleasure craft. From the docks of the Friday Harbor marina, **Trophy Charters** (© **360/ 378-2110;** www.fishthesanjuans.com) runs salmon fishing trips, starting from C$108 (US$95) per person. **Western Prince Cruises** (© **800/757-6732** or 360/378-5315; www.orcawhalewatch.com) offers nature and **whale-watching** expeditions from C$67 (US$59) for adults, C$44 (US$39) for children 12 and under. The 46-foot vessel accommodates up to 30 passengers and with plenty of indoor and outdoor seating, inclement weather is no deterrent. Tours are 3 to 4 hours. **Maya's Whale Watch Charters** (© **360/378-7996;** www.mayaswhalewatch.biz) take out smaller groups (6 passengers); 3-hour tours are C$67 (US$59) adults and C$56 (US$49) children 12 and younger. Guides are exceptionally wildlife-savvy, having written several wildlife books. They are also accomplished photographers who will give you tips beyond just point and shoot. **San Juan Kayak Expeditions** (© **360/378-4436;** www.sanjuankayak. com) has been in business near to 30 years, and will set you up for 3- and 4-day kayaking trips around the islands from C$455 to C$569 (US$399–$499) per person. They are the only folks to offer kayak-sailing, a combination of sale, paddle, and a following wind that has you traveling up to five times the distance. They also rent standard double kayaks for C$80 (US$70) per day.

San Juan Historical Museum   Housed in an 1890s wood-frame farmhouse, the museum includes a crowded collection of antiques, old photos, and American Indian artifacts, plus intriguing old farm equipment that makes you wonder how on earth they did what they purport to have done. Unless you're really into maritime "stuff," save your visit for a rainy day.

405 Price St., Friday Harbor (© **360/378-3949;** www.sjmuseum.org). May–Sept Thurs–Sat 10am–4pm; Sun 1–4pm; Mar–Apr and Oct Sat 10am–4pm; by appointment Nov–Feb. C$1.40 (US$1.20) for adults, C75¢ (US65¢) for children 6 to 18.

The Whale Museum   Although the maritime displays (other than the whale skeleton) are on the ho-hum side, a visit does give you a pretty good insight as to whale behavior: the difference between breaching, spy hopping, and tail lobbing, as well as the many vocalization patterns; listen to their songs on The Whale Phone Booth. If whale-watching is on your agenda, check out the photo collection with the names and identification markings of some of the 90 or so resident orcas in the area. The museum also has an orca adoption program to help fund ongoing research, and it operates a **24-hour hotline** (© 800/562-8832) to report whale sightings and marine mammal strandings.

62 1st St. North, Friday Harbor (© **360/378-4710.** www.whalemuseum.org). May–Sept daily 10am–5pm. Hours variable Oct–Apr. Call to confirm. C$6.85 (US$6) adults; C$5.70 (US$5) seniors; C$3.40 (US$3) children 5 to 18.

AMERICAN CAMP ⚓

When British and American settlers were tilling the soil of San Juan Island, soldiers on both sides attempted to stake a national claim to these fertile lands. Sovereignty was eventually settled and, although not entirely accurate, today Americans refer to that time as the British occupation. However you view it, the American Camp, 10km (6 miles) south of Friday Harbor, serves as a historic reminder of those early days. The windswept grassy peninsula is a wonderful place to spend a sunny summer afternoon. On any other day, though, the winds make it barren and rather inhospitable, though some might say deliciously lonely. Two buildings remain, an abandoned officers' quarters and a laundresses' quarters, along with a cemetery and a defensive fortification built by Henry M. Roberts, of *Roberts Rules Of Order* fame. A white picket fence circles the grounds, which include a Hudson's Bay Company farm on Grandma's Cove at the southern border of the park, along the water.

American Camp is really all about the great outdoors and limited facilities—you'll find a pit toilet along the way but little else. The approach road, Cattle Point Road, can get pretty busy with cyclists heading for the southernmost tip of the island, and trails throughout the park are popular for hikers, though none of them seem to get overcrowded. An on-site **Visitor Centre** (© **360/378-2902**) is open year-round daily 8:30am to 4:30pm. Admission is free.

Hiking Highlights

There are various routes to gain beach access, the easiest and most direct being from the respective parking lots and a 5- to 10-minute walk. These include **South Beach,** the longest public beach on San Juan Island, and a great place to see shorebirds and whales. The beach is mainly gravel, so shoes or sandals are a must. It's a short walk to reach the secluded **Fourth of July Beach** where, appropriately, eagles nest nearby. Getting to **Picnic Cattle Point,** arguably the prettiest beach on the island, is a precarious scramble down a rocky ledge, but again, only minutes from the parking lot. **Grandma's Cove** is a downhill stroll for half a kilometer to a picturesque beach. Use caution in descending the bluff, the gravelly soil gets very dry in summer and it's easy to lose your footing.

Prairie Walks are primitive tracks that crisscross the prairie and trace the bluff from Grandmas's Cove. It feels wild, and on a clear day, you can see views of Mount Baker, the Olympic and Cascade ranges, Vancouver Island and even Mount Rainier, 209km (130 miles) up Admiralty Inlet. Mind your step; watch for rabbit warrens. A more protected walk is the 2.4-km (1.5-mile) **Jakle's Lagoon Trail,** which travels along the old roadbed beneath a canopy of Douglas fir, cedar and hemlock trees.

Hardy hikers usually opt for the upward trail to reach **Mount Finlayson**—90m (295 ft.)—from where you can see the Coastal Mountains—as well as the Olympic and Cascade Ranges on the horizon and seascape below. *Tip:* From the parking lot, follow the trail along the ridge; you have a dense evergreen forest to your left and a prairie of golden grass down to the beach on your right. From the summit, choose the well-worn path on the east side of the bluff and you descend into a cool, thick forest and a network of trails that twist and turn along the shore of Griffin Bay and pass two saltwater lagoons. You can enjoy the best of both worlds—different as night and day—as the two trails connect in a 4-km (2.5-mile) loop. Birders come to the camp to catch a glimpse of the only nesting Eurasian skylarks in the U.S.

ENGLISH CAMP ✵✵

In sharp contrast to American Camp, English Camp is located in an area of protected waters, with maple trees spreading out overhead. About 16km (10 miles) from Friday Harbor, the site includes a restored hospital, a commissary, an impressive formal garden, and small white **barracks,** which are open to the public mid-May through Labor Day. The blockhouse, built right on the beach, served to protect the marines from marauding Natives, not Americans, and was later used as a guard house for miscreant troopers. You'll find interpretive displays on a hillside terrace overlooking the camp, close to where the officers' quarters were built. A small cemetery holds the graves of six British Marines who died accidentally during the occupation from 1860 to 1872 (there were no war-related casualties, other than the pig), and a trail leads through second-growth forests up to **Mount Young,** a fairly easy 198-m (650-ft.) ascent. A **Visitor Centre** (✆ **360/378-2902**) operates June through August, daily from 8:30am to 4:30pm. It is housed in what was once the officer's mess hall, and is staffed by rangers in period costume. At opening and closing times, these rangers create a fair to-do about raising the British Flag although it's lower than the American flag just up the hill. For information at any time of year, for English and American Camps, contact the **Park Headquarters,** 125 Spring St., Friday Harbor (✆ **360/378-2240**). Admission is free.

Hiking Highlights

Hiking here is not as rigorous as in American Camp. The easiest trail is **The Bell Point Trail,** a 1.5-km (1-mile) long, fairly level walk to Bell Point—it's a 3.2-km (2-mile) loop—for a view of Westcott Bay. If you like to harvest shellfish, check with the park ranger at the visitor center for locations, daily limits, and red tide warnings. Conversely, the **Young Hill Trail** climbs up to 198m (650 ft.) to the top of Young Hill for a panoramic view of the island's northwest corner. Novice walkers should take care to pace themselves, as most of the gain is in the last half kilometer. **Royal Marine Cemetery** is located about 46m (50 yards) off the Young Hill Trail, about a third of the way up. Five Royal Marines are interred here, and a memorial stone is in place for two other marines.

ROCHE HARBOR ✵✵

Roche Harbor is a heritage destination resort about 14km (9 miles) away from Friday Harbor, San Juan's commercial center. A favorite getaway of the late John Wayne, Roche Harbor is a mix of historic buildings, modern conveniences, and marine-related activities. Listed on the National Register of Historic Places, Roche Harbor was once the home of lime and cement tycoon John S. McMillin. In its heyday during the 1890s, the town had the largest limeworks west of the Mississippi, operating kilns that each burned 10 cords of wood every 6 hours—just to keep functioning. The remains of several kilns are still visible. Much of the lime sweetened the huge salt marsh that was filled in and became the tulip fields of the Skagit Valley.

The renovated **Hotel de Haro** still maintains much of its historic character, and a number of the heritage cottages used by workers in the lime kiln business have been converted to overnight lodgings. (See "Where to Stay").

The resort has some walks to enjoy: through pretty Victorian gardens beside the hotel, along the docks, and on some heritage trails that take you through the old lime quarries, past historic sites such as the woodyard, the site of the original company cottages, and onto the hillside, where you can take in views of the Spieden Channel, and

(*Moments*) Field of Sculptures

One of the San Juan Islands' newest features, the Westcott Bay Reserve (www. wbay.org) is an 8-hectare (19-acre) nature interpretive park filled with a rotating exhibit of more than modern sculptures in bronze, stone, wood, metal, glass and ceramics. The tall, dried grass shrouds one or two items, but perhaps it's left that way for "artistic expression"—who knows? The art is on loan to the park, and many can also be purchased from the artists. *Note:* If you missed the park at the turnoff heading down to Roche Harbor, there's a trail from the harbor back across the airstrip and cottages.

small San Juan islands. Some of the paths are paved with the same bricks that lined the original lime kilns. Pick up a trail map (C$1.14/US$1) at the hotel. The one walk you don't want to miss is to **The Mausoleum,** a bizarre McMillin family memorial that's about 20 minutes from the harbor. The structure itself is covered with Masonic symbols: an open, Grecian-style columned complex surrounds six inscribed chairs, each containing the ashes of a family member, set before a round table of limestone. Rumors abound as to why the seventh chair and column have been removed. Some say it was part of Masonic ritual, others believe a family member was disinherited. Or was it because the seventh member considered life to be everlasting?

Although open year-round, the resort is at its best in summer, not only for the landscaping but for the activities. Sea kayaking and whale-watching expeditions are available through the **Marine Adventure Centre,** and a naturalist guide hangs around to answer any questions about the local wildlife and terrain. The resort also becomes a showcase of local talent. By day, the resort's pathways and docks fill up with artists' booths displaying watercolors, oil paintings, photography, jewelry, knitted products, alpaca yarns, hand-made handbags, and pottery. You can even get your portrait painted. By night, **Island Stage Left,** a local outdoor theater company, takes to the boards with productions such as *The Merchant of Venice.* It can get a bit chilly by final curtain, so dress warmly, and bring bug spray and a blanket to sit on. Performances are free.

Roche Harbor promises to be even busier, with the 2007 opening of the resort's latest development: a "village" of rental town homes and a new spa hotel with 12 luxury guest suites and a full service wellness center.

LIME KILN POINT STATE PARK 🍁

Head due west from Friday Harbor, through the center of the island, and you'll wind up at Lime Kiln State Park. Named for an early lime-kiln operation on site (remnants of its old structures are still evident), this is the only park in the world dedicated to whale-watching. Researchers use the **Lime Kiln Lighthouse,** built in 1914 and listed on the National Register of Historic Places, to watch for whales and to determine whether passing boats are affecting their behavior. Other whale-watching enthusiasts crowd the bluff, or set up camp around picnic benches scattered along the beach. Your chances of sighting success are especially good in late August and early September, when major salmon runs head for the Fraser River spawning grounds. En route, they pass through **Haro Strait** in front of the park, along the west side of San Juan Island, attracting whales, which feed on them. You might spot orca, minke, and pilot whales, or their smaller cousins, harbor and Dall's porpoises. Bring your binoculars and cameras with telephoto lenses. There are 12 picnic sites and decent washroom facilities so it's a good family destination, especially since the trails are short (from less than half a mile to the longest at 2.5km (1.6 miles) and easy to navigate. The park is open year-round, daily from 8am to dusk. It operates a recorded information line, at © 360/378-2044.

PELINDABA LAVENDER FARM

More than 10,000 lavender plants grow in scenic rows on slopes leading to the forest's edge and make for a fragrant stroll on a hot summer's day. Just be sure to close the gate behind you. Designated "certified organic," the plants are transformed into essential oils, processed on site in a custom-built distillery, as well as handcrafted perfumes, soaps, candles, truffles, and other foodstuffs (see "Where to Dine," below). The original homestead cabin is now a tranquil three-room spa offering excellent lavender-oriented massage, facials, and a meditation space.

33 Hawthorne Lane. © 866/819-1911 or 360/378-4248. www.pelindaba.com. Free admission. May–Sept daily 10am–5pm; Oct–Apr Wed–Sun 10am–5pm. Closed Jan.

WHERE TO STAY

Friday Harbor House 🜂   This elegant hotel on the bluff above the harbor offers the finest modern accommodations on San Juan Island, and the best views of the harbor to boot. The inn is a welcome relief from all the Victorian-styled B&Bs found elsewhere on the San Juan Islands. The interior is distinctly West Coast, with lots of windows, wood, slate tiles, and plush carpets. And this goes for the rooms, too. A standout feature is a double-person (but noisy) Jacuzzi strategically situated so that you can see through into the bedroom, enjoying the views beyond. It's also within sight of the fireplace, so you can enjoy its warmth. All rooms have queen-size beds save for three new units, which each feature a king. The continental breakfast includes home-baked scones and muffins. If you're on the early morning ferry, park your car in the lineup and return to enjoy these goodies; and be sure to ask for a treat box "for the road." Harbor House Restaurant has also earned a reputation for a creative fine-dining restaurant (see "Where to Dine").

130 West St., Friday Harbor, WA 98250. © 360/378-8455. Fax 360/378-8453. www.fridayharborhouse.com. 23 units. May 24–Sept C$336–C$359 (US$295–US$315) standard; C$433 (US$380) king; C$386 (US$340) 1-bedroom suite. Oct–May 23 C$205–C$228 (US$180–US$200) standard; C$399 (US$350) king; C$302 (US$265) 1-bedroom suite. 2-night minimum stay required in summer and on weekends. Rates include continental breakfast. Extra person C$40 (US$35). Children 17 and under stay free in parent's room. AE, MC, V. **Amenities:** Restaurant. *In room:* TV/VCR/DVD, fridge, hair dryer, iron.

Friday's Historic Inn   This historic inn (circa 1891) is forever reinventing itself, and although currently a sassy little boutique hotel, it still manages to maintain the gracious atmosphere of yesteryear. Guest rooms are decorated in rich colors against light walls, and with a blend of modern and period furnishings. Every room is a different size and shape, as might be expected in an old building, but that's part of the charm. Four of the rooms share two bathrooms; the other 11 have private en suites. All bathrooms have heated floors. The Marrowstone Suite has a private outdoor Jacuzzi, and the Bainbridge Suite can sleep 7. The San Juan Suite is a favorite. It's near the top of the house and offers a kitchen, a private deck, and a bird's-eye view of the harbor. The inn is associated with The **Friday Harbor Inn** *(Value* (© **800/793-4756** or

360/378-4000), an upgraded 72-room motel down the road (think polished hard-wood floors versus shag carpet), and guests here have access to the motel's heated indoor swimming pool, hot tub, and sauna. *Note:* The inn is right downtown, 2 blocks from the ferry landing and from a couple of boisterous bars; noise can some-times be a problem.

35 1st St. (P.O. Box 2023), Friday Harbor, WA 98250. © **800/352-2632** or 360/378-5848. Fax 360/378-2881. www.friday-harbor.com. 15 units. June to mid-Sept C$170–C$193 (US$149–US$169) standard; C$227–C$307 (US$199–US$269) suite. Mid-Sept to May C$136–C$158 (US$119–US$139) standard; C$181–C$261 (US$159–US$229) suite. Rates include continental breakfast. Extra person C$23 (US$20). Children 3 and under stay free in parent's room. MC, V. **Amenities:** Lounge. *In room:* TV, minibar, coffeemaker, no phone.

Roche Harbor Resort 🐾🐾 *Kids*   A village unto itself, Roche Harbor offers many different kinds of lodging, as well as a marina large enough for 377 vessels, for seafar-ing guests. First, there is the century-old Hotel de Haro, where lace-trimmed beds, antiques, and roaring fireplaces transport you back to an earlier time. Originally a log bunkhouse, the hotel evolved into the distinctive three-story structure you see today, sophisticated enough to entertain company brass and dignitaries, including President Theodore Roosevelt (look for his signature in the guestbook). Suites have killer views, welcoming big beds, and large, claw-foot soaking bathtubs. Some single guest rooms share a bathroom. The one on the second floor contains the bathtub that John Wayne used to soak in. If you enjoy old and historic, The Haro delivers—slanted floors, crooked windows, and all. However, in addition to the hotel, there are nine former workers' cottages that have been converted into two-bedroom units close to the swim-ming pool, as well as one- to three-room condominiums and carriage houses. Cottages, carriage houses, and condos (which are expanding in 2007 with the addi-tion of 12 new spa suites) all have contemporary furnishings, full kitchen facilities, and of course, great views. Dining options are numerous, and include **McMillin's Restaurant** *(Overrated* housed in the former home of John S. McMillin, Roche Harbor Lime & Cement company president. The menu is expensive enough that you would expect the prime rib to be outstanding or presented with designer panache. It's good, but for better value for the money, opt for the less formal Madrona Grill downstairs *Note:* Either restaurant is a great place to view the nightly closing taps ceremony when half a dozen resort staff march up the main dock, music blaring over the loud speak-ers, to lower the flags.

4950 Reuben Tarte Memorial Dr., Roche Harbor, WA 98250. © **800/451-8910** or 360/378-2155. Fax 360/378-6809. www.rocheharbor.com. 60 units, some w/kitchens. Mid-June to Aug C$138–C$161 (US$121–$141) 16 with shared bathroom; C$184–C$209 (US$161–US$183) 4 with private bathroom; C$234–C$614 (US$205–US$539) condo-minium and carriage house; C$262–C$285 (US$230–US$250) cottage. Sept to mid-June C$80–C$98 (US$70–US$86) shared bathroom; C$98–C$114 (US$86–US$100) private bathroom; C$163–C$450 (US$143–US$395) condominium and carriage house; C$148–C$217 (US$130–US$190) cottage. Children 18 and under stay free in parent's room. AE, MC, V. **Amenities:** 3 restaurants; lounge; large outdoor heated pool; 2 tennis courts; playground; activities desk. *In room:* TV/VCR, coffeemaker, hair dryer.

Wildwood Manor B&B 🐾   New owners have added so many comfort touches to this manor inn that it ranks right up there with the best. A winding drive leads you through a canopy of evergreens to a picture-book country manor. The surrounding woods offer easy trails in which to wander, and the views include rolling hills down to the San Juan Channel. Common areas include a large living room with comfortable, oversize lounge chairs, floor-to-ceiling bookshelves lined with books and movie titles, hand-painted murals, hardwood floors, a large Georgian fireplace, and a refreshment station that includes candies, gourmet coffee, home-baked cookies, and chilled water with fresh cucumber slices. As soon as your feet hit the stairs, they sink into high-grade, plush carpeting that's also in every guest room. Beds have down duvets and high-quality linens, and furnishings include antiques alongside a flatscreen plasma TV. Bathrooms are stocked with everything from Q-tips to robes. Be prepared for a stellar breakfast—menu items change to guest preferences and may include items such as vanilla bean panna cotta with fresh strawberries or wild rice and goat cheese frittata. The warm and genuine hospitality extends beyond inn guests; there's a deer-feeding station near the front drive, frequented by entire families of deer for some good Kodak moments.

5335 Roche Harbor Rd. Friday Harbor, WA 98250. © **877/298-1144** or 360/378-3447. Fax 360/378-6095. www. wildwoodmanor.com. 4 units. May–Sept C$222–C$285 (US$195–US$250); Oct–Apr C$177–C$234 (US$155–US$205). **Amenities:** Lounge; refreshment bar; library, trails. *In room:* TV/DVD; Wi-Fi, hair dryer, no phone.

WHERE TO DINE

Duck Soup Inn *(Finds* PACIFIC NORTHWEST   Set in the woods overlooking a pond, the restaurant is housed in a former woodworking shed. Cozy booths and small tables create an intimate atmosphere, especially with the fieldstone fireplace, walls decorated with local art, and hurricane lamp sconces. The seasonal menu changes daily around the best island produce, meat, and poultry. It usually offers only four appetizers, two or three entrees, and a handful of decadent desserts. But don't be put off by the lack of selection: this is a case where less is definitely more. And even if you're a meat-and-potatoes diehard, chances are you'll find something unexpectedly delicious. It's the innovative breads and creative combinations that set this restaurant apart. For example, there might be tempura squash blossoms stuffed with goat cheese and thyme and served with spicy apricot orange jam, or Sri Lankan prawns with chilies, dates, lime, and dried mango, or roasted mission figs stuffed with blue cheese and topped with candied pecans and reduced balsamic. A small cocktail lounge is set to open in 2007.

50 Duck Soup Lane, Friday Harbor. © 360/378-4878. www.ducksoupinn.com. Reservations required. Main courses C$30–C$39 (US$26–US$34). AE, MC, V. Apr–Oct daily from 5:30pm. Closed Nov–Mar.

Harbor House Restaurant   With views looking down on Friday Harbor, this smart-casual restaurant is a popular spot for locals to celebrate special occasions. The menu changes weekly to take advantage of what's fresh and new on the island, though you can always expect flavorful homemade soups, imaginative salads with all sorts of edible herbs and flowers, and a catch-of-the-day special such as seared halibut with heirloom tomatoes, onion capers, white wine, olives, and basil, or the cod with lemon basil caper vinaigrette. The rack of lamb served with island-made goat-cheese pesto and the flame-broiled rib-eye steak with balsamic glaze and blue cheese crumble are two of their regular items, both served with mainstay garlic mashed potatoes. Desserts are different every night except for the signature home-made ice creams. One scoop of each flavor is the only way to go. Hotel guests have preferred seating; reservations are highly recommended. Ask about their special 4- to 6-course Wine Dinners, held periodically to showcase new dishes and local wines.

130 West St., Friday Harbor. © 360/378-8455. www.fridayharborhouse.com. Reservations recommended. C$22–C$39 (US$19–US$34); AE, MC, V. May–Sept daily from 5:30pm; Oct–Apr Thurs-Mon from 5pm.

Pelindaba Downtown   At first blush, you think this light and modern specialty store sells only lavender-based products, but push on through to the back and you'll find a food-service counter and a bright and airy restaurant-cafe. The lavender theme is carried through to lemonade, a lavender hummus (don't knock it until you've tried it), and a first-rate lavender cheesecake. Salads and sandwiches are good but it's the South African spiced soups that really set this eatery apart, in particular the goulash-style, lavender-free Ground Nut Soup. And you'll want to check out the lavender sugar, honey, syrup, salt, pepper, vinegar, and chocolates. *Pelindaba* is the Zulu word for "place of great gatherings," and it's appropriately named.

150 1st Ave. ⓒ **866/819-1911** or 360-378-6900. www.pelindaba.com. C$6.85 (US$6) MC, V. May-Sept daily 7am–7pm; Oct-Apr Mon–Thurs 7am–5:30pm, Fri–Sun 7am–7pm.

Steps Wine Bar PACIFIC NORTHWEST   Small, with burgundy walls that give it a jazzy atmosphere, this is the kind of eatery you'd expect to find in Seattle; its presence reflects the slow gentrification of Friday Harbor. The wine list offers more that 60 wines by the glass as well as an extensive specialty selection. Meals are tapas-style starters, small plates or large plates depending on how hungry you are. Many ingredients are from San Juan Island, as well as neighboring Waldron and Lopez islands, to create items such as beer-battered oysters, homemade yam gnocchi, seared Ahi tuna, grilled New York steak, and a crab-stuffed chicken breast that melts in your mouth. Desserts, too, won't disappoint, especially the flourless dark chocolate cake with caramel sauce and toasted peanuts.

The Alley, Friday Harbor Center. ⓒ **360/370-5959.** www.stepswinebarandcafe.com. C$21 (US$18). MC, V. Wed–Mon from 4 pm. Closed Tues.

3 Orcas Island

Named for the viceroy of Mexico in 1792, and not, in fact, for the orca whales common to its waters, Orcas Island is the largest (148sq. km/57 sq. miles), hilliest, and most beautiful of the San Juan Islands. Half the fun of exploring this island is traveling its roads, which, in addition to going up and down, twist and turn between hedgerows, fields, and orchards. Around any bend might lie a jewel of a bay or an unexpected hamlet filled with quaint cottages and wildflower gardens. You can climb to the top of **Mount Constitution,** in **Moran State Park,** where the panorama stretches from The Lions, over Vancouver, to Mount Rainier, south of Seattle, or stroll down lanes that give way to picturesque havens such as **Deer Harbor** and **Orcas Landing.** Early settlers logged, fished, and farmed, but today most of the island's 4,500 population are artisans, entrepreneurs, retirees, and eco-adventurers. In **Eastsound,** the heart of "commercial" activity on Orcas, you'll find horseback and kayaking excursions, in addition to galleries, restaurants, and some shops. The **Rosario Resort,** an elegant mansion that regularly graces the pages of travel magazines, is probably the island's most prominent landmark. Hiring 200 staff, it is the largest private employer on the islands (see "Where to Stay & Dine," below).

ESSENTIALS
GETTING THERE
Washington State Ferries dock at **Orcas Landing,** at the central southern peninsula of the island. See "Getting There," at the beginning of the chapter, for information about fares and schedules.

VISITOR INFORMATION

Stop in at **Orcas Island Chamber of Commerce,** Moran State Park, Olga Rd. (P.O. Box 252), Eastsound, WA 98245 (© **360/376-2273;** www.orcasisland.org), which operates from June to Labor Day (second Mon in Sept) daily from 8:30am to 4:30pm.

GETTING AROUND

Once there, **Orcas Taxi** (© **360/376-TAXI**) provides pickup and dropoff service throughout the island, year-round. From May to September, **Orcas Moped & Car Rental,** which has an association with M&W Auto on San Juan, (© **360/376-5266**) offers a limited number of midsize rental cars for about C$63 (US$55) a day. **Orcas Mopeds** (© **360/376-5266**), near the ferry landing, rents mopeds for C$23 (US$20) per hour or C$57 (US$50) per day; scootcars for C$46 (US$40) per hour and C$114 (US$100) per day. Bike rentals are available from **Dolphin Bay Bicycles** (© **360/ 376-4157**), located at the ferry landing, as well as from **Wildlife Cycles,** 350 North Beach Rd., Eastsound (© **360/376-4708;** www.wildlifecycles.com). Mountain bike and hybrid bike rentals are C$40 (US$35) per day. If time is of the essence, why not opt for a vintage biplane tour with **Magic Air Tours** (© **800/376-1929** or 360/376-2733; www.magicair.com) and get the lay of the land from the air. Trips are C$363 (US$295) for two people.

EXPLORING THE AREA
EASTSOUND VILLAGE

From the ferry dock, head due north 23km (14 miles) to **Eastsound Village,** at the center of the island. This is the commercial hub of Orcas Island, and it's both lovely to look at and a delight to stroll through. Catering to backpackers and the well-to-do alike, Eastsound sports galleries, potters, and a charming village green that hosts a number of special events. Check out the **Saturday morning market,** or watch a craftsperson whittle all manner of furniture and kitchen utensils with a foot-powered lathe at a pioneer display.

Eastsound is also where you'll want to base any **outdoor activities.** You may want to go horseback riding at **Walking Horse Country Farm,** 180 Westbeach Rd. (© **360/376-5306**). Each session costs C$68 (US$60), and includes a demonstration, some instruction, and an hour's trail ride. Private rides are C$114 (US$100). Another "horsey" experience, though not for riding, are the Clydesdales at **Once in a Blue Moon Farm,** 412 Eastman Rd. (© **360/376-7035;** www.onceinabluemoonfarm. com). They're local celebrities (along with the llamas that act as guardians of the farm's sheep and chickens) because of the carriage rides and haywagon tours around the 8 hectares (20 acres) of orchards, forests, u-pick strawberry fields and lovely gardens.

You can rent kayaks from **Shearwater Adventures,** 138 North Beach Rd. (© **360/ 376-4699;** www.shearwaterkayaks.com). Three-hour trips cost C$63(US$55) for adults, C$29 (US$25) for children 11 and under; full-day trips cost C$97 (US$85) per person. For a historical twist to kayaking, take a look at what **Osprey Tours,** P.O. Box 580, Eastsound, WA (© **360/376-3677**), has to offer. These folks use hand-crafted Aleutian-style kayaks and every kayaker is given an Aleutian whale-hunter's hat. Shaped like conical visors that resemble bird beaks, these hats served to disguise hunters, while their shape amplified the sounds of whales moving through the water. Osprey Tours specializes in private tours, and will accommodate families. Call for reservations and to arrange a venue based on your itinerary; one of their launch sites is right beside the ferry landing. Half-day trips cost C$88 (US$77) per adult; full-day trips cost C$137 (US$120); overnight trips start at C$228 (US$200). Children's rates are negotiable.

The **Orcas Island Historical Museum,** 5 North Beach Rd. (© **360/376-4849**), makes for a brief diversion, mainly for a look at the building itself. It comprises six one-room log cabins constructed by homesteaders in the 1880s. Between 1951 and 1963, cabins were disassembled and transported to Eastsound Village, where they were painstakingly reconstructed and connected to create the museum you see today. Admission is C$2.30 (US$2) for adults, C75¢ (US65¢) for seniors, students, and children 5 and up, C35¢ (US30¢) for children 4 and under. The museum is open June through September daily from 10am to 4pm.

MORAN STATE PARK

A favorite destination for visitor and islander alike, Moran State Park's 1,864 hectares (4,605 acres) offers a number of outdoor recreational activities, including camping, picnicking, canoeing and kayaking, hiking, horseback riding, and more. Over 48km (30 miles) of hiking trails, most built by the Civilian Conservation Corps (CCC), cover everything from easy nature loops like the 4.3-km (2.7-mile) walk around Cascade Lake to challenging out-of-the-way hikes such as the 7.6-km (4.7-mile) Mount Pickett Trail that ascends 3338m (1,110 ft.) through part of the largest tract of unlogged, old-growth forest in the Puget Sound Trough. Pick up a trail map from the Park Office at Cascade Lake. Unlike quieter Mountain Lake (that's where to put in for a quiet paddle, and fishing enthusiasts angle for trout), Cascade Lake gets a little like Grand Central Station in summer with canoe and paddleboat renters, picnickers, swimmers, day hikers setting off from the lakeside's many trailheads, and overnight campers. It's the only place in the park where you'll find bathhouses, kitchen shelters, and a sani-station. Call © **888/CAMPOUT** or 888/226-7655 for campsite reservations or visit www.parks.wa.gov. The park's landmark, **Mount Constitution,** is the highest point in the islands. Rising 734m (2,409 ft.) above sea level, the summit is reached by a steep, paved road, where you'll discover a 16-m (52-ft.) stone tower patterned after a 12th-century fortress. You can drive to the top; if you take your bike, you'll find the hard ride up rewards with an exhilarating ride back down. Because the gradient is so steep, the road is generally closed from mid-November to mid-April, as it can get slick and dangerous. Information on trails, campsites, and activities in the park is available from **Washington State Parks,** 7150 Cleanwater Lane, Olympia, WA 98504 (© **360/902-8844**). You can also go online to **www.orcasisle.com/ moran.**

DEER HARBOR

Lying at the end of a winding country lane, Deer Harbor has some of the best marine views in all of the San Juans, as well as a marina with showers and a laundry, boat charters, gift shops, and a new waterfront park. **Deer Harbor Charters** (© **800/544-5758** or 360/376-5989) offer year round 4-hour marine wildlife tours with a professional naturalist at C$56 (US$49) per adult and C$40 (US$35) per child under 14 years of age, while **Deer Harbor Marina** (© **360/376-3037**) can arrange for kayak, small boat, and bicycle rentals. The Resort at Deer Harbor (© **888/376-4480**), which lies just above the marina, recently converted to a complex of deluxe timeshare cottages so the only place left to stay in the area is the **Deer Harbor Inn** (© **877/377-4110** or 360/376-1040). It offers both lodge and private cottage accommodation,

Finds Get Potted

In operation for more than 60 years, **Orcas Island Pottery,** 338 Old Pottery Rd, Eastsound (© **360/376-2813;** www.orcasislandpottery.com) is one of the oldest potteries in the region and represents the work of almost two dozen potters. Look for a weathered log cabin festooned with colorful oversize pottery plates, and jewel-tone glazed vases in the garden. Inside is a working studio with artists throwing pots on the wheel, hand-building and glazing. **Crow Valley Pottery & Gallery,** 2274 Orcas Rd., Eastsound (© **360/376-4260;** www.crowvalley.com), is also housed in a log cabin, circa 1866, and showcases the works of more than 70 artists and craftspeople. Located in a renovated **strawberry** packing plant, **Olga Artworks,** Olga (© **360/376-4408;** www.orcasisland.com/artwork), is just east of Moran State Park, and features the work of more than 60 local artists displayed almost as creatively as the pieces themselves: on shelves made of railroad ties, benches of driftwood, and tree-stump pedestals.

unpretentious but comfortable (country quilts on the beds and paper cups in the bathroom versus down duvets and glasses), and only peek-a-boo harbor views, sometimes across the parking lot. The Inn does run a casual restaurant in the original 1915 building; serving mostly comfort foods and seafood, family-style with salad and soup.

WHERE TO STAY & DINE
VERY EXPENSIVE

Rosario Resort & Spa 🌟🌟🌟   This turn-of-the-century mansion, originally the private residence of shipping magnate Robert Moran, is worth the look even if you don't have the money to stay. Listed on the National Register of Historic Places, the building has been beautifully restored, and as befits a ship building, is still as solid and elegant as an ocean liner of the period. Walls are 30 centimeters (12 inches) thick and paneled with mahogany. Windows are inch-thick plate glass. And the mansion boasts 557sq. m (6,000 sq. ft.) of teak parquet floors that took craftsmen more than two years to lay. The music room features a Tiffany chandelier and a working 1,972-pipe Aeolian organ, which, when installed in 1913, was the largest organ in a private home in the United States. Don't miss the free hour-long concerts held nightly—they're entertaining, and reminiscent of when Moran used to play the complicated organ for his guests—only the real secret is, he never knew how to play. In winter, concerts are performed on Saturday evening only. The mansion is one of 10 buildings that make up the Rosario Resort & Spa, which is spread out over 3 hectares (8acres), and surrounded by several more acres of countryside. Guest rooms vary from standard accommodation either scattered along the waterfront in motel-style buildings or near the mansion, to one-and two-bedroom suites, with kitchens and private balconies, perched on the hillside. All are spacious (especially those on the hill), with bright, modern decor in neutral tones accented with floral-print accessories, and down duvets, and they offer terrific views of Cascade Bay. Hillside rooms also have fireplaces and sunken Jacuzzi tubs. The **Avanyu Spa** offers everything from early morning yoga and cardio workouts, to aromatherapy wraps, massage, and other personalized body treatments. There are three restaurants, suitable to all tastes and budgets. The Mansion Dining Room is the must-reserve, dress-up restaurant. The menu features popular steak and salmon dishes as well as organic island-grown produce, although its real pièce de résistance is its all-you-can-eat buffet. The wine list has many selections from local northwest wineries. In summer, a poolside bar and grill is also open. Rates drop for weekday stays year-round, and winter rates are more than 50% less than those charged in summer.

1 Rosario Way, Eastsound, WA 98245. ℂ 800/562-8820 or 360/376-2222. Fax 360/376-2289. www.rosarioresort. com. 116 units, some w/ fireplaces and Jacuzzis. July to mid-Sept C$272–C$341 (US$239–US$299) standard; C$409–C$797 (US$359–US$699) suite. Mid-Sept to June C$124–C$170 (US$109–US$149) standard; C$227–C$295 (US$199–US$259) suite. Extra person C$23 (US$20). Children 17 years and under stay free in parent's room. AE, DC, DISC, MC, V. Pets accepted w/prior approval. **Amenities:** 3 restaurants; lounge; small heated indoor pool; large heated outdoor pool; health club; spa; sauna; concierge; activities desk; car-rental desk; library; museum. *In room:* TV, VCR on request, dataport, kitchen, coffeemaker, hair dryer.

Spring Bay Inn 🌟🌟 *(Finds)*   It's a long drive on a dirt road to get here, but your efforts are amply rewarded. Situated on 23 hectares (57 acres) of woods, the Spring Bay Inn does what it can to showcase its setting, mainly through 270 custom windows that peek through the trees to stunning water views from every room. The angular Great Room has hardwood floors, an impressive fieldstone fireplace and vaulted ceiling, and the four guest rooms upstairs have wood-burning fireplaces, feather mattresses, down comforters, high ceilings, private bathrooms, and fresh flowers. The fifth guest room, the Ranger's Suite, downstairs, has 27 windows and its own outdoor Jacuzzi. In the morning, coffee, muffins, and fresh fruit are delivered to your door—a little sustenance for the 2-hour guided kayak tour to follow, included with the room rate. Brunch is served on your return. The innkeepers are an engaging pair of retired State Park Rangers, who go out of their way to share their knowledge and make beginner kayakers feel like pros.

464 Spring Bay Trail (P.O. Box 97), Olga, WA 98279. ℂ 360/376-5531. Fax 360/376-2193. www.springbayinn.com. 5 units. Year-round C$251–C$296 (US$220–US$260). Rate includes continental breakfast, brunch, and kayaking trip. AE, DISC, MC, V. **Amenities:** Lounge; Jacuzzi. *In room:* Fridge, hair dryer, no phone.

MODERATE

Cascade Harbor Inn   Situated among madrona trees, across the bay from Rosario Resort, this is a more affordable alternative (compare rates). Studio, one- and two-bedroom suites have a motel feel, with fully equipped kitchen including a fridge, microwave, and coffeemaker, making them a good choice for families and those indulging in longer island stays. The studio Murphy beds are surprisingly comfortable as are the sofa pullouts for additional guests. Every room has a great marine view and private balcony overlooking Cascade Bay. Only summer rates include continental breakfast.

1800 Rosario Rd., Eastsound, WA 98245. ℂ 800/201-2120 or 360/376-6350. Fax 360/376-6354. www.cascade harborinn.com. 44 units. June–Labor Day C$147–C$455 (US$129–$399); Sept–May C$74–C$227 (US$65–US$199). C$29 (US$25) extra person. AE, DISC, MC, V. Free parking. **Amenities:** Breakfast lounge; wireless Internet. *In room:* Fridge, hair dryer, microwave.

Doe Bay Resort & Retreat Center   Spread over 12 hectares (30 acres) of waterfront property, this resort is a throwback to the 1970s, offering a congenial, New Age atmosphere. There's a wide range of accommodation: rustic cabins (one-, two-, and three-bedroom configurations, some with no running water; others with fully equipped kitchen), yurts (canvas and wood structures) with skylights, treehouses (kids and romantics love them), greenhouse cabins, tents, limited RV sites, and a hostel. There are shared central bathrooms and a community kitchen. The fully equipped, self-contained "retreat house" accommodates ten. A wonderful, clothing-optional, three-tiered sauna and a creekside mineral springs Jacuzzi perch on a covered deck. Bring an oversize towel or two, and a flashlight. Sea kayak tours and bike rentals are available. The Cafe Doe Bay is decorated with lava lamps, and it dishes up good vegetarian and seafood selections, although you might have to wait a bit because service can be casual. The cafe is housed in a former general store and post office (built in 1908 and listed in the National Register of Historic Places). It's open daily in summer for breakfast, brunch, and dinner; with restricted hours in winter. Call to confirm.

107 Doe Bay Rd. (P.O. Box 437), Olga, WA 98279. ⓒ **360/376-2291.** Fax 360/376-5809. www.doebay.com. 64 units. June–Sept C$40 (US$35) tent and hostel; C$74–C$230 (US$65–US$210) cabin and yurt. C$513 (US$450) retreat house. Rates 20% lower Oct–May. MC, V. Pets accepted June–Sept C$23 (US$20). **Amenities:** Restaurant; Jacuzzi; sauna; limited water-sports rentals; bike rentals, massage, yoga classes. *In room:* No phone.

Orcas Hotel 🅐   Built in 1904 as a boarding house, this restored Victorian home is on the National Register of Historic Places, and overlooks the ferry terminal. Guest rooms aren't deluxe, but they're clean and comfortable, decorated with faux country quilts, earth tones, and period furniture. Some share bathrooms; others have private toilets but shared showers. The newer guest rooms have private balconies and Jacuzzis. For those who really want to get away from it all, there's also a small, self-contained cottage that sleeps six. Rates include a continental breakfast in the Orcas Café, which also has a grandstand veranda to wait out the ferry with a beer or a sandwich, later on in the day. Octavia's Bistro adjoins the hotel and serves a good selection of seafood, steaks, and pasta.

P.O. Box 155 (Orcas ferry landing), Orcas, WA 98280. ⓒ **888/672-2792** or 360/376-4300. Fax 360/376-4399. www.orcashotel.com. 12 units, cottage. May–Oct and year-round holiday weekends C$89–C$167 (US$78) standard; C$236 (US$208) with Jacuzzi. Nov–Apr C$101–C$138 (US$89–US$121) standard; C$162 (US$142) with Jacuzzi. Year-round C$143 (US$125) cottage. Extra person C$17 (US$15). AE, MC, V. **Amenities:** Restaurant; pub; lounge; VCR on request; nonsmoking. *In room:* TV, hair dryer, no phone.

Turtleback Farm Inn 🅐🅐   Set away from the water, the pastoral setting of Turtleback Farm is refreshingly bucolic with its lush meadows, duck ponds, and forests. Originally constructed in the late 1800s, the farmhouse has been completely redone and yet still retains a heritage feel, with lots of wood paneling, antiques, comfortable lounge chairs, and a living room that boasts a Rumford fireplace. Bedrooms tend to be on the small side but exude so much charm that you'll want to nest. Linens include woolen comforters and down pillows. Most en suites have claw-foot tubs. Orchard House, a new addition to the farm resembles a barn from the outside. Set in the apple orchard, it has four spacious rooms with king-size beds, completed with gas fireplaces, sitting/dining areas with TV/VCR, and private decks from which you can watch the farm's handful of sheep and cows, including some Scottish Highlanders, set the pace for the day.

1981 Crow Valley Rd., Eastsound, WA 98245. ⓒ**800/376-4914** or 360/376-4914. Fax 360/376-5329. www.turtle backinn.com. 11 units. C$171–C$279 (US$150–US$245); lower rates Nov–May. Extra person C$40 (US$35). MC, V. Children must be 8 and over to stay in Farmhouse. Nonsmoking. **Amenities:** Lounge; coffeemaker; iron; dataport. *In room:* No phone.

Finds Shaw Island

Shaw Island is the most remote of the accessible San Juan Islands, and makes for a terrific bike trip; most roads are paved. If you visit, however, take care to be as self-sufficient as possible, bringing along enough food, water, and other supplies to last. Home to approximately 230 permanent residents, most of Shaw Island's 20sq. km (7.7 sq. miles) are undeveloped. With the exception of a **wildlife refuge** and a tiny country park offering limited picnicking and camping facilities, the island is completely privately owned. Its store, **Shaw General Store,** on Blind Bay Rd. (*℃* **360/468-2288**) is, by law, the only commercial business allowed, which is why it acts as ferry terminal, grocery store, gas station, and post office. Although the store sells a number of tourist trinkets, it also boasts a surprising selection of gourmet items, such as mustards, herbs, and vinegars produced by the nuns of Our Lady of the Rock, a cloistered Benedictine order that runs a large dairy farm to the west. Although tours are rarely available, you are welcome to take in the beautiful marine-themed chapel, where mass is held each Sunday. Nearby, **The Little Red Schoolhouse** (listed on the National Register of Historic Places) is one of the few one-room schools still in use. Across the road, a tiny log cabin houses the **Shaw Island Museum**—a display of mostly old photographs and island artifacts. Whether you go by bike or car, there are enough sailings to and from Shaw to make a day trip possible. You'll need to check sailing times carefully, though, since arrivals and departures are a mix of eastbound and westbound destinations.

4 Lopez Island

Laced with country lanes, picturesque farms, and orchards, Lopez Island is just about as bucolic and pastoral as it gets. Cows and sheep are a common sight, as are bright fields of daffodils, tulips, lilies, and delphiniums. Home to approximately 2,100 people, and covering 76sq. km (30 sq. miles), Lopez has a rich agricultural heritage. Once known as the "Guernsey Island" for its exports of cream, eggs, and poultry, the land now supports more than 50 working farms. In summer, cyclists flock to the gently rolling hills, and birdwatchers take to the expanses of protected tidal flats to watch a myriad of shorebirds: horned grebes, double crested cormorants, yellow legs, peeps, ospreys, and peregrine falcons.

Spencer Spit State Park is a 56-hectare (138-acre) marine and camping park, named for the lagoon-enclosing sand spit on which it lies. Clamming, crabbing and saltwater fishing are among the park's most popular activities. It's also a sun-drenched picnic area with 37 sought-after standard camping sites at C$18–C$26 (US$16–US$23) per night March through October. Call *℃* **888-CAMPOUT** (888/226-7688) for reservation or visit www.parks.wa.gov. **Shark Reef Recreation Area** is a favorite spot from which to watch harbor seals, sea lions, and bald eagles diving for dinner. Or you can head for **Agate Beach,** one of the few beaches open to the public, and one of the most romantic places to watch the sun go down. The southernmost point, Iceberg Point, is another easy trail to the bluffs that edge the shore.

Come winter, Lopez Island seems to go into virtual hibernation, save for a fairly recent phenomenon: when one of the original Microsoft team built his compound here a few years back, techies followed, and vacation mega-houses have been popping up all along the waterfront ever since. Real estate prices are soaring. Lopez village has developed a new gentrified air, and now has street names and sidewalks. Lopez is, however, still the friendliest of the San Juan Islands. Waving to passing cars and cyclists is a time-honored local tradition.

ESSENTIALS

GETTING THERE

The ferry arrives at the northerly tip of the island. See "Getting There," at the beginning of the chapter, for information about fares and schedules.

VISITOR INFORMATION

The **Lopez Island Chamber of Commerce,** P.O. Box 102, Lopez, WA 98261 (℗ **360/ 468-4664;** www.lopezisland.com), distributes literature and maps in shops and galleries throughout the island.

GETTING AROUND

Folks on foot could be out of luck. Taxi service is an on–off affair (at time of printing, there was none available). Call the Chamber of Commerce (above) to get the latest scoop. One of the best bike routes around the island is a 48-km (30-mile) circuit that can be done in a day and is suitable for the whole family. If you don't have your own wheel power, here are some rental options: **Lopez Bicycle Works & Kayaks,** 2847 Fisherman's Bay Rd. (℗ **360/468-2847**), offers mountain bikes, tandems, and children's bikes, as well as repairs and sales.

EXPLORING THE AREA

Lopez Village is the business center of the island, and has a scattering of cafes, shops, a charming farmers' market (held Wednesday and Saturday), and, of course, real estate offices. The **Library,** 2225 Fisherman Bay Rd. (℗ **360/468-2265**), housed in a bright red and white 19th-century schoolhouse, is the *only* place to get the Sunday *New York Times, The Los Angeles Times,* and *The Wall Street Journal.* Copies are donated, which might mean you're reading 2-day-old news. Well, call it being on island time. Nonresidents pay a refundable C$11 (US$10) fee to check out books while on the island.

When you're browsing through Lopez Village, be sure to drop in to the **Soda Fountain & Pharmacy** (℗ **360/468-4511**), where you'll find an old-fashioned ice-cream parlor with a slew of fountain treats: killer banana splits, hand-dipped malts, and suck-'til-your-brain-hurts thick-and-creamy milk shakes. The place is a bit scruffy but the lunch counter is gossip central for Lopez locals, just in case you're interested in the lowdown on island life. The **Lopez Historical Museum,** 28 Washburn Place (℗ **360/ 468-2049**), houses artifacts such as a foot-powered cow-milking machine, and a 1903 Orient buckboard—the first car driven on the island. The museum puts out an island tour map of historic landmarks, which, believe it or not, has 34 destinations! You have to be a history nut to really appreciate this, though. Museum operating hours are sporadic, particularly in winter, although you can usually count on Friday through Sunday from 10am to 3pm. It's a fun 20-minute visit while you're wandering around the village. Admission is C$1.70 (US$1.50) for adults, C$1.15 (US$1) for children 18 and under.

Touring island farms is another fun excursion, especially if you're into market produce, herbs, or handwoven blankets. Call the **Lopez Community Land Trust** (℃ 360/468-3723) for information. If you're a wine lover, or are even just learning to love it, pay a visit to **Lopez Island Vineyards,** 724 Fisherman Bay Rd. (℃ **360/ 468-3644;** www.lopezislandvineyards.com). This small, family owned winery is the oldest in San Juan County, producing organically grown grapes and some pretty drinkable wines. Until recently, if you bought any wines with labels stating an origin of Friday Harbor or Orcas Island, they were tourist gimmicks. The wine was actually made in the Yakima Valley. These folks, however, have matured their early-ripening vines from the mid-1980s, so they now produce grapes that create more flavor. In addition to a Cabernet and Merlot, there's a medium-dry white apple-pear wine, as well as a full-bodied blackberry dessert wine, all of which are made on the premises. The vineyard is open for free tastings from April 15 to December 15, Friday and Saturday, from noon to 5pm. It's also open in July and August on Wednesday.

WHERE TO STAY

Edenwild Country Inn 🌿 This is the Victorian centerpiece of Lopez Village, complete with picturesque flower garden and large wraparound porch. Although the inn is not located on the water, many guest rooms have views of the San Juan Channel. Pleasant antique furnishings decorate the recently refurbished rooms, and there are quality bathroom amenities and delicious Bavarian chocolates at your bedside. Three guest rooms also have large wood-burning fireplaces. All have private bathrooms, some of which feature deep-soaker claw-foot bathtubs. Room 2 is the most comfortable, notable for its size and cozy sitting area, the family heirlooms (circa 1920), and vistas of Fisherman's Bay. In answer to the island's lack of cable TV, there are books everywhere—you can actually take them home thanks to Lopez's phenomenal recycling program. The European-style breakfast is generous, with plenty of cold cuts, cheeses, bread varieties, eggs, and fresh fruit.

132 Lopez Rd. (PO Box 271), Lopez Island, WA 98261. ℃ **800/606-0662** or 360/468-3238. Fax 360/468-4080. www.edenwildinn.com. 8 units. May–Sept C$170–C$182 (US$150–US$160). Rates 20% lower Oct–Apr. Rates include full breakfast. Extra person C$29 (US$25). AE, MC, V. Children under 12 not accepted. **Amenities:** Lounge; hair dryer and iron available. *In room:* Coffeemaker, no phone.

Inn at Swifts Bay 🌿🌿 Set among tall cedars above Swifts Bay, this elegant Tudor inn, formerly a summer home, offers luxury in a casual atmosphere. The entrance is a bit forbidding—the trees make everything seem so dark—but once inside, you'll notice California-style furnishings happily mixed with antique reproductions, and details such as goose-down comforters, fresh flowers, crocheted antimacassars, and needlepoint pillows. The overall appeal, though, might lean to guests age 50 plus. Shared areas are warm and inviting; the lounge contains a fireplace, a piano, decanters of sherry and port, many books, and a movie library of over 350 films. The two-person sauna and tiny exercise studio are unexpected finds, with just enough equipment to work up a sweat: a universal gym, treadmill, stationary bike, and some weights. Three of the comfortable guest rooms have fireplaces, fridges, and private bathrooms; the remaining two guest rooms share a bathroom. The breakfasts are feasts: crab cakes are the reputed favorite, although the hazelnut waffles with fresh

Lopez Island berries, potato galette with smoked salmon, and the inn's specialty, orange-cinnamon bread pudding, can't be far behind.

856 Port Stanley Rd., Lopez Island, WA 98261. ⓒ 800/375-5285 or 360/468-3636. Fax 360/468-3637. www.swifts bay.com. 5 units. Year-round C$125–C$143 (US$110–US$125) shared bathroom; C$200–C$239 (US$175–US$210) private bathroom. Rates include full breakfast. AE, DISC, MC, V. **Amenities:** Lounge; exercise room; Jacuzzi; sauna. *In room:* No phone.

MacKaye Harbor Inn   Originally built in 1904, and dramatically rebuilt 20 years later when it was the first island homestead to have electricity, the upgraded farm-house still retains much of its homey style. Rooms are large, ceilings are high, picture windows overlook the bay and there's a long porch. Decor and furnishings are unpretentious but comfortable, and an enclosed garden gazebo is a private sanctuary where guests can read, meditate, or enjoy watching the hummingbirds at the feeder. Rates include truffles and port in the evening, and a large continental breakfast with very wholesome muffins, hard-boiled eggs, fresh fruit, and granola. Guests have free use of 21-speed mountain bikes and can rent kayaks for C$29 (US$25) per day, or C$40 (US$35) for their entire stay. There are also two self-contained cottages on property, suitable for families.

949 MacKaye Harbor, Lopez Island, WA 98261. ⓒ 888/314-6140. Fax 360/468-2253. www.mackayeharborinn.com. 5 units, 4 with ensuite bath. C$154–C$222 (US$135–US$195). Rates are less in early spring. Retreat packages available. Rates include breakfast. MC, V. Closed mid-Oct to end Apr. **Amenities:** Lounge; kayak rentals; free use of mountain bikes. *In room:* Hair dryer, no phone.

WHERE TO DINE

The Bay Cafe 𝒌𝒌 *Finds* PACIFIC NORTHWEST   Located at the entrance to Fisherman's Bay, this bright, spacious restaurant is a delight. Colorful and contemporary art adorns the walls, while row upon row of windows give way to terrific sunsets and waterside views. The views are only outdone by the food: the ever-changing selection of seafood tapas is imaginative (the Dungeness crab and shrimp cakes with a citrus sesame soy sauce are to die for), and the entrees cover all the bases, with dishes to please carnivores, herbivores, and everything in between. The Thai curry is exceptionally good, as is almond-crusted Alaskan halibut with gingered boysenberries, and the

---

Moments **A Wonderful Walk**

Iceberg Point, at Lopez's southernmost coast, beyond Agate Beach, is located minutes away from MacKaye Harbor, and leads to some of island's most spectacular (and sometimes windy) coastline. But you need to pay attention to find it, and to make sure you're not an unwelcome visitor on private land. Park your car at the Agate Beach parking area and walk south to where the pavement ends. Go through the private gate onto the gravel road, past a large tree line on the right. When you come to a beach house on your left, turn right at the telephone on your right, down a well-driven driveway and through the metal gate. Continue down the grassy road, and stay left at the fork—or you'll be trespassing. This shaded trail passes huckleberry and blackberry bushes, and soon the forest opens up to Iceberg Point State Park. It's about a 20-minute walk and you'll want to spend at least an hour exploring the bluffs; more if you have a picnic.

(Fun Fact Birders Unite

On Orcas Island, the best birding spots include Killebrew Lake, Moran State Park, and the state parks at Obstruction Point, Point Dougherty, and Point Lawrence. On San Juan Island, you'll see the most birds if you hike up Mount Young at British Camp or trek along Mount Finlayson at American Camp.

The local chapter of the Audubon Society (www.sjaudubon.org) offers monthly bird walks that rotate between islands, and offers an open invitation to tag along. So lace up those boots—and don't forget to bring binoculars. Call ✆ **360/378-3068** for details.

---

pork tenderloin spiced with apple-wood-smoked bacon and peach barbecue sauce. Homemade soup and salad are included with your meal, which makes the menu particularly good value. There's a patio in summer. In winter, call ahead.

9 Old Post Rd., Lopez Village. ✆ **360/468-3700**. www.bay-cafe.com. Reservations required July–Aug. Main courses C$19–C$29 (US$17–US$25). AE, DISC, MC, V. May–Aug daily 5:30–10pm; Sept–Apr Wed–Sun 5:30–10pm (variable).

Love Dog Café *(Finds* ECLECTIC   Its name is derived from a 13th-century poem by philosopher Rumi: "There are love dogs in this world no-one knows the names of, give your life to be one." The chef-owner-storyteller is (self-)named White Bear for her white hair and somewhat stocky appearance. And the food is some of the best Italian fare in the San Juan Islands There are always half a dozen different pasta specials (pray that you're there for the Pesto Capellini) usually served family-style, as well as a couple of fresh fish features. In the morning, the cafe serves some of the best breakfasts too, and true to its eclectic nature is able to transform from an eatery serving burgers, quiche, and good salads by day, to quite a romantic spot at night, especially if you hit an evening with live jazz. Service can be on the slow side but it's worth the wait. All the basics and baked goods are made from scratch, and the desserts are delicious, especially the pot au chocolate or bread pudding with whiskey sauce.

1 Village Center, Lopez Island. ✆ **360/468-2150**. Main courses C$14 (US$12) dinner. MC, V. Open daily 6:30am–10pm (variable in winter).

Index

See also Accommodations and Restaurant indexes, below.

GENERAL INDEX

Abkahzi Garden (Victoria), 72
Aboriginal Journeys (Campbell River), 169
Accommodations. *See also* Children, accommodations
  Alert Bay, 175
  bed and breakfast, 7–8, 56, 59, 98, 99, 106, 119–120, 179
  best, 6–8
  booking online, 26
  Campbell River, 161–163
  "Canada Select," 35
  Cape Scott Provincial Park, 179–180
  Clayoquot Sound, 140–143
  Cortes Island, 169–170
  Courtenay & the Comox Valley, 153–155
  Cowichan Valley, 105–107
  expensive, 56–57
  Gabriola Island, 119–120
  Galiano Island, 200–202
  Gold River, 165
  Hornby & Denman Island, 157–158
  house-swapping, 36
  Lopez Island, 231–232
  Mayne Island, 205–206
  moderate, 57–58, 60–62, 227–228
  Nanaimo, 115–116
  Nootka Sound, 166–167
  Parksville & Qualicum Beach, 125–127
  Pender Island, 196–197
  Port Alberni & Bamfield, 131–133
  Port McNeill, 175
  Quadra Island, 168–169
  reducing rate, 35–36
  reservations hotline, 49
  room selection, 36–37
  Saanich Peninsula, 90–91
  Salt Spring Island, 188–189
  San Juan Islands, 220–222, 226–227, 230–232
  Saturna Island, 209–210
  Sooke Region, 98–100
  Telegraph Cove, 173–174
  tips, 35–37
  Tofino, 140–143
  Ucluelet, 143–144
  very expensive, 54–56, 226–227
  Victoria, 54–62, 58–62
  youth hostels, 61
  Zeballos, 172
Active Pass Lighthouse (Mayne Island), 43, 204
Adam's Fishing Charters (Victoria), 73
Adventure activities, 46–47
Afternoon tea, 62, 67, 89, 149
Agricultural Hall (Mayne Island), 43
Ahousaht Wildside Heritage Trail (Tofino), 135
The Ahous Trail (Vargas Island), 135
Air Canada, 48
Airfares, 25–26, 28–29
Airline bankruptcy protection, 21
Airlines, 29–30, 48–49
Airport bus service, 48
The Alberni Valley Museum (C. Vancouver Island), 130
Alcheringa Gallery (Victoria), 79
Alert Bay (Cormorant Island), 170, 172, 174–175
All Fun Recreation Park (Victoria), 77
All Sooke Day and Annual Festival of History, 19
American Automobile Association, 38
American Camp (San Juan Islands), 41
American Express, 15, 38, 53
Ancient Cedars Spa (Tofino), 5, 143

Annual Bald Eagle Count (Goldstream Provincial Park), 18
Annual Brant Wildlife Festival, 18
Antiques, 78
April Point Lodge (Quadra Island), 162
The Aquaterre Spa (Parksville/Qualicum Beach), 126
Arrowsmith Golf and Country Club (Qualicum Beach), 124
Artcraft (Salt Spring Island), 186
Art galleries, 68, 79
Art Gallery of Greater Victoria, 68
Art in the Park (Orcas Island), 20
The Artisans Courtyard (Courtenay), 150
Artists' Studios Open House (San Juan Island), 19
ATMs, 14, 15
Aurora Explorer, 3
Aveda Lifestyle Spa (Victoria), 59
Avis, 37

Bamfield, 132. *See also* Port Alberni & Bamfield
Bamfield Marine Sciences Centre, 132
Bars, 84–85. *See also* Restaurants Index
Bathtub Race, 19, 115
B&Bs. *See* Accommodations index
BC Ferries circle tour, 149
BC Forest Museum Park/BC Forest Discover Centre (Duncan), 103
BC Ministry of Environment, Lands, and Parks, 153
BC Open Sandcastle Competition, 19–20

Beaches
Botanical Beach (Port
Renfrew), 2, 44
Lopez Island (San Juan
Islands), 229–230
Mayne Island, 205
Parksville & Qualicum Beach,
123
Rathtrevor Beach Provincial
Park (Parksville), 2
Southern Vancouver Island,
96–98
**Beacon Hill Children's Farm
(Victoria), 77**
**Beacon Hill Park (Victoria), 44,
72**
**Beasley Fishing Charters
(Victoria), 73**
**Beaumont Marine Provincial
Park (Pender Island), 43, 195**
**Belfry Theatre Society
(Victoria), 83**
**Bellhouse Provincial Park
(Galiano Island), 199**
**The Bell Point Trail (San Juan
Island), 218**
**The Bengal Lounge (Victoria),
84**
**Bere Point Regional Park
(Malcolm Island), 175**
Big Bad Johns (Victoria), 84
**The Big Cedar Trail (Tofino),
135**
**Big Foot Organic Herb Farm
(Salt Spring Island), 188**
**Birding, 18, 105, 121, 134, 195,
205, 233**
**Blue Grouse Vineyards
(Duncan), 104**
**Boat Festival (Cowichan Bay),
19**
Boat tours, 166
Aurora Explorer, 3
Inside Passage, 10
Port Alberni, 130
**Bob's Taxi & Tours (San Juan
Island), 215**
Bookstores
Victoria, 79
**Born Free Bed & Breakfast of
BC, 54**
**Botanical Beach (Port
Renfrew), 2, 44, 95**
**Botanical Beach Provincial Park
(Port Renfrew), 98**
The Brant Festival, 121
Brewpubs, 62
**British Columbia Aviation
Museum (Saanich Peninsula),
88**

**British Importers Men's Wear
(Victoria), 80**
**Broken Group Islands (Pacific
Rim National Park), 22, 46,
130, 138, 139**
**Broken Island Adventures
(Bamfield), 132**
Broughton Inlet, 2
Budget car rental, 37
Bungee jumping, 113–114
Bus
from/to airport, 48
Buses, 51
tours, 75
Business hours, 38, 53
Bus travel, 30–31
**Butchart Gardens (Saanich
Peninsula), 10, 44, 75, 89**
**Butterfly Gardens (Victoria),
77, 89**
**Butterfly World and Gardens
(Parksville/Qualicum Beach),
131**
**Buttle Lake (Strathcona Provin-
cial Park), 153**

Cabbage Island Marine Park
(Saturna Island), 207
Cable Bay Trail (Nanaimo), 114
Calendar of events, 18–21
**Cameron Lake (Parksville/
Qualicum Beach), 129**
Campbell River, 158–164
accommodations, 161–163
fishing, 3, 160–161
restaurants, 163–164
transportation, 160
traveling to, 159
visitor information, 159
Camping facilities, 98
Campbell River, 162
Galiano Island, 199–200
kid-friendly, 162
Mayne Island, 205–206
Pacific Rim National Park, 140
Parksville & Qualicum Beach,
125
Salt Spring Island, 187
Tofino, 142
**Canadian Food Inspection
Agency, 13**
Canoeing, 73, 130. *See also*
Kayaking
**Cape Scott Provincial Park
(Port Hardy), 47, 178–179**
accommodations, 179–180
restaurants, 180
**Cape Scott Trail (Port Hardy),
3–4, 178, 179**

Car insurance, 22
Car rentals, 49, 51
Car travel, 31–35, 37, 51
**Case and Warren Winery (Port
Alberni), 130**
Casinos, 85
**Catala Charters (Port Hardy),
177**
**Cathedral Grove (Parksville/
Port Alberni), 4, 45, 129**
Cave tours, 124
**Cedar Hill Municipal Golf
Course (Victoria), 74**
Cellphones, 27
Central Vancouver Island
Gabriola Island, 118–120
map, 112–113
Nanaimo, 109–118
Pacific Rim National Park,
133–146
Parksville & Qualicum Beach,
120–128
Port Alberni & Bamfield,
128–133
Tofino, 133–146
Ucluelet, 133–146
**Centre of the Universe
(Victoria), 77**
**Channel Trail (Newcastle
Island), 115**
**Chapters Downtown (Victoria),
79**
Charles Baird (Victoria), 78
**Chemainus (Cowichan Valley),
102**
accommodations, 106
**Chemainus Theatre (Cowichan
Valley), 102**
**Cherry Point Vineyard
(Cowichan Valley), 103**
Children
accommodations, 56, 125–127,
161, 189–190, 196, 200,
201, 209–210, 221
camping facilities, 162
San Juan Islands suitability,
211
sights and attractions, 44,
70–71, 76–77, 89, 94, 103,
124, 149, 151, 166
traveling with, 12–13
China Beach, 95
Chinese New Year (Victoria), 18
**Chronicles of Crime (Victoria),
79**
Cinemas, 77
**Classic Car Museum (Courte-
nay), 151**
Classic Silverware (Victoria), 78

Clayoquot Sound, 10, 46, 135
  accommodations, 140–143
  restaurants, 144–146
Climate, 16, 49
Club and music scene, 85–86
Coastal Circle Route, 4
Coastal Island Fishing Adventures (Campbell River), 160
Cob houses, 204
Codfather Charters (Port Hardy), 177
Comox, 149–150
Comox Valley. See Courtenay & the Comox Valley
Comox Valley Art Gallery, 150
Concerts, 71, 82–83. See also Music, Musical events
Coombs (C. Vancouver Island), 128
Cordova Bay Golf Course (Victoria), 74
Cortes Island, 168
  accommodation, 169–170
Cortes Island Vacation Rentals, 170
Cottonwood Golf Course (Nanaimo), 114
Cougar Annie (Annie Rae-Arthur), 138
Courtenay & District Museum and Palaeontology Centre, 2
The Courtenay Museum & Paleontology Centre, 151–152
Courtenay & the Comox Valley, 147–156
  accommodations, 153–155
  attractions, 149–152
  public transportation, 149
  restaurants, 155–156
  traveling to, 148
  visitor information, 148
Cowichan Bay, 107
Cowichan Trading Company (Victoria), 79
Cowichan Valley, 44–45, 101–108
  attractions, 103
  visitor information, 103
Cowichan Wine & Culinary Festival, 20
Crafts, 226
  Victoria, 79–80
Craigdarroch Castle, 68–69
Credit cards, 15
Crow Valley Pottery & Gallery (Orcas Island), 226
Cruises. See also Boat tours
  Queen Charlotte Strait, 160
Crystal Cove Beach Resort (Tofino), 142

Cumberland (Courtenay/Comox Valley), 152
Cumberland Museum & Archives, 152
Currency and exchange rates, 14–15, 53
Customs, 13–14, 29
Cycling
  Galloping Goose Trail (Sooke), 44, 95
  Lopez Island (San Juan Islands), 230
  San Juan Island, 215
  in Victoria, 73

Dance clubs, 85–86
Dance performances, 83
Danceworks (Victoria), 83
Darcy's Wharf Street Pub (Victoria), 84
David Robinson Antiques (Victoria), 78
Deer Harbor Charters (San Juan Islands), 225–226
Deer Harbor Marina (San Juan Islands), 225–226
Deer Harbor (San Juan Islands), 41, 225–226
Della Falls (Strathcona Provincial Park), 153
Denman Hornby Canoes & Kayaks, 157
Denman Island. See Hornby & Denman Islands
Dentists, 38, 53
Dinner Bay (Mayne Island), 205
Dionisio Point Provincial Park (Galiano Island), 42
Disabilities, travelers with, 24
Discover Camping, 98, 125, 162, 187, 200
Discover the Past (Victoria), 76
Discovery Channel (Campbell River), 159
Discovery Expeditions (Telegraph Cove), 172–173
Diving, 166. See also Scuba diving
  Port Hardy, 177
  Zeballos, 171
Doctors, 38, 53
Dolphin Bay Bicycles (Orcas Island), 224
Dragon boat festival, 20
Driftwood Centre (Pender Islands), 194
Driver's licenses, 12
Drives, scenic, 4
Driving in Victoria, 51

Drugstores, 39, 53
Drumbeg Park (Gabriola Island), 119
Duncan, 44–45, 102
  accommodations, 105–106
Dunsmuir, Robert, 68–69
Duval Point Lodge (fishing camp), 177

Eagle Aerie Gallery (Tofino), 5, 134
Eaglecrest Golf Club (Qualicum Beach), 124
Eagle Feather Gallery (Victoria), 5, 79
East Point Regional Park (Saturna Island), 44, 208
East Sooke Coast Trail, 4, 96
East Sooke Regional Park, 96
Eastsound (San Juan Islands), 41
Edible British Columbia, 116
Edinburgh Tartan Shop (Victoria), 80
Electricity, 39
Elk Lake/Beaver Lake Park (Saanich Peninsula), 90
Emergencies, 39, 53, 54
English Camp (San Juan Islands), 41
Englishman River Falls Park (Parksville/Qualicum Beach), 123
E&N Trail (Nanaimo), 114
Entry requirements, 11–13
Essence of Life Spa (Victoria), 6, 81
Events calendar, 18–21
Expedia, 25

Fairs, 187
  agricultural, 20
Fairwinds (Parksville), 124
Faith Grant's Connoisseur Shop (Victoria), 78
Families with children
  accommodations, 56, 125–127, 161, 189–190, 196, 200, 201, 209–210, 221
  camping facilities, 162
  San Juan suitability for, 211
  Saturna Island, 209–210
  sights and attractions, 2, 24, 44, 70–71, 76–77, 89, 94, 103, 124, 149, 151, 166, 224
Family Cavern Tour (Qualicum Beach), 124

Fan Tan Alley (Victoria), 50
Fashion, 80
Female travelers, 24
Ferries, waltzing, 74
Ferry tours, 75, 149
Ferry travel, 30–35, 49, 53
    to Southern Vancouver Island, 88
Festival of Murals (Chemainus), 19
Festival of the Arts (Salt Spring Island), 19
The Filberg Lodge and Park (Comox), 149
Finnerty Gardens (Victoria), 72
First Nations, 101, 102, 103, 111, 174
    art galleries, 79
    culture and history, 5
    heritage, 169
    Quw'utsun Cultural Centre, 5, 45, 103
First Night (Victoria), 20–21
Fisherman's Wharf (Victoria), 44, 72
Fishing, 46
    Campbell River, 3, 46, 160–161
    Courtenay/Comox Valley, 152
    Galiano Island, 199
    Gold River, 165
    licences, 73
    Nootka Sound, 166
    Parksville/Qualicum Beach, 123
    Port Hardy, 177
    Tofino, 136
    Tyee Club, 158, 159
    Ucluelet, 136
    Victoria, 73–74
    Zeballos, 171
Fishing camps, 177
Flores Island (Tofino), 135
FOGO Folk Art Studio (Gabriola Island), 119
Forbidden Plateau (Strathcona Provincial Park), 153
Fort Rodd Hill & Fisgard Lighthouse (Victoria), 77, 94
Fran Willis Gallery (Victoria), 79
French Beach (Sooke Region), 97
Friday Harbor (San Juan Islands), 41
Frommers.com, 25

Gabriola Artworks, 119
Gabriola Island, 118–120
    accommodations, 119–120
    restaurants, 119–120
    transportation, 118–119

Galiano Bicycle, 199
Galiano Bluffs Park, 42, 199
Galiano Chamber of Commerce, 199
Galiano Island, 42–43
    accommodations, 200–202
    attractions, 199
    restaurants, 202–203
    transportation, 199
    traveling to, 198
    visitor information, 199
Galiano Island Kayaking, 199
Galiano Mopeds, 199
Galiano Water Taxi, 199
Galloping Goose Trail (Victoria-Sooke), 4, 44, 73, 95
Ganges (Salt Spring Island), 186–187
Gardens
    Butchart Gardens, 10, 44, 75, 89
    Cape Scott Provincial Park, 178–179
    Comox, 149
    Mayne Island, 205
    Parksville & Qualicum Beach, 122
    Port Alberni, 130
    Tofino, 134
    Victoria, 72–73
The Gardens at Government House (Victoria), 72
Gasoline, 39
Gay and Lesbian travelers, 24
    nightlife, 86
Georgina Point (Mayne Island), 205
The Glass Menagerie (Victoria), 78
Glenterra Vineyards (Cowichan Valley), 104
Go Galiano Island Shuttle, 199
Gold Mine Trail (Ucluelet), 136–137
Gold River
    accommodations, 165
    attractions, 165
    restaurants, 165
    traveling to, 164–165
    visitor information, 165
Goldstream Provincial Park (Victoria), 5, 18, 44, 96–97
Golf courses, 3, 46, 74, 114, 123, 136, 150–151, 153–154
Gray Line of Victoria, 75
The Great Canadian Adventure Company (Port Alberni/Bamfield), 132
The Great Canadian Beer Festival (Victoria), 20

Great Canadian Casino (Victoria), 85
Great Pacific Adventures (Victoria), 73
Green Point (Long Beach), 140
Greyhound Canada, 102
The Grotto Spa (Parksville), 6
Gulf Islands
    best of, 2–9
    in brief, 10–11
    calendar of events, 18–21
    car travel on, 37
    fast facts, 38–40
    Galiano Island, 198–203
    map, 43, 184–185
    Mayne Island, 203–207
    one-week getaway, 42–44
    Pender Islands, 193–198
    Salt Spring Island, 183–193
    Saturna Island, 207–210
    traveling to, 34–35, 182–183
    visitor information, 11, 183
Gulf Islands Brewery (Salt Spring Island), 188
Gulf Islands National Park Reserve, 194

Haig-Brown, Roderick, 46, 161–162
Half Moon Bay (Long Beach), 139
Harbour Air Seaplanes (Victoria), 76
Harbour Canoe Club (Victoria), 84
Harbour Festival (Victoria), 19
Harbour Quay (Port Alberni), 129, 130
Harbour Seaplane Islands Extravaganza, 75
Hardy Bay Boat Rentals (Port Hardy), 177
Hatley Park & Museum (Victoria), 72
Health concerns, 22–23
Helliwell Bay Provincial Park, 157
Heritage Tours and Daimler Limousine Service, 76
Hermann's Jazz Club (Victoria), 85
Hertz, 37
Hiking trails, 3–4
    Cable Bay, 114
    Cape Scott, 3–4, 47, 177, 179
    Channel Trail, 115
    E&N, 114
    extreme, 46–47

Hiking trails *(cont.)*
  Galloping Goose, 4, 44, 73, 95
  Gold River, 165
  Irvine, 90
  Juan de Fuca, 4
  Mallard Lake, 115
  Mayne Island, 205
  Merriman, 90
  Mount Washington Alpine
    Resort, 152
  Nootka Trail, 167
  Norn, 90
  Orcas Island, 225
  Parksville & Qualicum Beach,
    123
  Parkway, 114
  Peninsula, 95
  Port Hardy, 178
  San Juan Islands, 217, 218
  Saturna Island, 207, 209
  Shoreline Trail, 115
  Ucluelet, 136–137
  West Coast Trail, 130, 132,
    138–139
  Zeballos, 171
Hills Native Art (Victoria), 79
Holberg (N. Vancouver Island),
  178–179
Holidays, 16–18
HomeLink International, 36
Home of the Mars Water
  Bombers (Port Alberni), 130
Hornby & Denman Island
  accommodation, 157–158
  bicycling, 157
  provincial parks, 157
  restaurants, 157–158
  traveling to, 157
  visitor information, 157
Horne Lake Caves Provincial
  Park (Qualicum Beach), 2, 46,
  124
Horne Lake Caves (Qualicum
  Beach), 46
Horseback riding, 224
Hospitals, 39, 53
Hotel de Haro (San Juan
  Island), 218
Hotels. *See also* Accommoda-
  tions Index
  best, 6–7
Hotlines, 54
Hot Springs Cove (Tofino), 135
House-swapping, 36
Hughes Clothing (Victoria), 80
Hugo's Brewhouse (Victoria),
  84
Hush (Victoria), 86

I CA Folkfest (Victoria), 19
Iceberg Point (San Juan
  Islands), 4, 41, 232
IMAX theatre, 77
Immigration, 29
Inside Passage, 10, 171
Insurance, 21–22
The International Gay and
  Lesbian Travel Association
  (IGLTA), 24
International Sandcastle
  Competition, 121
Internet access, 27, 39, 54
Intrepid Theatre Company
  (Victoria), 83
Irvine Trail (Saanich Peninsula),
  90
Island Bicycles (San Juan), 215
Island Camping (Saanich Penin-
  sula), 90
Island Gourmet Safaris (Salt
  Spring Island), 188
Island Stage Left (San Juan
  Island), 219
Itineraries, suggested, 41–47

J ade Tree (Victoria), 80
Jamie's (Tofino), 137
Jamie's Whaling Station (Tofino
  & Ucluelet), 137
Japanese Garden (Mayne
  Island), 205
Jay's Clayoquot Ventures
  (Tofino), 136
Jazz Fest International
  (Victoria), 19
Jedediah Marine Park
  (Parksville/Qualicum
  Beach), 123
Jewelry, 80–81
Johnstone Strait Whale Inter-
  pretive Centre (Telegraph
  Cove), 172
Jordan River (Sooke Region), 97
Journeywoman, 24
Juan de Fuca Trail, 44, 95
The Juan de Fuca Trail (Sooke-
  Port Renfrew), 4

K abuki Cab (Victoria), 44,
  75–76
Kayaking
  Bamfield, 132
  Broken Group Islands, 2, 130
  Clayoquot Sound, 137
  Denman Island, 157

  Galiano Island, 42–43, 199
  Gold River (N. Vancouver
    Island), 165
  Nanaimo, 116
  Orcas Island, 224
  Parksville/Qualicum Beach, 123
  Pender Islands, 43–44, 195
  Port Hardy, 178
  Port McNeill, 176
  San Juan Islands, 216
  Saturna Island, 207, 208
  Telegraph Cove, 172
  Victoria, 73
  Zeballos, 171
Kayak Pender Island, 194
Kenmore Air Seaplane (San
  Juan Islands), 212
The Kids' Guide to Victoria, 77
Kingfisher Oceanside Resort &
  Spa (Courtenay), 150
The Kingfisher Oceanside Spa
  (Courtenay), 6
King Pacific Lodge (fishing
  camp), 177
Kitty Coleman Woodland
  Gardens (Comox), 149
Kwagiulth Museum and
  Cultural Centre (Quadra
  Island), 168
Kyoquot Sound, 165–167

L ady Rose Marine Services
  (Port Alberni), 130
Ladysmith, 106–107
Laidlaw Coach Lines, 102
Lance's Sportfishing Adven-
  tures (Tofino), 136
Langham Court Theatre
  (Victoria), 84
Last Minute Golf Hotline
  (Victoria), 74
Latin Caribbean Festival
  (Victoria), 19
Legends (Victoria), 85
The Library (Lopez Island), 230
Lighthouses, 43, 77, 94, 136,
  208, 219
Lime Kiln Lighthouse (San Juan
  Island), 219
Lime Kiln Point State Park (San
  Juan Island), 219–220
  whale-watching, 3
Liquor laws, 38–39
Little Hustan Caves (Zeballos),
  171
Little Qualicum Cheeseworks
  (Parksville/Qualicum Beach),
  122

The Little Red Schoolhouse
(San Juan Islands), 229
Live to Surf (Tofino), 137
Long Beach (Pacific Rim
National Park), 22, 45, 138,
139
Lopez Bicycle Works & Kayaks
(San Juan Islands), 230
Lopez Community Land Trust,
231
Lopez Historical Museum (San
Juan Islands), 230
Lopez Island Chamber of
Commerce, 230
Lopez Island (San Juan Islands),
41
   accommodations, 231–232
   beaches, 229–230
   restaurants, 232–233
   transportation, 230
   traveling to, 230
   visitor information, 230
Lopez Island Vineyards (San
Juan Islands), 231
Lost-luggage insurance, 21–22
The Lucky Bar (Victoria), 85
Luge run, 152
Lyall Harbour (Saturna Island),
208

Mackay Whale Watching
(Port McNeill), 174
The Madrona del Mar Spa
(Galiano Island), 6
Magic Air Tours (Orcas Island),
224
Majestic Ocean Kayaking
(Ucluelet), 137
Malahat (S. Vancouver Island),
105
Malaspina Galleries (Gabriola
Island), 119
Mallard Lake Trail (Nanaimo),
115
Marine Adventure Centre (San
Juan Island), 219
Marine Drive bike path
(Victoria), 73
Maritime Discovery Centre
(Port Alberni), 129
Maritime Museum of British
Columbia (Victoria), 69–70
Markets, 20, 81, 128, 186, 194,
204, 224
Market Square (Victoria), 81
Mars Water Bombers (Port
Alberni), 130
The Mausoleum (San Juan
Island), 219

Maya's Whale Watch Charters
(San Juan Island), 216
Mayne Island, 43
   accommodations, 205–206
   attractions, 204
   restaurants, 206–207
   transportation, 204
   traveling to, 203
   visitor information, 203
Mayne Island Community
Chamber of Commerce, 203
Mayne Island Museum, 43, 204
Mayne Kayaks & Canoes, 204
McLean Mill National Historic
Site (Port Alberni), 131
McPherson Playhouse
(Victoria), 83
Meares Island (Tofino), 135
Medical insurance, 21
Medical requirements, 12
Medicine Beach (Pender
Islands), 195
Merridale Ciderworks
(Cowichan Valley), 104
Merriman Trail (Saanich Penin-
sula), 90
Microbreweries, 20, 84
M.I.D.A.S. Taxis (Mayne Island),
204
Milner Gardens & Woodland
(Parksville/Qualicum Beach),
122
Mineral World & Scratch Patch
(Victoria), 77
Miners Bay (Gulf Islands), 43
Miniature World, 24
Miniature World (Victoria), 44,
70, 77
Miracle Beach Provincial Park
(Campbell River), 162
Money matters, 14–15
Montague Harbour (Galiano
Island), 42–43
Montague Harbour Marina
(Galiano Island), 199
Montague Harbour Provincial
Marine Park (Galiano Island),
199–200
Montague Provincial Park
(Galiano Island), 42
Moonstruck Organic Cheese
(Salt Spring Island), 188
Mopeds
   Orcas Island, 224
   San Juan Island, 215
Moran State Park (San Juan
Islands), 41, 225
Morning Bay Vineyards (Pender
Island), 43–44, 194

Morningstar Golf Club
(Parksville/Qualicum Beach),
124
Mothership Adventures (Port
McNeill), 176
Mountaineering, 46
Mt. Arrowsmith Regional Park
(Parksville/Qualicum Beach),
123
Mount Constitution (Orcas
Island), 225
Mount Douglas Park (Saanich
Peninsula), 90
Mount Finlayson (San Juan
Island), 217
Mount Maxwell Provincial Park
(Salt Spring Island), 183
Mount Parke Park (Mayne
Island), 204
Mount Warburton Pike
(Saturna Island), 209
Mount Washington Alpine
Resort (Courtenay/Comox
Valley), 152
Mount Young (San Juan Island),
218
Munro's (Victoria), 79
Music
   jazz, rhythm and blues, 85–86
Musical events, 82–83, 121
   classical, 20, 83
   jazz, 19
   Latin Caribbean, 19
   multicultural, 19
   opera, 83
M&W Auto (San Juan), 215
Mystic Beach (Sooke Region), 97

Nanaimo, 109–118
   attractions, 110–111
      Newcastle Island, 114–115
      Protection Island, 114
   transportation, 110
   visitor information, 110
Nanaimo Bar, 118
The Nanaimo Bastion, 111
Nanaimo District Museum, 111
Nanaimo Golf Club, 114
Nanaimo Marine Festival, 19
Neighborhoods in Victoria,
50–51
Newcastle Island (Nanaimo),
114–115
Newcastle Island Provincial
Park (Nanaimo), 114–115
Newspapers, 39, 54
New Year celebrations
   Chinese, 18
   First Night, 20–21

Nightlife, 82–86
    club and music scene, 85–86
    gay and lesbian, 86
    performing arts, 82–84
Nimmo Bay Resort (fishing
    camp), 177
Nootka Charters (Gold River),
    165
Nootka Sound, 165–167
    accommodation, 166–167
    restaurants, 166–167
    traveling to, 166
    visitor information, 166
Nootka Sound Charters, 166
Nootka Trail, 166
Nordic trails, 152
Norn Trail (Saanich Peninsula),
    90
Northern Vancouver Island
    Campbell River, 158–167
    Cape Scott Provincial Park,
        176–180
    Cortes Island, 167–170
    Courtenay & the Comox
        Valley, 147–156
    Gold River, 158–167
    Hornby & Denman Islands,
        156–158
    Kyoquot Sound, 158–167
    map, 150–151
    Nootka Sound, 158–167
    Port Hardy, 176–180
    Quadra Island, 167–170
    route to Port Hardy, 170–176
    Tahsis Sound, 158–167
North Island Daytrippers (Port
    Hardy), 177
North Island Dive & Charters,
    177
Not Just Pretty (Victoria), 80

Oaks Vineyard (Salt Spring
    Island), 188
Ocean Explorers Diving
    (Nanaimo), 112
Ocean River Sports (Victoria),
    73
Ocean's Edge (Ucluelet), 136
Oceanside. See Parksville &
    Qualicum Beach
Odyssey Kayaking (Port Hardy),
    178
Old Cemetery Society of
    Victoria, 76
Old Country Market (Port
    Alberni), 128
Old School House
    (Parksville/Qualicum Beach),
    122

Old Vogue Shop (Victoria), 78
Olga Artworks (Orcas Island),
    226
Olga (San Juan Islands), 41
Olympic View Golf Club
    (Victoria), 74
Once in a Blue Moon Farm
    (Orcas Island), 224
Opera, 83
Orbitz, 25
Orcas Island Chamber of
    Commerce, 224
The Orcas Island Historical
    Museum, 225
Orcas Island Pottery (San Juan
    Islands), 226
Orcas Island (San Juan Islands),
    41
    accommodations, 226–228
    Eastsound Village, 224–225
    Moran State Park, 225
    outdoor activities, 224–225
    transportation, 224
    traveling to, 223
    visitor information, 224
Orcas Moped & Car Rental, 224
Orcas Mopeds, 224
Orca Spirit Adventures
    (Victoria), 75
Osprey Tours (Orcas Island),
    224
Otter Bay Marina (Pender
    Islands), 194
Outdoor activities, 73–75,
    111–114, 177–178
Outdoor Rappel
    (Parksville/Qualicum Beach),
    125
Outlooks for Men (Victoria), 80

Pacific Opera Victoria, 83
Pacific Rainforest Adventure
    Tours (Parksville/Qualicum
    Beach), 122
Pacific Rim National Park, 3,
    10, 18, 22, 45, 95, 138–140
Pacific Rim Whale Festival
    (Tofino/Ucluelet), 18, 136
Pacific Surf School (Tofino), 137
Pacific Undersea Gardens
    (Victoria), 44, 70, 77
Painter's Lodge Holiday & Fish-
    ing Resort (Campbell River),
    161
Paradise Meadows Loop Trail,
    152
Parking
    in Victoria, 51

Parksville, 46
    Horne Lake Caves Provincial
        Park, 2
    Rathtrevor Beach Provincial
        Park, 2
Parksville & Qualicum Beach,
    120–128
    accommodations, 125-127
    attractions, 122
    camping, 125
    restaurants, 126, 127-128
    traveling to, 121
    parks, 122-125
    visitor information, 121
Parkway Trail (Nanaimo), 114
Parliament Buildings (Victoria),
    70
Passports, 11, 12
The Patch (Victoria), 80
Patos Island Lighthouse (Sat-
    urna Island), 208
Pearl Spa (Victoria), 58
Pelindaba Lavender Farm (San
    Juan Islands), 41, 220
Pender Island Chamber of
    Commerce, 194
Pender Islands, 43–44
    accommodation, 196–197
    North Pender, 194–195
    restaurants, 197–198
    South Pender, 195
    transportation, 194
    traveling to, 193–194
    visitor information, 194
Pender Island Taxi & Tours, 194
Peninsula Trail (Sooke Region),
    95
Penny Farthing Pub (Victoria), 84
Performing arts, 82–84
    dance, 83
    theatre, 82–84, 102
Pets, traveling with, 13
Pheasant Glen Golf Resort
    (Qualicum Beach), 124
Pioneer Waterfront (Nanaimo),
    110
Planning trip online, 25–26
Poets Cove Marina (Pender
    Islands), 195
Poets Cove (Pender Islands), 44
Police, 54
Port Alberni & Bamfield,
    128–133
    accommodations,131-133
    attractions, 129-131
    restaurants, 131-132
    traveling to, 128-129
    visitor information, 129
Port Browning Marina (Pender
    Islands), 195

Port Hardy, 10
outdoor activities, 177–178
traveling to, 170–171
Port Hardy Museum, 176
Port Hardy Visitor Information
Centre, 171, 176
Port McNeill
accommodation, 175
attractions, 174
restaurants, 175
Port McNeill Visitor Informa-
tion, 171
Port Renfrew, 98
Botanical Beach, 2
Port Renfrew Recreational
Retreat, 98
Post office, 40, 54
Potteries, 226
Potter's Place (Courtenay), 150
Prince of Whales (Victoria), 75
Prior Centennial Provincial Park
(Pender Islands), 195
Prism Lounge (Victoria), 86
Profish Adventures (Campbell
River), 160–161
Protection Island (Nanaimo),
114
Provincial Legislature (Victo-
ria), 44
Puget Sound Express, 214

Quadra Island
accommodation, 168–169
attractions, 168
traveling to, 167
visitor information, 167
Qualicum, 46
Qualicum Beach. See Parksville
& Qualicum Beach
Qualicum Beach Harvest of
Music, 121
Qualicum Beach Memorial, 124
Queen Charlotte Strait, 160
Quw'utsun' Cultural Centre
(Duncan), 5, 45, 103

Races
marathon, 20
sailing, 18–19
Radar Hill (Long Beach), 139
Radio, 40
Rainforest Kayak Adventures
(Tofino), 137
Rappeling, 46
Rathtrevor Beach Provincial
Park (Parksville), 2, 46,
122–123
Recollections (Victoria), 78

The Red Jacket (Victoria), 85
The Reef (Victoria), 84
Rental cars, surfing for, 26
Restaurants. See also Restau-
rants Index
best, 8–9
expensive, 62–63, 64
inexpensive, 63–64, 64–68
moderate, 63–64, 64–68
tipping, 40
Rippingdale's Fishing (Camp-
bell River), 161
Robinson's Outdoor Store
(Victoria), 74
Robson Bight Ecological
Reserve, 173
Robson Bight (Port McNeill), 5,
47
Roche Harbor (San Juan
Islands), 41
Roesland (Pender Islands), 195
Rollins Art Centre and Gardens
(Port Alberni), 130
Romanoff & Co. (Victoria), 78
Ronning Gardens (N. Vancouver
Island), 178–179
Royal British Columbia
Museum (Victoria), 2, 10, 44,
70–71, 77
Royal London Wax Museum
(Victoria), 71, 77
Royal Marine Cemetery (San
Juan Island), 218
Royal Roads University
(Victoria), 72
Royal Theatre (Victoria), 82
Royal Victorian Marathon, 20
Ruckle Provincial Park (Salt
Spring Island), 44, 187

Saanich Fall Fair, 20
Saanich Peninsula, 87–93
attractions, 88–90
Sacred Mountain Lavender
Farm (Salt Spring Island), 188
Safety, 22–23, 54
Sailing, 74
Sail Piraeus Adventures
(Victoria), 74
Salt Spring Cheese Company,
188
Salt Spring Island, 44
accommodations, 188–189
attractions, 186–187
restaurants, 191–193
transportation, 186
traveling to, 186
visitor information, 186
Salt Spring Island Dollars, 183

Salt Spring Island Fall Fair, 187
Salt Spring Marina, 187
Salt Spring Vineyards & Winery,
188
Sandcastle competition, 19–20,
121
Sandy Island Provincial Marine
Park, 157
San Josef Bay Trail (Port
Hardy), 178
San Juan Airlines, 212
San Juan Historical Museum,
216
San Juan Island
accommodations, 220–222
American Camp, 217
best of, 2–9
English Camp, 218
hiking, 217, 218
restaurants, 222–223
transportation, 215
traveling to, 215
visitor information, 215
San Juan Island Chamber of
Commerce, 215
San Juan Island Express, 214
San Juan Island National His-
torical Park, 215
San Juan Islands
in brief, 10–11
calendar of events, 18–21
car travel on, 37
fast facts, 38–40
itinerary, 41–42
Lopez Island, 229–233
map, 42, 213
Orcas Island, 223–229
San Juan Island, 215–223
traveling to, 35, 212
visitor information, 11, 214
San Juan Islands Visitor Information Services, 11, 214
San Juan Kayak Expeditions,
216
San Juan Taxi, 215
San Juan Transit, 215
San Juan Vineyards, 215
Sante Spa (Victoria), 6, 81
Sapphire Day Spa (Victoria), 81
Saturday Market (Pender
Islands), 194
Saturna Island, 44
accommodations, 209–210
attractions, 208–209
transportation, 208
traveling to, 208
visitor information, 208
Saturna Island Vineyards, 44,
207, 208, 209
Saturna Sea Kayaking, 208

Schooner Beach Trail (Long Beach), 137, 139
Scottish Dance Society, 83
Scuba diving, 111–112, 132
Seafun Safaris Whale Watching (Victoria), 75
Sea kayaking, 47
Sea Magnolia (Victoria), 81
Sea Orca Whale Watching (Port McNeill), 174
Sea-renity Spa, 100
Seatac International Airport, 48
Sea to Sky Expeditions, 138
Sea Wharf Kayaks (Victoria), 73
Second Beach, 97
Senior travelers, 25
Shakespearean Festival (Victoria), 83
Shark Reef Recreation Area (Lopez Island), 229
Shaw General Store (San Juan Islands), 229
Shaw Island Museum (San Juan Islands), 229
Shaw Island (San Juan Islands), 41, 229
Shearwater Adventures (Orcas Island), 224
She She Bags (Victoria), 80
Shi Studio (Victoria), 81
Shopping in Victoria, 78–79
Shoreline Trail (C. Vancouver Island), 115
Sidney Historical Museum (Saanich Peninsula), 89
Silva Bay Shipyards School (Gabriola Island), 119
Six Gill Adventures (Port Alberni), 130
Skiing, 152
Smoking, 40
Smoking Lily (Victoria), 80
Snow tubing park, 152
Soda Fountain & Pharmacy (Lopez Island), 230
Sointula (Malcolm Island), 171, 174, 175
Sointula Museum, 175
Sombrio Beach, 98
Sooke Potholes Provincial Park, 96
Sooke Region, 93–101
    accommodations, 98–100
    attractions, 94–95
    beaches, 96–98
    hiking trails, 95
    parks, 96–98
    restaurants, 100–101
    traveling to, 94
    visitor information, 94

Sooke Region Museum, 94–95
Sooke Region Museum Visitors Information Centre, 94
Sound Passage Adventures (Pender Islands), 194
South Beach Trail (Ucluelet), 137, 139
Southern Vancouver Island
    attractions, 88–90, 94–95
    Cowichan Valley, 101–108
    map, 92–93
    Saanich Peninsula, 87–93
    Sooke Region, 93–101
The Spa at Delta Victoria, 81
The Spa at Ocean Point, 6
Spas
    best, 5–6
    Courtenay & the Comox Valley, 154
    Galiano Island, 201
    Orcas Island, 226–227
    Parksville, 46, 126
    Pender Islands, 196
    Saanich Peninsula, 90
    Salt Spring Island, 190–191
    Sooke, 100
    Tofino, 143
    Victoria, 5, 6, 58, 59, 81
Spelunking, 46, 165, 171
Spelunking Adventure (Parksville/Qualicum Beach), 124
Spencer Spit State Park (San Juan Islands), 41, 229
Spider Lake Park (Parksville/ Qualicum Beach), 123
Spinnakers Brewpub (Victoria), 62, 84
Sporades Tours (Galiano Island), 199
St. Mary Magdalene Anglican Church (Mayne Island), 43, 204
Starfish Glass Works (Victoria), 79–80
Steamers (Victoria), 86
Sticky Wicket Pub (Victoria), 62
The Sticky Wicket (Victoria), 85
Storm watching, 136, 145
Strathcona Provincial Park (Courtenay & Comox Valley), 152–153
Stubbs Island Charters (Telegraph Cove), 172
Student travelers, 25
Studio Tour (Salt Spring Island), 186
Surfing, 22, 46, 97, 98, 137
Surf Sister (Tofino), 137

Susie's Mopeds (San Juan Island), 3, 215
Suze Lounge & Restaurant (Victoria), 85
Swans Brewpub (Victoria), 62, 85
Swiftsure Weekend (Victoria), 18–19
Symphony Splash (Victoria), 20, 83

Tahsis Sound, 165–167
Tahtsa Dive Charters (Nootka Sound), 166
Tall Ship Adventures (Victoria), 74
Tallyho Horse Drawn Tours (Victoria), 75–76
Taxis, 48, 51
    Lopez Island, 230
    water, 90, 183, 199
Tea. See Afternoon tea
Telegraph Cove, 47, 172–174
    accommodations, 173–174
    outdoor activities, 172–173
    restaurants, 174
Telegraph Cove Sea Kayaking, 172
Telephones, 40
Theatre, 82–84, 102, 219
Theatre Inconnu (Victoria), 83
Thomas Cook, 15
Thomson Park (Saturna Island), 207
Thunderbird Park (Victoria), 72–73
Tide Rip Tours (Telegraph Cove), 172
Time zone, 40
Tipping, 40
Tofino, 45
    accommodations, 140–143
    exploring, 134–135
    restaurants, 144–146
    side trips, 135
    traveling to, 133–134
    visitor information, 134
The Tofino Botanical Gardens, 134
Tofino Sea-Kayaking Company, 137
Toilets, 40
Top Bridge (Parksville/Qualicum Beach), 123
Totem poles, 45, 101, 102, 149, 174
Tourism Association of Vancouver Island, 11
Tourism British Columbia, 11

Tourism Victoria Visitor Information Centre, 49
Tours
    bus, 75
    cemetery, 76
    driving, 4, 44–46
    guided cave, 124
    organized, 75–76
    self-guided cave, 124
    self-guided walking, 102
    specialty, 75–76
    walking, guided, 76
    wildlife, 199
Train travel, 30, 37–38, 49, 102–103
Transportation, 51–53
Traveler's Aid International, 39
Traveler's checks, 15, 53
Travel insurance, 21
Travelocity, 25
Travel with Taste (Saanich Peninsula, Cowichan Valley), 104
Tribune Bay Provincial Park (Hornby Island), 157
Trip-cancellation insurance, 21
Trophy Charters (San Juan Island), 216
Trumpeter Swan Festival (Comox Valley), 18
Tyee Club (Campbell River), 158, 159

Uchuck III, 3, 166
Ucluelet, 46, 135–138
    accommodations, 143–144
    fishing, 136
    golfing, 136
    restaurants, 145–146
U'Mista Cultural Centre (Alert Bay), 5, 174
Uno Festival of Solo Performance (Victoria), 83
Upana Caves (Gold River), 165

Vancouver International Airport, 48
Vancouver Island
    adventure itinerary, 46–47
    best of, 2–9
    calendar of events, 18–21
    car travel on, 37
    fast facts, 38–40
    map, 17, 32–33, 45, 47
    traveling to, 34
    visitor information, 11
Vanity Fair Antique Mall (Victoria), 79

Vargas Island (Tofino), 135
Venturi-Schulze Vineyards (Cowichan Valley), 104
Vesuvius (Salt Spring Island), 187–188
VIA Rail, 49
Victoria
    accommodation, 54–62
    attractions, 68–71
    Butchart Gardens, 44
    Chinatown, 50
    city layout, 49–50
    city tour, 75
    climate, 49
    Craigdarroch Castle, 44
    Downtown, 50
    fast facts, 53–54
    Inner Harbour, 44, 50, 54–58
    James Bay, 51
    map of downtown, 52
    neighborhoods, 50–51
    Oak Bay, 51
    Old Town, 50
    outdoor activities, 73–75
    parks and gardens, 72–73
    Provincial Legislature, 44
    public transportation, 51–53
    restaurants, 62–68
    Ross Bay, 51
    tours, 75–76
    traveling to, 48–49
Victoria Bobby Walking Tours, 76
Victoria Bug Zoo, 2, 10, 24, 71, 77
Victoria Clipper, 214
Victoria Dragon Boat Festival, 20
Victoria Fringe Festival, 83
Victoria Harbour, 74
Victoria Harbour Ferry, 53, 75
Victoria International Airport, 48
Victoria Operatic Society, 83
Victoria Symphony Orchestra, 20, 71, 83
Victoria Theatre Guild, 84
Vigneti Zanatta (Cowichan Valley), 104, 108
Vinoteca (Cowichan Valley), 104–105
Violette Veldor (Victoria), 81
Visa (credit card), 15
Visa (travel document), 12, 29
Visa Waiver Program, 12
Visitor information, 11

Walkabout Historical Tours (Victoria), 76
Walking Horse Country Farm (Orcas Island), 224

Walking tours
    self-guided, 102
Warburton Pike (Saturna Island), 209
Washington State Ferries, 212
Water taxis, 90, 183, 199
Weather, 40
Websites
    bed and breakfast, 54
    women travelers, 24
West Coast Trail (Pacific Rim National Park), 3, 10, 95, 130, 132, 138–139
Westcott Bay Reserve (San Juan Island), 219
Westcott Bay Sculpture Park (San Juan Islands), 41, 219
The West End Gallery (Victoria), 79
Western Prince Cruises (San Juan Island), 216
The Whale Museum (San Juan Island), 216
Whale-watching, 3
    Clayoquot Sound, 46
    Pacific Rim National Park, 18
    Port McNeill, 5, 172, 173, 174
    San Juan Islands, 3, 216, 219
    Sooke Region, 98
    Tofino/Ucluelet, 136, 137
    Victoria, 75
White Hart Pub (Gabriola Island), 119
The Wickaninnish Beach & Interpretive Centre (Long Beach), 139
Wildlife Cycles (Orcas Island), 224
Wildlife viewing, 5, 18, 114, 132, 137, 172, 195. See also Birding, Whale-watching
    Clayoquot Sound, 46
    Galiano Island, 199
    Gold River, 165
    Lopez Island, 229
    Mayne Island, 205
Wild Pacific Trail (Ucluelet), 3, 46, 136
WildPlay at the Bungy Zone (Nanaimo), 2, 113
Wild West Coast
    itinerary, 44–46
    map, 45
Willowbrae Trail (Long Beach), 139
Willow Stream Spa (Victoria), 5, 81
Winchester Galleries (Victoria), 79
Windsurfing, 97

Wineries, 43–44, 45, 103–105, 130, 188, 194, 207, 215, 231

Winter Cove Marine Park (Saturna Island), 207

Winter sports, 152

W&J Wilson (Victoria), 80

World Parrot Refuge (Port Alberni), 128

Young Hill Trail (San Juan Island), 218

Youth hostels, 61

Zeballos, 171
  accommodation, 172
  restaurants, 172

Zeballos Village Museum/ Visitors Information Centre, 171

ACCOMMODATIONS

Abigail's Hotel (Victoria), 7, 58

Admiral Inn (Victoria), 60

The Aerie (Malahat), 105, 107

The Aerie (Victoria), 8

Alert Bay Lodge, 175

Anchor Inn & Suites (Campbell River), 161

Anchor Point B&B (Salt Spring Island), 188–189

Andersen House B&B (Victoria), 56

Anne's Oceanfront Hideway B&B (Salt Spring Island), 189

Bahari Vacation Apartments (Qualicum Beach), 125

Beach Acres Resort (Parksville), 125–126

Beaconsfield Inn (Victoria), 58

The Bedford Regency (Victoria), 60–61

Bellhouse Inn (Galiano Island), 200

Best Western Barclay Hotel (Port Alberni), 131

Best Western Dorchester Hotel (Nanaimo), 115

Best Western Westerley Hotel (Courtenay), 153

Bird Song Cottage/Castlebury Cottage (Chemainus), 106

Blue Vista Resort (Mayne Island), 205

Bodega Ridge Resort (Galiano Island), 200

Breezy Bay B&B (Saturna Island), 209

Brentwood Bay Lodge & Spa (Victoria), 6, 90

Cable Cove Inn (Tofino), 140

Canadian Princess Resort (Ucluelet), 143

Cascade Harbor Inn (Orcas Island), 227

Clayoquot Wilderness Resort, 6, 140–141

Cliff Pagoda (Galiano Island), 200–201

Cloud 9 (Salt Spring Island), 189

Coast Bastion Inn (Nanaimo), 115–116

Coast Discovery Inn & Marina (Campbell River), 161

Coopers Cover (Sooke), 8, 98

Crown Isle Resort (Courtenay), 3, 150, 154

Cusheon Lake Resort (Salt Spring Island), 189–190

Dalewood Inn (Port McNeill), 175

Deer Harbor Inn (Orcas Island), 225

Delta Victoria Ocean Pointe Resort and Spa, 54–55

Doe Bay Resort & Retreat Center (Orcas Island), 227–228

Driftwood Village Resort (Galiano Island), 232

Edenwild Country Inn (Lopez Island), 231

Fairburn Farm Culinary Retreat & Guesthouse (Duncan), 8, 105–106

The Fairmont Empress (Victoria), 6, 55, 67

Friday Harbor House (San Juan Island), 7, 220

Friday Harbor Inn (San Juan Island), 220

Friday's Historic Inn (San Juan Island), 220–221

Galiano Inn & Spa, 201

The Gatsby Manor (Victoria), 56

Glen Lyon Inn & Suites (Port Hardy), 179

Grand Hotel Nanaimo, 116

Haida-Way Motor Inn (Port McNeill), 175

Haig-Brown House (Campbell River), 161–162

Hartmann House B&B (Sooke), 98–99

Hastings House (Salt Spring Island), 7, 190

Haterleigh Heritage Inn (Victoria), 57

Hemlock House Lodge (Swanson Island), 175

Heron's Landing (Campbell River), 162

Hidden Cove Lodge (Telegraph Cove), 173

Hollyhock (Cortes Island), 169

Hornby Island Resort, 158

Hospitality Inn (Port Alberni), 132–133

Hotel Grand Pacific (Victoria), 55–56

Humboldt House B&B (Victoria), 59

Hummingbird Lodge B & B (Gabriola Island), 119–120

Inn at Swifts Bay (Lopez Island), 7, 231–232

Inn at Tough City (Tofino), 141

Inn on Pender Island, 196

Island Time B&B (Galiano Island), 201

James Bay Inn (Victoria), 57

Kingfisher Oceanside Resort & Spa (Courtenay), 154

Laurel Point (Victoria), 57

Long Beach Lodge Resort (Tofino), 141

MacKaye Harbor Inn (Lopez Island), 232

The Magnolia Hotel & Spa (Victoria), 59

Maquinna Resort (Tahsis), 166

Markham House B&B and Honeysuckle Cottage (Sooke), 99

Mason's Lodge (Zeballos), 172

Mayne Island Eco Camping, 205–206

Middle Beach Lodge (Tofino), 141–142

Miraloma on the Cove (Saanich Peninsula), 91

Oceanfront Grant Resport & Marina (Cowichan Bay), 107

Ocean Island Backpackers Inn (Victoria), 61

Oceanside Inn (Pender Island), 196

Oceanview B&B (Port Hardy), 179

Oceanwood Country Inn (Mayne Island), 7, 206

The Old Farmhouse B&B (Salt Spring Island), 190

Orcas Hotel, 228

Pacific Sands Resort (Tofino), 142

Pacific Shores Resprt and Spa (Parksville/Qualicum Beach), 126

Painted Turtle Guesthouse (Nanaimo), 116

Painter's Lodge Holiday & Fishing Resort (Campbell River), 7, 162

Pioneer Inn Riverside RV Park (Port Hardy), 179

Poets Cove Resort & Spa (Pender Island), 7, 196

Point No Point Resort (Sooke), 99

Prancing Horse (Malahat), 105

Prior House B&B Inn (Victoria), 59

Quarterdeck Inn & Marina Resort (Port Hardy), 180

Ramada Huntingdon Hotel & Suites (Victoria), 56

Ridgeview Motor Inn (Gold River), 165

Roche Harbor Resort (San Juan Island), 2221

Rosario Resort & Spa (Orcas Island), 6, 226–227

The Royal Scot (Victoria), 57–58

Sage Cottage (Mayne Island), 206

Sahhali Serenity Ocenfront B&B Inn (Pender Islands), 7, 196–197

Salt Spring Island Village Resort, 193

Salt Springs Spa Resort, 190–191

Saturna Lodge & Restaurant, 209

Shangri-La Oceanfront B&B, 197

Sky Valley Inn (Salt Spring Island), 191

A Snug Harbour Inn (Ucluelet), 143–144

Sonora Resort, 6–7, 163

Sooke Harbour House, 99–100

Sooke Harbour House (Vancouver Island), 8

Spinnaker's Guest House (Victoria), 61

Spring Bay Inn (Orcas Island), 227

Strathcona Park Lodge & Outdoor Education Centre (Campbell River), 154–155

Sund's Lodge (Malcolm Island), 175

Surf Lodge (Gabriola Island), 120

Swans Hotel (Victoria), 61–62

Tahsis Motel, 167

T'ai Li Lodge (Cortes Island), 169

Tauca Lea Coast Resort (Ucluelet), 144

Telegraph Cove Marina & RV Park, 173

Telegraph Cove Resorts, 173

Tigh-Na-Mara Seaside Resort & Spa (Parksville), 126–127

Tsa-Kwa-Luten Lodge & RV Park (Cortes Island), 168

Turtleback Farm Inn (Orcas Island), 8, 228

Victoria Marriott Inner Harbour, 60

The Westcoast Trail Motel (Port Renfrew), 98

Westin at Bear Mountain (Victoria), 60

Wickaninnish Inn (Tofino), 6, 142

Wickaninnish On the Beach (Tofino), 142

Wildwood Manor B&B (San Juan Island), 7–8, 221–222

Wisteria Guest House (Salt Spring Island), 191

Woodstone Country Inn (Galiano Island), 7, 202

Yellow Point Lodge (Ladysmith), 106–107

RESTAURANTS

Acme Food Company (Nanaimo), 117

The Aerie (Malahat), 46, 107

Atlas Cafe (Courtenay), 155

Atrevida! (Galiano Island), 202

Auntie Pesto's Café (Salt Spring Island), 191–192

Aurora (Pender Island), 197

Azuma Sushi (Victoria), 64–65

Baan Thai (Campbell River), 163

Baan Thai (Victoria), 65

Bamfield Inn, 132

Barb's Place (Victoria), 63

The Bay Cafe (Lopez Island), 232–233

Beach House Cafe (Qualicum Beach), 127

Black Fin Pub (Courtenay), 155

Black Olive (Victoria), 65

The Blethering Place Tearoom (Victoria), 67

Blue Crab Bar & Grill (Victoria), 8, 62–63

Blue Fox Café (Victoria), 65

The Blue Heron Restaurant (Zellabos), 172

Blue Poppy Restaurant (Butchart Gardens, Saanich Peninsula), 89

Boat Basin Lounge and Restaurant (Ucluelet), 145–146

Butchart Gardens Dining Room (Saanich Peninsula), 67, 89

Cafe Brio (Victoria), 64

Café Mexico (Victoria), 65

Camille's (Victoria), 65–66

Cedar Restaurant (Parksville), 126

Crow & Gate (Cowichan Bay), 107

Da Tandoor (Victoria), 66

Deep Cove Chalet (Saanich Peninsula), 8, 91

Dinghy Dock (Protection Island), 114

DOCK 503 Waterfront Café (Sidney), 91

Duck Soup Inn (San Juan Island), 9, 222

The Fairmont Empress (Victoria), 62, 67

Fire & Water Fish and Chop House (Victoria), 60

Fisherman's Wharf (Victoria), 44

Floyd's Diner (Victoria), 66

The Genoa Bay Café (Duncan), 108

Glen Lyon Restaurant (Port Hardy), 180

Harbor House Restaurant (San Juan Island), 222

Harbour Grill (Campbell River), 164

Harvest Restaurant (Port Alberni), 132

Hastings House (Salt Spring Island), 192

Herald Street Caffe (Victoria), 66

Hope Bay Café (Pender Island), 197–198

House Piccolo (Ganges), 9, 192

Hummingbird Pub (Galiano Island), 202

Il Terrazzo Ristorante (Victoria), 64

The Islander (Pender Island), 198

IV's Quarterdeck Pub (Port Hardy), 180

The James Bay Tea Room & Restaurant (Victoria), 63

Kalvas (Parksville), 127

Killer Whale Café (Telegraph Cove), 174

Kingfisher Oceanside Restaurant (Courtenay), 155

La Berengerie (Galiano Island), 202

The Landing West Coast Grill (Parksville/Qualicum Beach), 126, 127

The Latch (Sidney), 91–92

Legends (Campbell River), 162

Lighthouse Pub & Restaurant (Port Renfrew), 98

Love Dog Café (Lopez Island), 233

Lure Seafood Restaurant and Bar (Victoria), 55

Mac and Mortiz (truck) (Galiano Island), 203

Mahle House (Nanaimo), 117

The Mark (Victoria), 63

Masthead Restaurant (Cowichan Bay), 107–108

Matterson House (Ucluelet), 146

Mayne Inn, 206

McMillin's Restaurant (San Juan Island), 221

Memories at the Inn (Pender Island), 196

Milanos (Nanaimo), 117

Moby's Marine Pub (Salt Spring Island), 192

Mom's Cafe (Sooke), 100

Monte Christo on the River (Courtenay), 155–156

Murchie's Tea and Coffee (Victoria), 67

My Thai Café (Victoria), 66

Oceanwood Country Inn (Mayne Island), 206–207

Old Customs House Restaurant & Inn (Alert Bay), 175

Old Saltery Pub (Telegraph Cove), 174

Pagliacci's (Victoria), 8, 67–68

Pastimes Sports Bar and Grill (Port Alberni), 131

Pelindaba Downtown (San Juan Island), 223

Pescatore's Fish House (Victoria), 63

Point Ellice House (Victoria), 62, 67

Pointe Restaurant (Tofino), 9, 143, 144

Polly's Pub (Port Alberni), 132

Raven Street Market Café (Salt Spring Island), 192–193

rebar Modern Food (Victoria), 68

Restaurant Matisse (Victoria), 64

Ridge Neighbourhood Pub/Restaurant (Gold River), 165

Riptide Marine Pub & Grill (Campbell River), 164

Rock Cod Café (Cowichan Bay), 108

Santiago's (Victoria), 63–64

Sanuk Restaurant (Victoria), 59

Saturna Lodge & Restaurant, 209–210

Scarlet Ibis Pub (Holberg), 178

The Schooner on Second (Tofino), 144

Shady Restaurant Waterfron Pub & Restaurant (Qualicum Beach), 127–128

Shelter Restaurant (Tofino), 9, 144–145

Silva Bay Bar & Grill (Gabriola Island), 120

Silverado Steak House (Courtenay), 156

Six Mile Pub (Sooke), 100

SoBo Restaurant (Tofino), 134, 145

Sooke Harbour House, 100–101

Spar Tree Pub (Tahsis), 167

Spring Water Lodge (Mayne Island), 207

Stamps Cafe (Port Alberni), 131

Steps Wine Bar (San Juan Island), 223

Stonehouse Pub (Sidney), 92–93

The Sushi Bar at the Inn at Tough City (Tofino), 8

Sushi Bar at Tough City (Tofino), 145

Tania's Tapas Bar & Grill (Nanaimo), 118

Thatch Neighbourhood Pub (Hornby Island), 157

Tomato Tomato (Courtenay), 156

Toscanos Trattoria (Comox), 156

Tree House Cafe (Salt Spring Island), 193

Triskell Restaurant & Creperie (Parskville/Qualicum Beach), 128

Vinoteca (Duncan), 108

Wah Lai Yuen (Victoria), 66

Wesley Street Cafe (Nanaimo), 118

White Heather Tea Room (Victoria), 67

The Wickaninnish Restaurant (Ucluelet), 146

Wisteria Restaurant (Galiano Island), 203

FROMMER'S® COMPLETE TRAVEL GUIDES

Alaska
Amalfi Coast
American Southwest
Amsterdam
Argentina & Chile
Arizona
Atlanta
Australia
Austria
Bahamas
Barcelona
Beijing
Belgium, Holland & Luxembourg
Belize
Bermuda
Boston
Brazil
British Columbia & the Canadian
  Rockies
Brussels & Bruges
Budapest & the Best of Hungary
Buenos Aires
Calgary
California
Canada
Cancún, Cozumel & the Yucatán
Cape Cod, Nantucket & Martha's
  Vineyard
Caribbean
Caribbean Ports of Call
Carolinas & Georgia
Chicago
China
Colorado
Costa Rica
Croatia
Cuba
Denmark
Denver, Boulder & Colorado Springs
Edinburgh & Glasgow
England
Europe
Europe by Rail
Florence, Tuscany & Umbria

Florida
France
Germany
Greece
Greek Islands
Hawaii
Hong Kong
Honolulu, Waikiki & Oahu
India
Ireland
Israel
Italy
Jamaica
Japan
Kauai
Las Vegas
London
Los Angeles
Los Cabos & Baja
Madrid
Maine Coast
Maryland & Delaware
Maui
Mexico
Montana & Wyoming
Montréal & Québec City
Moscow & St. Petersburg
Munich & the Bavarian Alps
Nashville & Memphis
New England
Newfoundland & Labrador
New Mexico
New Orleans
New York City
New York State
New Zealand
Northern Italy
Norway
Nova Scotia, New Brunswick &
  Prince Edward Island
Oregon
Paris
Peru
Philadelphia & the Amish Country

Portugal
Prague & the Best of the Czech
  Republic
Provence & the Riviera
Puerto Rico
Rome
San Antonio & Austin
San Diego
San Francisco
Santa Fe, Taos & Albuquerque
Scandinavia
Scotland
Seattle
Seville, Granada & the Best of
  Andalusia
Shanghai
Sicily
Singapore & Malaysia
South Africa
South America
South Florida
South Pacific
Southeast Asia
Spain
Sweden
Switzerland
Tahiti & French Polynesia
Texas
Thailand
Tokyo
Toronto
Turkey
USA
Utah
Vancouver & Victoria
Vermont, New Hampshire & Maine
Vienna & the Danube Valley
Vietnam
Virgin Islands
Virginia
Walt Disney World® & Orlando
Washington, D.C.
Washington State

FROMMER'S® DAY BY DAY GUIDES

Amsterdam
Chicago
Florence & Tuscany

London
New York City
Paris

Rome
San Francisco
Venice

PAULINE FROMMER'S GUIDES! SEE MORE. SPEND LESS.

Hawaii

Italy

New York City

FROMMER'S® PORTABLE GUIDES

Acapulco, Ixtapa & Zihuatanejo
Amsterdam
Aruba
Australia's Great Barrier Reef
Bahamas
Big Island of Hawaii
Boston
California Wine Country
Cancún
Cayman Islands
Charleston
Chicago
Dominican Republic

Dublin
Florence
Las Vegas
Las Vegas for Non-Gamblers
London
Maui
Nantucket & Martha's Vineyard
New Orleans
New York City
Paris
Portland
Puerto Rico
Puerto Vallarta, Manzanillo &
  Guadalajara

Rio de Janeiro
San Diego
San Francisco
Savannah
St. Martin, Sint Maarten, Anguila &
  St. Bart's
Turks & Caicos
Vancouver
Venice
Virgin Islands
Washington, D.C.
Whistler

FROMMER'S® CRUISE GUIDES

Alaska Cruises & Ports of Call

Cruises & Ports of Call

European Cruises & Ports of Call

FROMMER'S® NATIONAL PARK GUIDES

Algonquin Provincial Park
Banff & Jasper
Grand Canyon

National Parks of the American West
Rocky Mountain
Yellowstone & Grand Teton

Yosemite and Sequoia & Kings
  Canyon
Zion & Bryce Canyon

FROMMER'S® MEMORABLE WALKS

London
New York

Paris
Rome

San Francisco

FROMMER'S® WITH KIDS GUIDES

Chicago
Hawaii
Las Vegas
London

National Parks
New York City
San Francisco

Toronto
Walt Disney World® & Orlando
Washington, D.C.

SUZY GERSHMAN'S BORN TO SHOP GUIDES

France
Hong Kong, Shanghai & Beijing
Italy

London
New York

Paris
San Francisco

FROMMER'S® IRREVERENT GUIDES

Amsterdam
Boston
Chicago
Las Vegas

London
Los Angeles
Manhattan
Paris

Rome
San Francisco
Walt Disney World®
Washington, D.C.

FROMMER'S® BEST-LOVED DRIVING TOURS

Austria
Britain
California
France

Germany
Ireland
Italy
New England

Northern Italy
Scotland
Spain
Tuscany & Umbria

THE UNOFFICIAL GUIDES®

Adventure Travel in Alaska
Beyond Disney
California with Kids
Central Italy
Chicago
Cruises
Disneyland®
England
Florida
Florida with Kids

Hawaii
Ireland
Las Vegas
London
Maui
Mexico's Best Beach Resorts
Mini Mickey
New Orleans
New York City

Paris
San Francisco
South Florida including Miami &
  the Keys
Walt Disney World®
Walt Disney World® for
  Grown-ups
Walt Disney World® with Kids
Washington, D.C.

SPECIAL-INTEREST TITLES

Athens Past & Present
Best Places to Raise Your Family
Cities Ranked & Rated
500 Places to Take Your Kids Before They Grow Up
Frommer's Best Day Trips from London
Frommer's Best RV & Tent Campgrounds
  in the U.S.A.

Frommer's Exploring America by RV
Frommer's NYC Free & Dirt Cheap
Frommer's Road Atlas Europe
Frommer's Road Atlas Ireland
Great Escapes From NYC Without Wheels
Retirement Places Rated

FROMMER'S® PHRASEFINDER DICTIONARY GUIDES

French

Italian

Spanish